ROME'S WORLD: THE PEUTINGER MAP RECONSIDERED

The Peutinger Map is the only map of the Roman world to come down to us from antiquity. An elongated object full of colorful detail and featuring land routes across Europe, North Africa, and the Near East, it was mysteriously rediscovered around 1500 and then came into the ownership of Konrad Peutinger, for whom it is named. Today it is among the treasures of the Austrian National Library in Vienna. Richard J. A. Talbert's *Rome's World: The Peutinger Map Reconsidered* offers a long overdue reinterpretation and appreciation of the map as a masterpiece of both mapmaking and imperial Roman ideology. Here, the ancient world's traditional span, from the Atlantic to India, is dramatically remolded; lands and routes take pride of place, whereas seas are compressed. Talbert posits that the map's true purpose was not to assist travelers along Rome's highways, but rather to celebrate the restoration of peace and order by Diocletian's Tetrarchy. Such creative cartography, he demonstrates, influenced the development of medieval mapmaking. With the aid of digital technology, this book enables readers to engage with the Peutinger Map in all of its fascinating immensity more closely than ever before.

Richard J. A. Talbert is William Rand Kenan, Jr., Professor of History and Classics at the University of North Carolina, Chapel Hill, where he has taken the lead in establishing the Ancient World Mapping Center. He is the author of several books, including *The Senate of Imperial Rome* and the collaborative *Barrington Atlas of the Greek and Roman World*.

Mezzotint of Franz Christoph von Scheyb in an aristocratic pose as Secretary for Lower Austria, a post he occupied from 1739 onward. Here we see him proudly unrolling his full-size engraving of the Peutinger map, published in 1753, so that Vienna (*Vindobona*) rather than Rome occupies the central position.

ROME'S WORLD

THE PEUTINGER MAP
RECONSIDERED

RICHARD J. A. TALBERT

University of North Carolina, Chapel Hill

in association with Tom Elliott,

assisted by Nora Harris, Gannon Hubbard,
David O'Brien, and Graham Shepherd

with a contribution by Martin Steinmann

CAMBRIDGE
UNIVERSITY PRESS

CAMBRIDGE UNIVERSITY PRESS
Cambridge, New York, Melbourne, Madrid, Cape Town, Singapore,
São Paulo, Delhi, Dubai, Tokyo, Mexico City

Cambridge University Press
32 Avenue of the Americas, New York, NY 10013-2473, USA

www.cambridge.org
Information on this title: www.cambridge.org/9780521764803

First published 2010

Printed in the United States of America

A catalog record for this publication is available from the British Library.

Library of Congress Cataloging in Publication data

Talbert, Richard J. A., 1947–
Rome's world : the Peutinger map reconsidered / Richard J. A. Talbert.
p.   cm.
Include bibliographical references and index.
ISBN 978-0-521-76480-3 (hardback)
1. Peutinger table.   2. Early maps – Rome.   3. Roads, Roman.   I. Title.
GA304.Z53T35   2010
912.37–dc22   2009023313

ISBN 978-0-521-76480-3 Hardback

Additional resources for this publication at www.cambridge.org/9780521764803

This book is dedicated to the memory of my parents,

John (d. September 2, 2007)

and Susan (d. September 25, 2007),

who did not live to see its completion

CONTENTS

ONLINE CONTENTS

www.cambridge.org/9780521764803

MAPS

A Peutinger map: seamless whole, in color, with overlaid layers prepared by Nora Harris (*use with Appendix 8*)

B (i) Peutinger map: monochrome photographs of each of the eleven parchments as taken at full size or more in 1888 by Carl Angerer and Alexander Göschl

(ii) Peutinger map: digital color photographs of each of the eleven parchments as taken at full size by the Österreichische Nationalbibliothek in 2000 (the components of Map A)

Outlines on *Barrington Atlas* base (*use with Appendix 9 and Figure 7*):

C Peutinger map Rivers

D Peutinger map Routes

E Antonine Itinerary (*ItAnt*) Journeys

F Bordeaux Itinerary (*ItBurd*) Journeys

DATABASE

Peutinger map names and features, with Commentary (*use with Appendix 7*):

FEATURES AND NOTICES
    Complete list by grid square
    Complete alphabetical list
    Names and notices in red ink
    Complete list by reference number

LISTS BY FEATURE TYPE
    Networked names, no symbols
        Complete alphabetical listing
        Alphabetical listings by initial letter
    Networked symbols, named
        Complete alphabetical listing
        Alphabetical listings by initial letter
    Networked symbols, unnamed
        Listing by reference number
    Unnamed or illegible features
        Listing by reference number
    Isolated names
        Complete alphabetical listing
        Alphabetical listings by initial letter
    Isolated symbols, named
        Complete alphabetical listing
    Isolated symbols, unnamed
        Listing by reference number
    Islands
        Complete alphabetical listing
        Alphabetical listings by initial letter
        Listing by reference number

Mountains
    Complete alphabetical listing
    Listing by reference number
Peoples
    Complete alphabetical listing
    Alphabetical listings by initial letter
Regions
    Complete alphabetical listing
    Alphabetical listings by initial letter
Rivers
    Complete alphabetical listing
    Alphabetical listings by initial letter
    Listing by reference number
Special features and notices
    Complete alphabetical listing
Water, other than rivers
    Complete alphabetical listing
    Alphabetical listings by initial letter
    Listing by reference number

SYMBOL CLASSIFICIATION

WORKS CITED

CONCORDANCES OF REFERENCES

NAMES AND FEATURES NOT NOTED IN THE BARRINGTON ATLAS AND DIRECTORY

LIST OF PLATES, FIGURES, AND TABLE

In asterisked instances, where a Plate comprises several images, only one appears in the printed book.

PLATES

FIGURES

TABLE

PREFACE AND ACKNOWLEDGMENTS

Experience and accident mixed with frustration and optimism have combined to launch this study. I probably read about its object first in one of my schoolbooks, the 1961 revision of *Everyman's Classical Atlas* introduced by J. Oliver Thomson ("As a map this ribbon is absurd, but its aim is only to give roads with their stations . . ."), and over time I grew accustomed to the illustrations of one segment or another seen in publications of all kinds about Roman history and culture. Once I became seriously engaged with cartography from the 1980s, my awareness of the importance of the Peutinger "Table" or Map sharpened correspondingly. As the *Barrington Atlas* took shape during the 1990s, I witnessed at first hand the heavy dependence that many contributors laid upon this "absurd" survival for place-names and routes across the entire Roman world. At the same time, when I ventured into the emerging debate about Romans' "map consciousness" or the lack of it, colleagues' widespread preference for excluding this item from consideration on the grounds that it should be viewed as a diagram rather than a map came to seem less and less justifiable. I was for a long time incredulous that no full-scale presentation and analysis of it had appeared since World War I. Although color photographs had eventually been published in 1976, many scholars had still not abandoned their reliance upon the more accessible nineteenth-century lithographed drawings. In addition, the map's segments continued to be numbered in two different sequences, while any system of reference for individual features had yet to be devised. Above all, a new evaluation of the map was lacking; no alternative had been proposed to the age-old dismissal encapsulated in Thomson's pithy summation of 1961.

By the late 1990s, therefore, I was convinced that the challenge of attempting to present the Peutinger map afresh and to rethink its character and purpose might repay the inevitable risks. Now, a decade later, with the work ready for publication at last, I dare to think that the struggle has been justified. To imagine that my conclusions will meet with universal acceptance would be unrealistic, but if nothing else the new approaches on which they are based may deter scholars from persisting complacently with the claim that the map is a mere road diagram of minimal cartographic or cultural significance. Issues of its design, context, purpose, and impact raised here can no longer be ignored. A rich, layered context now emerges for the map. This identification leads in turn to a refined grasp of the map's long-term impact and its importance in the history of cartography. Moreover, tools are developed that permit everyone to study the map closely and to refer conveniently to each of its components.

From the outset, the creation of these tools has demanded collaboration, skills, and labor on an extensive scale. As has become painfully clear to those who have dared to work with the map over the centuries, it is the most exacting of taskmasters, but at the same time an unfailingly alluring one. In the twenty-first century, as I soon came to realize, it would be less practical and less affordable than ever to present the map in print as a single item, especially at full size and in color. Once some formidable technical obstacles were overcome, however, electronic publication has proved itself well suited to the purpose. In this connection, no one has done more than Tom Elliott to demonstrate to me the extraordinary potential of digital technology and to overcome the countless obstacles arising from its application. His vision and persistence are beyond praise; it is hard to imagine how this work could have been accomplished without them, and I am deeply grateful to him. I am keenly aware, too, that electronic publication of the map is contingent upon authorization from the Austrian National Library to reproduce its scanned images; lasting thanks are due to the library for its alacrity in granting this request. No less is Princeton University Press to be thanked for permitting the use of geo-registered raster images of a substantial "mosaic" of maps from the *Barrington Atlas*. Cambridge University Press is to be thanked above all. I am especially grateful that my editor, Beatrice Rehl, and her colleagues have shared my enthusiasm for a hybrid format, which allows the book's text matter to be presented both electronically and in a printed volume for readers' convenience.

To an embarrassing degree, completion of this book has depended upon collaborative effort and support from individuals and institutions on both sides of the Atlantic. I welcome the chance to thank them all at last, however inadequately. An appropriate order can hardly be determined, but without doubt the University of North Carolina, Chapel Hill, should be mentioned first, in particular for generous financial support, for its outstanding libraries, and for its sponsorship of the Ancient World Mapping Center, where almost all the digital work on the map was done. At different stages over several years, Nora Harris, Gannon Hubbard, David O'Brien, and Graham Shepherd played key roles in this exacting, complex activity at the Center under Tom Elliott's direction; assistance was also rendered there by Jeffrey Becker, Andrew Hull, Joshua Moffitt, Elizabeth Robinson, Brian Turner, and Sarah Willis. David O'Brien's work was supported by an award from the Loeb Classical Library Foundation. I realize that it can seem invidious to name only certain staff members within Chapel Hill's libraries when all have been so supportive; at the same time, it is impossible for me not to mention Sellers Lawrence, Celia Pratt, and John Rutledge for their exceptional service. Among academic colleagues over the years at Chapel Hill and at Duke nearby, I thank especially Robert Babcock, Tolly Boatwright, David Ganz, George Houston, Terence McIntosh, Michael McVaugh, Fred Naiden, Francis Newton, Grant Parker, William Race, Werner Riess, Philip Stadter, and Siegfried Wenzel; among my former students I thank Ricky Law and Sonia Wilson.

Beyond Chapel Hill, an ever-widening circle of friends and colleagues across a range of disciplines has generously informed, influenced, corrected, and sustained me in multiple ways: Emily Albu, Gregory Aldrete, Pascal Arnaud, Peter Barber, Niccolò Capponi, Brian Campbell, Martin Cropp, Raymond Davis, Gianluca Del Mastro, Catherine Delano-Smith, Adelheid Eubanks, Patrick Florance, Patrick Gautier Dalché, Helen Hardman, Paul Harvey, Nicholas Horsfall, Keith Lilley, Natalia Lozovsky, Michael Maas, Neil McLynn, Eckart Olshausen, Michael Rathmann, Gerald Stone, Jennifer Trimble, John Wilkes, and the late, much lamented David Woodward. Again, gratitude demands that a few individuals be singled out for special mention. Ekkehard Weber, a new friend, could not have been kinder or readier to help a less senior colleague who aimed to supersede his own invaluable work on the map. Nor could Kai Brodersen, an old friend, have been more supportive, despite the growing divergence in our estimation of Romans' worldview. Benet Salway, too, has been the most perceptive and tactful of critics, ever ready to join in appraising and modifying fresh approaches and ideas, however raw. A lead from Marjeta Šašel Kos transformed my understanding of significant, ill-documented episodes in the map's history during the early nineteenth century, and she and her husband, Peter Kos, made my visit to Ljubljana in this connection a most memorable and productive one. Expertise of a different character has been offered by Martin Steinmann, who agreed to evaluate the map from a paleographer's perspective, thus illuminating an aspect of fundamental importance that has been woefully neglected and lies beyond the capacity of a historian; without Steinmann's exemplary and unselfish contribution, this book would not be complete. Its value would also have suffered if it had not been possible for the technology supporting the presentation of the map as a seamless whole (Map A) to be skillfully upgraded in 2009 by Tom Elliott and Sean Gillies with joint hosting by New York University's Institute for the Study of the Ancient World and the Digital Library Services Team.

Thanks are due to several libraries, above all to the National Library of Austria, Vienna, and to the successive directors of its Handschriftensammlung, Ernst Gamillscheg and Andreas Fingernagel, for granting the privilege of three visits to inspect the map itself, two on my part and one by Martin Steinmann. Other libraries (and in some instances individual staff members) to be thanked are: Library of Congress, Washington, DC; New York Public Library (Alice Hudson); Widener Library, Harvard University (David Cobb); Newberry Library, Chicago (James Akerman); British Library, London; Royal Geographical Society Library, London (Francis Herbert); Bodleian Library, Oxford (Nick Millea); John Rylands University Library, Manchester; Robinson Library, University of Newcastle; Bibliothèque de l'Université Mons-Hainaut, Belgium (Christine Gobeaux); Stadtbibliothek, Trier, Germany (Reiner Nolden); Universität Basel Library, Switzerland; American Academy in Rome Library (Christina Huemer); Slovenian National Library, Ljubljana (Jasna Hrovat); also the National Museum of Slovenia, Ljubljana (Polona Bitenc).

Fellowships from the American Council of Learned Societies, the J. S. Guggenheim Memorial Foundation, and the National Humanities Center (Goheen Fellowship) played a vital and much appreciated role in the launching of my research for this book; a Harley Research Fellowship in the History of Cartography, held in London, advanced its completion.

I could never have reached the point of completion, however, without the support, patience, and skills of my wife, Zandra, and our two sons, Daniel and Patrick. Responsibility for any shortcomings remains mine alone. Unlike some of the map's previous editors, I lack the confidence to claim that all slips in its presentation have been eliminated, despite my best efforts.

Chapel Hill, NC
July 2009

ABBREVIATIONS

AE	*L'Année épigraphique*
BAtlas	R. J. A. Talbert (ed.), *Barrington Atlas of the Greek and Roman World*, with *Map-by-Map Directory* (Princeton [NJ] and Oxford, 2000)
CAH	*The Cambridge Ancient History*
CIL	*Corpus Inscriptionum Latinarum*
CRAI	*Comptes Rendus des séances de l'Académie des Inscriptions et belles-lettres* (Paris)
FGH	F. Jacoby, *Die Fragmente der griechischen Historiker* (Berlin and Leiden, 1923–)
GGM	C. Müller (ed.), *Geographi Graeci Minores*, 2 vols. and maps (Paris, 1855, 1861)
GLM	A. Riese (ed.), *Geographi Latini Minores* (Heilbronn, 1878)
Gött. gel. Anz.	*Göttingische gelehrte Anzeigen*
HistCart	*The History of Cartography, vol. 1: Cartography in Prehistoric, Ancient, and Mediaeval Europe and the Mediterranean*, ed. J. B. Harley and D. Woodward (Chicago, 1987); *vol. 3: Cartography in the European Renaissance*, ed. D. Woodward (Chicago, 2007)
ILS	H. Dessau, *Inscriptiones Latinae Selectae*, 3 vols. (Berlin, 1892–1916)
ItAnt	*Imperatoris Antonini Augusti Itineraria Provinciarum.* In O. Cuntz (ed.), *Itineraria Romana*, vol. 1 (Leipzig: Teubner, 1929); see also Appendix 9
ItBurd	*Itinerarium Burdigalense.* In P. Geyer (ed.), *Itineraria et Alia Geographica*, Corpus Christianorum Series Latina 175 (Turnhout [Belgium], 1965), 1–26; see also Appendix 9

ItMarit	*Imperatoris Antonini Augusti Itinerarium Maritimum.* In O. Cuntz (ed.), *Itineraria Romana*, vol. I (Leipzig: Teubner, 1929)
ItMiller	K. Miller, *Itineraria Romana: Römische Reisewege an der Hand der Tabula Peutingeriana dargestellt* (Stuttgart, 1916)
JRA	*Journal of Roman Archaeology*
JRS	*The Journal of Roman Studies*
Killy	W. Killy (ed.), *Literaturlexikon. Autoren und Werke deutscher Sprache*, 15 vols. (Gütersloh/Munich, 1988–93)
LTUR	E. M. Steinby (ed.), *Lexicon Topographicum Urbis Romae* (Rome, 1993–2001)
MEFRA	*Mélanges d'Archéologie et d'Histoire de l'Ecole Française de Rome*
NP	*Der neue Pauly: Enzyklopädie der Antike* (Stuttgart, 1996–2008); English ed., *Brill's New Pauly* (Leiden, 2002–)
PIR[2]	*Prosopographia Imperii Romani saec. I. II. III*, 2nd ed. (Berlin and Leipzig, 1933–)
Pliny, *NH*	Pliny the Elder, *Naturalis Historia*
Ptol., *Geog.*	A. Stückelberger and G. Grasshoff (eds.), *Ptolemaios: Handbuch der Geographie*, 2 vols. (Basle, 2006)
RAC	*Reallexikon für Antike und Christentum*
RE	Pauly-Wissowa-Kroll, *Real-Encyclopädie der classischen Altertumswissenschaft* (Stuttgart, 1894–1978)
SEG	*Supplementum Epigraphicum Graecum*
TAVO	*Tübinger Atlas des Vorderen Orients* (Wiesbaden, 1977–94)
TLL	*Thesaurus Linguae Latinae*
Weber, *Kommentar*	Volume accompanying E. Weber, *Tabula Peutingeriana, Codex Vindobonensis 324* (Graz, 1976)

INTRODUCTION

S ELDOM ARE VISITORS to the Manuscript Collection of Austria's
National Library in Vienna permitted to inspect its set of eleven
parchment segments that together form an elongated, squat, and not quite
complete map of the Roman world, the so-called Peutinger map. The bold
manipulation of landmasses, the detailed plotting of land routes with names
in Latin, and the vibrancy of the color on most of the segments are just
three among the wealth of impressive features that at once strike the viewer.
Here is a major map that in its reshaping of continents recalls the futuristic
Atlantropa project devised by Herman Sörgel (1885–1952).[1] Altogether,
however, it is a map without close match in any period or culture world-
wide. Not least because autopsy is inevitably such a rare privilege,[2] the
primary purpose of this book is to render the map more widely accessible
and more comprehensible with the support of up-to-date scholarship and
technology. At the same time, the opportunity is taken to reconsider the
map's design, purpose, history, and significance in the light of current ideas
and methods.

The book proceeds on the basis of the long-standing view that the map
itself is not an original creation, but a copy at several removes of a lost
Roman forerunner. Such copying is the typical means by which texts from
antiquity have been preserved. Even so, a vast range of classical authors'
works no longer survives. Of those that do, an alarmingly high number are
preserved in just a single copy, and there is no manuscript of any classical
text that survives from its author's own time, or even close to it. Roman
production of maps (especially large ones) was never as prolific as that of
texts. So it is hardly a surprise that a mere couple even remotely comparable to this one have survived, both of them as original stone monuments
in fact (now fragmented), rather than through copying by scribes. In the
present case, while any serious study has to consider the circumstances
and context both of the original Roman map and of the successive copies

now lost, it is as well to bear in mind from the outset that all conclusions reached can be no more than conjecture. This is hardly good cause to be deterred, however. After all, the map's plight is shared by countless material objects from antiquity and later, which have likewise been set adrift. In this connection a confession by Antoine Lancelot, the first scholar to take a close interest in what has come to be called the Bayeux Tapestry, may readily be appreciated. In the early 1720s, when he first saw incomplete drawings of part of it that lacked even the briefest explanatory note, he frankly admitted his inability to identify the nature of the object, let alone where it might have come from. It might, he thought, be "a bas relief, a sculpture around the choir of a church, round a tomb, on a frieze, a fresco, a design for windows or even a tapestry."[3]

The production, early history, and discovery of our sole surviving copy of the map are in turn virtually a blank record. Only once it had the good fortune to be rescued from obscurity early in the sixteenth century and safeguarded in the private library of Konrad Peutinger at Augsburg, Germany, did we begin to become informed. Among many other preoccupations, Peutinger was actively engaged in assisting the Holy Roman Emperor Maximilian I to forge a historical link for himself with the Roman Empire and its rulers. In general, moreover, humanists of the period were eager seekers of new materials for the study of classical antiquity and its heritage. Lectures on Tacitus' *Germania* given by Konrad Celtis in the 1490s fired widespread interest in this text for the first time after its rediscovery about forty years earlier.[4] Meanwhile, alongside the emergence of a German national identity, a new awareness of scientific cartography and its global application was also developing.[5]

Around 1500, it seems, Celtis stumbled upon the map. Understandably enough, his extraordinary new find, of a most unusual type, thrilled fellow humanists. The limited circle who first gained the opportunity to inspect the map at once seized upon it to further their researches into the history of the Germans or their studies of place-names. "There are various conjectures on this issue," explained Beatus Rhenanus about the naming of Boulogne in antiquity, "but the military map which we have seen at the Augsburg residence of our friend Konrad Peutinger removes all our doubts."[6] Another scholar, who had not been able to inspect the map, nonetheless reflected optimistically: "Learned men were beginning to reckon that with this map as the arbiter of territorial disputes, able to overrule every objection, it would be possible for many of the almost everlasting disagreements among geographers to be resolved, and for many of the knots that seemed to defy disentanglement in books by historians to be untied."[7]

The issue of who had commissioned the original map became a favorite topic for speculation — a Roman emperor, it was readily assumed, but which one? The full span of the first four centuries A.D. from Augustus to Theodosius was wide open, and has been revisited repeatedly ever since. The impossibility of achieving consensus on this issue (in the sixteenth century, or indeed down to the present) in turn contributed to long-standing lack of agreement on a name by which to refer to the map, a difficulty only compounded by the lack of any term in classical Latin that indisputably equates to "map." The very first sentence, no less, of the preface introducing the first publication of any part of the map alludes to inconsistency in naming it. For a noun, on the one hand, *tabula* – otherwise commonly used to refer to a large piece of parchment stretched on a frame or fastened to a wooden tablet – relatively soon came to be preferred to *charta* (chart) or *itinerarium* (itinerary). For a much longer time, on the other hand, there was no agreement on an apt descriptive phrase or adjective (one or more) such as *Augustana* (from Augsburg), *Itineraria*, *Militaris*, *Provincialis*, *Theodosiana*. However, references to the map commonly did include some mention of Konrad Peutinger, its owner from a very early stage after the rediscovery. It was the adjective *Peutingeriana*, therefore, that frequently came to be attached to *tabula* – either alone, or with one or more others – and was certainly the most distinctive indicator for purposes of identification. Hence arose the formulation *Tabula Peutingeriana*, or "Peutinger Table," for which I substitute the less latinate and more immediately informative "Peutinger map." "Map" also serves to remove any chance of misconception that the object in question is a piece of furniture or set of statistics.

It was not unalloyed good fortune that the map came into Konrad Peutinger's possession, devoted bibliophile though he was. To be sure, he treated it with the utmost pride and respect, and was mindful of the stipulation by which it had been bequeathed to him, namely, that on his death he should make it publicly available – in a library, for example. In fact he sought to do more, and sooner, by attempting to have the map engraved for publication, a pathbreaking step for his day. In the event, however, his successive efforts were thwarted. Quite apart from the map's sheer size – 672 cm wide by 33 tall (or approximately 22 × 1 ft.) – the difficulties of first elucidating all its complex details, and of then reproducing them flawlessly, presented engravers with unfamiliar and almost insuperable challenges. In addition, willingness aside, it was not always possible for an engraver to work directly from the map; instead, he might have to be supplied with drawings made by others. It would be these renderings that he then engraved, thus opening up further scope for error. Moreover, as was acknowledged right from the sixteenth century, it was simply not feasible for an engraver to capture the exact style of the map's smaller lettering, especially if his commission was to deliver a scaled-down image. Nor was it practical for any publication to reproduce the map's coloring, integral part of its presentation though that is. Such limitations could not be overcome, and they were to bedevil even the most painstaking of intentions to reproduce the map faithfully for publication through the nineteenth century. Even today, they continue to make themselves felt, insofar as the type of image chosen as a convenient illustration of the map is often still a drawing.

When pondering the map's checkered history of publication from its discovery to the present, it is sobering to realize that only once during these five centuries (in the 1750s) was it engraved at full size by an engraver on the spot who first made his own tracing of it. Unfortunately he reproduced lettering less ably than line work, these errors went uncorrected, and the outsize, costly volume did not sell. Over a century later, one expert could venture the depressing opinion that even then (in the 1860s!) the most reliable presentation of the map remained the first engraving published of it in its entirety, in 1598, although this is little over half-size and the hasty job of an engraver who never set eyes on the map itself. It was this engraving that several subsequent publications were content to reuse or reengrave time and again. With the aid of lithography, two improved presentations of the map – one full-size, the other two-thirds – did eventually come to be produced in the late nineteenth century, even incorporating the map's colors, albeit in somewhat rudimentary manner. The problem of the prohibitive outlay entailed in preparing any presentation of the map remained intractable, however. Costs, in turn, undermined the forward-looking scheme to issue a set of high-quality (monochrome) photographs of each of the map's eleven parchment segments in 1888; few of these sets went into circulation because they had to be priced so high. Not for almost another century did a set of color photographs at last become available, as recently as 1976.

In short, for obvious enough reasons, it has proven an unremitting struggle in various related respects – artistic, paleographic, technological, financial – to present the Peutinger map satisfyingly and accurately for those unable to inspect it in person. No less have scholars continued to struggle over equipping their fellows with the kind of supporting apparatus that was already considered invaluable in the sixteenth century. The nature and scope of some of the desirable elements for this purpose are more easily settled than others. Compilation of a gazetteer of all the names marked on the map, for example, gives rise to fewer conceptual and organizational dilemmas than the preparation of a commentary. For the latter purpose, which features and names are to be singled out for attention? In which order should they be treated, and how extensively? Much to its credit, a preliminary publication (1591) of a limited part of the map offered a commentary and gazetteer that together respond to such fundamental issues in well-judged ways. But the immense task of publishing a commentary on the entire map was not accomplished successfully – after several failures – until 1825. This work was already outdated when it appeared, however, and the continued advancement of knowledge on all fronts during the nineteenth century both encouraged further efforts and slowed them down. Only the effort by Konrad Miller in Germany succeeded in fact. His work was eventually published in Stuttgart in 1916 and has still to be superseded.

Today, Miller and his work, impressive as it is, appear to be the epitome of traditional approaches to scholarship in general and to the map in particular since its discovery four centuries earlier. Miller labored alone as an amateur enthusiast; the images of the map on which he relied were drawings; and his lines of enquiry hardly diverged from those established in the sixteenth century. He never queried the conviction that the map was created exclusively for practical purposes, and his principal concern was to test the accuracy of its land routes and accompanying distance figures. At the same time – like all scholars before the present generation – he showed next-to-no concern for the entire dimension of the map's design and presentation from a cartographic perspective, an omission that in turn calls into question his overconfident reconstruction of its lost Western end.

Beyond all doubt, therefore, an effort to present the Peutinger map anew and to rethink it has long been overdue. But, until very recently, viable means by which to branch from the traditional path and to develop alternative ways forward seemed elusive. Now, however, four related but very different stimuli have together removed long-standing obstacles and encouraged an advance. First, the *Barrington Atlas of the Greek and Roman World*, published by Princeton University Press in 2000, has at last furnished comprehensive, informed maps of classical antiquity's physical and cultural landscapes according to modern norms. Before, in the absence of such maps, a satisfactory cartographic lens through which to interpret the Peutinger map today had for too long been lacking. However, to continue considering a Roman map largely in relation to the scientific perspectives and accumulated knowledge of the twentieth or twenty-first century is no longer appropriate. Fortunately, second, the ongoing *History of Cartography* project initiated by Brian Harley and David Woodward during the 1980s has offered fruitful new models for the interpretation of mapmaking in premodern cultures, with stress on the need to evaluate such activity above all within its contemporary intellectual and social context. Third, my own immersion in mapmaking as director of the project that produced the *Barrington Atlas* has enabled me to penetrate for the first time the over-looked, but vital, process by which the Peutinger map was conceived and made. Finally, fourth, the growing capacity and robustness of digital technology over the past decade have now furnished versatile means to present and analyze the map that in a print medium are either prohibitively expensive or quite unattainable. The Stanford Digital Forma Urbis Romae Project (http://formaurbis.stanford.edu), launched in 1999, has set an instructive example in this respect. In retrospect, the fact that the last systematic presentation of the Peutinger map dates as far back as 1916 may hardly seem surprising from a practical viewpoint. The new digital technology has proven literally a godsend for informative dissemination and study of such an unwieldy, complex item.

The new technology is the reason why the present work was conceived as a digital product from the outset. It not only displays the map at full size and in color as a seamless whole, but also adds multiple layers, which deconstruct its components as well as label and highlight names and features. Accordingly, the map may be examined in greater or lesser detail on screen, and the layers may be displayed in any combination or removed altogether. Associated with this display is a database with entries and commentary for over 3,500 individual names and features. In addition, for the modern viewer's perspective, the routes followed by the Peutinger map and Antonine and Bordeaux Itineraries, as well as the identifiable rivers appearing on the map, are all traced on a mosaic of *Barrington Atlas* maps.

However, limits have been set for the scope of the commentary associated with the database. In particular, quite deliberately no attempt has been made to expand upon local matters – for example, the history of a place, the style of its name, the accuracy of a distance figure, or the course of a route on the ground – in the way that Miller and his predecessors did. For further investigation of these and related questions, the *Barrington Atlas* and its *Map-by-Map Directory* are simply cited as the best single resource in the first instance. The vast scope of the map's coverage and its mass of detail make it a Herculean, not to say Sisyphean, labor to tackle local matters. Given today's range of scholarly reference tools, such unrewarding duplication of effort becomes a counterproductive diversion when so much else of importance about the map has long remained neglected. The perils of entrapment in local matters may be clearly perceived in the length (421 pages) and density of just one recent exemplary monograph devoted to routes in a single region for which the map furnishes vital testimony.[8] This said, however, the electronic format of the present work's database equips it with the potential to become the framework where others from here on may usefully graft further comments to individual entries.

Following this Introduction, five chapters and a conclusion seek to elaborate upon a range of questions that should concern all scholarly users of the map. Chapter 1 addresses the map's discovery around 1500, its ownership thereafter, and the successive struggles to publish it and to provide commentary. These stages, with their multiple ramifications, have never been described so fully or objectively. Nor has their wider significance been recognized as a classic example of the formidable challenges facing all efforts to reproduce a large, complex map at any period before the development of color photography and printing. Chapter 2 breaks fresh ground by offering a detailed, long overdue analysis of the map's paleography, not least with a view to determining what claims may fairly be made about where this surviving copy was made, and when. Chapter 3 probes the decisions underlying the design of the map and the principles by which it is presented; for these purposes, its physical and cultural components are closely examined in turn. Chapter 4 tackles the vital but enigmatic issue of the extent to which the surviving copy – as a reflection of work by one copyist after another – succeeds in reproducing the original map now lost. Chapter 5 focuses squarely on fundamental issues associated with the lost original: its likely sources, date, authorship, context, and purpose. Finally, the Conclusion reflects upon the map's place within classical cartography, its subsequent circulation, and its impact upon medieval mapmaking.

The interpretation of the map and its influence that emerges forms a radical, not to say provocative, departure from established opinion. I dare to regard the map as having been part of a decorative scheme for a specific public space inside some imperial palace of the Tetrarchic period, when the Roman Empire was ruled by Diocletian and three coemperors (around A.D. 300). The unknown mapmaker's purpose is seen as primarily artistic and celebratory, not practical or geographic; no one was ever seriously expected to plan a long journey or a military campaign from this map. Rather, its viewers were invited to marvel at the sweep of Roman power and civilization, and to be engaged – even teased – by the strikingly elongated representation of the known world from the Atlantic to as far as India, where the city of Rome dominates at the center, landmasses are manipulated and much open water drained. To quote the Tetrarchs' own rhetoric, the world seen here is one now – thanks to their exertions – "in tranquility, placed in the lap of a most profound calm, as well as benefiting from a peace that was toiled for with abundant sweat." Far from being just a rather dull itinerary diagram recording land routes – an artistically and culturally isolated product – the map embodies the traditional ideals of the *pax Romana* and creatively projects Late Antique taste, ideas, and values.

Moreover, the map's innovative design and content are seen to have made a widespread impact that continued to be felt for many centuries. In particular, medieval "world maps" (*mappaemundi*), while original creations in their own right, are at the same time also products of the creative inspiration projected by the Peutinger map. Henry VIII, king of England from 1509 to 1547 – as it happens, almost exactly the same period as Konrad Peutinger's ownership of the map – took with him on his royal progresses "a mappa mundi in parcheament," which formed part of "the Removing Guarderobe . . . attendaunt at the Courte uppon the kinges most Roiall personne where the same for the tyme shall happen to be." Nor was this the only *mappamundi* that Henry owned; maps were a regular feature of his court ceremonials and diplomatic conferences. Had he seen the Peutinger map, he would surely have grasped its value to a ruler. So too would have his earlier namesake, Henry III (reigned 1216–72), who is said to have positioned a *mappamundi* on the wall behind his throne in the Painted Chamber at Westminster (destroyed by fire in 1263).[9]

If the unapologetically controversial views advanced in this book can act to arouse lively debate across disciplines as well as closer attention to

Roman cartography and worldview, this will be a welcome outcome for a lengthy and daunting endeavor. For too long now, the Peutinger map has been awaiting fresh vision, from new and wider perspectives.

PRESENTATION OF THE MAP

Reference to the map is offered in various forms:

> Map A presents the map full-size in color as a seamless whole by assembling the digital photographs presented individually as Map B (ii) below. Layers overlaid on Map A identify and distinguish the map's components. Appendix 8 offers a Guide.
>
> Map B (i) presents the map's eleven segments individually, as photographed in monochrome in 1888. Each is full-size, or very slightly enlarged; see further Chap. 1, sec. 5.
>
> Map B (ii) presents the map's eleven segments individually, as photographed digitally full-size in color in 2000.
>
> Database with Commentary containing entries for individual features and names. Appendix 7 offers a Guide.
>
> Map C outlines the Peutinger map's rivers on a "mosaic" of *Barrington Atlas* bases, eastward as far as the Euphrates and Tigris. Appendix 9 offers a Guide.
>
> Map D outlines the Peutinger map's routes on a "mosaic" of *Barrington Atlas* bases, up to Maps 87 and 89. Appendix 9 offers a Guide.

As an aid to comprehensibility, the transcription of the map's lettering throughout has been simplified as follows:

> (i) "Display capitals" and "capitals" are not distinguished; see further Chapter 2.2 (b) (i);
>
> (ii) the alternate forms of **s** (round and tall) are all transcribed as round;
>
> (iii) the alternate forms **u** and **v** are all transcribed as **v**;
>
> (iv) stops marked before or after words and numbers, as well as dots above **y**, are normally ignored;
>
> (v) where the initial letter of a word appears to be a capital, it is transcribed as such. However, where a letter *within* a word written in minuscule appears to be a capital, it is *not* transcribed as a capital. The copyist has a quirky habit of frequently introducing such capitals within words, as explained in Chapter 2.2 (c) and illustrated immediately below. Even so, there are many instances where it is unclear whether the form of a letter really is to be regarded as a capital. More generally, the appearance of capitals within words creates a strange and disorienting impression upon today's readers without particularly enhancing their appreciation of the map. Hence my decision on balance has been to refrain from further complicating the presentation in this way. As an illustration of

the practice that I have decided *not* to adopt, note the following sample names from Segment 1A:

1A1   Ad taVM, SinomaGi
1A2   BReVodVRo, TeRVanna
1A3   CoNDaTE, DVRocassio, IVLioMaGo, LvRa, PeTRVM viaco, TeVceRa
1A4   AQVis SeGeSTe, Baca coneRVio
1A5   AtVaca, Colo(nia) TRaiaNa, coRtovallio, Fl. RiGeR, Vet-eRibVs.

CHAPTER ONE

THE SURVIVING COPY

HISTORY, PUBLICATION, SCHOLARSHIP

THE "PEUTINGER MAP," which this study presents and analyzes, is today universally, and in my view correctly, considered to be no more than the sole surviving copy of a lost original. That original map – which is Roman in character even if not necessarily in date – must be this study's eventual concern, but it can only be approached through the copy, which is therefore addressed from many different perspectives in Chapters 2 through 4. This preliminary chapter establishes an essential foundation by treating the copy's discovery around 1500, its ownership over the next half millennium to the present, and above all the successive efforts to publish it and comprehend it.

1. DISCOVERY AND BEQUEST TO KONRAD PEUTINGER[1]

The earliest testimony to the copy – the surviving Peutinger map – is its bequest to Konrad Peutinger in the will of Konrad Pickel (or Bickel; latinized as Celtis or Celtes); this was made on January 24, 1508, shortly before his death on February 4 at age forty-nine:[2]

> Item. Ego lego d(omi)no doctori Conrado Peutinger Itinerarium Antonini Pii, qui etiam eundem nunc habet; volo tamen et rogo, ut post eius mortem ad usum publicum puta aliquam librariam convertatur. [Plate 1]

> I bequeath to Mr Dr Conrad Peutinger the *Itinerarium Antonini Pii*, the very same item that is at present in his possession; I wish, however, and request that after his death it should be turned over to public use, such as some library.

Celtis was a passionate, unscrupulous collector of manuscripts both on his own behalf and that of the emperor Maximilian I (1459–1519);

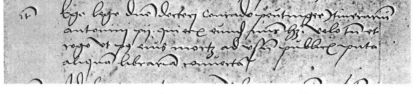

PLATE I. Extract from Celtis's will made on January 24, 1508. Photo: Archiv der Universität Wien.

geography and mapping featured among his special interests.[3] There is no explicit testimony to how or where he obtained this particular map (evidently for himself), nor to why he chose to bequeath it thus. Holes indicate that at some stage it had been displayed,[4] and so just possibly the actual sight of it drew his attention. Moreover, a similar map – acquired at the Council of Basle during the 1430s, it was said – is known to have been displayed in the bishop's anteroom at Padua in 1495 (and maybe earlier too).[5] If Celtis had somehow known of it,[6] such awareness might well have prompted him to be on the lookout in Germany for the exemplar from which it was copied, or another copy. Should that conjecture be accurate, it follows that he might have been intrigued and surprised to realize that his discovery is instead a variant of the map displayed in Padua. Even so, despite tireless speculation over the centuries, it still remains impossible to say either where, or exactly when around 1500, he found this Peutinger map.[7]

If Celtis did obtain the map by false pretences, his own defense would no doubt be the nub of the argument that he made in 1501 – with fluent rhetoric – to Frederick the Wise, Elector of Saxony, in the preface to his publication of the Roswitha (Hrotsvita) manuscript at the Benedictine monastery of St. Emmeram. The promise he made to return this manuscript there was never kept:

Quo circa dum vidissem multa preclara et illustria exemplaria tamquam aegregia et optima quedam de nobis spolia ab Italis e germania in italiam delata ibique impressa. Cogitabam ego ad me hominem in media germania et hercinia natum, et qui primus inter germanos litterarum ornamenta et insignia ac imperialem laurum a caesare, tuo princeps illustrissime Friderice ductu et monitu, accepissem, successionis et hereditatis iure spectare debere, ut latentes in obscuro codices velut venator egregius elicere. Germanisque meis tanquam opipera quedam offerrem, quibus illi veterum nostrorum patrum et progenitorum circa litteras et religionem christianam nostram diligentiam et iuges labores viderent et intelligerent, Conmiseratione quadam ductus et priscorum germanorum laboribus mirum immodum conpaciens, ut quae illi magnis impensis et vigiliis, dum ante annos septingentos Rhomanas litteras, prius enim graecis usi fuimus, cum religione christiana suscepimus scripsissent, Illa iam seculorum nostrorum ignavia et incuria, dum speciosa vicia sequimur, a coeli iniuria pulvere pro litterarum studiis situ et carie et ut cum gemitu dicam a blaptis etiam non satis tuta essent. Accessit mira mihi quaedam historiarum germanicarum vicinarumque nobis nationum cupido.

Therefore, when I saw that many famous and brilliant manuscripts, like so many fine and first-rate spoils of ours, were being removed by Italians from Germany to Italy and printed there, I thought to myself that a man born in the heart of Germany in Hercynia and the first German to receive, on your initiative and advice, most illustrious Prince Frederick, the laurel from the emperor as the ornament and symbol of letters should be duty-bound by right of succession and heritage like a skilled hunter to ferret out those codices now lying in obscurity and to present them to my fellow Germans as something to be admired so that they might observe and understand the industry and patient labors which our fathers and progenitors of old devoted to literature and the Christian religion. I was stirred with regret and deep sympathy for the labors of the ancient Germans who wrote these manuscripts with great expense and trouble over seven hundred years ago when we first learned Latin letters (for we at first used Greek letters) together with the Christian religion; for these manuscripts are now, through the ignorance and carelessness of our own times, in which we follow specious vices, not sufficiently protected from damaging weather, dust, mold, and even (it pains me to say) insects, instead of being preserved for literary studies. In addition I feel some special passion for the history of the German nation and of those bordering it.[8]

Nothing is known either of when or why Celtis conveyed the map to his friend, the prominent jurist, collector, and scholar, Konrad Peutinger (1465–1547), *Stadtsschreiber* (city secretary) of Augsburg,[9] although summer 1507 may be considered a possibility, because Celtis is attested as visiting Augsburg at that time. Confirmation that it was beyond doubt the map that Celtis gave to Peutinger, not some other document or text, comes from the latter's own catalog of his library, in which he records:

Antonini itinerarium . . . : hoc idem in Charta Longa a Celti nobis Testamento legata. [Plate 2]

The *Antonini itinerarium* . . . . : this being the same in a long map bequeathed to us by Celtis in his will.[10]

In line with the wish expressed by Celtis in his will, Peutinger twice set plans in motion for the copying and publication of the map, having gained the necessary permission (*privilegium impressorium*) from the emperor Maximilian for the latter step on March 1, 1511.[11] In the first instance, however, he was evidently not satisfied enough to continue

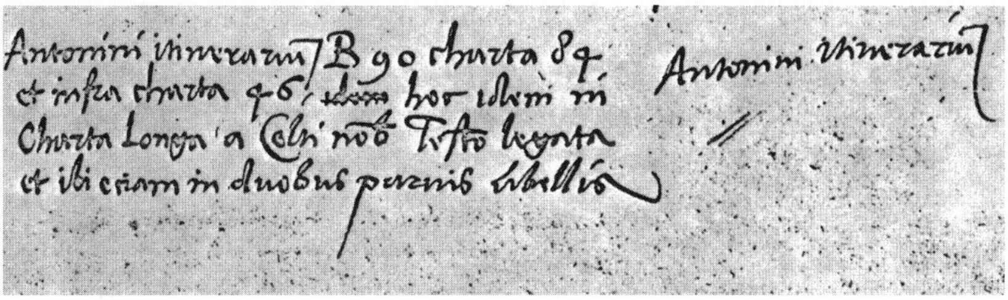

PLATE 2. Inventory entry made by Peutinger. Photo: Bayerische Staatsbibliothek, München. Clm 4021 c, fol. 6r.

the work. As will emerge, all that was ever published from it (and not until 1591) are two anonymous artists' sketches of the leftmost portion of the map. In the second instance, another artist, Michael Hummelberg, duly fulfilled his commission to copy the map full-size, challenging task though he found it to be.[12] He undertook it at the specific request of the renowned humanist and historian of the early Germans, Beatus Rhenanus (1485–1547).[13] Proud of having reproduced the map faithfully without introducing corrections or improvements, by May 1526 Hummelberg was preparing to hand over his eighteen sheets to a pair of engravers;[14] but he died a year later without having done this, it seems, and the sheets subsequently disappeared.[15]

Peutinger willingly showed the map to friends and rejected all overtures to part with it, rebuffing even an approach from Francis I, king of France (r. 1515–47). Hummelberg records the memorable occasion, but does not date it (presumably between 1515 and 1519), in a letter written to Beatus Rhenanus on January 13, 1526:

> Superioribus annis, praesente divo Maximiliano, Orator Regis Gallorum pro hac tabella Peutingero obtulerat LX. Coronatos; cui ille: Placerent quidem coronati nummi, sed vetustatis hoc monumentum magis placet, quam ulla pecunia, qua vel aestimari possit vel vendi. Collaudavit Caesar et responsum, et Peutingerum munere donavit caesareo.

> Years ago, in the presence of his late majesty Maximilian [died 1519], the French king's spokesman had offered Peutinger 70 crowns for this map. His response was that while he would certainly value the cash, this monument of antiquity was worth more to him than any money, beyond all possible valuation or sale price. The emperor both praised this response and made a princely gift to Peutinger.[16]

Understandably, however, the impact that the map made during Peutinger's lifetime remained altogether limited,[17] and then, in the decades following his death in 1547, would shrink to nothing.

(a) Welser (1591)

Peutinger had bequeathed his library to his four sons with the stipulation that it was not to be divided, and it was in fact to remain in the family's possession until the death of the last male descendant, Desiderius Ignaz von Peutingen (1641–1718),[19] who bequeathed it to St. Salvator's College, a Jesuit institution in Augsburg. In 1546, however, fear for the library's safety on the outbreak of war had prompted Peutinger to order its removal to a more secure location. Not until 1548 (after his death) was it brought back to Augsburg, its 2,200 volumes inevitably in disarray, and thereafter a complete fresh inventory was not taken until 1597.[20] Marcus Welser (Velserius, 1558–1614) – [21] member of another leading Augsburg family related to the Peutingers through Konrad's marriage to Margarita Welser and a humanist, author, and publisher – went in search of the map once he returned to Augsburg in 1584 after residing in Venice. He was prompted in part by Abraham Ortels (Ortelius, 1527–98),[22] the famous maker and publisher of maps at Antwerp, the European center for such activity in the late sixteenth century. As it happened, not only was Ortels's family from Augsburg, but he also maintained a keen lifelong interest in ancient history and geography.

However, Peutinger's second son, Christoph, who inherited his father's library after the death of his elder brother Claudius Pius in 1552, had politely rebuffed even the enquiry about the map made by his friend Johan Roma at Ortels's urging. Roma reported Christoph's reaction to Ortels on June 25, 1583:

> . . . se nihil magis in votis habere, quam tibi, tuique similibus eruditis viris, in re praesertim tam honesta gratificandi, sed me non ignorare, quam huiusmodi res difficiles sint inventu, cistas enim plures diversis chartis, tabulis, ac scripturis plenas, quas nunquam vidit extare, ac ob id se nescire, unde initium quaerendi facere debeat. . . .

> . . . his greatest desire was to satisfy you and learned men like you in such a particularly worthy cause; but I should be aware how difficult items of this type are to locate, since there is a quantity of boxes full of various papers, documents, and writings which he has never seen, hence he does not know where he should so much as begin a search. . . . [23]

This approach by Roma had been recommended to Ortels by Adolphus Occo in a letter dated November 5, 1582; here Christoph Peutinger is described as "homine misanthropo," who only admits "familiarissimos et intimos" to the library.[24] Welser did eventually succeed in gaining admittance, and in 1587 he discovered there the two anonymous sketches – mentioned above – commissioned by Konrad Peutinger. These he arranged to be engraved and published (uncolored) by Aldus Manutius in Venice in 1591, under the title *Fragmenta tabulae antiquae, in quis aliquot per Rom. provincias itinera. Ex Peutingerorum bibliotheca.* "Tabula" — Welser's choice of descriptive noun — typically denotes a large piece of parchment, often stretched on a frame or fastened to a wooden tablet.[25] [Plate 3a, b]

Welser not only opens the *Praefatio* (pp. 5–16) to his publication with a recollection of the tribute repeatedly paid to the importance of the map by Konrad Peutinger's friend, the scholar Beatus Rhenanus, but he also concludes the volume's text (pp. 58–60) with a reproduction of relevant *Testimonia* by both Beatus Rhenanus and two other scholars. As Welser goes on to say in the *Praefatio*, Beatus Rhenanus' exploitation of the map fired others with a powerful desire to see it.[26] Even so, Peutinger (Welser explains) never brought it to publication, and since his death it could no longer be found. Despite the best efforts of searchers, all that had emerged were two anonymous sample sketches reckoned to have been made from the map on Peutinger's instruction. Now that these two were in Welser's hands, he had resolved to publish them, as there was no knowing when in the future, if ever, anything more of the map might come to light. The limitations of the sketches, however, called for a commentary, which Welser also committed himself to provide.

Much about the sketches no doubt puzzled Welser, and understandably so. The engraving of the first ("SCHEDA PRIOR") is a sheet approximately 38 cm wide and just under 17 cm high ($15 \times 6\frac{1}{2}$ in.).[27] Its coverage extends no farther leftward than Ridvmo in Britain, nor farther right than Colo Tra (where the name breaks off) in 1A5. This sketch omits anywhere in mainland Europe that is placed lower than Lemvno, and does not extend as far down as Africa; indeed, toward its bottom and far right the sketch is simply blank. From the many spelling errors, Welser rightly conjectured that the artist had been prone to read names carelessly. Roman numerals have been converted into arabic figures. It is equally evident that the artist has taken the liberty of rendering symbols in a contemporary sixteenth-century style. Two further significant deviations on his part that Welser could not have grasped are enlargement of symbols and tracing of routes as sinuous lines rather than as predominantly straight stretches divided by sharp downward turns or "chicanes."

At just over 20 cm (8 in.), the engraving of the second sketch, a sheet folded into the volume, is less wide than the first; but it is considerably taller — just over 28 cm (11 in.), with almost a further 3 cm ($1\frac{1}{4}$ in.) to accommodate the title "SCHEDA POSTERIOR," which runs along the bottom. While this second sketch, too, extends leftward to Ridvmo (spelled "Riduno" here), it goes no farther right than Adullia, Duretie, Bibona, Lomiuio (as these names are spelled). Corresponding coverage of Africa *is* offered in this instance, however, and no substantial part of the sheet is left blank. Latin numerals are retained. Otherwise, this second sketch takes similar liberties to those of the first, although in distinct enough ways to suggest that the two artists were different individuals working quite independently. The second artist, too, enlarged symbols and rendered them in his own sixteenth-century style. His routes also are sinuous line work – rather less sinuous than that of the first artist, it is true, but still showing no appreciation for the correspondence between place-names and straight stretches marked off by chicanes that the mapmaker intended. Last but not least, the spelling of many names is careless: notably, "Bouilla" is written for "Bononia."

If Konrad Peutinger had commissioned these sketches in the hope that either of the artists, or both, would demonstrate the capacity to produce a satisfactory copy of the entire map, we may readily appreciate (as Welser could not in 1591) why he preferred to postpone the initiative. This

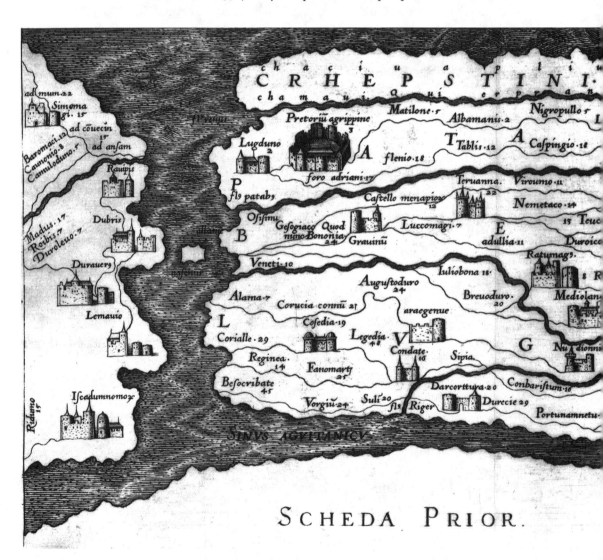

SCHEDA PRIOR.

said, the puzzle remains that Peutinger seemingly failed to demand more painstaking attention to accurate reproduction of the map in all its aspects, and that the artists on their part treated such concerns so cavalierly. Given that Michael Hummelberg did gain authorization to complete his copy of the map, his rendering, by contrast, must no doubt have found acceptance; but the loss of his material removes the opportunity to compare his efforts with the earlier sketches by the other two artists.

After some discussion of Roman itineraries and roads in his *Praefatio*, Welser proceeds to offer an extensive scholarly commentary (*Explicatio*), name by name, for each sketch. The first of these commentaries (pp. 17–48) is longer than the second (pp. 49–57), because the latter only addresses those names not already found on the first sketch. Following the *Testimonia* mentioned above, a two-page *Index Nominum* concludes the volume.

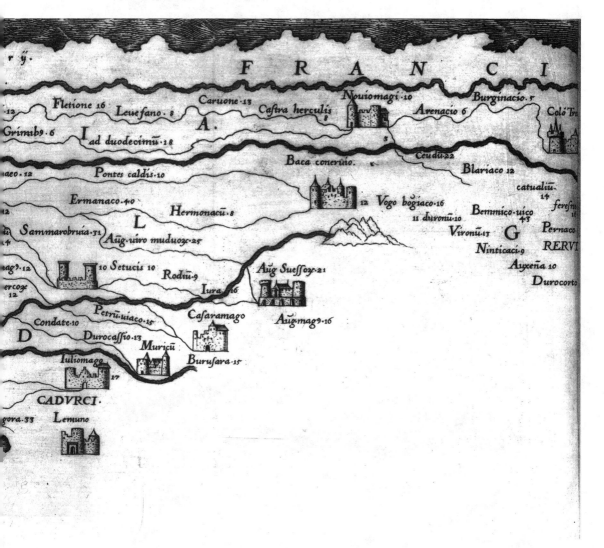

PLATE 3a. Sketch published by Welser, 1591. Photo: Universität Basel.

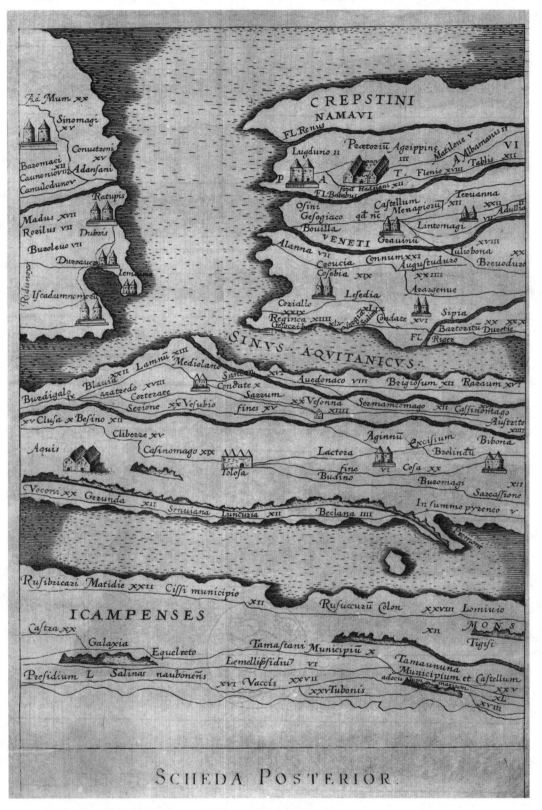

PLATE 3b. Sketch published by Welser, 1591. Photo: Universität Basel.

(b) Welser and Moretus (1598)

Meanwhile the map itself continued to elude Welser until 1597, when he wrote to Ortels in Antwerp on July 2:

> Euangelia para, mi Orteli, euangelia: debes certe. Tabula illa sive itineraria, sive provincialis, sive cuiuscumque illa nominis, quam te per aliquot viginti annos opinor quaerere, cuiusque nos olim schidia tuo consilio magni adeo fecimus, ut aeri incise publico dederimus, Deo bene iuvante, tandem inventa est, aliquo meo labore, nonnulla etiam invidia, sed omnia tanti sunt. Autographum domi habeo, satisdato de incolumi restituendo iis quorum interest, nam postquam me eius mirifice cupidum animadverterunt, rem prius neglectui habitam, suo primum pretio aestimare coeperunt. Apographum inde religiosissime confectum ad te cogito mittere, sed temporis aliquam moram patienter feras oportet, quod pictor, cuius in hoc genere expertus diligentiam inprimis probo, nunc nobis vacare non possit, brevi tamen vacaturus spero.

> Prepare to rejoice, my dear Ortelius, to rejoice: you surely should. That document, be it an itinerary, or regional [map], or whatever other name it should go by, the one that I believe you have been seeking for some twenty years, sketches of which on your advice I once valued highly enough to have engraved on copper and published, with God's good help has finally been found, with some effort on my part, as well as a degree of resentment, but it is all worth as much. I have the original at home, after making a pledge for its safe return to those whose concern it is. Indeed, having realized my extraordinary eagerness for it – an item previously treated with neglect – they have begun to appreciate it at its own value for the first time. I next mean to send you the most accurately rendered copy, but you are obliged to be patient and tolerate some delay for a time, because the artist whom I consider more painstaking at this kind of skilled task than any other cannot be free for our work at this point; but I hope that he will be free shortly.[28]

Welser commissioned the Augsburg artist Johannes Moller to make a half-size rendering of the entire map, which was dispatched to Antwerp. Prior to his death on June 28, 1598, Ortels entrusted the publication to Johannes Moerentorf (Moretus). Proofs from the eight anonymous copper-engraved plates (which in turn render the map at just over half-size) were read against the original in Augsburg by Welser. Each plate measures about 51 cm (20 in.) in width, and shows the map 18.5 cm ($7\frac{1}{4}$ in.) tall within its margins; plates are lettered A–H sequentially at bottom center or thereabouts as space permits. Occupying the leftmost 16.5 cm ($6\frac{1}{2}$ in.) of the first plate are the title and dedication:

> *Tabula itineraria ex illustri Peutingerorum bibliotheca quae Augustae Vindel. est beneficio Marci Velseri septemviri Augustani in lucem edita. Nobilissimo viro*

Marco Velsero R. P. Augustanae septemviro Ioannes Moretus typographus Antverp.
S. P. D.

Tabula itineraria from the distinguished library of the Peutingers situated at Augsburg, brought to light by the good efforts of Marcus Velser, councillor of Augsburg. Dedicated to the most noble Marcus Velser, councillor of the city of Augsburg, by Ioannes Moretus, printer at Antwerp, at his own expense.

Appended to this title and dedication is a tribute by Moretus to Welser dated December 1, 1598: [Plate 4]

Hanc tabulam, vir nobilissime, non mittimus ad te, sed remittimus, aquam scilicet e tuo fonte. Tu eam ad Ortelium nostrum (heu, nuper cum dolore litteratorum defunctum) descriptam miseras, tua cura inter Peutingeri schedas repertam et erutam: ideoque iure ad te redit. Ipse Ortelius, haud

procul a fato, ita mihi mandaverat: et mea sane voluntas et tui cultus eodem ducebant. Accipies igitur privatam olim tuam, nunc publicam per te omnium tabulam: et si gratum carumque defunctum habuisti, quaeso ut etiam hoc postremum ab eo munus.

Most noble sir, we do not so much send you this document as send it back, like water from your own fountain. You it was who had sent a copy of it to our Ortelius (recently deceased, alas, to scholars' sorrow), after it had been found by your efforts among Peutinger's manuscripts and rescued: rightly thus it returns to you. Ortelius himself, as death approached, had therefore entrusted it to me, and my commitment and your concern forged ahead together. So you are to accept this document that once was your private property, but now by your efforts belongs to all. And if you esteemed the deceased (Ortelius) as a kind, dear, man, I ask that you consider this, too, a final gift from him.

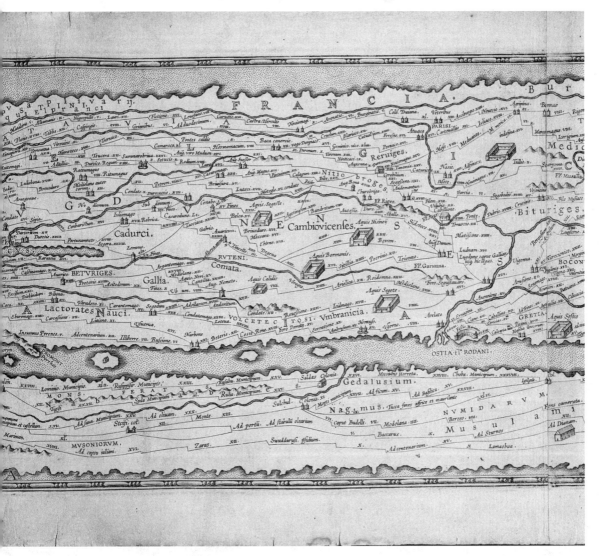

PLATE 4. The 1598 engraving of the entire map half-size printed by Moretus (first plate). Photo: Bibliothèque, Université de Mons-Hainaut, Mons.

Once Moretus had dispatched to Welser a handful of first copies made in great haste from these eight plates at the end of December 1598, he then proceeded to add a ninth plate of Latin text (only 24 cm [9$\frac{1}{2}$ in.] wide) for the print run proper of 250 uncolored copies.[29] This text in two columns – simply headed SPECTATORI S. and allegedly written by Welser –[30] celebrates the recent discovery of the entire map and briefly reflects upon its authorship and scope, as well as explaining certain features of the engraving.[31]

The engraving and publication of an entire historic map in this way merit recognition as an unprecedented initiative of lasting importance.[32] Indeed, as will emerge,[33] almost three centuries later (in the 1860s) Ernest Desjardins was to claim that the 1598 "facsimile" had still to be surpassed, even though it was made at only about half-size and from an artist's rendering rather than from the map itself, which stayed in Augsburg. Certainly there is no denying that despite the reduced size – or perhaps because of it – the engraver has successfully striven to present a very clear and tidy presentation of the map's detail; the control of names and line work in the vicinity of yconio (9B2), for example, is remarkable.

At the same time, however, these very merits of the engraving act to misrepresent the map, which in fact falls well short in clarity and comprehensibility. No doubt it was Welser himself whose editorial zeal ensured that only in the rarest instances should the lettering for a name be left incomplete. As a result, in the Aegean barely a single island lacks its full name, and similarly complete nomenclature is to be found in the Nile Delta, although both these areas of the map are poorly preserved on our copy. Needless to add, the assurance given in the final paragraph of the SPECTATORI S. text that the engraving represents a wholly faithful reproduction of the map in Augsburg – with no corrections or "improvements" introduced – is exaggerated. Rather, there was a deliberate intention on the part of those responsible for the engraving to render it as accessible and satisfying as possible to users. An unfortunate consequence of this effort is that, because no distinction is drawn between lettering that could be read on the map and restored lettering, it becomes impossible to gauge how much more of it was visible to Welser than to any of his successors down to the present. In the late nineteenth and early twentieth centuries Konrad Miller[34] would maintain that the 1598 engraving (not to mention what he identified as Hummelberg's drawing) preserves lettering and other features that subsequently faded from view. Some deterioration of this type seems by no means implausible, but its extent is beyond recovery. The difficulty of speculating about it is only compounded by instances where Welser can be seen to reject lettering still plainly visible today in order to "improve" upon it: note, for example, his Port Salonitanus (5A3) where on the map itself capital C as the first letter of the second word is not in doubt, nor v as its fifth letter.

Welser did at least evidently succeed in demanding from the artist Johannes Moller a far higher degree of accuracy in copying line work and symbols than Peutinger had been able to secure from either of the artists whose sketches Welser published in 1591, when the map itself still eluded him. Even so, the engravings derived from Moller's drawings, like the sketches published in 1591, suggest that he envisaged the settlement symbols as sixteenth-century turrets, and consequently added two or more small upper window slits to them as embellishment. The accuracy of the line work for coasts, rivers, and routes is generally satisfactory, but there is often still room for improvement, and egregious slips can be found. Among the latter is a failure to complete the route from unnamed symbol no. 33 (4B4) to Adnovas (4B5), with the consequent omission of three names and two distance figures.[35]

On November 18, 1598, enclosing a proof of the map provided by Moretus, Welser wrote to Paul(lus) Merula (1558–1607),[36] professor of history and librarian at Leiden University, with a pressing plea that he undertake to prepare a commentary on it in its entirety.[37] Merula's reply of February 1, 1599, declining this invitation is not preserved, but it was evidently gracious enough to tempt Welser to repeat his plea in a letter dated September 1, 1599.[38] Merula remained adamant, however, as emerges from the prefatory section "LECTORI MEO S. dico" of his *Cosmographiae Generalis Libri Tres* (Leiden, 1605). Here he acknowledges Welser's repeated efforts to persuade him to undertake a commentary on the map, but confesses himself deterred by the complexity of the task ("negocium involutum labor difficilis") together with the map's vast scope.[39] In the course of the *Cosmographia* he does take into account information gained from the map, but Welser's hope that he would focus on it more directly was never to be fulfilled. In fact, no commentary on the entire map would achieve publication for a further two centuries and more.

(c) Reuse of the 1598 Plates

Moretus' eight plates presenting the map (headed by the *Tabula Itineraria* title and tribute to Welser) were reissued – along with the Antonine and Bordeaux Itineraries – in the second volume of *Theatrum Geographiae Veteris* by Petrus Bertius (Bert), professor at the University of Leiden and *cosmographus* to King Louis XIII of France, published at Amsterdam in 1619.[40] The large page-size (26 cm wide × 42 [$10\frac{1}{4}$ × $16\frac{1}{2}$ in.]) permits two of the plates (one above the other) to occupy a doublespread. Each of the four spreads in fact comprises a single sheet, with only titles printed on the intervening pages, so that in principle the map could be reassembled in strip form. This presentation of the *Tabula Itineraria* is preceded (on a single page) by the *Testimonia* that form pages 58–60 of Welser's 1591 volume, and is then followed by that entire volume (reprinted on twenty pages) except for the *Index Nominum*; the two sketches form separate sheets, each folded in at the start of its respective *Explicatio*.

The eight 1598 plates were again used to include the map in the 1624 edition of *Theatrum Orbis Terrarum Parergon, sive veteris geographiae tabulae commentariis geographicis et historicis illustratae* published at Antwerp in Ortels's name by Balthasar Moretus (son of Johannes). Here, too, as in Bertius' volume, the page size (28 cm wide × 46 [11 × 18 in.]) permits two plates to occupy a doublespread.[41] These four spreads are distributed through three reprinted texts comprising (in order, spread over seven pages): the Praefatio from Welser's 1591 *Fragmenta tabulae antiquae*; the SPECTATORI S. text[42] from the 1598 *Tabula Itineraria*; and the Testimonia from the 1591 *Fragmenta tabulae antiquae*.

Joannes Janssonius (Jansson) at Amsterdam had the 1598 plates reengraved, with the original dedication replaced by: "Tabula Itineraria ex illustri Peutingerorum Bibliotheca quae Augustae Vindelicorum Beneficio Marci Velseri Septem-viri Augustani in Lucem edita." Jansson first issued them in his *Accuratissima Orbis Antiqui Delineatio sive Geographia Vetus, Sacra, et Profana* in 1652.[43] The set of eight plates, each measuring 50 cm wide × 18 ($19\frac{3}{4}$ × 7 in.), offers just the entire map headed by a short title and occupies four successive doublespreads. These spreads are single sheets with nothing printed on the intervening pages, so that the map could be reassembled in strip form. Two subsequent works by Jansson that expanded upon his *Accuratissima* also included this presentation of the map: Part VI of his *Novus Atlas sive Theatrum Orbis Terrarum* from 1658, and his *Atlas Major* from 1662.[44]

A 1682 volume of almost a thousand pages published in Nuremberg, *Marci Velseri Opera in Unum Collecta*, brings together writings by Marcus Welser or closely associated with him. The editor Christoph Arnold includes the following items relevant to the Peutinger map:

(pp. 705–72) The entire *Fragmenta tabulae antiquae* (1591) except for its Index Nominum. Arnold's page size (20 cm wide × 32 [8 × $12\frac{1}{2}$ in.]) permits Scheda Prior at its original size to be accommodated across a doublespread without the need for a righthand foldout. Scheda Posterior, too, is virtually unchanged in size, occupying a single page here, though cramped on all sides, and indeed losing its original edges. Between pp. 727 and 771, copies of the *Tabula Itineraria* (1598) engravings are interspersed, presented as one single page at the start (p. 727), followed by eleven doublespreads. The new plates prepared for the purpose are all are approximately 18 cm (7 in.) tall, and on each page the map has a width of approximately 16 cm ($6\frac{1}{4}$ in.). Miller notes that many slips by the engraver have gone uncorrected.[45]

(pp. 773–74) The dedication and SPECTATORI S. text from the *Tabula Itineraria* (1598). The text is now titled DISSERTATIO ANONYMA SPECTATORI S., some minor changes in punctuation are made, and the opening sentence of the final paragraph is expanded.[46]

(pp. 775–84) The text entitled *Germania* from Petrus Bertius, *Theatrum Geographiae Veteris*, vol. 2 (1619). By this means, as Arnold explains,[47] readers may gain information on at least part of the map (spanning six segments, he claims) that extends Welser's systematic guidance (here reprinted) for

the limited area covered by the two sketches. Arnold's inclusion of Bertius'
Germania text underscores the point that, during almost a century since the
full publication of the Peutinger map in 1598, a successor had yet to expand
the scope of Welser's commentary even partially. In the early eighteenth
century, too, several initiatives with this aim never came to completion for
one reason or other.[48]

The original edition of Nicolas Bergier, *Histoire des grands chemins de*
l'empire romain (Paris, 1622) included three scholarly, albeit general, chapters on the Peutinger map, including some comparison with the Antonine
Itinerary (Book 3, chaps. 7, 8, 9 = pp. 320–38), but there is no reproduction of even part of the map. However, when the work was reissued
over a century later in two volumes (Brussels, 1728), the map was added
at the end of the second on eight plates bound in as righthand pullouts
on thick paper.[49] The engraving used for the reissue is 18 cm (7 in.) in
height. On the lefthand page facing the first pullout, the 1598 SPECTATORI
s. text is reprinted with this title. An *Avertissement* by the printer in the
front matter to volume 1 explains that the Peutinger map plates are those
of Jansson/Horn reengraved (i.e., the 1598 plates now at second remove),
and that the only alterations to Bergier's text are corrections or additions
that he himself had recorded in his own copy of the original edition.

3. CHANGES OF OWNERSHIP, REAL (1714–1738) AND THREATENED[50]

Despite being the single most famous and precious item in Peutinger's
collection, the map itself evidently remained neglected and was even pre-
sumed lost again during the seventeenth century. However, in July 1714 –
prior to Desiderius Ignaz von Peutingen's bequest of his ancestor's library
to St. Salvator's College the following year – the Augsburg councillor
Wolfgang Jakob Sulzer successfully discovered the map, "squalore et situ
obductam, et, non certe pro dignitate, in obscuri cuiusdam anguli latebris
reconditam" ("found overlaid with dirt and decay hidden away in the
recesses of some dark corner, where it assuredly did not deserve to be").[51]
Sulzer then urged that this extraordinary treasure receive far more respect-
ful treatment in the future. Ignaz von Peutingen's reaction was that the map
warranted a new owner, and he accordingly disposed of it to the noted
Augsburg bookseller, Paul Kühtze (or Küz), for a substantial (unspecified)
sum. In 1715 Kühtze placed a long, curious, and by no means altogether
accurate, notice in the *Leipziger Wochentliche Post-Zeitungen von gelehrten*
Neuigkeiten confirming that the map itself – not a copy – was in his hands,
and inviting enquiries:[52] [Plate 5]

Augsburg. Zu denen *Itinerariis antiquis*, so *Ricciolus Hydrogr. reformat. 1.III.*
cap. 3. p. 53. anführet, zum E(xempel?) des *Antonini, Aethici* und anderer,

gehöret allerdings die *tabula itineraria*, so *Conradus Peutingerus* in seiner *Bibliothec* aufbehalten, und dahero *Peutingeriana* genenet worden. Sie ist in dem *Originale* unter denen letzten *Imperatoribus* gezeichnet, und von dem *Conr. Protuccio Celte* in einer *Bibliothec* auf seinen Reisen gefunden worden, von dem sie *Peutingerus* ohne Zweiffel gehabt, wie er denn unterschiedenes daraus die gelehrte Welt lesen lassen. Ob nun wohl dieselbe ein grosses Verlangen bezeiget, diese *Tabulam* gantz und gar zu haben, weil man un(d) zwar nicht ohne Grund davor gehalten, daß sie viel schwere Knoten in *Geographicis* so wol als *Historicis* aufzulösen dienen würde, so hat doch *Peutingerus* dieses Verlangen aus unbekandten Ursachen nicht gestillet. Es hat auch niemand anders dieselbe nur zu sehen bekommen können, ob man sich gleich höchstes Fleisses darum bemühet. Alles, was man nach seinem Todte unter seinen *Manuscriptis* finden können, sind 2 Risse gewesen, so nach dieser *tabula* nachgezeichnet worden, welche *Marcus Velserus* herausgegeben und mit Anmerckungen erläutert hat. Sie finden sich in seinen *Operibus p. 726 seq.* Ob diese *tabula* noch vorhanden, haben viele in Zweiffel

Teutſchland.

Augsburg. Zu benen Itinerariis antiquis, ſo Ricciolus Hydrogr. reformat. l. III. cap. 3. p. 53. anführet, zum E. des Antonini, Aethici und anderer, gehöret allerdings die tabula itineraria, ſo Conradus Peutingerus in ſeiner Bibliothec aufbehalten, und dahero Peut.ngeriana genenet worden. Sie iſt in dem Originale unter denen letzten Imperatoribus gezeichnet, und von dem Conr. Protuccio Celte in einer Bibliothec auf ſeinen Reiſen gefunden worden/ von dem ſie Peutingerus ohne Zweiffel gehabt/ wie er denn unterſchiedenes daraus die gelehrte Welt leſen laſſen. Ob nun wohl dieſelbe ein groſſes Verlangen bezeiget, dieſe Tabulam gantz und gar zu haben/ weil man un zwar nicht ohne Grund davor gehalten, daß ſie viel ſchwere Knoten in Geographicis ſo wol als Hiſtoricis aufzulöſen dienen würde, ſo hat doch Peutingerus dieſes Verlangen aus unbekandten Urſachen nicht geſtillet. Es hat auch niemand anders dieſelbe nur zu ſehen bekommen können, ob man ſich gleich höchſtes Fleiſſes darum bemühet. Alles, was man nach ſeinem Todte unter ſeinen Manuſcriptis finden können/ ſind 2 Riſſe geweſen, ſo nach dieſer tabula nachgezeichnet worden/ welche Marcus Velſerus herausgegeben und mit Anmerckungen erläutert hat. Sie finden ſich in ſeinen Operibus p. 726. ſeq. Ob dieſe tabula noch vorhanden, haben viele in Zweiffel ziehen wollen. Marcus Velſerus ſelbſt redet davon als von einer ungewiſſen Sache. Hr. M. Chriſtian Hübner und Hr. Jo. Gottfried Gregorii halten dieſelbe gar vor verlohren/ gleichwie aus des erſtern Diſſertatione de ſtudio Geographico in genere §. 113. p. 17. und des letztern Tractate von denen vornehmſten alten und neuen Land-Charten cap. IV. §. 7. p. 31. zu erſehen iſt. Alleine es iſt wohl eher geſchehen, daß man Dinge verlohren geſchätzet/ die nichts deſto weniger in guten Händen geweſen. Dergleichen hat man uns auch von dieſer tabula berichtet. Denn ein Liebhaber deutſcher Antiquitäten hat Gelegenheit gehabt, ſich an einem gewiſſen Orte nach dieſen Monumento umzuſehen, und iſt, wie uns zugeſchrieben worden/ ſo glücklich geweſen/ dieſelbe anzutreffen. Er hat dieſelbe mit der in Velſeri Operibus befindlichen Copie genau verglichen/ und eine völlige Übereinſtimmung wahrgenommen. Inſonderheit äuſſert ſich alles an derſelben/ was Velſerus p. 709.-716. und NB. p. 772.773.774. davon geſchrieben. Dahero denn gedachter Liebhaber nicht zweiffelt, daß ſolches nicht das wahre Original derſelben ſeyn ſolte / ja vielmehr glaubet/ jedermann werde ihm Beyfall geben/ wenn er daſſelbe in der Nähe ſehen ſolte. Daferne jemand weitere Nachricht davon einzuholen Luſt hat, der kan ſich an Hn. Paul Kühtzen/ berühmten Buchhändler in Augsburg, addreſſiren/ welcher ihm genugſame Anleitung darzu geben wird.

ziehen wollen. *Marcus Velserus* selbst redet davon als von einer ungewissen Sache. Hr. *M. Christian Hübner* und Hr. *Jo. Gottfried Gregorii* halten dieselbe gar vor verlohren, gleichwie aus des erstern *Dissertatione de studio Geographico in genere §. 113. p. 27.* und des letztern *Tractate* von denen vornehmsten alten und neuen Land-Charten *cap. IV. §. 7. p. 31.* zu ersehen ist. Alleine es ist wohl eher geschehen, daß man Dinge verlohren geschätzet, die nichts desto weniger in guten Händen gewesen. Dergleichen hat man uns auch von dieser *tabula* berichtet. Denn ein Liebhaber deutscher *Antiqui*täten hat Gelegenheit gehabt, sich an einem gewissen Orte nach diesen *Monumento* umzusehen, und ist, wie uns zugeschrieben worden, so glücklich gewesen, dieselbe anzutreffen. Er hat dieselbe mit der in *Velseri Operibus* befindlichen *Copie* genau verglichen, und eine völlige Übereinstimmung wahrgenommen. Insonderheit äussert sich alles an derselben, was *Velserus p. 709.–716.* und *n(ota) b(ene) p. 772.773.774.* davon geschrieben. Dahero denn gedachter Liebhaber nicht zweiffelt, daß solches nicht das wahre *Original* derselben seyn solte, ja vielmehr glaubet, jedermann werde ihm Beyfall geben, wenn er dasselbe in der Nähe sehen solte. Daferne jemand weitere Nachricht davon einzuholen Lust hat, der kan sich an Hn. Paul Kühzen, berühmten Buchhändler in Augsburg, *addressi*ren, welcher ihm genugsame Anleitung darzu geben wird.

Augsburg. Among the ancient itineraries – Ricciolus . . . cites as examples those of Antoninus, Aethicus, and others – there definitely belongs the *tabula itineraria* kept by Conrad Peutinger in his library, so that it came to be called "Peutingeriana." The original was drawn under the last emperors and discovered in a library by Conrad Protuccius Celtes on his travels; without doubt it was from him that Peutinger obtained it and permitted the scholarly community to read extracts from it. The scholarly community has displayed a strong desire to possess this Tabula in its entirety, as scholars have held with good cause that it may be used to solve many difficult problems in both geography and history; for reasons that are unknown, however, Peutinger did not satisfy this desire. Nobody else was even able to see it, despite making the greatest of efforts. All that could be found among his manuscripts after his death were two sketches traced from this Tabula, which Marcus Velser published and commented upon with notes. These are to be found in his *Opera*. . . . Many people wished to doubt whether this Tabula still existed. Marcus Velser himself speaks of it as an unresolved issue. Hübner and Gregorius go so far as to consider it lost, as is evident both in Hübner's *Dissertatio de studio Geographico in genere* . . . and in Gregorius' *Tractate von denen vornehmsten alten und neuen Land-Charten* . . . – except it so happened that things were thought to be lost which were nonetheless in good hands all along. This is what was reported to us about the Tabula. As a lover of German antiquities wrote to us, because he had the opportunity to search for this monument in a certain place, he was very happy to come across it. He made a close comparison with the copy to be found in Velser's *Opera*, and recognized a full correspondence between the two, which becomes particularly clear in what Velser wrote about it, pp. . . . No enthusiast would doubt that the Tabula is not the genuine original [of Peutinger's map], but believes instead that anyone who was to see it close up would concur with him. Anyone caring to obtain further information can apply to Herr Paul Kühze, well-known book dealer in Augsburg, who will provide detailed guidance.[53]

Keen interest was shown by potentially formidable bidders, including the senate of Leipzig itself and the duke of Braunschweig-Wolfenbüttel. It is unclear why the sale was only completed in 1720, although Kühtze's death before he had disposed of the map seems the most likely explanation; it was his executor or heirs who made the sale, presumably after an interval.[54] Why the successful purchaser proved to be Prince Eugen of Savoy (1663–1736) is equally obscure, especially when the price he is known to have paid – 100 (gold) ducats, equivalent to a high imperial official's annual salary – hardly seems beyond others' reach. On September 20, 1717, he wrote a letter – still preserved [Plate 6] – "au camp de Semlin" outside Belgrade (after the Turkish defeat there) addressed to (Karl Gustav) Heraeus, imperial "Inspecteur des antiquités," expressing interest in the acquisition of "les Tabula Peutingeriana de Theodose en original écrites sur le velin."

There need be no doubt that the eventual choice of bidder must have involved more than merely financial considerations. Quite apart from his prestige as a general, Prince Eugen truly was a zealous collector of books and manuscripts.[55] Indeed, the celebrated funeral oration delivered for him by the papal nuncio in Vienna, Domenico Passionei (1682–1761),[56] praised the pride he took specifically in acquiring the map:

> E perchè io non debbo esser indifferente alle brame di tutti quei valent'Uomini, che in Paesi da questo lontani, vanno registrando ne'fasti della erudizione i ragguagli della più scelta letteratura; accennerò loro in passando, ch'egli non perdendo mai di vista lo scopo principale del suo profitto, si affaticò, e con tutta ragione, per conseguire l'unico esemplare di quella famosissima Carta, la quale a guisa d'una Terra nuovamente scoperta, come l'America, porta dopo due Secoli, il Cognome del celebre Peutingero, che per averla tratta fuora dalle tenebre, in cui giaceva sconosciuta, e sepolta, può chiamarsi il suo fortunato ritrovatore. E tanto Eugenio sì adoprò, e tanto fece, che no avendo risparmiato, nè offerte, nè recompense, n'ottenne finalmente il bramato possesso.

> And because I ought not to be backward to satisfy the Desires of those most worthy Men, who, in Countries far distant from this, go registering in the pride of Erudition, Informations of the choicest Literature, I shall remark to them as I pass along, that he never losing Sight of the principal Scope of his Design, labour'd, and that with great Reason, to obtain the only Copy

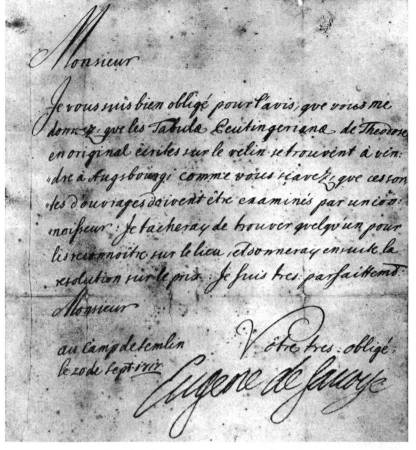

PLATE 6. Prince Eugen's letter dated September 20, 1717. Photo: © Bildarchiv, Österreichische Nationalbibliothek, Wien. Autogr. 14/61–1.

of that famous Map, which, like a Land newly discover'd, as was *America*, carries, after two Ages, the Name of the celebrated *Peutingerus*, who having drawn it forth from the Obscurity in which it lay unknown and buried, might call himself its fortunate Retriever. So much did EUGENE strive, and so much do, that neither sparing Offers, nor Rewards, he at last gain'd the desired Possession of it.[57]

Following Prince Eugen's sudden death, in 1737 his entire library was purchased from his niece and heir, Victoria, by the emperor Charles VI. Hence in 1738 the map came to the Hofbibliothek in Vienna,[58] which from 1920 has been Austria's National Library.

The map still remains in the library's Handschriftensammlung, cataloged as Codex Vindobonensis 324.[59] However, it would be a mistake to assume that external events from the mid-eighteenth century onward have not threatened it there. On the contrary, as one of the library's most prized treasures, in times of crisis its security has been a matter of concern at the highest level. In April 1797, when Vienna was under threat of capture by French forces, the map was one of twenty precious manuscripts packed up for immediate evacuation. This crisis was ended by the peace treaty signed at Campo Formio in October; but the precautions were evidently renewed in late 1800, until peace was agreed at Lunéville in February 1801.[60] At the end of October 1805, when orders were again issued for the packing and immediate removal of the library's greatest treasures, the map was one of three specifically named. In the event, the cases of treasures were hidden in the city rather than being moved elsewhere, and the library was not plundered by Napoleon's army during its brief occupation of the city from mid-November 1805 to mid-January 1806.[61]

There was a less happy outcome when French forces reoccupied Vienna in mid-May 1809, because a substantial proportion of the library's holdings was now removed to Paris (later recovered). However, the map escaped this ignominy, because it was in the fourteen cases of treasures already evacuated from the library to Hungary at the end of April – and by road rather than river, in order to reduce the possibility of any damage from damp.[62]

In mid-century, the map had the good fortune to remain unharmed by the outbreak of fire that did serious damage to the library on October 31 in the turbulent year 1848.[63] Later still, throughout World War II, it was among the great quantity of items stored in the cellars of the library and the Neue Burg nearby. Although there had been bomb damage, the immediate vicinity of the library otherwise escaped relatively unscathed when Russian forces occupied Vienna in April 1945. According to one horrifying rumor, however, this vicinity was to have been designated the last bastion of resistance.[64]

4. PUBLICATION (MID-18th CENTURY TO THE 1870s)

(a) von Scheyb (see Frontispiece)

After the map came to the Hofbibliothek, it was the Austrian scholar, poet and administrator Franz Christoph von Scheyb (1704–77)[65] who soon took what would prove to be the landmark step of commissioning a new engraving of it for publication. This was executed in Vienna by Salomon Kleiner (1703–61), in principle with special concern for accuracy. He began by tracing the entire contents of the map onto oiled paper, as von Scheyb explains in characteristically rhetorical style (*Praefatio*, p. x):

> Quippe ut, quod intendi, exactissime praestarem, exercitatissima ad id usus sum manu viri eximii Salomonis Kleiner geometrae et architecti ad id genus delineationum aptissimi. Is ne lacunam, hiatum, linoleam, punctum vel oblitteratum apicem transiliret; chartam oleo tinctam adeoque pellucidam archetypo superimposuit, inque illa, quidquid oculis percipi poterat, attentissimo calamo designavit, ac tandem apographum hoc meum labore tam indefesso ad umbilicum duxit, ut nemo illud aliis signis, quam quibus nova

ab antiquis differre solent, vetustatis nimirum rubigine, qua membranae authenticae oblitteratae sint, ab hac possit distinguere. Animo tamen necdum constiti. Segmenta singula in aes incisa et chartae impressa ad ipsam rursus Peutingerianam Tabulam tanquam ad lineam, ac iterum iterumque revocavi, examinavi, et quod sedulitas stili, invita descriptoris manu, forte transgressa est, vel immutavit; ea qua potui, adcuratione emendavi.

In order to achieve my aim of making a most accurate copy, I employed for the purpose the highly experienced hand of that outstanding individual Salomon Kleiner, surveyor and architect, most skilled at this type of drawing. In order not to omit any hole, gap, dash, stop, or damaged stroke, he placed paper soaked in oil and thus transparent over the exemplar, and with the most alert penmanship he traced onto this everything visible; eventually, by such tireless efforts, he made this apograph of mine its identical twin, leaving it possible for anyone to tell it apart from the original only by those signs which typically distinguish new from old, such as the foxing from age that has damaged genuine parchments. Even so, I was still in no mood to relax. Once the individual segments had been engraved on copper and printed on paper, I brought them back time and again to the Peutinger Table itself as if to a model, I inspected them, and whatever the application of the blade, through the unresponsiveness of the engraver's hand, had by chance omitted or altered, this so far as possible I carefully corrected.

The edition – entitled *Peutingeriana Tabula Itineraria Quae in Augusta Bibliotheca Vindobonensi Nunc Servatur Adcurate Exscripta* – was published in Vienna by the imperial printer and bookseller Johann Thomas Trattner in 1753. It is a substantial volume that includes several sections of text (each paginated separately): a learned and effusive six-page *Dedicatio* to the Empress Maria Theresa;[66] a six-page *Praefatio*; two pages of *Testimonia* to the accuracy of the copy;[67] a sixty-nine-page *Dissertatio de Tabula Peutingeriana* divided into six chapters;[68] and a twelve-page *Index* or gazetteer.[69] Last but not least in the volume comes the map itself, at full size. Von Scheyb's presentation of it comprises twelve folio doublespreads,[70] each thus slightly less wide than one of the eleven parchments being reproduced.[71] [Plate 7]

Von Scheyb's twelve doublespreads of the map were issued uncolored, but they incorporate indicators designed to convey to viewers (again for the first time) a useful impression of how and where color features. As he explains:

Curavi praeterea, ut, quemadmodum Archetypus variis coloribus ornatus est; ita etiam iisdem haec mea folia possint adumbrari. Quamobrem tota Tabula, quantum varietate rerum licuit, methodo, qua Heraldi, ut vocantur, colores aeri incisos exprimere solent, delineata est: *Mare* scilicet, *et flumina* lineis a sinistra ad dexteram declivibus exprimuntur, ut *viridis* coloris sint. *Montes* atque *aedicularum latera* punctis conspersa sunt, ut *flava*;

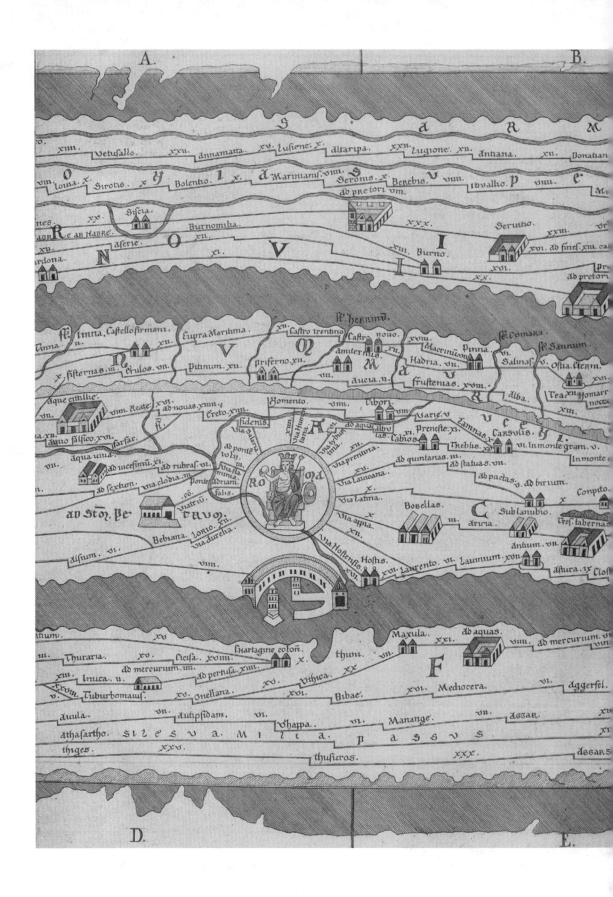

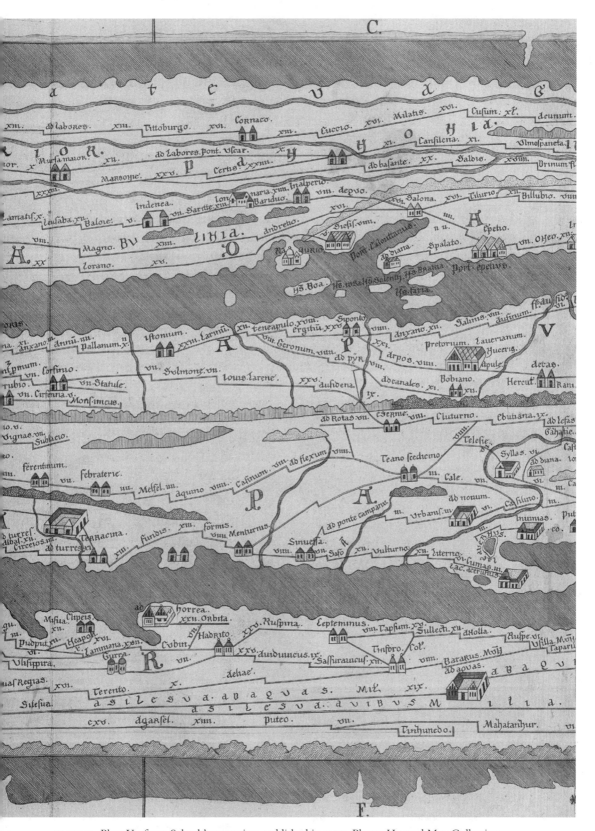

PLATE 7. Plate V of von Scheyb's engraving, published in 1753. Photo: Harvard Map Collection.

alii quoque *montes* lineis promiscuis et punctis designantur, ut *subfusculo colore* adumbrentur. *Tecta* lineis rectis parallelis in quamcumque partem ductis elucent, ut *rubra*; *viae* omnes lineis rectis duplicibus ducuntur, ut *rubrae*; *litterae* denique majusculae lineis transversis quasi transparentes, ut quoque *rubrae* appareant; aliae vero nigro colore quasi opacae sunt, ut *nigrae* maneant. Quae singillatim in foliis meis tam facili negotio conspiciuntur, ut possessor, qui exemplar suum, observata hac ratione, coloribus exornari mandaverit, ipsam Autographi imaginem uno in conspectu habere sibi videatur.

Given that the exemplar is decorated in various colors, I ensured besides that these sheets of mine too could be shaded to match. Hence, so far as the complexity of its subject matter permits, the entire Table is marked out by the method which heralds (as they are termed) typically use to denote colors in bronze engravings: thus the *sea* and *rivers*, *green* in color, are represented with lines sloping from left to right. A pattern of dots over *mountains* and the *sides of structure-symbols* signifies *yellow*. Also, other *mountains* are demarcated with lines and dots indiscriminately to signify that they should be shaded in a *dark color*. On *roofs*, straight parallel lines regardless of direction signify *red*. All *routes*, drawn with double straight lines, are *red*. Capital *letters*, drawn with sloping lines and left open in effect, should appear as *red* too, while others essentially closed by use of black should remain *black*. To view the individual shadings on my sheets is such a straightforward matter that anyone who owns a copy, and gives instructions for it to be decorated in color in accordance with this system, may feel himself to be gazing at a true likeness of the original.[72]

Von Scheyb's edition eventually became the target of such harsh criticism from scholars eager to correct its shortcomings that respect for its merits and its overall importance has been unfairly diminished.[73] To be sure, von Scheyb overstated both his own and Kleiner's attention to accurate reproduction of the map. His predilection for high-flown, loquacious rhetoric came to be considered irksome, and the tendency of his discussions to stray far from the map and closely related topics met with impatience. His arguments associating the map with Theodosius I could readily be challenged. Nonetheless, his engravings placed engagement with it on a fresh and much improved footing. After all, the sole previous presentation, produced in haste a century and a half before, was only about half-size, and had been engraved in Antwerp from an artist's copy while the map itself remained in Augsburg. By contrast, von Scheyb, his engraver, and the map were together in Vienna; the presentation is made at full size; and it reflects the map's coloring. Moreover, von Scheyb provided a complete gazetteer. The three last-mentioned features, it should be understood, are all new, and there is no doubting their fundamental long-term value to any study involving the map.

The previously mentioned provocative claim made by Desjardins in the 1860s that the 1598 engraving offers a rendering of the map superior to that of von Scheyb is extreme and unjustified. On the one hand, it is most unfortunate that von Scheyb's work was needlessly marred by his failure to identify and correct misreadings of names and figures by Kleiner, some of them egregious. As it turned out, too, the damage done by this failure was to prove longer-lasting than could possibly have been anticipated in the 1750s. On the other hand, it is a merit that Kleiner made a painstaking effort to reproduce exactly what could be read on the map, without supplementing or correcting as Welser had done. In addition, Kleiner's line work is without question more accurate than that on the 1598 engraving.

On publication, von Scheyb's grand volume – produced at his expense alone and inevitably priced high in view of the exceptional costs – attracted disappointingly few purchasers, thus placing him under severe financial pressure. Eventually, in 1767, he incurred further expense by taking the desperate step of dispatching five hundred copies to postmasters throughout Europe.[74] No doubt an accompanying note requested that each copy be placed in the hands of the appropriate local scholar or learned society; by this means the volume could at least become more widely known and valued.[75] Even so, sales cannot have risen appreciably, because the following year (1768) von Scheyb concluded negotiations to dispose of the remaining stock, along with the engraver's copperplates for the map, to the Academia Palatina that had been founded by Karl Theodor, Kurfürst of the Pfalz, at his capital, Mannheim, in 1763. It was through a long-standing acquaintance with the honorary president, Johann Schöpflin (1694–1771), that von Scheyb happened to be aware of the academy and of its special interest in the Rhineland's Roman past. Schöpflin was delighted with the purchase – for which Karl Theodor paid 2,000 florins – and thought that von Scheyb ought to be equally pleased. At the least, he was no doubt gratified to be elected to the academy as *socius extraordinarius* (foreign member) in the same year, 1768.[76]

Von Scheyb had a further reason to cultivate a mutually rewarding relationship with the academy. In 1766 he completed a painstaking Latin commentary on the map (arranged alphabetically) that runs to over 1,600 folio pages in manuscript, and naturally he anticipated difficulty in arranging for its publication. In the March–April 1766 issue of a Leipzig journal[77] he explained the background, offered an outline table of contents, and called for subscriptions to fund publication; if this initiative failed, he added, the entire manuscript could be purchased for 300 (gold) ducats. Predictably enough, the initiative did fail, and no purchaser came forward. Von Scheyb then tried to interest the academy in undertaking the publication. Schöpflin was in principle favorably disposed and even commissioned the printing of twelve trial pages. At the same time, he was shocked by many features of the style and presentation. As he wrote to the secretary of the academy, Andreas Lamey (1726–1802):

> On ne sçauroit imprimer l'ouvrage de Scheyb tel qu'il est; il faut en eliminer les barbarismes, soloecismes et autres incongruités avant de le mettre sous presse; sans cela le public seroit scandalisé.

> It would be out of the question to publish Scheyb's work in its present state; before it is sent to press, its barbarisms, solecisms, and other oddities must be removed. Otherwise readers would be outraged.

Schöpflin asked the director of the Mannheim Antiquarium (and member of the academy), the abbé Casimir Häffelin (1737–1827), to make appropriate revisions. However, he formed a very negative opinion of the map. As he later explained:

> ... l'aspect de la table de Peutinger fait une sensation désagréable sur moi, et me donne une idée peu favorable des talens et de l'intelligence du géographe qui l'a entreprise et exécutée d'une maniére si peu correcte et si bizarre.[78]

> ... the sight of the Peutinger Table makes me feel upset, and gives me a hardly favorable impression of the talents and intelligence of the geographer who undertook it and produced it in a fashion so far from correct and so strange.

For his part, von Scheyb, in frustration and disappointment, demanded the return of his manuscript. Once he eventually received it, he resubmitted it to the professor of Greek at Utrecht University, the young Rijklof van Goens (1748–1810), but here too no publication resulted.[79] As Häffelin later summed up the matter: "Mais l'impression n'eut pas lieu. L'auteur est mort depuis et son ouvrage avec lui" ("But there has been no publication. The author has since died, and his work with him").[80] Today, the manuscript (MS 9509), along with associated materials (MSS 9374, 9498, 9501), is held by the National Library, Vienna.

(b) Mannert

Von Scheyb's remaining stock and copperplates might never have been heard of again but for some extraordinary twists of fate that can be reconstructed in outline, if not always in detail. The story is summarized by Friedrich Thiersch and Conrad Mannert in a revised presentation of the map that eventually appeared in 1824, but their oblique account calls for elucidation and reassessment. One key to a more balanced understanding is surviving correspondence between Thiersch in Munich and Batholomäus Kopitar in Vienna that has not been adequately appreciated in this connection.[81]

In 1777 Karl Theodor inherited Bavaria, and so proceeded to make Munich his capital. The Academia Palatina, however, remained where it was until Mannheim was occupied by Napoleon's forces. Only then, in 1800, were its collections and possessions moved to Munich and incorporated into the Bayerische Akademie der Wissenschaften there.[82] Amid the hurried removal preparations, it somehow happened that von Scheyb's copperplates were carelessly included with surplus items offered for disposal at auction. Not until after they had been purchased for melting down was attention drawn to the mistake, and the Academy in its humiliation then had to pay a much higher amount than the sale price in order to reclaim them from such an ignoble fate.[83]

Sooner or later the remaining stock of von Scheyb's edition was sold off, and the retrieved copperplates were left to gather dust. What eventually revived attention to them was the sheer accident of a lasting friendship between the classicist Friederich Thiersch (1784–1860)[84] and Bartholomäus (Jernej) Kopitar (1780–1844).[85] Thiersch became "secretary" of the Bavarian Academy's section for philosophy and philology during summer 1814, and later that year in this capacity he was sent to Paris to reclaim items removed there during the Napoleonic period. Kopitar, despite his junior status as a member of the imperial library's staff only since 1810, was Thiersch's counterpart from Vienna. Their visits to Paris coincided for three to four months, and they kept in close touch thereafter.

In a letter to Thiersch dated January 22, 1819, Kopitar warmly recalls their period spent together, when presumably the Peutinger map had arisen in conversation as a topic of mutual interest. Kopitar had been aware of the map and its importance at least as early as 1809. In this year – when he had moved from his native Ljubljana to Vienna but was not yet a member of the library staff – he had fulfilled a request from his fellow Slovene, Valentin Vodnik (see next subsection), for a copy of von Scheyb's edition, and he enclosed with it a severely critical essay, *Anmerkungen über die Tabula Peutingeriana*, written in 1768 by Joseph Benedikt Heyrenbach (1738–79);[86] this essay was held in manuscript by the Hofbibliothek.[87] In fall 1815 Kopitar assisted Vodnik when the latter visited Vienna in order to check the accuracy of von Scheyb's engraving against the map itself. Thereafter, in circumstances unknown, he sent to a friend in Breslau, the classicist and librarian Johann G. 'Saxo' Schneider (1750–1822),[88] Vodnik's list of many errors in von Scheyb's engraving. From March 1816, when Kopitar was given overall charge of the Hofbibliothek's manuscripts, the Peutinger map even became his direct responsibility.[89]

It would have been natural enough for Kopitar, at some point, to formulate the idea of issuing a corrected version of von Scheyb's engraving, provided a sponsor could be enlisted, the copperplates found, and ownership of them secured.[90] Hence he opens the last part of his letter to Thiersch on January 22, 1819, by suddenly exclaiming:

Die Platten der Scheybschen Tabula Peutingeriana sind in Ihrer Bibliothek! Wie erwünscht wäre eine *neue verbesserte* Aufl. Scheyb muss alles den Kupferstechern, *ohne* alle Controlle überlassen haben; so oft ist im *eigensten* Verstande ein **x** für **v** und umgekehrt, in den Ortsdistanzen! item Scheyb hat aus XI Segmenten (das erste fehlt seit jeher) ganz neue XII gemacht! Und nach solchen Quellen muss man arbeiten, und sich närrisch combiniren, weil der Herausgeber sorglos war.[91]

The plates of Scheyb's Tabula Peutingeriana are in your library! How welcome a *new, improved* edition would be. Scheyb must have handed over everything to the engravers *without* exerting any control; an **x** has been *most* willfully substituted for a **v** in the distance figures so often! Again, Scheyb has made an unprecedented 12 segments out of 11 (up till now the first has been missing)! And these are the kinds of sources one has to work with, and put together in a frenzy, because the editor was careless.

Thiersch did not reply until July 11, 1819.[92] He confirmed that, as Kopitar had thought, the Academy did in fact hold von Scheyb's copper-plates. Moreover, it had now approved the preparation of a revised edition, which Konrad Mannert (1756–1834)[93] had willingly consented to undertake. He seemed a most appropriate choice: a Fellow of the Academy, professor of history at Ingolstadt University in Landshut, Bavaria,[94] and noted for his extensive publications in ancient history as well as in geography, both ancient and modern. In particular, his *Geographie der Griechen und Römer* was issued by the Leipzig publisher Hahn in ten volumes between 1820 and 1831. Thiersch quotes the letter of acceptance written by Mannert, where the latter emphasizes how vital it would be that he personally should check every letter, line, and dot to ensure an accurate reproduction of the map.

However, because of his age and other unspecified reasons, Mannert was not willing to make the journey to Vienna. Thiersch evidently sympathized, and so in his most effusive prose he broached the delicate question of whether authorization might possibly be secured to send the map on loan to Munich. A mere ten days later, on July 21, 1819, Kopitar replied that only in the most exceptional circumstances, with authorization from the highest level, could any of the library's materials be removed from the building. He added that, were *he* to find himself in Thiersch's position, he would at least offer to convey the desired item personally to Landshut (or wherever) with every possible security precaution. And even then, he asks, were the Bavarian Academy to receive a request for such a special loan, how would it react, especially after its recent experience of how the French handle others' property?[95] There Kopitar let the matter drop, until on August 18, 1819, he urged Thiersch to send Mannert to Vienna in October and not earlier, because the library was closed for vacation in September.[96]

A passing mention in another letter sent by Kopitar to Thiersch on January 19, 1820, indicates that the matter was still unresolved.[97] It evidently remained so until April 12, when Thiersch put a new proposition to Kopitar. As Mannert would not go to Vienna in order to check the map, and as the Bavarian authorities were declining to cover the costs of a new edition for which a check was not undertaken, Thiersch now begs Kopitar to furnish a detailed assessment – if possible, illustrated by some egregiously careless segment – of how much correction von Scheyb's engraving requires. With this assessment in hand, signed and sealed by Kopitar and ideally by the prefect of the library too,[98] Thiersch hopes to revive the project.[99]

On April 26, 1820, a very short letter from Kopitar explains that he knows of a comparison already made between von Scheyb's engraving and the map, which is currently in the hands of Johann Schneider in Breslau. He wants Thiersch to treat the letter as a specific record of this information in the event of any future legal challenge.[100] Thereafter, however, Schneider did return the comparison at Kopitar's request, and on August 9, 1820, Kopitar apologizes for delay in sending it on to Thiersch. He had simply not found time to organize the material (as he had been hoping), so now forwards it just in its original state – requesting Thiersch either to send him back an organized copy or to commit it to print. Last but not least, he continues to maintain that Mannert should make a personal check:

> Um Sie nicht länger warten zu lassen, sende ich hier das *Original* von Vodnik, . . . mit der Bitte, mir davon eine ordentliche *Abschrift*, oder einen Abdruck zukommen zu lassen, damit diese Arbeit nicht etwa *ad acta* verkomme. Ich kann in der Eile nicht nachsehen, ob Vodnik bemerkt, dass Scheyb aus den *11* Segmenten des Originals, ganz eigene *12* gemacht hat. Vielleicht wäre es am besten, zuerst diese Vodnik'sche Collation auf *einem Bogen in Scheyb's Format* drucken zu lassen; dann aber noch den Altmeister Mannert hieher zu schicken, dessen Kennerauge vielleicht noch manches bemerken wird, was Vodnik's Franziskaner Bequemlichkeit entgangen ist. Aber im *September* haben wir Ferien, die den *1ten October* aufhören. Darnach möchte Mannert seine Reise einrichten.

> So as not to keep you waiting longer, I send here Vodnik's *original*, . . . with the request that you arrange for a tidy *copy* to be made for me, or have one printed, so that this work is not put aside and forgotten. I am too pressed to check whether Vodnik notices that Scheyb has made *12* quite separate segments from the *11* of the original. Probably it would be for the best to have this collation by Vodnik printed *on a sheet in Scheyb's format*; then, however, still send the Grand Old Man Mannert here, because his expert eye would probably notice a few things that Vodnik's Franciscan slackness missed. *September*, however, is our vacation, which ends on *1st October*. Mannert should plan his trip accordingly.[101]

Most regrettably, there is now a large lacuna in the surviving correspondence between Kopitar and Thiersch, which only resumes on May 7, 1825, when Kopitar confirms the library's receipt of Mannert's published volume.[102] Even so, it is possible to reconstruct at least an outline of developments in the interim with some confidence. A compromise must have been reached whereby Mannert would indeed not go to Vienna himself, but would contribute an essay to the revised edition; this he delivered, signed and dated 1821. Meantime Kopitar would undertake to ensure that Vodnik's list of errors be rechecked and drawings made of whatever the Academy's engraver would need to correct on von Scheyb's plates.

In fact Kopitar proceeded to delegate these demanding tasks to a very junior member of the library staff, Friedrich von Bartsch (1798–1873). The assignment was in principle appropriate, insofar as von Bartsch had joined the staff (in 1814, aged precisely fifteen and a half) to assist his father, Adam (1757–1821), in curating the collection of copperplates;[103] but otherwise young Friedrich lacked special skills or training. Kopitar, preoccupied with his own duties and his work on Slavic languages and literature, evidently exercised no supervision; Mannert's shirking of responsibility can hardly have inspired him to go to special trouble. In any event, the Academy remained unaware of this laxity, and it understandably accepted without demur the recommendations for its engraver returned by von Bartsch.[104] These in turn evidently sufficed to procure the necessary funding for the revised edition. The engraver, J. B. Seitz,[105] added his name and the date 1822 at the bottom right of the final plate, under the declaration "Denuo collatum et emend" ("Checked anew and corrected").

The page size of Mannert's edition – issued by his Leipzig publisher, Hahn, in 1824 rather than from Munich –[106] is 29 cm wide × 40 ($11\frac{1}{2} \times 15\frac{3}{4}$ in.), and each of the twelve plates is presented as a doublespread printed on a single sheet. The intervening pages are kept blank, so that the purchaser has the option of reassembling the map in strip form. The plates are uncolored, but Mannert does reprint (p. 37) von Scheyb's statement of how he conveyed color, so this feature of the latter's presentation is maintained. The text accompanying the plates opens with a six-page Praefatio by Thiersch explaining why and how this revision of von Scheyb's edition had been commissioned and executed. Multiple errors (distance figures in particular) noted by Vodnik that cannot otherwise be identified through the index are listed. Mannert's essay follows (44 pp.). It begins with the briefest outline of the circumstances that lay behind the new edition, and in nine numbered sections then discusses a variety of topics – in particular the purpose, authorship, and date of the original map. A date around A.D. 230, under Alexander Severus, is proposed (p. 16), but consideration is also given to the possibility that it is original medieval work. The character of the map and its history from circa 1500 onward are treated too. The essay concludes with a clarification of how Mannert's edition differs from von Scheyb's, and with what is termed in effect an appendix on the Geographer of Ravenna. Following the essay, von Scheyb's index of names is reprinted, but with corrections of his readings added and marked as such.

Mannert offers sound practical reasons for not providing an extended commentary on the map:

Explicationem singularum Tabulae viarum atque locorum in hac succincta operis universi descriptione nec exspectabit lector nec exspectare potest; in magnam voluminis molem enim nostra excresceret dissertatio, et ob nimium pretium quo solvenda esset Tabulae nova editio, impedimento magis quam emolumento foret eam sibi comparare volentibus. Quod si quis tamen cujuscunque notatu dignioris loci notitiam comparare sibi cupit, adeat meum de geographia Graecorum et Romanorum opus, inventurus quae suo desiderio satisfaciant; ibi enim inter caetera ad geographiam illustrandam subsidia, Tabulae quoque rationem habui, omni qua fieri potuit cura.

In this concise description of a comprehensive work no reader would or should expect a commentary on the map's individual routes and places. This essay would expand into a great heavy volume, the cost would exceed what the production of this new edition can bear, and prospective purchasers would be deterred rather than attracted. Anyone wishing to acquire a treatment of the more notable places should turn to my work on the geography of the Greeks and Romans, where they can be sure of finding whatever they desire – including, among other assistance for elucidating geography, my own very painstaking explanation of the map.[107]

Understandably enough, Mannert seems not to have been aware of the effort by Mathias Peter Katancsich in Hungary to provide a commentary (see sec. 4 [e] below). By sheer coincidence the latter's first volume and the Bavarian Academy revision of von Scheyb's engraving both appeared in the same year, 1824. It was to prove more damaging that Mannert was just as unaware of the many shortcomings of Bartsch's recommendations. The whole purpose of the Bavarian Academy's initiative was diminished as a result. But Mannert remained adamant in his refusal to go to Vienna to inspect the map himself, and Kopitar – who had deplored careless editing in his letter of January 22, 1819 – omitted to supervise Bartsch's work. Only decades later was attention to be drawn to its inadequacies, long after both Mannert and Kopitar had died.

(c) Vodnik

As it happens, work by Valentin Vodnik (1758–1819)[108] – to whose energy and sharp eye the Bavarian Academy owed so much – offers instructive insight into the copying of the Peutinger map that has so far gone unrecognized. Born, like Kopitar, near Ljubljana, he joined the Franciscans and became a priest, but in the late 1790s he abandoned this calling and taught, first classics, later history and geography, in a Ljubljana college. With encouragement from the intellectual leader baron Sigismund (Žiga) Zois (1747–1819), Vodnik developed a keen interest in the Roman and pre-Roman antiquities of his country. Napoleonic occupation of Slovenia – which culminated in the formation of the Illyrian Provinces in 1809, with Ljubljana as capital – by chance acted to deepen this interest, because it was keenly shared by the French commissaire des guerres, first at Udine from 1806, and then at Treviso from 1808, Etienne-Marie Siauve

XIIII. Votusallo. XXII. annuma... XII. Lusione. X. Vltarisa XXII. Lugione. XII. antiana. XII. Donatia

Iouia. X. Sirotis. X. Praetorio ... Maternis ... scrofas. X. Berebis. Iovallio. VIIII. Mus...

Sistia. Burnomilia. XXX. I. Seruitio. Urban...

Re ab Mädre. Vertis. XII. XI. Praeno. Ad fines. XIII.

Aquetittillie.

fl. hertinu.

fl. Tinna. Castellofirmani. Cupra Meritima. XII. Castro trentino. Castro noua. XVIII. fl. Comara. fl. Sannum.

Tinna. II. XII. Piserno. XIII. Amiternus. XII. Pinna. VII. Salinas. V. Ostia eterni.

Fiscenas. III. Enlos. VII. E. fl. VIII. Auria. II. Amsternias. XVIII. Nomare...

Reate. Vapouas. XIIII. Ereto. Nomento. VIIII. Tibori. Varie. Vmnas. Carsulis.

Aquipulssica. farfar. via... Treblis. XV. in monte gran. N.

Aquia niua. Aduicesimum. XI. adrubras. via prenestina. Adquintanas. ad Antnas. VII.

ad Sextum. via clodia. via... Ad Adrano... ROMA. via Latina. Bobellas. III. Aricia. Sub Lanubio. X.

ad Sim. Pe. +C. Bobiam. Loria. XVII. via Latina. X. Antium. VII.

Alsium. VI. via aurelia. via Appia. Hostis. Laurento. VI. Lauinium. XVII. Astura.

VIIII.

minatium. XV. Chartagine. Con. Maxula. XXI. Ad aquas. Ad mercurium.

III. Thuraria. XX. Cicisa. XVIII. Huni. VII. IX. VIIII.

XIII. Inuca. II. Ad mercurium. ad portus. Vthica. XX. Bibae. XVI. Mediocre. VI. Aggersel.

V. Tuburbomaius. XV. O. ellas. XII. XVI. XVI.

Auila. VII. Autispidam. VI. Manange. VII. Aggar. XIIII.

Athasartho. Silesua. Ni. Passus. XII.

XXV. thusuros. XXX. Aggar S.

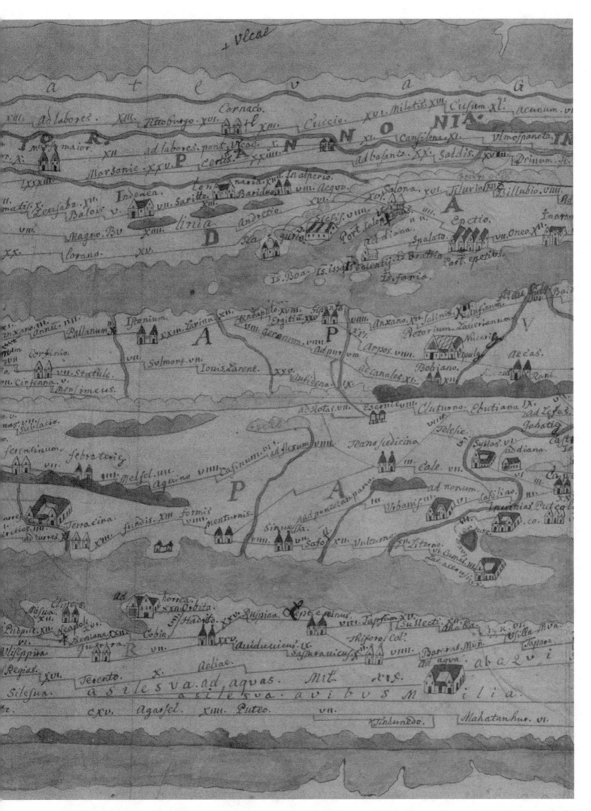

PLATE 8. Von Scheyb's engraving as copied by Vodnik in 1809; see further Appendixes 2 and 3. Photo: Narodni Muzej Slovenije, Ljubljana.

(1757–1812).[109] A former cleric like Vodnik, and almost his exact contemporary, Siauve traveled through Slovenia with him in search of antiquities, most notably in 1809.

That same year, when Siauve wished to consult the Peutinger map, he searched in Zois's library for a copy of von Scheyb's engraving and was disappointed to find none.[110] Zois accordingly wrote to his former close associate, Kopitar, now in Vienna, asking him to purchase a copy. None was available, however, and the best that Kopitar could do – after a long search – was to borrow a copy from the library of the Discalceate Carmelites, which was to be returned by New Year 1810; this he sent to Ljubljana on October 10, 1809.

When Vodnik was able to inspect the copy of the map, he was no doubt immensely excited by it and at the same time deeply frustrated by the need to return it so soon, with no prospect of securing another copy. He took the bold decision, therefore, to make his own copy, even coloring it. All this he accomplished promptly with the assistance of two of his pupils (unnamed), before Zois returned the borrowed volume to Vienna a month late, at the end of January 1810. In circumstances that remain obscure, Vodnik's remarkable copy of the map eventually came to the National Museum in Ljubljana (Narodni Musej Slovenije) sometime during the late nineteenth century, and it remains there today.[111] [Plate 8]

At the same time as he fulfilled Zois's request for a copy of von Scheyb's volume, Kopitar also took the initiative in arousing concern about how accurately it reproduced the map, because he enclosed a manuscript copy of Heyrenbach's severe assessment of it made in German in 1768.[112] Because Siauve could not read that language, Vodnik made a Latin summary of Heyrenbach's essay for him, and two very similar handwritten versions of it dated 1809 are held by the Slovenian National Library in Ljubljana.[113] [Plate 9]

Once Austrian rule was reimposed in Ljubljana in 1813, Vodnik was obliged to retire prematurely because of his close association with the French authorities. This release at least left him free to study von Scheyb's engraving further, which he proceeded to do in fall 1815 by actually bringing his copy of it to the Hofbibliothek in order to make a thorough comparison with the map itself. Fortunately, the record of this eight-day inspection that he inscribed in the lower margin near the righthand end of his copy survives: "Nemitz et Vodnik contulerunt cum Orig 4 tum 5. 6. 7. 9. 10. 12. [..] Octobris 1815." Nemitz, or Neshics, was a helper found by Kopitar, who later refers to him dismissively in a letter to Thiersch.[114]

Vodnik's copy shows that the practice he adopted in Vienna was first to highlight a slip by circling it in pencil; in many instances he then made the appropriate correction in ink. Names and numbers, rather than line work, seem to have been his principal concern. As a result of his check, Vodnik evidently identified the need for seventy-seven adjustments to von

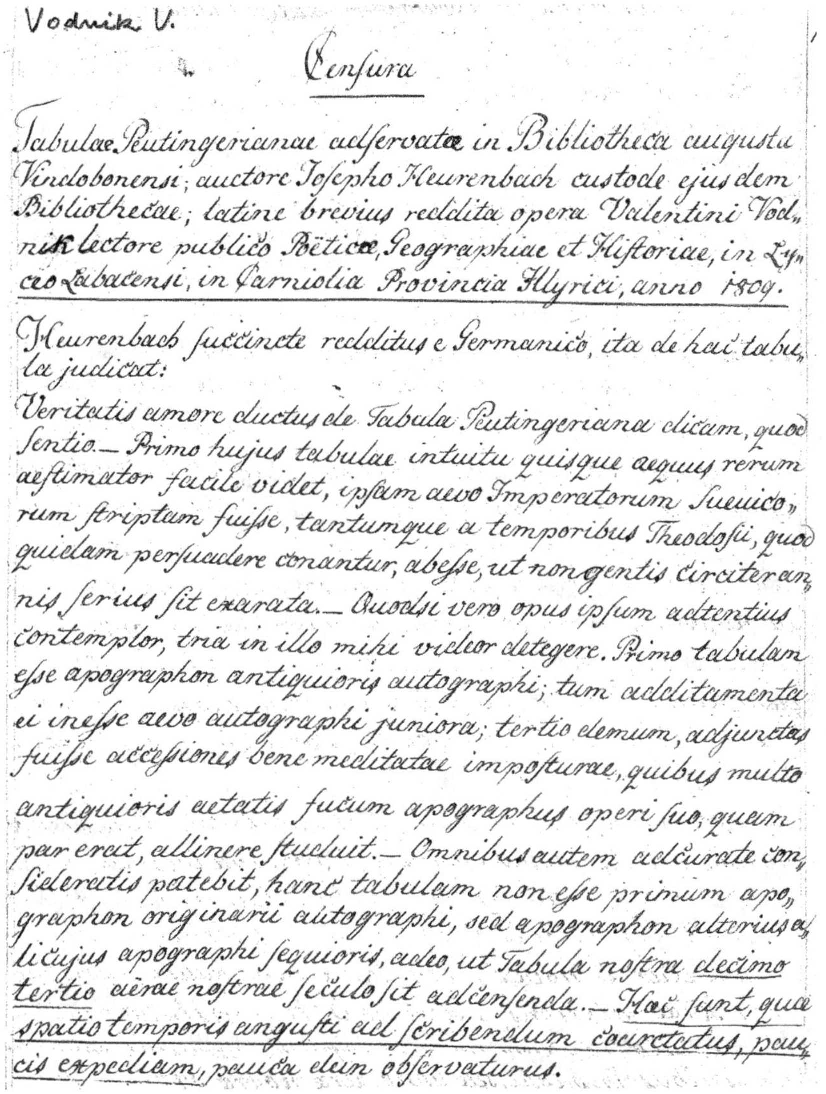

Vodnik. V.

Censura

Tabulae Peutingerianae adservatae in Bibliotheca augusta Vindobonensi; auctore Josepho Heurenbach custode ejusdem Bibliothecae; latine brevius reddita opera Valentini Vodnik lectore publico Poëticae, Geographiae et Historiae, in Lyceo Labacensi, in Carniolia Provincia Illyrici, anno 1809.

Heurenbach succincte redditus e Germanico, ita de hac tabula judicat:

Veritatis amore ductus de Tabula Peutingeriana dicam, quod sentio.— Primo hujus tabulae intuitu quisque aequus rerum aestimator facile videt, ipsam aevo Imperatorum Suevicorum scriptam fuisse, tantumque a temporibus Theodosii, quod quidam persuadere conantur, abesse, ut non gentis circiter annis serius sit exarata.— Quodsi vero opus ipsum adtentius contemplor, tria in illo mihi videor detegere. Primo tabulam esse apographon antiquioris autographi; tum additamenta ei inesse aevo autographi juniora; tertio demum, adjunctas fuisse accessiones bene meditatae imposturae, quibus multo antiquioris aetatis fucum apographus operi suo, quem par erat, allinere studuit.— Omnibus autem accurate consideratis patebit, hanc tabulam non esse primum apographon originarii autographi, sed apographon alterius alicujus apographi sequioris, adeo, ut Tabula nostra decimo tertio aerae nostrae seculo sit adscribenda.— Haec sunt, quae spatio temporis angusti ad scribendum coarctatus, paucis expediam, pauca dein observaturus.

PLATE 9. Vodnik's Latin summary of Heyrenbach's essay, written in 1809 (transcribed in Appendix 4). Photo: Vodnik Valentin: *Censura Tabulae Peutingerianae*. Narodna in univerzitetna knjižnica, Ljubljana. Rokopisna zbirka. Sign.: Ms 1443.

Scheyb's engraving. For whatever reason, these corrections were not well organized in whatever form Vodnik had deposited them in the imperial library. Kopitar nonetheless sent them in that form to Johann Schneider in Breslau, and then requested their return in 1820 when asked by Thiersch to identify the shortcomings in von Scheyb's engraving. In consequence, Vodnik's careful work gained importance and visibility that long outlived him. In principle, Mannert, as well as Cristianopoulo and Katancsich could all have fulfilled his role or reinforced it during the first quarter of the nineteenth century. Unfortunately, for a variety of reasons none did, and such reinforcement began only in the 1860s.

(d) Cristianopoulo

An Italian scholar-cleric in Iesi, whose passion for the map matched Vodnik's, experienced comparable difficulty in securing a copy of von Scheyb's volume and likewise went to extraordinary lengths to address the problem. He was Podocataro Cristianopoulo (Johannes Dominicus Podocatharus Christianopulus). Fired by enthusiasm for ancient geography in general, and specifically by a wish to improve upon Peter Wesseling's handling of distance figures in his 1735 edition of the Antonine and "Jerusalem" itineraries (see sec. 4 [e] below), he was eager to acquire a copy of the latest edition of the Peutinger map for the purpose, reckoning that it would be a mistake to pursue his project without it. But for long his hopes were dashed:

> Sed Vindobonensis Editionis, quum rarissima evasisset, exemplum habere, pene desperabamus. Verumtamen diu sollicite conquisitum, illud tandem Amici Vindobonae commorantis, qui sibi diu antea comparaverat, quo ipse multo aquisierat pretio, beneficio singulari obtinuimus; monuitque nos, venalia exempla reperiri omnino nulla, at si aliquod forte inveniretur, aureis vel viginti coemi oportere.[115]

> But I almost despaired of acquiring a copy of the Vienna edition because of its extreme rarity. After a prolonged period of anxious searching, however, I finally obtained one through the exceptional kindness of a friend staying in Vienna, who had purchased a copy for himself long before, acquiring it at a substantial price. He advised me that absolutely no copies could be found for sale, and that if by chance one should surface, it could be expected to cost twenty gold pieces.

As a result of this experience, Cristianopoulo resolved to make von Scheyb's edition available once more to the scholarly community by producing a matching edition. Moreover, it was his good fortune to have a brother, Franciscus, who was a prominent public figure – "qui Anconae pro Veneta Republica, per totam Pontificiam Adriatici maris oram *Consulis*, quem ajunt, Magistratum gerebat" ("who held the office of the Venetian Republic's *consul*, as it is termed, at Ancona for the entire Adriatic seaboard of the Papal States") –[116] and was willing to cover the costs of preparation and publication. However, there proved to be no engraver in whose accuracy Cristianopoulo felt confidence for this demanding purpose, especially as he was aware of the limitations of earlier engravings of the map. Yet it so happened that he himself had some taste and talent for engraving, so he determined to be his own engraver. As a preliminary step, he explained:

> Chartam igitur adeo perlucidam, quae vitri claritatem imitaretur, haud quidem oleo, ut moris est, sed alia a nobis excogitata ratione paravimus, in qua egregie calamo scribitur, neque paginas ullas, quamvis diutius illis adhaereat, commaculat. (ibid.)

I therefore prepared – not with oil in the usual way, but by another means of my own devising – very vitreous paper with the transparency of glass, which a pen can write on efficiently without marking any pages even though they are pressed together for some time.

Cristianopoulo then proceeded to engrave, checking repeatedly for accuracy, of names and numbers especially. The length of time that the work took him is not stated, but it must have been well over a decade. He does mention that both the engraving and the composition of the text were completed by 1796 (p. xv), and he quotes in full (p. 29) a perceptive letter of April 18, 1785, from Giuseppe Garampi (1725–92), the learned papal nuncio in Vienna and former Vatican archivist,[117] responding to a request to inspect the map and address concerns about the drawing of margin lines. Cristianopoulo never seems to have had the opportunity to visit Vienna and inspect the map himself.

Once everything was ready in 1796, however, Cristianopoulo's hopes of proceeding to publication were dashed by external events:

At calamitas, quae universas Italiae Regiones, ac Venetam potissimum afflixit, ipsamque Rempublicam sustulit, uti cujusque ordinis civium, ita etiam amantissimi Fratris fortunas remque familiarem totam foedissime subvertit; Litteratique homines inopia retrahere se ab studio, ac in otium transdere coacti, pene ad famem rejecti sunt. Itaque ereptis iis, quae diximus adjumentis, omnem ferme Operis nostri edendi spem abjeceramus.[118]

But the disaster that struck all the regions of Italy did its severest harm in the Veneto and overthrew the Republic itself. As a result, citizens of every rank – my dearest brother included – had their circumstances and entire family affairs most cruelly undermined. Want forced men of education to abandon scholarship and instead to be without employment, almost driven into starvation. So with the support previously mentioned snatched away, I virtually abandoned all hope of publishing my work.

Thereafter, funding for publication was at long last forthcoming locally through his bishop, Stefano Bellini. Cristianopoulo then settled for producing his work in Iesi, rather than in Venice or Rome as he had once planned, and in a more modest format. Hence his *Tabula Itineraria Militaris Romana Antiqua Theodosiana, et Peutingeriana Nuncupata quam ex Vindobonensi editione clar. Viri Christophori de Scheyb anni MDCCLIII accurate descripsit* came to be published by Vincentius Cherubinus in Iesi ("Aesii in Piceno") in 1809. With its sturdy paper stock, specially chosen,[119] and a new typeface ordered from Venice,[120] the volume is a handsome product, far from negligible in appearance, although the page size (just over 28 cm × 42 [11 × 16$\frac{1}{2}$ in.]) does call for the twelve engravings of the map to be righthand foldouts (two folds) rather than doublespreads. [Plate 10]

Cristianopoulo's text has four components – a dedication to bishop Bellini (pp. v–x); a *Praefatio* explaining the background to his project,

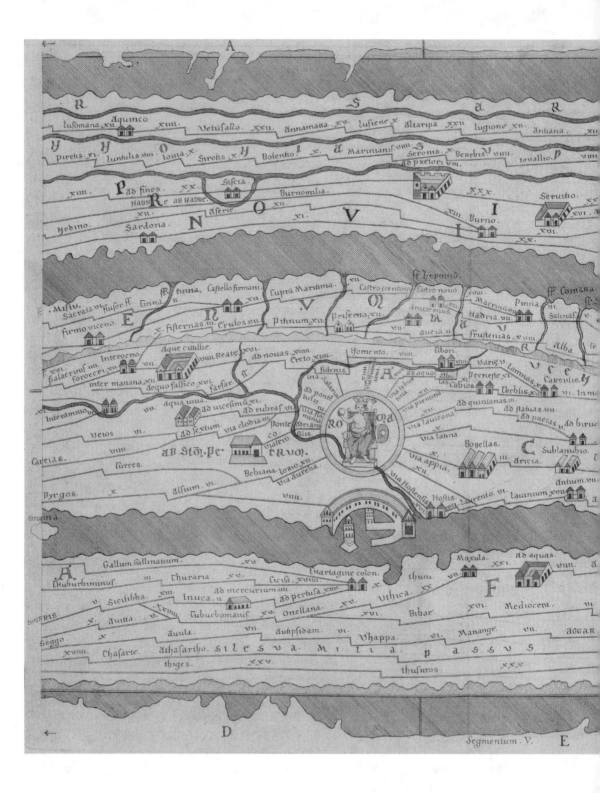

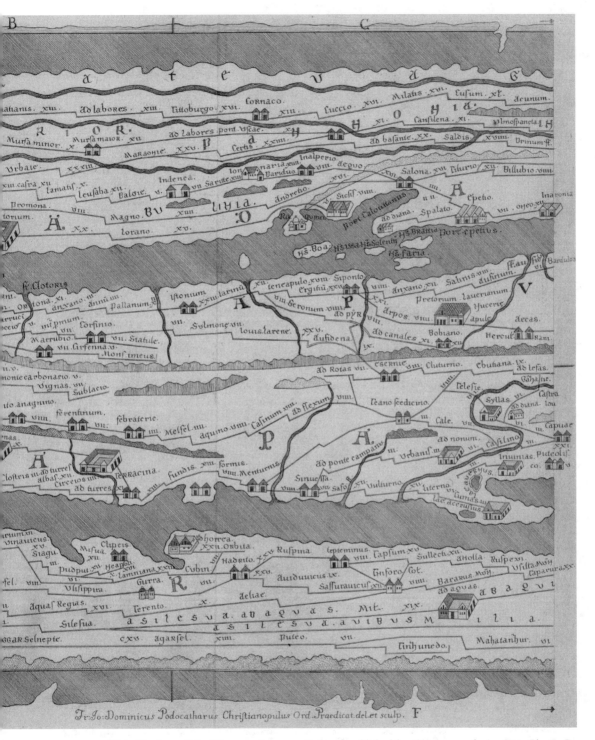

PLATE 10. Plate V of von Scheyb's engraving as copied and published by Cristianopoulo in 1809. Photo: By permission of Houghton Library, Harvard University. Smyth GSB 3.18*.

its character and uneven progress (pp. XI–XVI); a *Dissertatio in Tabulam Peutingerianam Editionis Italicae Primae* (pp. 1–68); and a revision of von Scheyb's index, followed by notes on the changes proposed (pp. 1–XXXVII). Three components of the *Dissertatio* stand out. First, it documents the energy with which Cristianopoulo has compared points of difference in the engravings published by von Scheyb and Horn[121] in particular. Second, at considerable length and with special attention to letter forms (even a full-page *Tabula Palaeographica*, facing 32), it rebuts von Scheyb's view that the map is an original document rather than a copy. And third, at great length (from 33 onward) it offers a wide-ranging analysis of the distance units used by the map and other relevant sources, and of their equivalence to contemporary units (with a comparative table facing 44). These emphases duly demonstrate Cristianopoulo's devotion to scholarship,[122] and they match well enough the scope of von Scheyb's *Dissertatio* for those with the good fortune to have read it. But here Cristianopoulo seems to confine himself unduly to his original limited purpose of improving Wesseling's handling of distance figures. To readers deprived of von Scheyb, however, the choice of aspects singled out for fullest explanation and discussion is perhaps less than ideal. Nowhere, for example, does Cristianopoulo expand upon his decision to adhere to the tradition of representing the map as "military" in character.

Cristianopoulo's volume evidently did not fulfill its aim of making the map accessible again as a replacement for von Scheyb's presentation of it. Such a work published obscurely in Iesi by an otherwise unknown author stood little chance of gaining widespread attention.[123] Mannert[124] says that he had not seen a copy, and that his knowledge was limited to a notice published in 1817.[125] Later, d'Avezac, too, failed to trace a copy, but offers a summary of the same notice.[126]

(e) Katancsich

Meantime, a professor and librarian in Hungary, the Franciscan Mathias Peter Katancsich (1750–1825),[127] had determined to achieve the challenging goal – still unfulfilled – of providing for the entire map the type of systematic commentary that had accompanied Welser's initial publication of the two sketches in 1591.[128] During the late 1780s and early 1790s Katancsich painstakingly prepared his own copy of von Scheyb's presentation of the map and colored it as von Scheyb had indicated. With the aid of maps by the leading French cartographer Jean Baptiste Bourguignon d'Anville (1697–1782) on the one hand, and the inspiration of Peter Wesseling's 1735 edition and commentary on itineraries and comparable material on the other,[129] he then exploited the limited scholarly resources at his disposal to comment on every name and feature throughout the entire map. Most of the references are to ancient authors and to respected geographers and cartographers such as d'Anville and his forerunner Philipp Clüver (1580–1623).

Katancsich proceeds by continent in the first instance, in the order Europe (vol. 1), Asia, and Africa (vol. 2). At the start, in *Tabulae Itinerarium*, the "routes" on the map are summarized place by place in the style of the Antonine Itinerary.[130] At the end, two indexes list the (ancient) names on the map, and the modern place-names to which the commentary refers. The commentary alone – without the opening notice,[131] Prooemium, route summaries, and indexes – runs to 731 pages in volume 1 and 625 in volume 2. In addition, twelve sheets reproducing Katancsich's copy of von Scheyb's edition of the map were prepared by two engravers at Pest, Samuel Lehnhardt (sheets 1–4) and Ferenc (= Franciscus) Karacs (sheets 5–12),[132] and colored by hand. The color palette, although bright, remains limited and unsubtle. In consequence, while the colorfulness that is so integral to the map does feature here for the first time in a publication, the rendering of it is in fact far from full or accurate.[133] [Plate 11]

On completion of the manuscript, the time, effort, and expense needed to bring such an immense, complex work to publication must all have been exceptional. Prolonged delay did ensue, because the work was approved for publication by the Royal Hungarian Academy, Buda, at its expense in 1803, yet it did not appear until 1824 (vol. 1) and 1825 (vol. 2 and map sheets) under the title *Orbis Antiquus ex Tabula Itineraria quae Theodosii Imp et Peutingeri Audit ad systema geographiae redactus et commentario illustratus.* The print run was a hundred copies. To judge by Katancsich's opening notice, the cause of the delay was the predictable one of the Academy's facing difficulty in assigning the necessary funds. It cannot have helped, however, that Katancsich's health had broken down by 1800, when his request to retire was granted. Although he did continue with his studies, he evidently never left his room for the next twenty-two years. This self-imposed seclusion may in turn explain why he evidently never traveled to Vienna to check his copy against the Peutinger map itself and to inspect its coloring.[134] Because it so happened that the Bavarian Academy's far leaner and less costly presentation of the map also appeared in 1824, Katancsich's work never gained the attention that it merited. For all its shortcomings, it is nonetheless a Herculean, forward-looking achievement – the first publication to reproduce the map in color, to provide a commentary on all its names and features, and to determine the modern equivalent names for the ancient ones marked.

(f) Fortia d'Urban

The next contribution of importance, however, was to be even more consistently neglected, although it, too, broke fresh ground.[135] It is not an edition of the map itself, but rather a tabulation of its routes (such as Katancsich had furnished), together with what remains till now the only attempt to represent them on a set of modern maps of the Roman world. The work was commissioned by the extraordinary aristocrat Agricol Fortia d'Urban (1756–1843),[136] but only published posthumously in 1845

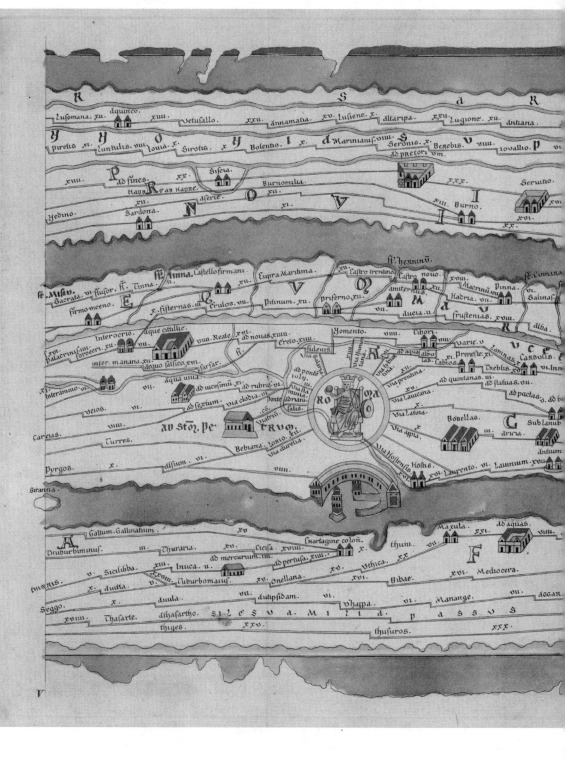

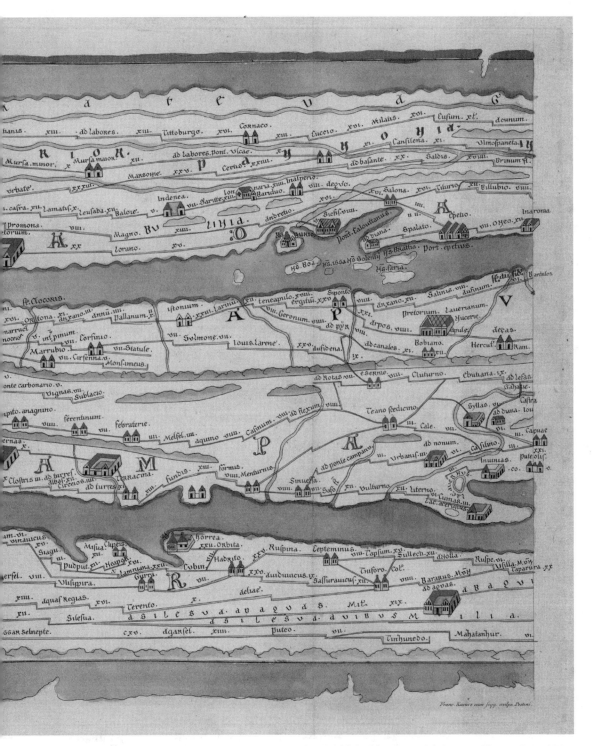

PLATE 11. Plate V of von Scheyb's engraving as copied and published by Katancsich in 1825. Photo: Harvard Map Collection.

by the Imprimerie Royale, Paris: *Recueil des Itinéraires Anciens comprenant l'Itinéraire d'Antonin, la Table de Peutinger et un choix des périples grecs, avec dix cartes dressées par M. le Colonel Lapie.*[137] The "text" comprises lists (in four columns) of the "routes" in each of these sources in turn, place by place, appending the modern equivalent name where possible and stating the distance figure for each stretch as it appears in Roman numerals in the source, together with the arabic-numeral equivalent, as well as the actual distance on the ground in Roman miles (arabic figures) as calculated by Lapie. The Peutinger map section (pp. 197–320) takes Rome as its starting-point – Katancsich, by contrast, starts from the lefthand edge of the map – and comprises 235 numbered routes; it is followed, moreover, by an alphabetical listing of those names to be found on the map which are detached from its route network.

The *Préface* to the volume – signed by Emmanuel Miller (1812–86) – explains (p. 1) that Lapie's maps "devaient être mises en rapport avec le texte, et représenter toutes les positions, toutes les localités, toutes les dénominations géographiques contenues dans l'Itinéraire d'Antonin, dans la Table de Peutinger et dans les Périples grecs" ("should be linked with the text and represent all the places, all the regions, all the geographical names contained in the Antonine Itinerary, Peutinger Table, and [for a separate tenth map] Greek *periploi*").

The maps for the Roman Empire comprise a 3 × 3 set (numbered 1–9 in horizontal sequence) that can be assembled to form one piece. Each map is a bifolio sheet with a single vertical fold, printed on one side only, with no overlap of coverage, and with a conspicuous border drawn to mark the edges of the set. Map coverage is as much as 51.5 cm wide × 37.5 ($20\frac{1}{4}$ × $14\frac{3}{4}$ in.) on a sheet. Assembled, the nine sheets span approximately 150 cm wide by 109 (60 × 43 in.), within which some space is reserved for insets, explanatory data, and so on. The prime meridian for the graticule runs through Paris. Rendering of elevation is limited, but mountain ranges are shown by hachuring. Only ancient names are marked, very legibly engraved however tiny they may be. Notably, an attempt is made to mark even names and notices from the Peutinger map that are not associated with its route network. [Plate 12]

No scale figure is stated for the main map (nor for any of the insets), but it is in fact approximately 1 : 3,400,000.[138] On sheet 6 the width of the main map is slightly reduced to accommodate a "bleed" toward the bottom right, 2.6 cm (1 in.) in width, which extends the coverage to Ctesiphon and Babylon, as well as to Vologesia. Sheet 7 only continues coverage of the main map at its very top (as far south as Autolole in Africa). Otherwise it accommodates a substantial small-scale map that ranges from Amastris in Asia Minor to the mouths of the Ganges; the scale is approximately 1:11,000,000. At bottom right on sheet 8 appears the key to the eight styles in which route line work is drawn throughout:

PLATE 12. Detail from Sheet 5 of Lapie's map of the Roman Empire, published in 1845. Photo: Andover-Harvard Theological Library, Harvard Divinity School.

Itinerarium Antonini; Burdigalense; Tabula Peutingeriana
Itin Ant; Tab. Peuting.
Itin. Antonini
Tabula Peutingeriana
Itin Burdigal et Anton
Itin Burdigalense
Itin Burdigal; Tab Peuting
Viae Romanae, de quibus silent scriptores veteres.

Inevitably, these eight variants are by no means easy to differentiate, because the line work is always thin and its presentation in color impractical (even so, purchasers could add color themselves). A further challenge to the user is the fact that in some regions – Italy and Crete, to name but two – the quantity of data to be accommodated pushes both the chosen scale and the skill of the engraver[139] to their limits. In addition, naturally, there is scope for disagreement about rendering of landscape, placement of names and routes, and so forth. As always, too, new findings created constant pressure for revision. The *Préface* explains that revision was undertaken for North Africa and Asia Minor even before the maps were issued; meantime sheet 1 at least, dated 1834, had already been printed.

Such concern only underlines the favorable reputation enjoyed by the experienced cartographer, Colonel Pierre Lapie (1777–1850),[140] not to mention that of the classical scholars led by Emmanuel Miller who supplied the ancient data. In retrospect, they all seem to have been unduly modest about the ambitious and pathbreaking character of their collaborative achievement. What they had achieved marks an extraordinary advance – the production of a large, modern representation of the Roman world on which the Peutinger map's routes, as well as those of the Antonine Itinerary and Bordeaux Itinerary, are traced in detail and integrated. None of this data had been mapped out thus before, nor has a map been produced since that features it all. Even so, the undeserved fate suffered by Lapie's maps was to be all but ignored initially, and thereafter forgotten.

(g) Desjardins

In 1855, when explaining his plans for three volumes of *Geographi Graeci Minores* to be published by Firmin-Didot in Paris, the experienced editor Carl Müller (1813–94) wrote of including in the third "appendicis loco . . . geographi latini, itineraria, tabula Peutingeriana."[141] For whatever reason, however, no third volume ever followed the first two (1855, 1861). Even so, it would seem that Müller did work on the map,[142] and in the early 1870s still anticipated bringing the results to publication. William Smith, in the Preface to his *Atlas of Ancient Geography*[143] dated November 1874, states:

> The chartographical part of the Classical Atlas is based, first, upon Strabo, the text of which has been much improved in the edition published at Paris,

with a critical commentary, by Dr. Charles Müller, in 1853; secondly, upon the improved edition of the Geographi Minores, also published at Paris by the same Editor; thirdly, upon a comparison made by Dr. Müller of the edition of the Tabula Peutingeriana, published by the Academy of Munich, with the original of this unique work, which is preserved in the Library of Vienna; and lastly, upon a collation, made by Dr. Müller, of more than fifty manuscripts of the geography of Ptolemy. . . .

In the text pages of Smith's *Atlas* that were entitled "Sources and Authorities for the Maps" and only delivered in the 1870s, Müller himself often cites the Peutinger map, finally stating with reference to Map 29 Asia Minor:

In so far as there is doubt about fixing the course of the ancient roads, and the towns situated on them, we refer the reader, for the reasons of our opinion, to the commentary on the Tabula Peutingeriana, which will appear shortly.[144]

An ambitious attempt to improve on all previous editions was undertaken by Ernest Desjardins (1823–86),[145] professor of geography and the ancient history of the East at the École Normale, Paris, who received the financial support of France's minister of public education in 1868, and later that year (December 1) addressed him a six-page *Rapport* explaining the background and the plan of work. Desjardins had been shocked by a report from Alfred Maury, published in 1864, demonstrating that a comparison of the representation of Gaul in Mannert's 1824 edition with the map itself revealed multiple shortcomings.[146] Desjardins, too, personally inspected the map in Vienna and corrected his copy of the 1824 edition from it. In his opinion,[147] as mentioned above, this edition failed to improve von Scheyb's presentation of the map and left the 1598 engravings, despite their limitations and reduced scale, as still the scholar's best recourse.[148]

Most astonishing of all for Desjardins on his visit to Vienna in 1867 must have been an encounter with Friedrich von Bartsch – by now "Second Custos" of the library, on the verge of retirement –[149] which clarified at long last why the intended revision of von Scheyb's engraving was so unexpectedly flawed. Looking back almost half a century (before Desjardins was even born, in 1823), both men settle for a philosophical perspective:

M. Bartsch, qui vit encore, ne se piquait pas, surtout alors, d'être savant ni même géographe. A défaut de connaissances spéciales, il lui eût fallu posséder, du moins, quelques notions de paléographie et avoir cette application à bien faire, qui ne se rencontre, pour un tel travail, que chez ceux qui y prennent plaisir et dont l'ardeur est soutenue par cette sorte d'attrait que l'amour de la science peut seul répandre sur les travaux en apparence les plus ingrats. Dieu nous garde donc de rendre responsable le jeune graveur viennois de tant de fautes et d'omissions qu'il n'a pas vues, qu'il n'a pu voir

A

1

2

Vindobona
Carnunto
Varuno
Sabarie
N O R I C
M
O
Parentio
Pola
Silno
Acervone
L
I
B
Carsatica
Ravenna
Curva cesena
P
I
Volsinis
Tuscana
Aquas Passaris
Ameria
Castello amerino
Tarquinis
Mindo
Graviscæ
Castro
I
A
Membione
Ad turres
Cerva

A

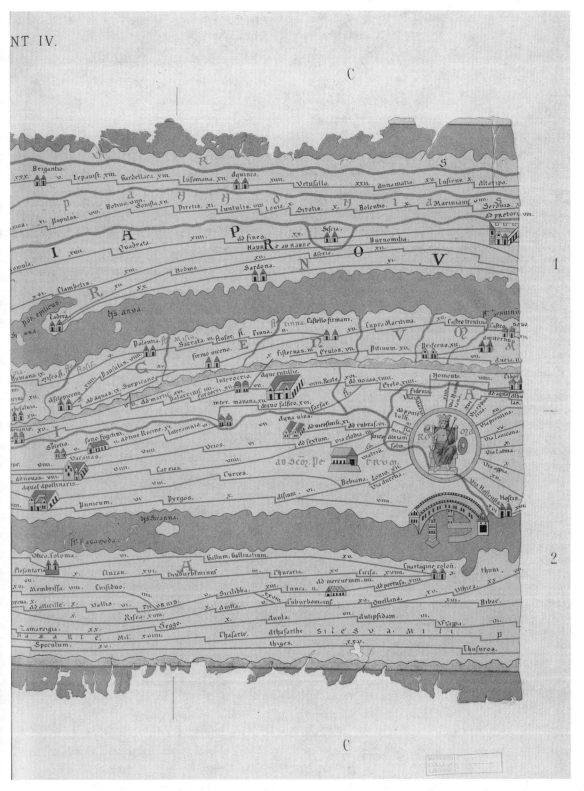

PLATE 13. Plate IV of Desjardins's lithograph, published in 1869. Photo: Harvard Map Collection.

et qu'il a laissées subsister dans les planches que l'Académie de Munich et le nom de Mannert couvrent de leur responsabilité.[150]

Mr. Bartsch, who is still alive, made no claim to be (especially back at that time) a scholar or even a geographer. In the absence of specialized expertise, he would have needed to possess, at a minimum, some grasp of paleography and the kind of capacity to apply it effectively, which for such a task is only found among those who take pleasure in it and whose passion is sustained by the type of appeal that love of learning alone can bestow on the seemingly most unrewarding tasks. Heaven forbid therefore that we should hold the young Viennese engraver responsible for so many errors and omissions that he did not spot, and was not capable of spotting, and that he left remaining on the plates for which the Munich Academy and the name of Mannert claim themselves responsible.

Desjardins did consider commissioning photographs of the map and working from them, but ultimately rejected this idea.[151] His edition, entitled in brief *La Table de Peutinger, d'après l'original conservé à Vienne*, was planned to comprise a total of eighteen *livraisons*, and began to appear in 1869. In the event, however, only fourteen were published (by Hachette, Paris),[152] and by that stage (in 1874) far more than a further four would have been needed for completion. At least the fourteen do include the entire map, with its eleven parchment segments in order – as separated in 1863 – presented full-size as a separate bifolio (i.e., single-sheet) doublespread at the end of each of *livraisons* 1–11. The printing process was the novel one of color lithography (in Desjardins's own words, "chromogravure sur pierre"), using five inks to create seven colors in all; consequently, a total of fifty-five stones was required. [Plate 13] The result is thus both the first publication of the map as eleven segments, and the first printing of it all in color – impressive work to be sure, but still no less expensive to acquire than previous editions had been.[153]

The commentary on each name and feature remains incomplete. No part of Africa is ever treated, but otherwise the coverage extends from the lefthand edge of the map to Sicily in 254 dense, double-folio, three-column pages (page size 36.5 cm × 53 [$14\frac{1}{4}$ × $20\frac{3}{4}$ in.]), and onward to the names of physical features in *Bassin du Danube et Europe Orientale* for six pages (255–60), before ceasing literally in mid-word.[154] Desjardins's title pages promise for each name "le dépouillement géographique des auteurs anciens, des inscriptions, des médailles et le résumé des discussions touchant son emplacement," and he duly addresses these matters, and more, in truly breathtaking detail. As a typical example, the entry for Benevento[155] extends to just over five columns, quoting inscriptions in both Samnite and (at length) Latin, explaining the attested magistracies of the city, and altogether overwhelming the reader with information far from directly relevant to a focus on the map. It seems no wonder that in time Desjardins felt unable to continue his work on the commentary amid his other preoccupations, or that the state's support was withdrawn, or both. Perhaps, too, his enthusiasm cooled once he had covered Gaul (the region of greatest interest to him)[156] and Italy. At any rate, the "Introduction historique et critique" promised in the *Rapport* (p. VI) did not appear, let alone any index, or any summary of the "routes" followed (such as Katancsich offers).

A welcome new feature, however, are three of the maps on which Desjardins promised to show readers ancient and modern place-names, with distinctive marking of those names that appear on the Peutinger map. These three maps (all in color) outclass Lapie's work, although the scale used for Gaul is smaller than his. They comprise Gaul as a single turn-page at 1:4,545,500 [Plate 14];[157] northern Italy (to Rome), as a bifolio spread at 1:923,000, with inset Submoenium Urbis at 1:580,000; and southern Italy and Sicily as a bifolio spread at 1:923,000, with inset Campaniae Pars Media at 1:455,000. Desjardins promised another type of map too – "carte établissant la conformité des indications générales de la Table avec les connaissances présumées des Romains sous Auguste (*Orbis Pictus d'Agrippa*)" – but none was ever issued. Eventually, however, a considerable amount of

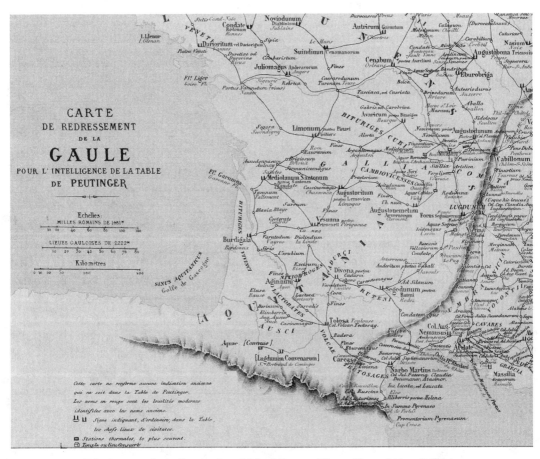

PLATE 14. Detail from Desjardins's map *Gaule*, published in 1874. Photo: Harvard Map Collection.

text that Desjardins must surely have prepared for the abandoned "Introduction historique et critique" did achieve publication in chapter 6 of the fourth volume of his *Géographie historique et administrative de la Gaule romaine*, issued posthumously in 1893.

5. PUBLICATION (1880s TO THE PRESENT)

Konrad Miller (see further sec. 6 below) also employed lithography to produce a more accurate and affordable revision of von Scheyb's engraving than Desjardins had achieved.[158] This he issued in 1888 (from Maier, Ravensburg) as *Die Peutingersche Tafel* in conjunction with a book, *Die Weltkarte des Castorius genannt die Peutingersche Tafel*, from the same publisher dated the previous year. The lithograph is a single foldout piece in color (formed by a series of sheets gummed together), reproducing the map at two-thirds its actual size with the heading CASTORI ROMANORUM COSMOGRAPHI *tabula quae dicitur Peutingeriana*. [Plate 15] Along the bottom, at appropriate spots below selected ancient names marked on the map, the modern equivalent name for each is added in italic. Also added here, in standard type, are the ancient names (as inferred by Miller) for many of the unnamed symbols on the map.

Miller's lithograph was reissued in 1892 by the British publisher Williams and Norgate (London and Edinburgh) as *Map of the World by Castorius generally known as Peutinger's Tabula*.[159] When Miller's commentary appeared in his *Itineraria Romana* (= *ItMiller*) in 1916, *Die Peutingersche Tafel* was expanded and reissued at the same time,[160] although the map is reproduced at only half its original size and uncolored. However, the imaginative reconstruction of the single parchment that in Miller's view served to complete the lefthand side of the map is now added as an integral part of the lithograph; it had originally been published separately – larger and colored – in 1898 [Plate 16].[161] The 1916 version of *Die Peutingersche Tafel* was republished unaltered in 1929,[162] and again in 1962,[163] although in the latter instance color was returned to the entire map except the reconstructed lefthand end. Finally, in 2003, the 1962 presentation of the entire map was reissued at two-thirds its actual size.[164] Parts of Miller's lithograph of the map have been reproduced in many publications.[165]

Although it remains widely available and is unquestionably superior to its forerunners, Miller's *Die Peutingersche Tafel* in its turn should not be regarded as an infallibly reliable reproduction of the map. Glaring errors or omissions are rare, to be sure; omission of the route connecting Avgusta Tavrinor(vm) and Eporedia (2B5) is therefore an exceptional oversight.[166] There are plenty of smaller discrepancies, however. In at least two instances, Miller's lithographer – working from von Scheyb's twelve-plate engraving but now dividing the map differently – evidently failed to achieve a smooth continuation between a pair of the previous plates. In consequence, at Miller's V 4 the lettering for THURRIS becomes jumbled; the Risca stretch has an extra chicane added to it; the S and "eggo" of Seggo are separated; "Mil(ia) XVIIII" is placed too far left, and an extra chicane is introduced after it; likewise the Speculum stretch acquires an extra chicane. Similar errors are introduced into Miller's XI 2 for the same reason. The righthand parts of all three "special notices" stand lower than they should, and "inopiam" has even acquired an additional (redundant) i; the name Metita is spread over two route stretches, when there should be only one. More generally, it is beyond the capacity of the lithograph to capture the many tiny variants in the map's presentation of symbols.[167]

In principle, the need to rely upon engraved or lithographed reproductions of the map was largely removed once the Hofbibliothek commissioned the publication of a set of photographs of all eleven parchments, a pathbreaking initiative on its part.[168] These photographs were taken and published in 1888 by the Viennese firm of Carl Angerer (1838–1916)[169] and his brother-in-law Alexander Göschl (1848–1900).[170] Each photograph is mounted on a sturdy, loose card, and they are numbered Segmentum I–XI. A title card (*Peutingeriana Tabula Itineraria in Bibliotheca Palatina Vindobonensi asservata nunc primum arte photographica expressa*), and a folder-case of heavy board with the first three words of the title stamped in gold on the front, are the sole accompanying components. The intention must have been to show each segment at full size in plain view without distortion, but users are not warned that the process adopted has in fact acted to create very slightly enlarged images. The degree of this enlargement (when it occurs) varies unaccountably, extending a segment's height by up to a centimeter or so, or width by up to almost three, or both.

In practice however, despite their remarkable quality, these photographs[171] did not remove the need for reliance upon engraved or lithographed reproductions of the map. The photographs were an extremely expensive set, rarely acquired (it seems) even by libraries.[172] Because the photography is monochrome, lettering on land stands out with exceptional clarity against the pale parchment background; but quite the reverse applies to lettering in water, where the contrast between the black of the former and the greenish tint of the latter is so slight.

The set of photographs, each reduced to approximately three-quarters their original size, is reproduced in Youssouf Kamal's *Monumenta Cartographica Africae et Aegypti*, vol. 2, fasc. 2 (Cairo, 1932); but this publication – for all its generous size and lavish presentation – is a rarity. Thirty-five years later, the photographs were next appended to Annalina and Mario Levi, *Itineraria Picta. Contributo allo studio della Tabula Peutingeriana* (Rome, 1967), as eleven pull-out plates; the reduction in their size here is considerable, however (40 × 22 cm [$15\frac{3}{4}$ × $8\frac{1}{2}$ in.]), and the quality of the images disappointing. The set was appended more recently to Luciano Bosio, *La Tabula Peutingeriana* (Rimini, 1983), with a better quality of image,

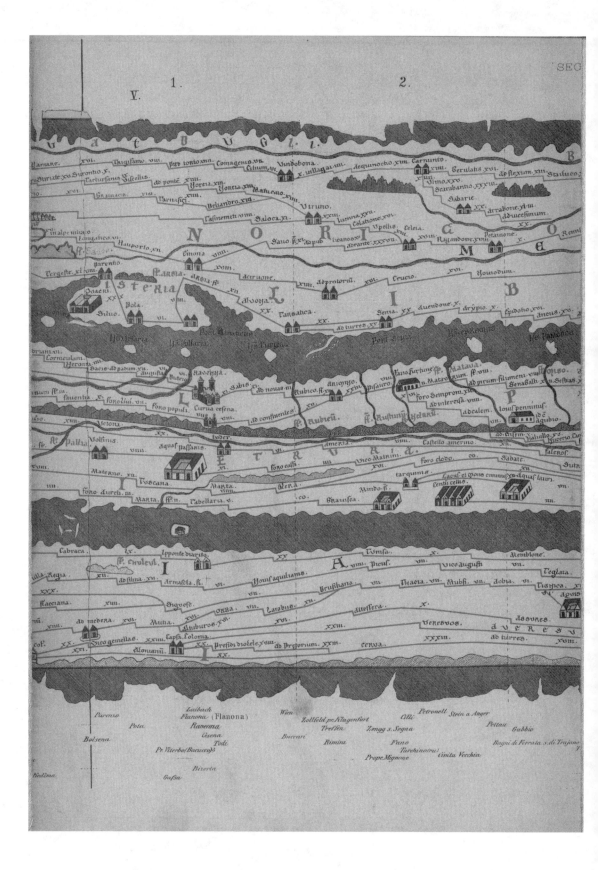

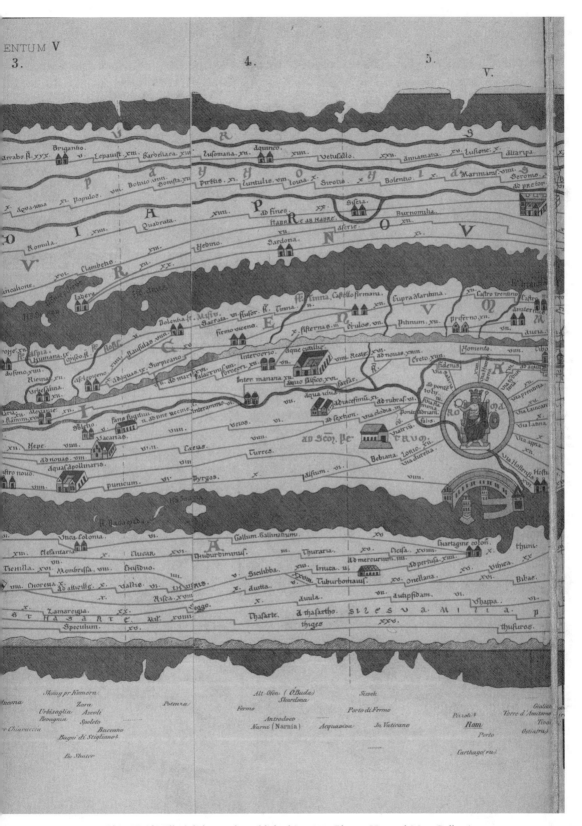

PLATE 15. Plate V of Miller's lithograph, published in 1888. Photo: Harvard Map Collection.

CASTORI TABVLAE dictae PEVTINGERIANAE segmentum primum
temporum iniquitate perditum quantum fieri potuit reconstruxit C. Miller.

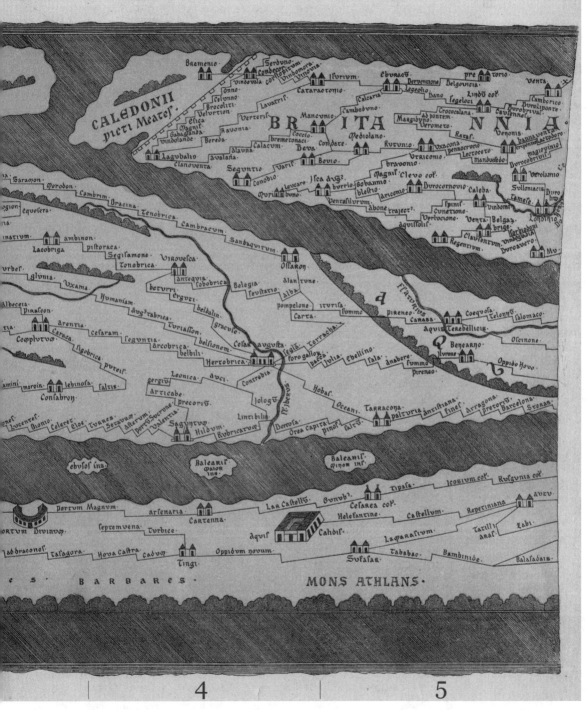

4   5

PLATE 16. Lost Western end of the Peutinger map as reconstructed by Miller in 1898 and discussed in Appendix 5. The numbers and dividers for five vertical subdivisions (added here) only appeared for the first time in the 1916 reissue of *Die Peutingersche Tafel*, together with modern equivalents (not shown here) for selected place names. Photo: Davis Library, University of North Carolina, Chapel Hill. Tafel 5 in K. Miller, *Mappaemundi: Die ältesten Weltkarten*, vol. 6. Stuttgart, 1898.

but with each parchment severely reduced to no more than 26 × 14 cm ($10\frac{1}{4}$ × $5\frac{1}{2}$ in.) so as to fit the book's page size.

Only in the 1970s – after almost a century – were new photographs of the map taken and published, moreover in color at last. In fact two sets of full-size color photographs were published in quick succession and (it seems) quite independently of one another. The earlier set, issued in 1976 by Ekkehard Weber,[173] is of superior quality, and has rightly become the primary resource for close study of the map. There is a photograph for each parchment, and the eleven are bound as a book that opens upward. Above each of these color photographs (and thus on the reverse of the preceding page) there appears a duplicate image, but monochrome, and with approximately 2 to 7 cm ($\frac{3}{4}$ to $2\frac{3}{4}$ in.) of the preceding and following parchments placed immediately adjacent on either side (marked off by white dividing lines). In addition, two loose sheets offer four sketch maps, each at a different scale. Between them these four span southern England to Sri Lanka, marking principal ancient settlements on modern outlines, with equivalent modern names as well as modern nations' names and boundaries; routes are absent, however, except for where they fan out from the city of Rome itself.

The distinctive feature of the second set of color photographs published by Annalina and Mario Levi in 1978 – one for each parchment in fact – is that they are joined together to present the map in its original, single-piece format. A wooden roller is attached at each end to form a scroll. The result is truly striking. At the same time, however, the photographs lack the sharp definition of Weber's set, and the paper chosen for printing them is unavoidably less sturdy (since it must be rolled up). Moreover, the lavishness of the production and its consequent high price – the scroll lies in a casket with an accompanying book, La "Tabula Peutingeriana" –[174] have made this item a rarity.

6. KONRAD MILLER'S ITINERARIA ROMANA (1916)

Konrad Miller (1844–1933) was an energetic, talented scientist, schoolteacher, and priest who developed a remarkably broad range of interests.[175] However, he was neither a trained classical scholar nor even a professional academic. Instead, it was newfound enthusiasm for Roman archaeology that attracted him to the map and led (as noted above) to the publication in 1887 of a book entitled *Die Weltkarte des Castorius genannt die Peutingersche Tafel*, followed at once by a lithograph of the map itself. Miller termed the book an "einleitender Text," designed to serve as "Grundlage und Vorarbeit" for a commentary to follow. Later, he would claim that there was already a complete draft of this commentary by 1887. However, rather than proceeding to bring it to publication without delay, he gave priority instead to publishing medieval world maps and related items. As a result, the work *Mappaemundi: Die ältesten Weltkarten* appeared in six fascicles between 1895 and 1898 (from Roth, Stuttgart). Not until 1916 in fact did the long projected commentary finally appear from Strecker and Schröder, Stuttgart, entitled *Itineraria Romana: Römische Reisewege an der Hand der Tabula Peutingeriana dargestellt*.[176] It completely superseded Katancsich's work, and has itself yet to be superseded. Appreciation of its distinctive nature, as well as of its limitations, is therefore essential.[177]

For the most part, the introductory section (from XIII to LIII) reprints Miller's 1887 book, with some adjustment to rebut the criticism leveled at its stance on controversial issues, especially that of the original mapmaker's identity.[178] Miller maintains his earlier idiosyncratic practice of numbering the map's surviving eleven parchments as II to XII,[179] on the reckoning that just a single parchment to the left is missing. Other aspects treated in detail are the discovery of the map and previous scholarship on it, the date of the original, its intended purpose, and the character of its symbols and other features. Thereafter, in addition (LIV–LXXV), Roman itineraries known from texts or inscriptions are laid out and briefly discussed (in particular, the so-called Antonine Itineraries for land and sea).

The commentary itself occupies 480 double-columned pages (with numbering by column). In accordance with *Itineraria Romana* as the choice of title, it firmly reflects Miller's conviction[180] that the map was above all intended as a practical tool for travelers' use. Two short "chapters" catalog water features (XIII) and the peoples beyond the Roman Empire named on the map (VII) respectively. Otherwise, however, the overriding concern is to test the accuracy of the map's routes and distance figures against surviving material or documentary testimony for conditions on the ground. Miller's organizational principle, broadly speaking, is to divide up the map on the basis of eleven Late Roman administrative regions or dioceses, with a "chapter" for each, in order: Britain; Gaul; Spain; Italy; Illyricum; Dacia, Macedonia, Thrace; Pontus; Asia; Oriens, with continuation through Parthia to India; Egypt and Libya; and Africa (from Libya westward to Morocco). Within each of these "chapters," Miller then follows 141 routes (*Strecken*) of his own devising, place by place.

Naturally Miller, like his predecessors, had to develop some viable means of presenting the map's vast, confusing maze of routes, and his choice is an original one with Late Roman roots. But at the same time its prescriptive nature needs to be recognized.[181] The map itself marks no boundaries, nor does it record the names of Late Roman dioceses. Most of Miller's routes are equally artificial. On the map, no distinction is made between, say, major and minor roads, and the entire network remains seamless. At every junction where there is more than one onward route, users of the map are left to make their own choice. Miller's *Strecken*, by contrast, must impose choices. Moreover, while justifiable enough from the traveler's perspective, these choices may run counter to the way in which the route network appears to have been laid out on the map, from left to right. *Strecke* 17c, for example,[182] which begins by proceeding to the right from Burdigala, then reverses at Aginnum by turning back leftward to Tolosa, rather than continuing to Bibona. By the same token, for an appreciation of how the routes in Africa from Alexandria westward were laid out, it might have been preferable to present them from left to right; but for the most part Miller chooses otherwise.

Miller's prescriptiveness is again apparent in his readiness to restore or rewrite lettering, as well as to redraw line work, in instances where he identifies omission, error, or confusion. Such steps he almost invariably takes with reference to his own lithograph of the map in preference to the photographs published in 1888.[183] In general, too, he offers little or no discussion, so that his reasoning may remain frustratingly obscure.[184] Meantime, in an effort to give the commentary a geographical and cultural scope far beyond anything that a study of the map calls for, he fills individual entries for places with information about alternative ancient names, historical background, archaeological finds, and more.[185] It is true that he must have learned by example to keep his practice in this regard much more restrained than that of Desjardins. Even so, simply to refer readers to standard reference works for such extraneous information might have been more appropriate; but that is not Miller's didactic way, unless, ironically, his readers seek precise text references to ancient authors whom he names as sources. For these, readers are directed (p. LXXVI) to consult Albert Forbiger's *Handbuch der alten Geographie*.[186]

Last but not least, Miller's eagerness to map the routes he devised is admirable, and he offers over three hundred hand-drawn sketches for the purpose. Two respects in which he might conceivably have done more raised special difficulties, however. First, the addition of even minimal color to these sketches could have greatly improved their accessibility, but the expense of coloring any maps was no doubt prohibitive, and there was the clear warning that such costs could be reckoned to have contributed to the suspension of Desjardins's publication. Second, a set of maps at a consistent scale representing the Roman world in all its immensity would have been invaluable to Miller's readers, but this too demanded further high outlay. There did exist Lapie's set published in 1845, which even marked the Peutinger map's routes. Yet for whatever reason Miller neither reproduced, let alone adapted, this set. Two passing references confirm his knowledge of it,[187] though they do next to nothing to bring it to readers' notice. It is true that in *Die Peutingersche Tafel* as expanded in 1916 – although not in *Itineraria Romana* itself – readers gain the opportunity to see twelve pages of successive overview sketches marking the Peutinger map's routes across most of the Roman world on modern bases. Even so, these pages repeatedly reflect the multiple limitations characteristic of Miller's sketch maps in general: they are drawn at various different scales (almost never specified on these pages), with minimal rendering of landscape, and with modern names presented in a cursive script very resistant to decipherment. In short, for all Miller's concern to raise his readers' cartographic awareness, the results are disappointing.

7. SCHOLARSHIP SINCE 1916: OVERVIEW[188]

After almost a century, Miller's comprehensive presentation of the map has still to be superseded. The only subsequent edition on which work is recorded was an initiative by Otto Cuntz (1858–1932). He refers to it in the brief Praefatio to his *Itineraria Romana* I (Leipzig: Teubner, 1929), and his draft materials were known to Joseph Schnetz (1873–1952) – editor of *Itineraria Romana* II as it eventually achieved publication in 1940 – who mentions them at the opening of his Praefatio. No one, however, continued Cuntz's work on the Peutinger map after his death.

At different times Wilhelm Kubitschek (1858–1936), Annalina and Mario Levi, and Ekkehard Weber might all conceivably have developed comprehensive presentations, but they preferred instead to make alternative contributions. Kubitschek, in addition to his long, harsh reviews of Miller's work, devoted almost nineteen dense columns of the *Real-Encyclopädie* to the map (s.v. "Karten"),[189] and these were later reinforced with almost eight more by Friedrich Gisinger.[190] The Levis' principal contribution is an entire monograph, *Itineraria Picta. Contributo allo studio della Tabula Peutingeriana* (Rome, 1967), devoted to the map's pictorial symbols. The interpretation it favors may no longer be found convincing, but its differentiation and classification of the symbols are of lasting value.[191] The Levis' later book, *La "Tabula Peutingeriana,"*[192] offering almost 150 pages of text, is written to accompany a full-size color reproduction of the map, and for the most part limits itself to a descriptive treatment of the map's features, especially its symbols and its routes region by region. Weber's *Kommentar* is similarly designed as a concise accompaniment to his set of full-size color photographs published in 1976. The avowed purpose of this *Kommentar* – which it amply fulfills – is no more ambitious than to provide a wide-ranging, up-to-date synthesis within less than twenty-five double-columned pages of text.

Luciano Bosio's 1983 study *La Tabula Peutingeriana: Una descrizione pittorica del mondo antico*[193] is notable, as the title indicates, for its attempt to shift attention away from the route network to physical landscape features. These form Bosio's primary focus, along with the symbols, and his treatment is the first to be illustrated so effectively in color. Altogether, throughout the book appear about fifty photographs (of multiple shapes and sizes, both reduced and enlarged) taken from the map.

In an extensive *thèse d'état* entitled "La cartographie à Rome,"[194] Pascal Arnaud devotes a substantial chapter to the map, articulating at the start[195] the hope that aspects other than origins and route network may at last claim overdue attention from scholars. While he rightly identifies

Bosio's study as promising in this regard, it must be said that the scope of his own treatment remains largely traditional.[196] The same applies to the contributions made by Mauro Calzolari, Manlio Magini, and Francesco Prontera to the 2003 volume *Tabula Peutingeriana: Le antiche vie del mondo* edited by Prontera, as well as to the overview offered by Pierre Herrmann in *Itinéraires des voies romaines de l'Antiquité au Moyen Âge*.[197] Likewise discouraging is the limited treatment of the map offered by Oswald Dilke in Harley and Woodward's *History of Cartography*,[198] and subsequently by Kai Brodersen in his *Terra Cognita: Studien zur römischen Raumerfassung*.[199] This said, Brodersen's brevity has to be seen as a consequence of his larger, provocative contention that Roman culture had little use for maps, while in all likelihood a fresh approach of the type encouraged by the History of Cartography project could not have been realistically expected of Dilke, for all his energy and learning.[200]

Today, however, there is no good reason to defer attempting a fresh approach, and such a shift forms a primary purpose of the present study. Meantime, naturally, the map remains of fundamental importance to scholars engaged at every level – continental, regional, local – by the network of land routes across the Roman Empire and beyond to the East.[201]

THE SURVIVING COPY

THE MATERIAL OBJECT AND ITS PALEOGRAPHY

THIS CHAPTER IS the first of three to examine the surviving copy of the Peutinger map from multiple perspectives. Here the copy as material object forms the focus of attention together with its paleography, which has never before been accorded the close scrutiny that Martin Steinmann devotes to it in section 2. Paleography, in turn, forms the basis for him to consider what may be determined about the exemplar of our copy (that is, the version of the map from which it was made); the copyist(s); and the date and place where the copy was produced. Chapter 3 then analyzes the design and character of the map, and Chapter 4 considers how faithfully the surviving copy reproduces the lost original.

1. MATERIAL, CONDITION, AND CONSERVATION
Coauthored with Martin Steinmann

Today, the map is most often thought of as eleven separate sheets of parchment, probably vellum.[1] This is by no means an inaccurate view, but it is equally important to bear in mind that from the outset the eleven were joined to form a long strip. For this purpose, they were not sewn together – as was more typical medieval practice – but glued. A narrow strip at one end of a sheet was overlapped, and thus hidden, by a corresponding strip at the end of the adjacent sheet. [Fig. 1] Because all the hidden strips are blank, we can be sure that the full extent of the parchment base required for the map was prepared before copying began. The overlaps for the four leftmost sheets do in fact correspond with those for the four rightmost, even if altogether the arrangement of overlaps seems to lack consistency. Three sheets (2, 5, 10) have an overlap on both sides; one (4) has an overlap only to the left; three (6, 7, 8) have an overlap only to the right; and four (1, 3, 9, 11) have no overlap at all. The vertical line drawn to mark off a very distinct margin at the lefthand end of the first sheet acts to confirm that our copy of the map never extended farther in this direction. There is no such margin or line at the righthand end of the eleventh sheet. It is just conceivable, therefore, that the map did continue on to one or more additional sheets now lost. More probably, it did in fact end abruptly thus, or a margin became lost at some stage when the map was removed from display on, say, a wall or a cylinder.

Because each sheet is today laid on acid-free paper and kept in a sealed container (see below), it is impossible to handle the parchment or to inspect the back of it. However, it seems to be vellum of good quality, with the map presented on the flesh side.[2] No writing or other mark on the back has ever been reported. Slightly differing figures for the dimensions of the sheets have been published, as is only to be expected when none is exactly rectangular or straight-edged. Even so, all are approximately 33 cm (13 in.) tall, and vary between 58 ($22\frac{3}{4}$ in.) and 70 ($27\frac{1}{2}$ in.) in width. For precision, the measurements taken by Weber[3] before the sheets were sealed in their containers may be regarded as the most reliable:

1. 33 cm tall × 59.8 wide (without margin 56.3 wide)
2. 33.5 × 62.8 (without margins 59.9)
3. 33.5 × 65.6
4. 33 × 61.8 (without margin 60)
5. 33.2 × 62.8 (without margins 59.2)
6. 33.5 × 60.6 (without margin 59.1)
7. 32.8 × 64.3 (without margin 62)
8. 33.7 × 58 (without margin 56.4)
9. 33 × 61.7
10. 33.4 × 70.2 (without margins 65.5)
11. 33 × 66

Total width: 693.6 cm ($22\frac{3}{4}$ ft.), or without margins 671.7 (22 ft.)

From the outset there were already several holes[4] and large tears here and there among the sheets, and some were sewn up by the parchment maker in the course of preparing the sheets for the copyist.[5] Over time, further damage of various kinds has occurred, and has often been repaired with linen and paper.[6] Successive creases, stains, blots, and the like, have left their mark too.

Although attention has not been drawn to them previously, certain holes clearly visible in the borders above and below the map seem best explained as having been made in order to fasten the map to a wall, say, or a frame, with sizeable nails of rectangular shape.[7] Wherever this was done, it would have happened before Celtis discovered the map. If it had remained on display thus for a considerable period, the varying intensity of light to which it was exposed along its entire length could in part account for the

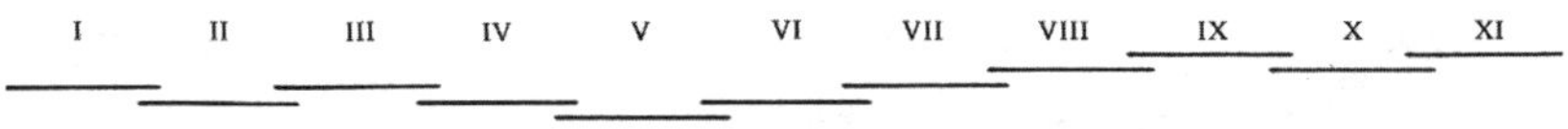

FIGURE 1. Overlapping of the map's eleven parchments. Line drawing from E. Weber, *Kommentar* (volume accompanying *Tabula Peutingeriana, Codex Vindobonensis 324*), p. 20. Graz, 1976.

notable differences in the degree of fading and soiling that has occurred (see further below). In any event, the holes are our only clue to how the map was kept for at least some of the time during the centuries before its discovery by Celtis.[8]

How the map was kept in the libraries of Konrad Peutinger and Prince Eugen for the next two and a quarter centuries is likewise uncertain, although there is never a hint of it being set up on display. During this period, rather, it was clearly subject to rolling and unrolling, as well as being stored rolled up and undisturbed for years on end.

Once the map came to the Hofbibliothek, the prefect Nicolò de Forlosia – concerned to minimize damage – placed it on a revolving cylinder, as von Scheyb personally attests:[9]

Anno demum 1741 quo idem Cl. Forlosia Caes. Bibliothecae Praefecti munus obiret, is membranas, quoniam senio et squalore ita erant affectae, ut revolvendo frustulis dissilientibus frangerentur; glutine super tela aptari, me quoque praesente, quam diligentissime curavit, uti deinceps circa taedae Cylindrum convolutae et volvi ab intuentibus, et tuto servari perpetuo possint.

The parchments were suffering so much from decay and dirt that rolling and unrolling them caused damage, with tiny pieces breaking off. Thus eventually, in the year 1741, when Forlosia assumed his position as Prefect of the library, he took the greatest care – in my presence moreover – to ensure that a cloth backing be attached with glue so that thereafter, with the parchments wrapped around a pinewood cylinder, viewers could turn this and the parchments could be kept unharmed indefinitely.[10]

The precise workings of this arrangement are beyond recovery,[11] although they were presumably comparable to the one described for the Bayeux Tapestry early in the nineteenth century: "The tapestry is coiled round a cylinder, which is turned by a winch and wheel."[12] It is again uncertain just how differently the map came to be displayed through the mid-nineteenth century. In a work published in 1859, Edward Edwards states that the map was to be found in "the great hall of the Library," occupying the ninth of "ten glazed cases in which are exhibited some of the choicest rarities of the collection."[13] Yet by the time Alfred Maury made his visit in August 1862, the map was evidently in its own room, again under glass, and partly unrolled.[14]

Separation of the parchment sheets in the interests of better preservation is known to have been considered by the library authorities in 1846. Only in fall 1863,[15] however, was this step taken, and the sheets placed in boxes. After World War II – if not earlier, possibly around 1937 – the sheets were each kept inside a pair of glass panes, and a steel container was then made for them.[16] A conservation initiative begun in 1978[17] transferred each sheet to its own sealed plastic container with a clear top punctured by airholes to allow "breathing."[18] There has also been an effort to darken the underpinning of gaps, rather than leaving them exposed in white as in the 1976 photographs. Inevitably, this darkening can act to increase the difficulty of determining the extent of damage suffered by a sheet. As a precaution against further fading, nowadays the sheets are very seldom exposed to light; so access to any of them is only granted most sparingly.

When all this is said, it is important to recognize that the parchment and the inks selected for making the surviving copy have proved remarkably resilient over eight centuries. The degree of rough handling on the one hand, and neglect on the other, to which the map has been exposed fall well short of those suffered by two comparable medieval masterpieces, the Bayeux Tapestry[19] and the Hereford Cathedral Mappamundi.[20] The Peutinger map can only have benefited from being left undisturbed for some very long periods. For that reason and others, by far the greater part of it overall remains impressively clear, vivid, and engaging to the viewer.

2. PALEOGRAPHY
Martin Steinmann

(a) Drawing

As explained above, the full extent of the parchment base that the map required was prepared before copying began. Because at various points colors and inks either overlap or remain distinct from one another, it is possible to reconstruct the sequence of most stages in the copying. In this instance the method chosen was evidently neither to prick the exemplar and then to apply pounce to the holes created, nor to prick both the exemplar and the new parchment.[21] Instead, the map was copied layer by layer. It simplified the transfer process if the exemplar and the new parchment were placed parallel to one another, so that the copy was directly below the model, and a copyist then had only to measure distances from the upper or lower edge.

In this instance water features were applied first, with a greenish color. Major river courses were represented by two parallel lines, and the space between them was then filled in with a thinner shade of the same color. Seas and lakes were later edged with black ink. The original color for the water is still visible in only a few places, specifically ones where a parchment sheet had the margin of an adjacent sheet glued under it. By contrast, large expanses have become more or less discolored and dark-brown. Clearly, the color contains copper compounds, and not only have these permutated, but they have also attacked the parchment, rendering it brittle and partly destroying it.[22] The map is especially affected in this way along its top and bottom; the blank margin there, along with stretches of open water, is often broken off.

Either the mountain ranges or the larger cities were drawn next; it is impossible to determine the order. The larger cities appear in the form of pictorial symbols ("vignettes") for buildings of various types, or as fortified cities with ramparts and towers. These symbols were first sketched with lighter ink and in a finer pen; then they were retraced with darker ink, details were added, and they were colored in light-red, brownish-yellow, and blue shades.[23] The large, figurative representations of Rome, Constantinople, and Antioch were also created using the same technique, although they were drawn with a thicker pen.[24] The symbols become more uniform in design, and less elaborate, toward the right of the map. In observing this shift, Weber[25] felt unsure whether the exemplar itself was not only already simplified in the East but also drawn with less detail there, or whether the copyist began his work on the left and devoted less effort to it as he proceeded toward the right.

In a further step, the links between cities were then drawn in as red lines. These halt on reaching symbols, so do not cut through them. In many instances, however, the symbols were clearly forgotten and were then added next to routes or on top of routes already drawn. These additions are often rendered smaller or simpler, or are left incomplete,[26] but otherwise they do not seem fundamentally different from their full-size counterparts. Along the routes, the successive stages for a journey are marked by sharp turns (chicanes), confirming that there was no intention to furnish an accurate representation of movement across the landscape. Red lines occur in addition along some river courses, always on one side only; their meaning is unknown.[27]

(b) Scripts

(i) *Types and Their Functions*

Once the drawing was done, the writing on the map was copied with red and black ink. The red ink used for this purpose is somewhat darker and more pasty than that used to mark the routes, while the black more or less matches the black used for outlining and finishing the symbols.[28]

The copyist used three types of script: minuscules, capitals, and display capitals. The first two types are each written with a pen. Display capital lettering, on the other hand, is drawn in such a way that the strokes of a letter overlap and are exaggerated; often there is no telling whether a pen has been used or a brush.

Black minuscules are used for place-names, and red for labeling rivers. From Segment 8 onward, the copyist begins to furnish descriptive notices in red minuscules of notably larger size: for example, *Desertvm v(bi) qvadraginta annis erraver(vn)t filii isrl(is) dvcente Moyse* (8C5);[29] *Babylonia* (10C4);[30] *Hic Alexander Responsvm accepit Vsq(ve) qvo Alexander* (11B4–11B5).[31]

The capital script is used for naming peoples, regions, mountains, and lesser expanses of open water (as in 7B1, for example). Two of the three cities distinguished by large symbols are also labeled thus in red, ROMA and ANTIOCHIA; *Constantinopolis*, by contrast, is labeled in minuscules (likewise red). To the left of Rome, AD SCM PETRVM (4B4) stands out in red capitals, as does HIC LACVS TRITONVM (7C5) likewise. Distance figures are written out in full in very small capitals along stretches in 4C and 5C; minuscule script, however, is used for the same purpose in 10C. The words in capitals are seldom separated, and even then not by much.[32]

Display capitals indicate large geographical units: provinces, landmasses, large expanses of open water (as across Segments 6–7, for example). Words rendered thus are widely spaced, and the choice of red ink or black reflects a concern that the sequence from one letter to the next should be clear rather than representing any hierarchy of meaning.

In text manuscripts, the normal practice was for the copyist to write the text itself in black ink first, and then in a second stage to draw initial letters, display elements, and highlights all in red. On the map, by contrast, the names in red, and perhaps also the black display capitals, were evidently written at an early stage of the work, in any case before the place-names in minuscules.[33] It also makes sense to assume that the river names in red minuscules were written early, and that only later – during his work on the place-names – did the copyist add in black ink those river names which he noticed had been overlooked, such as three in 6C2–6C3. When all this is said, it remains possible that further lettering in red was added only at a third stage, after two prior ones where the copyist had worked in red and black.

(ii) *Forms*

Display capitals appear partly straight – comparable in form to lettering in classical inscriptions – and partly round, with forms derived from uncial script that almost become distinctive letter forms in their own right (normally termed "Lombard" in the late medieval period): in MACEDONIA (6A3–7B2) compare the rigid **E** with the **D** and the **N** that follow. Where the copyist has several varieties for the same letter at his disposal, he plainly made a point of not using the same form twice in the same word: note **N**, for example, in LVGDVNENSES (1A1–1B5), and **M** in MESOPOTAMIA (10B3–10B5).

Letters in capital script have the same forms as the capitals in minuscule script. They are written with a pen, without flourishes and similar decorative elements. **F** has a double shoulder in its upper horizontal stroke: see, for example, 6A3 *INFERIOR*.

The minuscule script is clear, and at first sight seems to be the work of an experienced scribe without pretensions to calligraphy. Upon closer inspection, however, it appears rather irregular, and in specific instances positively hesitant or shaky: for example, observe the irregular interior shapes in the letter **o**. In general, the formation of the copyist's minuscule script exhibits characteristics that are partly Gothic, partly older (see further below). Ascenders are short in relation to the minims, although the letters themselves are fairly wide. They often touch one another and create lattice-work as in, for example, *Pitinvm* (4B5) and above it *Maritima*. On the other hand, the so-called biting of opposed round letters is lacking; at the most, there is slight overlap. In *Tibori* and *Adponte ivlii* (both 4B5), for example, note that the lobes of **b** and **o**, and **p** and **o**, respectively, do not overlap.[34]

The final vertical strokes of **m** and **n** are mostly broken, though at times completely round: for a broken instance, observe **m** in *Advicesimv* (4B4). Their shafts stop flat on the baseline – note, for example, *Bebiana* (4B5) – or make a slight turn to the right. This turn is often somewhat more pronounced on the last shaft: note the **m** in *Pitinvm* (4B5). In rare cases the last two vertical strokes of **m**, or both the vertical strokes of **n**, are broken: see for example, *Interamnio* and *Fisternas* (both 4B4). In *Tyberias* (9C2), even the **i** has a foot beneath it, a so-called quadrangle.

Long shafts begin mostly with a light stroke from the left, as in, for example, the double **l** and the **s** of *Castello firmani* (4B4); however, they never have an additional stroke, which would build a wedge or a forking. Cursive elements are absent: the three letters **f**, **r**, and long **s** do not extend below the baseline, nor are their shafts curved at the base.

Observations on the forms of individual letters:

For the most part the copyist uses the "round" **d** derived from uncial. At the same time, instances of the "straight" form are far from rare: for example, in *fidenis* (4B5). On the round **d**, the top end is sometimes curved back and capped with a decorative stroke that slopes upward to the right, as in, for example, *Rvdas* (5B4).

e with a cedilla occurs commonly in this hand (ę, "e caudata" = ae).

The lower part of **g** has a hook, which is often closed by a hairline, as in, for example, *agvbio* (4B3).

Diacritical strokes above **i** only occur where needed for comprehension, for example with double **i**, as in *Danvbii* (7A5), *filii* (8C5), or after double **n**, as in *Iovis penninvs ide agvbio* (4B2–4B3).

r often ends in a slim – sometimes barely visible – decorative stroke at its top right, as in, for example, *Interocrio* (4B4), *Priferno* (4B5).

The "round" **r** – attested since antiquity after **o**, and common in the fully developed Gothic script after all letters rounded on the right side – only occurs on the map in the abbreviation -*rvm* (see below): for example, *Arephilenor(vm)* (the upper instance of that name in 7C2).

The "round," or uncial, **s** familiar today mostly appears at the end of a word – as in *Adnovas* (4B5) – but the "tall" form occurs there often too, as in *Adrvbras* (4B5). Within a word, the tall form is the norm for **s**; the round form is not common there.[35]

x is written in three strokes – that is to say, its upper-right and lower-left parts are not sections of the same stroke: see, for example, *Ad Sextvm* (4B4).

y is sometimes written with the traditional dot above the letter – as in *Via tẏbvrtina* (4B5) – sometimes without it, as in *Pyrgos* (4B4).

For lower-case **z**, the form used is always the tall one, unfamiliar today. It resembles **h** with a long stroke at the top of the shaft: see *Vzappa* (4C5).

Abbreviations are used only sparingly:

am, vm signified by a macron over a vowel following **m** or **n**, as in *Advicesimv̄* (4B4);

e with macron for *est*, as in *Hoc ē [st] templ[vm] asclepy* (7C5);

i with macron for *in*, as in . . . *accepervnt ī[n] monte* . . . (8C5);

l with an upward-slanting stroke through the shaft for *–lia*, as in *MIŁ* (4C4); or for *–lvm*, as in *Templ* (5C5); or for *–lis*, as in *Hadrianopoł* (7C4); or for *–onia*, as in *Thisdro Coł* (5C3);

p with macron subscript for *per*, as in . . . *meotidi p(er) qvem* . . . (7C5);

t with an abbreviation stroke shaped like an arabic 2 occurs once for *dicitvr* (7C1);

figure **2** slashed by a vertical stroke for *–rvm*, as in *Arephilenor* (7C2);

7, a figure familiar today as seven, in a few instances signifies *et* (and), as in *Tvrris 7 taberna* (7C2);

figure **9** in superscript form for *–vs*, as in *Scinaloc* (7C1);

& (ampersand) is not found;

abbreviation through superscript letters does not occur.

(c) Exemplar

It is natural, and important, to consider what may be deduced about the exemplar, that is, the version of the map from which our surviving copy was produced. First, the vertical line drawn to mark off a very distinct margin at the lefthand end of our copy must surely indicate that the exemplar, too, never extended farther in this direction. Moreover, such a clean break could imply that the exemplar in turn had been produced on parchment. Papyrus by contrast is prone to fray much more jaggedly and, in any event, it seems most unlikely that a Late Antique papyrus roll of the map's ample dimensions would survive far into the Middle Ages.

There is really no knowing how accurate and legible a rendering of the map the exemplar itself was, and hence how far our copy's many slips and omissions merely reflect flaws already present in the exemplar or damage suffered by it. The notable absence of a name and symbol for the city of Alexandria in Egypt, for example (only its lighthouse appears inconspicuously in 8C3), could suggest that the exemplar was damaged hereabouts, if not elsewhere too.

Because the copyist's letter forms correspond throughout to those common around 1200 (see further below), it follows that he was not endeavoring to reproduce an older script. "E caudata" (ȩ), for example, is entirely common around 1200, but it would be expected to be used at the most sporadically in a Late Antique or Carolingian exemplar. This said, the copyist's minuscule script does reflect one distinct idiosyncracy. I know of no other manuscript in which so many letters within words written in minuscules appear as capitals. Most of the alphabet is represented thus: **R** especially, as well as **A, B, D, G, H, L, M, N, Q, S, V,** and **Z.** Such mixing of minuscule and capital letters is almost all confined to geographical names.[36] It is rare in the descriptive notices,[37] and altogether occurs unevenly across the map – notably more often on Segment 6, for example, than on Segment 9. It is just conceivable that the mixing was somehow supposed to illustrate the appearance of the geographical names on the original map. Another possibility is that the mixing indicates a failure on the part of the copyist to transcribe the exemplar accurately. Even so, nothing more can be said when neither the form of the letters overall nor the capitalization of particular ones corresponds to any earlier recognizable script, Late Antique or otherwise. Moreover, consistency was hardly a prime concern: for example, the name Abrostola occurs twice on different routes not far apart (8B4), but its **r** is minuscule in one instance, capital in the other.

One capital ligature is peculiar to the map: the abbreviation for *Insvla* begins with an **N** whose first shaft is lengthened at the top and stands for a preceding **I**, as in *Ins. Sasonis* (6B3). This kind of abbreviation would only be expected to be found in inscriptions and is highly unusual in book writing. However, our copyist does also use it once in another context: *In his locis scorpiones nascvntvr* (11C3).

Two comparable idiosyncratic features concerning stops may be observed, both of which our copyist may well have been just reproducing uncritically from the exemplar. The first is the frequent inclusion of stops between the words in geographical names comprising two or more words: for example, *Aqvas.Passaras* (4B1), *Vtica.Colonia* (4C3). In Roman manuscripts the practice of separating words by stops did not continue beyond the second century A.D., although it remained common in many inscriptions even into the Middle Ages. By presenting several of these names in this way, therefore, our copy of the map gives them something of an epigraphic character. Again, there is a marked contrast with the map's descriptive notices, where the words are never divided by stops. The second idiosyncratic feature is the way in which Roman numerals – in fact one or more letters fulfilling this function – are presented. It was regular scribal practice to signify that such letters were serving as numerals by setting them between two stops. On the map, however, where the layout calls for blank space to be left between a place-name and the distance figure relating to it, the mapmaker sets the first of the two stops immediately after the place-name rather than immediately before the distance figure.

Finally, a "false" spelling may contribute a valuable insight. In the seven instances where a distance figure is only a single mile, the copyist writes .*co*. with a macron above, as in 4B5 to the left of Rome itself.[38] Plainly, **M** for *mille [passuum]* should be meant, and the confusion is only readily explicable if a curved uncial **m** appeared in the exemplar. While undue weight should not be attached to this one usage, the fact remains that uncial was the most common type of script for complex Late Antique handwriting, and it is therefore a reasonable inference that it was used in the exemplar for our copy of the map.[39]

(d) The Copyist

In considering what may be deduced about the copyist, it is only right to begin with the issue of whether the artwork and the writing that the map required are the work of a single individual or of a pair. There is no easy answer. Generally speaking, for the production of illuminated texts both possibilities are well attested.[40] For certain, our copy of the map was produced in one continuous process. It does not exhibit later medieval additions, amendments, or corrections.[41] Nor apparently, after the copying was done, was it checked against the exemplar by another individual, useful though that regular step would have been. It does seem evident enough that all the writing – in the various scripts and colors – is the work of the same hand; there are no significant differences.

Whether the artwork was done by this hand too, however, is another matter, and the dissimilar nature of the two tasks leaves us without a basis for comparison. It might be tempting to attribute to a writer those drawings seemingly added as afterthoughts, which are cruder and more cramped than those copied in the regular way: consider, for example, the curious cliffs in 2B3.[42] On the other hand, the towers and roofs of some of the structures drawn in black are not much more accomplished. Equally, it might be reckoned that the artwork, writing, and afterthoughts are so closely integrated that a division of the work between an artist and a writer would not have been at all practical; hence the copying of the map could be regarded as the work of a single individual. This said, it must be acknowledged that any such conclusion still remains open to doubt.

Many names on the map are known to be incorrect, the accuracy of the cartography can also sometimes be doubted, and (as we have seen) the writing itself exhibits certain idiosyncrasies. Even so, the means are lacking to gauge how far these quirks and shortcomings were carried over from the exemplar, or stem from damage to it. At least it is plain that the map was not fundamentally edited by our copyist in the course of his work.

Nor is there any sign of a scholar attempting to remedy obvious mistakes, let alone to add to outdated names the ones current in the Middle Ages. The map as it survives is genuinely a copy, not a revised version of its exemplar. If it was indeed copied by a single individual, he seems most likely to have been an artist who could write but was no scholar. As such, he was indeed an appropriate choice for the formidable task that the copying of such a large and complex masterpiece represented. David Woodward's characterization of the makers of *mappaemundi* and their work may be noted in this connection:

> *Mappaemundi* were regarded as paintings in the early Middle Ages. Since their makers were map painters rather than cartographers in the modern sense of the word, the methods, tools, and materials used for these maps were those of the medieval artist in general. In particular, since the vast majority of these maps were produced for manuscript books, the techniques involved are indistinguishable from those used in manuscript illumination.[43]

The cost of the actual materials that the copying of the map called for would hardly have been far out of the ordinary. What truly mattered, rather, were space, light, time, and great skill. The inks used do not appear to have been very expensive ones, and even a slim book would require considerably more parchment than the map. The time needed would depend not least upon the season and the copyist's other commitments. In a monastic environment at least, there were unlikely to be more than about five hours in the day free for scribal work, and perhaps as few as three in some houses; low temperatures or bad light, or both, might often halt such work during winter.[44]

(e) Date and Place of Production

Our copyist's writing reflects the transition from later Carolingian minuscule to Gothic script.[45] In the course of this development, a constantly changing variety of traditional and new forms appear both in combination and in parallel, and care must be exercised not to draw rash conclusions from individual forms. A comprehensive study of the development is lacking; currently, the most detailed presentation is by Karin Schneider.[46] Although she limits her scope to German-language manuscripts, most of the characteristics she describes also occur in Latin ones. Moreover, the workmanlike style of many German manuscripts matches that of the map. Paleographical evaluation of the map is hindered, however, by its lack of any long, continuous text and the absence of all book decoration.

On the basis of the scripts used, there is no cause to dispute the general consensus that our copy of the map was produced in the last quarter of the twelfth century or in the first quarter of the thirteenth.[47] The likeliest match for the map is script of the first quarter of the thirteenth century as presented by Schneider.[48] In it there is a slight preponderance of early characteristics, so that a date around A.D. 1200 also seems reasonable. Unless the map can be linked to a specific center or at least to a particular region, a more precise conclusion about its date is not possible.

Regrettably, the means to determine a specific production center seems lacking at this point. As to a regional tradition, while the use of **y** with or without the traditional dot above the letter can offer no clue,[49] the copyist's devotion to the "tall" form of **z** could point to the south German region or Alsace.[50] A distinctive feature of the map's presentation warrants attention in this connection: except in the large symbol for Antioch, trees are shown only as part of the drawings for SILVA VOSAGVS (2A2–2B2) and SILVA MARCIANA (2A5–3A1). Because both these areas – the Vosges mountains and Black Forest respectively – are heavily forested, it is tempting to infer that their presentation is embellishment by a copyist familiar with the general region. Even so, there is still no telling whether he was our copyist or a predecessor.

An attempt has also been made to locate the exemplar for our copy of the map at the island monastery of Reichenau on Lake Constance.[51] This identification must remain a speculative one, however, which can be neither confirmed nor refuted beyond doubt. In principle it would have been possible for our copy to be produced at Reichenau or indeed at Murbach in southern Alsace (both Benedictine foundations). At both, to be sure, there were Late Antique manuscripts, and the transmission of the map must date back to that period. This said, even if the exemplar was at Reichenau or Murbach, it does not follow that the copyist had to be based there, especially as neither monastery was still a noted center of scholarship and book production by 1200. By contrast, abbeys such as Salem near Konstanz (a Cistercian foundation) and Weingarten near Ravensburg (Benedictines of the Hirsauer Reform) were flourishing at this date, and it is conceivable that the copyist came from one of them, to name but two possibilities among many. Until fresh evidence surfaces, the exemplar's location must remain an enigma.[52] Moreover, the copy was not necessarily made for purposes of scholarship or instruction. It is equally possible to imagine, say, the Hohenstaufen (Staufer) monarchy in Swabia taking an interest in a Roman world map, and a copy being commissioned by one of its nobles.[53] All this too, however, is pure speculation.

(f) Postmedieval Adjustments

As argued above, the copying of the map was one continuous process. The only further markings identifiable are few, all of them added very lightly. The natural assumption is that all date to the sixteenth or early seventeenth centuries, although it remains conceivable that one or other of the corrections was made by the copyist. The markings comprise one or more letters to complete or correct spellings,[54] the addition of "missing" ancient names[55] as well as of modern equivalents for ancient ones marked,[56] and also the addition of missing line work on a route in 10B5.[57] At least some of these additions have been attributed to Konrad Peutinger himself, but it is impossible to be sure; there are too few words for reliable analysis of the handwriting. Last but not least, part of a grid is visible; some copyist must have drawn it and no doubt intended to erase it, but never did.[58]

85

Chapter 2.
The Surviving Copy:
The Material Object
and Its Paleography

THE DESIGN AND CHARACTER
OF THE MAP

T HIS CHAPTER – THE second of three that examine the surviving copy of the Peutinger map from multiple perspectives – is divided into four principal sections. These consider the fundamentals of the map's design; the mapmaking practice that it reflects; and the map's various physical and cultural components, with special reference to the route network and associated pictorial symbols. Because, remarkably, no such detailed analysis of the map from a specifically cartographic viewpoint has ever been attempted, this chapter in its turn breaks new ground and may thereby contribute to the broader history of cartography. Uniting the chapter's sections is a concern to elucidate the range and quality of expertise that the map's cartography displays, as well as to identify what may be deduced about the aims that its maker had in mind. Findings here are incorporated into the wider appraisal of the context and purpose originally intended for the map, which is to follow in Chapter 5. The analysis in the present chapter depends upon the unverifiable assumption that the surviving copy does represent a sufficiently accurate rendering of the lost original as to permit a reliable discussion of *its* design and character by reference to the copy alone. To some degree or other, this assumption is likely to be flawed, and hence the issue of the copy's divergence from the lost original is specifically addressed in Chapter 4. In the absence of detailed testimony beyond the single copy, however, there is no alternative means by which to proceed.

1. FUNDAMENTALS OF THE MAP'S DESIGN

Despite its vital importance, the design of the map is a topic that has been virtually ignored to date. Current consensus holds that the route network – a linear representation of place-names and distance figures to be found in itinerary listings especially – forms the map's basis, with physical features only being added thereafter as "decoration." In consequence, the argument contends, the result is simply a diagram, not a map.[1] By the same token, many of the settlements on this network that are marked by pictorial symbols could in principle be considered to form the basis of the map, insofar as these settlements are positioned accurately enough within the physical landscape. But then any such claim overlooks the fact that the routes linking them are merely adapted to occupy the intermediate space available. It seems quite impossible, therefore, that either the route network itself or the settlements most closely associated with it form the basis of the map. It is inconceivable that the symbols marking these settlements could have been laid out prior to any physical landscape, above all because of the map's quite unconventional shape.

In my view, the map is no mere diagram. Rather, it does have a cartographic basis, and it represents an extraordinarily bold, mature achievement crafted to fulfill a range of purposes on several levels. Despite its unusual shape, the design is a single, cohesive one.[2] In discussing it here, I term the maker(s) or designer of the lost original as "the mapmaker" (singular, male), purely as a practical short form of reference. The maker of the surviving copy − "our copy" − I refer to likewise as "the (or our) copyist," thereby distinguishing "him" from the succession of previous, similarly anonymous copyists. Whenever I refer to "the copyists" (of the map), the context should make clear whether this generalization is intended to include "our" copyist, or to exclude him.

(a) Shape and Scope

As already noted,[3] the map's shape is extreme: it is everywhere about 33 cm (13 in.) in height for its full surviving width of about 672 (22 ft.). There is no knowing to what further width the original extended at its lost lefthand end, nor whether the copy's righthand end is even that of the original. It is certain that in the former connection there are sound reasons to reject Miller's claim that only a single parchment of the width used by our copyist (say, 60 cm [$23\frac{1}{2}$ in.]) has gone missing, thus making the original map about 732 cm (24 ft.) wide overall. In fact the ingenious and widely accepted reconstruction of the lost western end that Miller published in 1898 is altogether flawed. As Appendix 5 demonstrates in detail, it unnecessarily compresses the presentation of Great Britain and the Iberian peninsula, and it ignores several of the mapmaker's cartographic principles.

Not only must the map's extreme shape represent a deliberate, conscious decision on the part of its maker, but he also chose (in my view) to site Rome at the center, where the city would occupy a dominant, pivotal position from both horizontal and vertical perspectives. By definition, with our surviving copy incomplete, this choice is beyond proof and has largely been out of favor ever since Miller − with his lack of concern for map design − rejected it.[4] But as early as 1526 Michael Hummelberg assumes it,[5] and it is hard to imagine any Roman with an artistic bent designing a map of such exaggerated shape, which features Rome so prominently, without seizing the opportunity to make it the center point.[6] Taking Rome as the center, therefore, for the width left of the city to correspond to what survives to its right (approximately 432 cm [$14\frac{1}{4}$ ft.]), the existing 240 cm (8 ft.) to the left would need to be supplemented by a further 190 cm ($6\frac{1}{4}$ ft.) or so, in effect three parchment segments (see Fig. 2). In what is now missing there, the mapmaker surely included more of Great Britain, if not all of it, and completed his coverage of the Mediterranean and its surrounding lands.

The map itself need not have continued all the way to the lefthand end. Conceivably, there was also some combination of caption, list, and dedication placed there. Because so magnificent a map was no doubt produced for one or more patrons, or at their request, a dedication could well be expected – as Moretus made to Welser when he issued the first printed edition of the map in 1598.[7] The lefthand end is a natural choice for the placement of such a dedication (as Moretus chose), although by no means the only one possible. Ptolemy, in his *Geography*, supplied as a caption for his main map a summary of its scope that amounts to three full pages of a modern translation.[8] A list of total distances between principal settlements could also be placed appropriately at the map's lefthand end; such totals are a typical, and undeniably useful, component of written itineraries.[9]

Broadly speaking, however, the western limit set for the map is likely to have been the Atlantic Ocean, while, in our copy at least, the eastern limit is India and Insvla Taprobane. The former limit is a natural choice, the latter a distinctly bold stretch. A less distant eastern endpoint, such as Spasinou Charax at the head of the Persian Gulf, would have permitted better balance to the left and right of Rome at the center, but could not offer such decisive closure for the map on land. It was in any case the span from the Atlantic to India that traditionally framed the Roman worldview at its most expansive.[10] Thus the map's scope can be loosely described as the *orbis terrarum* in Latin, or *oikoumene* (inhabited world) in Greek,[11] with deft exclusion of shadowy marginal regions, in particular Arabia, East Africa, and China. This scope can in turn also be regarded as *orbis Romanus* or even *imperium Romanum*, that is, "the (part of the) world claimed by Rome," "Rome's dominion," or "Rome's sway." Further demarcation is skillfully provided by a band of open water.[12] Its outer limit on the map is defined by a margin top and bottom; coastline marks its inner limit, except along much of the bottom. Here, from the start of Segment 1 to the start of Segment 9, an unbroken mountain range (no. 11) fulfills this purpose instead, until the Red Sea is reached, which then leads into the Indian Ocean.

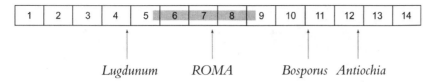

FIGURE 2. Placement of Rome and Italy (shaded area) within the original map, assuming Rome to be its center point.

(b) Landscape Base[13]

Far from being regarded as merely a "decorative" feature of the map, the principal elements of physical landscape need to be seen as its fundamental underpinning. At a minimum there are three: coastlines (defining both mainland and islands); principal rivers; principal mountain ranges.[14] All the map's other features are marked in reference to these three, just as the geographer Strabo recognized in the early first century A.D. (2.5.17):

Πλεῖστον δ᾽ ἡ θάλαττα γεωγραφεῖ καὶ σχηματίζει τὴν γῆν, κόλπους ἀπεργαζομένη καὶ πελάγη καὶ πορθμούς, ὁμοίως δὲ ἰσθμοὺς καὶ χερρονήσους καὶ ἄκρας· προσλαμβάνουσι δὲ ταύτῃ καὶ οἱ ποταμοὶ καὶ τὰ ὄρη. διὰ γὰρ τῶν τοιούτων ἤπειροί τε καὶ ἔθνη καὶ πόλεων θέσεις εὐφυεῖς ἐνενοήθησαν καὶ τἆλλα ποικίλματα, ὅσων μεστός ἐστιν ὁ χωρογραφικὸς πίναξ. ἐν δὲ τούτοις καὶ τὸ τῶν νήσων πλῆθός ἐστι κατεσπαρμένον ἔν τε τοῖς πελάγεσι καὶ κατὰ τὴν παραλίαν πᾶσαν.

It is above all the sea that delineates the land and shapes it, by forming gulfs and open water and straits, and likewise isthmuses, peninsulas, and promontories, with assistance from both rivers and mountains. These are the features that have molded our conception of landmasses and peoples as well as the favorable locations of cities and the various other elements that fill our geographical map. Among these elements, too, is the plethora of islands both dispersed across open water and all along the coastline.

Given the shape of his frame, the mapmaker concluded that only by removing considerable expanses of open water could he ensure adequate coverage of landmasses. As a result, the Bay of Biscay, the Mediterranean, the Adriatic, the Black Sea, the Red Sea, the Indian Ocean, and the Caspian Sea are all reduced to relatively narrow channels; the Aegean Sea is compressed, and the Hellespont and Propontis are effectively eliminated. By contrast, the Bosporus, which divides the continents of Europe and Asia is made broader than necessary, and thereby emphasized.[15]

Open water is removed, but not necessarily the names for parts of it, nor of islands within it. The retention of such names is especially extensive within the Adriatic and Black seas; the same may be said of islands within the Adriatic and Aegean seas. The mapmaker clearly attached importance to both types of feature, and in all likelihood he derived them from one or more maps that represented open water in fuller detail.[16] However, most islands are shown no more than small, with a stylized, token shape. Sicily, Crete, and Cyprus are the only islands rendered large and with a route network in place. In each of these instances, the narrow channel of the Mediterranean is widened to permit insertion of the island; the same is done for the Peloponnese.

It is a surprise that the mapmaker did not present Sardinia likewise. It engages him sufficiently to mark and name four offshore islands to its left and a further two to its right.[17] Sardinia itself is shown as approximately 8 cm wide by 1.5 high (3.1 × 0.6 in.), and could readily have been extended in width to match Sicily, which is made 21 cm wide by 4 ($8\frac{1}{4}$ × $1\frac{1}{2}$ in.) at its greatest height, allowing sufficient space to run three parallel routes from left to right.[18] Moreover, the upper shoreline of the Mediterranean could have been raised without strain to give Sardinia similar depth to that of Sicily; we may compare how below Sicily the lower Mediterranean shoreline is depressed to admit the island of Djerba (unnamed).[19]

As it is, the mapmaker drastically shrinks Sardinia and foregoes the opportunity to show its extensive route network, which happens to be well attested from the Antonine Itinerary and from the survival of over 150 milestones.[20] It is true that presentation of Sardinia's network might be thought to pose more difficulty than those of Sicily, Crete, or Cyprus, insofar as it runs mainly north–south whereas theirs all run west–east; but Sardinia as it appears on the map is already "turned" with its east coast uppermost. Possibly the mapmaker was restrained by the corresponding need to consider how Corsica should be presented in relation to Sardinia. Even so, he possessed ample ingenuity to devise a placement for Corsica other than its present one between Sardinia and the upper shoreline of the Mediterranean. If he plotted the physical landscape base from left to right,[21] it is conceivable that when encountering Sardinia – the first of the Mediterranean's large islands – he was strangely cautious about what space to allow for it. He restricts himself to marking seven isolated place-names on the island, one of them (Tvrribvs) with a symbol. The only other islands on which he marks isolated place-names are Corsica (one name) and Djerba (four). The islands of Rhodes (9B1) and of Taprobane (11C4), too, are each shown sufficiently large to accommodate one or more names, but none is marked on either.[22]

The mapmaker must have foreseen that he would need to manipulate the principal landmasses to a greater or lesser degree in order to accommodate them within such a squat map frame. An associated challenge was to provide an equal spread of territory to the left and to the right of Rome as the map's central point, when India is so much more distant than the Atlantic (see Fig. 3). At the same time the mapmaker needed to ensure that, so far as possible, each region was rendered neither too small to fit all the requisite names, features, and routes within it satisfactorily, nor too large for this purpose. It is impossible to say just how full or sound a grasp he already possessed of routes, in particular at the first stage when he laid out the physical landscape base. On balance, it seems rather more likely that he only gained a comprehensive awareness as he proceeded – especially if his attempt to show routes was a novel initiative —[23] and that by an advanced stage he could do little to adjust for mismatching coverage.

Not only was Italy the Roman heartland, but there would also be an especially dense network of routes to mark there, fanning out in all directions from Rome itself. As it happened, to give Italy pride of place – occupying about one-third of the map, in its very center [Figs. 2 and 3] – was advantageous both for the mapmaker's layout and for the intended impact of his work upon viewers.[24] The Italian peninsula, defined by the Adriatic and Mediterranean seas, was in any case a landmass uniquely well suited to elongated presentation on a map of this extreme shape. More generally, Italy was a vital asset in the struggle to match the less extensive territory that could be shown to the left of Rome with the greater extent to its right. Hence Italy is laid out to spread over two meters ($6\frac{1}{2}$ feet) and more, from the righthand end of Segment 2 almost as far as halfway into Segment 6. Toward its end, the peninsula is split into two prongs together narrower than its main body. As a result, the mapmaker could take the opportunity to fit an elongated island of Sicily here between the lower coastline of the lower prong and the North African coastline.[25]

Britain, largely lost in the surviving copy, would need to have been turned on its side to fit the map's shape, with its east coast evidently to the top like that of Sardinia, and thus the north (lost) to the left. Gaul is similarly manipulated, with its north coast turned left to face southern Britain, and then, after a long narrow inlet for the Sinvs Aqvitanicvs (1B1–1B2), its west coast facing southwest Britain above. The quantity of routes and other cultural data across Gaul is dense overall, but seems mostly well enough matched to the space assigned for the region.

With considerable ingenuity the mapmaker compressed the regions facing the empire's Rhine and Danube frontiers to occupy the top of the

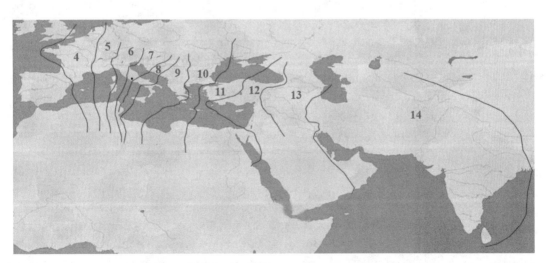

FIGURE 3. The map's coverage from the Atlantic to India set against a modern map outline, assuming the loss of three parchment segments, or equivalent, at the left. Map by Christos Nüssli.

map until the mouths of the Danube are reached near the righthand end of Segment 7. This vast area gains improved definition from the righthand end of Segment 3 onward with the appearance of the Adriatic Sea, which continues far into Segment 6, where the Italian peninsula ends. Routes in Dalmatia run immediately above the upper Adriatic shoreline.

Once the Adriatic merges with the Mediterranean (on Segment 6), the mapmaker again had a deeper unbroken landmass at his disposal. He exploited it to introduce a gentle downward curve of the Danube (no. 15A) so that the river now flows less close to the map's upper coastline. Into the space opened up by this means above the river, he then fitted Dacia and the routes there. Below the river, however, the coverage he wished to provide of Moesia and Macedonia is notably squeezed and elongated, so that Piraeus (Pyreo) lines up with Tessalonic(a)e and Philippis, and the island of Cytera appears just offshore below Tessalonic(a)e.[26] The part of this region that the mapmaker subjected to the most drastic shrinkage is central Greece, where the center of the world at Delphi in the traditional Greek view[27] is even omitted altogether. Perhaps this sacrifice was made readily enough in a map so dominated by Rome. It was in any case quite impossible to do justice to central Greece, given the map's shape and other constraints. At least there could hardly have been special difficulty in securing adequate information about routes there. Nearby, the routes laid out within the Peloponnese come close to straining the limited space assigned to it.

Thrace is fitted below the Black Sea (which extends from midway across Segment 7) and continues over to the Bosporus (8A1); in consequence this region receives quite ample coverage. Because it requires no great depth, however, below Thrace the mapmaker took the opportunity to widen the Mediterranean again in order to provide generous space for Crete.[28] The Black Sea – its lower coastline broken by a wide Bosporus between Europe and Asia – continues to the middle of Segment 9 and, like the Adriatic earlier, acts as a valuable divider. No route continues along its upper coastline for a long way beyond Tomis (7A4), placed just to the left of the Danube mouths; a route only resumes toward the far end of this coastline once Trapezvnte (9A2) is reached.

The mapmaker's decision to present the Black Sea as a narrow "horizontal" channel had major repercussions. In effect it constrained him from tilting the landmass of Asia Minor in the way that he manipulated Britain, Gaul, Sardinia, and Italy. Instead, he duly set the north of Asia Minor along the lower Black Sea coastline. To do so seems only natural; no special difficulty is created by presenting Sicily, Crete, Cyprus, and, in particular, North Africa in this way too. In the case of the Black Sea to the right of the Bosporus, however, severe consequences arise for thus accommodating Asia Minor to the map's extreme shape.[29] The region of the Bosporus itself, as well as of the Propontis and Hellespont notionally, *is* tilted to face left. But Asia Minor's western[30] and southern coasts[31] are then rendered as one, to form the Mediterranean's upper coastline. The latter of these coasts is conspicuously compressed, being assigned only about half the former's length. It surely follows that this unsatisfying alignment of Asia Minor contributes to the patent limitations that the presentation of cultural data in its interior exhibits.

The far end of the Mediterranean coincides with the placement of Antiochia (9B4). Immediately prior, the open water channel is widened to allow the inclusion of Cyprus in the same way that space was created for Sicily and Crete. Alexandria (unnamed symbol no. 56 in 8C3) and the Nile Delta as far as Pelvsio (8C4) are intended to feature prominently like Antiochia, although the mapmaker takes the creative liberty of placing them, not at the end of the Mediterranean, but earlier. In consequence, the entire stretch of coast from the Nile Delta to Selevcia and Antiochia[32] is shifted to become the final section of the lower Mediterranean coastline on the map.

North Africa from its lost lefthand end onward as far as Alexandria forms a substantial self-contained part of the map, with its length in effect dictated by the layout of Europe above. The placements of both Chartagine colon (= Carthage, 4C5), directly below Rome, and of Alexandria are surely to be considered the pivotal choices, which in turn determine the layout of the route network. A corresponding "anchor city" for the network at the lefthand end of the map is lost. Even so, there can be no doubt that at several stages the width available for the mapmaker to mark successive stretches on some of his routes in North Africa far exceeds what the relevant names and distance figures require. In consequence, stretches of exaggerated length both before Chartagine on Segments 2 and 4, and after it on Segment 5, cannot be avoided.[33] At the same time the map's squatness makes it impossible to reflect the depth of territory traversed in various directions by the routes shown here. The impression given that these all proceed smoothly eastward across North Africa is inevitably misleading.

The same false impression is even more patent in Egypt, where the map's shape offers no means to reflect the depth of the region, nor the south–north course of the Nile and of the long route associated with it, let alone the southeast direction of the route from the river to Pernicide portvm (= Berenice, 8C5). The river and the route associated with it are both laid out from the left,[34] because the space here (unlike that to the right in 8C5 and beyond) is not needed for any other purpose. In addition, this placement permits those who "read" the map from left to right to engage with the river at the earliest opportunity, and to follow it from its source.

Beyond the Mediterranean, the mapmaker exhibits a less confident grasp of the landscape, and he is now seriously hampered both by earlier decisions and by the realization that there is insufficient space for everything he would like to include here. He may also be calculating that his audience will care least about the representation of this region, and thus will not object to its especially severe compression in the interests of balancing the coverage of territory to the left and right of the city of Rome at the center. After all, only by reducing yet further the coverage of lands east of the city (or even east of the Bosporus) within the Roman Empire can the design devote more space to lands beyond in that direction.

By now the mapmaker has allowed the landscape to lose its cohesion, and it is hard to see how it could be regained. At the top, the uppermost of three routes from Trapezvnte (9A2) proceeds a considerable distance across the map to Sebastoplis (10A2). This is a route that should follow the Black Sea coast;[35] instead, it is placed entirely to the right of it. Below this route, and again to the right of the Black Sea, are laid out routes in eastern Asia Minor extending as far as Samosata (10B3) on the Euphrates. Meantime, further below, routes proceed to the right from Damaspo (= Damascus, 9C3) and Antiochia (9B4) to Palmyra (9C5), Zevgma (10C3), and Samosata, a layout severely warped by the decision to run the eastern shore of the Mediterranean to the left of Antiochia; in consequence Damaspo is placed well to the left of Antiochia.

The fact that the different components of the larger region immediately beyond the Mediterranean do not coalesce is only the prelude to graver shortcomings.[36] Thereafter, beyond the Euphrates, Mesopotamia is hopelessly compressed and distorted, with its northern part − where Roman interests lay − forming the main focus of attention, and Babylonia (= Babylon, 10C4) and Selevcia (10C4) both being situated close to the shore of the Indian Ocean. Regions further east are represented in token fashion at best. Ecbatana[37] and Persepolis,[38] too, are situated along the shore of the Indian Ocean; Ecbatana serves as a key nodal point because routes farther east can only be reached through it. The Caspian Sea is shown,[39] but its situation is too remote to assist the mapmaker in presenting related cultural features in the way that he exploits the Adriatic and Black seas. The Indian subcontinent, reduced to a modest size indeed along with its river Indus (no. 136), is notionally tilted like other landmasses already noted, so that its western coast (the only one documented here in the regular way) runs along the bottom of Segment 11. Ironically, however, at the same time as the mapmaker foreshortens the landscape so much, his presentation of routes beyond the Euphrates suggests that he is struggling against a lack of sufficient space for some of them. To an unprecedented extent, he now resorts to sloping routes vertically rather than maintaining the regular horizontal layout. Perhaps he had not expected to have so much relevant data at his disposal here as turned out to be the case.

In considering both mountain ranges and rivers it can prove difficult, if not impossible, to distinguish between those which are fundamental components of the physical landscape base and those more likely to have been added later after the placement of other features. The distinction is in any event artificial, and of only limited significance. More important is an appreciation that certain mountain ranges and rivers act as defining landscape features along with coastlines. No route crosses the Apennines, for example, between Iria (3B1) and Adcalem (4B2). In addition to the Apennines, the fundamental mountain ranges are the Alps[40] and the Taurus,[41] and in all probability the Pyrenees too, although our copy of the map only preserves their eastern end.[42]

The fundamental rivers without doubt include the longest, such as the Rhine, Rhône, Danube, Po, Tiber, Nile, Euphrates, Tigris, and Ganges. There seems every likelihood that the mapmaker marked their courses on the map before any cultural features. How early some other rivers may have been marked, despite their prominence, is not so self-evident: among these are, for example, the Riger (1B2), Garvnna (1B1), [Savvs],[43] Orontes,[44] and the two unnamed rivers flowing into the Black Sea either side of Trapezvnte.[45] The case of the Patabvs (no. 3) – far from unique – serves to illustrate the quandary. It seems likely, but remains impossible to establish, that the mapmaker drew its course in relation to that of the Renvs (no. 2A), *before* he laid out the pair of routes from Lvgdvno (1A1) to Noviomagi (1A4) and the single continuation on to Colo Traiana and Veteribvs (1A5). In drawing the Patabvs, therefore, he may have been purposely demarcating space for these routes.

Altogether, it is possible to gauge from the surviving copy how the mapmaker addressed the multiple challenges of furnishing the vast coverage he desired – centered upon the city of Rome in particular and Italy in general – within an extraordinarily elongated frame. He concluded that certain sacrifices had to be made and shortcomings tolerated, most notably the removal of much open water, a lack of depth in North Africa, and increasing compression of the lands east of the Bosporus. Some coasts and settlements had to be situated absurdly close to one another,[46] therefore, while others appeared unnaturally far apart,[47] and the route network is affected accordingly. These are consequences of the map's shape that informed viewers need to understand and make allowances for.[48]

2. MAPMAKING PRACTICE

There seems good reason to imagine (as already mentioned) that the mapmaker, in order to establish the fundamentals of his creation, exploited earlier maps that sought to show and name the principal elements of physical and cultural (man-made) landscape with a fair degree of accuracy. As we turn next to consider different aspects of his mapmaking practice, it is as well to bear in mind that here, too, he must have been influenced by this exposure to earlier cartography, although the degree of its impact can no longer be measured because no closely relevant examples survive.

Fortunately, however, three other maps do survive, albeit incomplete, and as originals rather than copies.[49] So the mapmaking practices they reflect may prove instructive, even if in all three cases the scope and content happen not to match those of the Peutinger map. First, the so-called Orange cadaster in fact comprises three separate parts of the large-scale record engraved on stone for public display at ancient Arausio (modern Orange in the Rhône valley). This checkerboard plan made to document how the city's surveyed land was divided and held represents a standard type, in this instance made during the late first century A.D.[50] Second, the immense so-called Marble Plan of Rome (18 m [59 ft.] wide × 13 [42½ ft.] high) is another display piece, but probably a far more unusual one, produced around A.D. 200 and covering (when complete) almost the entire wall of a great hall at a generous scale that evidently was standard for urban surveys (1:240).[51] What the plan presents is a somewhat simplified, but still meticulous, record of literally every ground-floor feature throughout the city.[52] By contrast, third, the "Dura shield" map is a parchment fragment of the early/mid third-century A.D., part of a design that may have decorated a shield. It features the Black Sea and its surrounding coasts as a map would, marking settlements and rivers along with names and distance figures.[53]

(a) Orientation

The fundamental choice of a north orientation must be seen as a deliberate one on the part of the mapmaker, and by no means to be taken for granted. In principle, a south orientation might have suited his purpose equally well, and either south or north could readily appeal to viewers whose worldview was dominated by the Mediterranean as an elongated central feature.[54] A typical boast on the part of the city of Rome's wealthiest residents, says the fourth-century historian Ammianus Marcellinus in a mocking passage,[55] was to claim that they owned vast estates from farthest east to farthest west. North happens to match Ptolemy's recommendation,[56] but the fact is that Greek and Roman cartography never reached consensus on the issue.[57] Thus the three Orange cadasters vary in their orientation,[58] the Marble Plan of Rome is oriented south-southeast,[59] and the "Dura shield" south.[60] The numbering of the Roman Republic's thirty-one "rural" tribes evidently followed the order in which routes fanned out from Rome, starting from the Via Ostiensis to the southwest and then proceeding anticlockwise.[61]

The Peutinger map's north orientation can never make more than a general impression, because the extreme shape so severely restricts the north–south dimension. Reliable correspondence to the compass points, therefore, must often be abandoned. The three routes already mentioned proceeding to the right – or seemingly "eastward" – from Trapezvnte (9A2) offer a telling illustration. The topmost of the three does in fact go east on the ground (albeit along the Black Sea coast rather than beyond it); but the next route goes directly south, and the lowest directly west. More broadly, the same lack of correspondence can be found in much of Africa as the map has to present it. Another consequence of the severe reduction of any vertical dimension is that a region designated "Inferior" is liable to be shifted to the right of its "Svperior" counterpart rather than appearing "above" it (that is, on the ground, farther from Rome).[62]

(b) Scale

By its very nature, no map can lack a sense of scale, and the maker of ours clearly had this sense. However, as he also realized, any expectation of a uniform scale – a preoccupation of scientific cartography – was out of the question in this instance because of the map's extreme shape and selectivity. The concern here, rather, had to be the more challenging one of allotting each region the coverage it merited for fulfillment of the map's overall aims, without any jarring transitions from one region to the next. Hence Italy in particular is presented as disproportionately large, while eastern regions beyond Roman territory at the far right of the map are severely shrunken. One can only admire the quiet deftness with which the various shifts in "scale" were accomplished. If the mapmaker dared to reckon that the great majority of his viewers would hardly be disturbed or confused by the choices he made for showing the different regions, in all likelihood he was right.

(c) Color

If our copy[63] reproduces the mapmaker's choices, then his palette was evidently limited, but effective. The surface on which the map is drawn – vellum in the case of our copy – remains uncolored as a plain background, and the mapmaker hardly introduced more than four colors: black, green, red, and brown. Black demarcates coastlines (including lakes)[64] and mountain range symbols; it is also used to write most names and (with red and brown) for creating symbols. Green fills all space demarcated by coastlines to signify open water (including lakes); rivers, too, are green line work. Red is used for all margin lines and route line work, for some names (rivers especially), and – with black and brown – for creating symbols.[65] The intermittent appearance of a red line along certain river courses on Segments 1 to 4 is a puzzling oddity.[66] The claim has been made that the extra line may signify, for example, the navigability of these stretches of river, but it is added too randomly for such an interpretation to be persuasive. In my view it is no more than a copyist's impulsive attempt at embellishment that came to be abandoned.[67]

Brown is used in symbols[68] and as a fill for some mountain ranges. Since brown nowhere seems to be integral to the map's presentation but is only decorative, it may conceivably have been introduced as a copyist's embellishment. There is similar uncertainty concerning blue, which only fills the center of some large bath/spa symbols and decorates the special symbols – undoubtedly embellished by copyists – for ROMA and Constantinopolis. It might seem unlikely that the mapmaker would include blue in his palette only to employ it so little. Alternatively, such sparing use could have been deliberate. The bath/spa symbols, already large, would thereby become still more eye-catching, to the delight of patrons and other viewers with a fondness for such resorts.

Quite apart from the issue of whether brown or blue featured in the original design, there is cause to question whether it incorporated *any* color. The fact is that, strictly speaking, none is needed for comprehension of the map's physical and cultural components, because the styles for presenting line work, names, and symbols are already clearly distinguishable by other means without color. This said, given the powerful enhancement the use of color furnishes, it does seem needlessly extreme to envisage that the opportunity to incorporate it was rejected. Nonetheless, it remains conceivable that the styles employed here had been developed in the first instance for maps that were not to be colored.

(d) Line Work

The different types of line work are readily distinguishable by weight, color, and style. All open-water coastlines are thin, black, and quite deeply serrated; minor variations occur in the character and depth of this serration, but these seem to have no significance. Lake shorelines, too, are thin and black, and most are serrated, although less deeply. In the case of some small lakes, as of some small islands in open water, no attempt is made to serrate and the shoreline is left smooth.[69] Line work for mountain ranges is thin, black shading into brown, straight along the bottom, and more or less sharply serrated above; again, the minor variations readily detectible in this serration seem to be without significance.[70] Mountain ranges are rendered more conspicuous when filled with a color rather than left hollow; but whether they are filled, and if so with which color, seem to have been merely matters of embellishment.[71] In the course of a long range, changes of color may occur.[72] River line work is always green, usually thick, and curved or wavy. It can run freely in any direction, as the flow direction arrows overlaid on Map A show.

Margin lines are thin, red, and straight, and by definition they occur only at the top and bottom of the map frame (and no doubt at either end, too, in the original). In any case, they are readily distinguishable from route line work, which is similarly thin and red but interspersed at frequent intervals by sharp downward turns or "chicanes."[73] Route line work is also kept so far as practicable either horizontal or no more than slightly sloping. It must not overrun rivers or shoreline; hence copyists have been liable to omit it when this prospect arises.[74] Without doubt the mapmaker's concern was not just to differentiate river and route line work clearly, but also to help viewers to comprehend the route network's complexity. He was well aware that, were he to permit routes to range across the map in every direction with the same freedom that he granted to rivers, then the clarity he sought to achieve could no longer be maintained. Even so, potential confusion was liable to ensue where it would otherwise be appropriate to run a river and a route in parallel. The disruptive separation of the Rhône (no. 9A) from several of the communities along it between Lugdunum and the river mouth starkly illustrates the difficulty.[75] In some other instances, by contrast, no special difficulty for the map's layout arises in keeping a river and parallel route side-by-side, as along the Rhine (no. 2A) in Segments 1 and 2.

The left-facing, "north" coast of Gaul offers an apt illustration of the mapmaker's aversion to laying out routes "vertically" for any great distance. Routes originate from this coast, but none runs along it; the same applies to the west coast of Asia Minor, as well as to the coast of India at the map's righthand end. Rather, so far as possible, the mapmaker wants to present routes running "horizontally." The inclusion of long gulfs that cut more or less horizontally into landmasses reinforces this perspective: the Sinvs Aqvitanicvs (1B1–1B2) cutting into Gaul, for example, three gulfs into Greece (Segment 6), and others into Asia Minor (8B2), Egypt (8C4), and Persia (11C1). It might be argued that in any case constraints of space precluded the inclusion of a "tall", "western" coast for Sicily, for instance, or the Peloponnese, or Cyprus. The same is not true, however, of the west coast of Asia Minor, nor of the east coast of the Mediterranean; any "vertical" dimension for the latter coast is purposely eliminated. There is indeed a vertical route to be seen in the surviving part of Britain, but it is no more than two short end-branches off what must originally have been a longer horizontal route. West of the Euphrates, the one exceptional instance where the mapmaker brings a route down a coastline at a pronounced slope is along the Adriatic in Epirus (6B3).

Inland, likewise, in the surviving part of the map, routes that proceed at a pronounced slope for a considerable distance are rare. What may at first glance seem to be a striking case occurs from Baca conervio (1A4) to Dvrocortoro to Andemantvnno to Cabillione to Lvgdvno (1B5), if a downward continuation is followed at each of the three intermediate junctions named. It is more appropriate, however, for the sections of route linking each pair of junctions here to be regarded as no more than connectors between longer routes that proceed more or less horizontally; short connectors of this type occur often. It is true that no such alternative viewpoint is valid for several routes beyond the Euphrates on Segments 10 and 11, which do very visibly slope. But here – in this respect, as in others – the mapmaker is self-evidently relaxing some of the constraints he has adhered to thus far in the surviving part of the map.

No line work style is required for any boundary or frontier, even a fortified one, because the mapmaker opted to omit such features altogether. Needless to add, plenty of indicators confirm his awareness of boundaries between communities and provinces.[76] Their exclusion was a conscious choice.[77] Their placement would certainly have been complicated by the map's extreme shape, and it might well have sometimes proven awkward to distinguish them from the routes, which without doubt matter more for the mapmaker's purposes in this instance.

(e) Lettering and Its Placement

All lettering, and by extension numerals, on our copy are in the Latin alphabet. It is natural to infer that a transliteration of some names was made directly from the Greek,[78] but there is no knowing when exactly that shift occurred or under what circumstances. It could certainly have happened even before the making of the original map. No less indeterminable is the extent to which our copy reproduces the lettering styles used for the original, although it might seem optimistic to expect a close resemblance.[79] There is perhaps a stronger likelihood, however, that copyists have maintained much of the original's sizing and placement of lettering. Even so, it still may prove awkward to determine where word breaks were meant to occur, in particular when a name begins with prepositions such as "ad" or "in." The difficulty could conceivably date back to the original map; in any event it, too, seems not to have been of special concern to our copyist.

The lettering for all names placed in open water, and also for most names elsewhere, is black. However, river names – equally distinguishable because they begin "Fl." – appear in red when placed on land.[80] For regions and peoples, the lettering may vary considerably in size, and such names may be in either black or red. The choice of color for them seldom seems to be more than a matter of achieving some variety.[81] Occasionally, however, it must reflect an effort to avert confusion between adjacent or overlapping names.[82]

For certain, neither lettering style nor color is deployed to distinguish the names of a people or region from those of a settlement. This distinction stems, rather, from association with route line work or a symbol (or both). A name without this association is most likely to be a people or region. Yet these two types of name, in turn, are not distinguished from one another. Even more unfortunately, they cannot be securely distinguished from any settlement that is marked only with a name (no symbol) and placed in isolation from the route network. A more scientific style of cartography could remedy this shortcoming once and for all by always associating any such settlement name with a point symbol. But it is striking that the mapmaker studiously denied himself this simple expedient of using point symbols. At least, whatever his reason for completely dispensing with them, the impact of their absence is in practice mitigated by his lack of concern to mark settlements isolated from the route network.[83]

To aid viewers' comprehension no doubt, names are marked horizontally so far as possible.[84] Where a route has to slope slightly, names are placed to match; but in the few instances where a route takes a steep plunge, the relevant names are not turned correspondingly.[85] Lettering should not overrun any symbol or line work,[86] unless this proves unavoidable;[87] a name may straddle such an obstacle, but had to be divided for the purpose.[88] Equally, the lettering for a name and for its associated distance figure had to appear on the same level, with the route line work for the stretch below; it was considered undesirable for the route line work to run above the distance figure (or worse, the name).[89] Moreover, the name of any land feature[90] or river should not extend into open water.[91]

Ideally, a river is named at its source, or as close thereto as practicable. However, several rivers that the map presents flowing right to left – hence the viewer proceeding from the left encounters the mouth first – are named at the mouth[92] and even again at the source.[93]

Where the area encompassed by a people or region or sea calls for naming in display capitals spread out, each letter is placed individually with an eye to ensuring that the intervals between all the letters of the name do not vary unduly. If it at all possible, these letters are also not to overrun any line work or other name.[94] Therefore, peoples, regions, and seas were presumably among the last features to be marked on the original map. In no instance is a loop or line drawn to demarcate their extent. Instead, the spread of the name itself fulfills that function.[95] For the name of a people, region, or sea to be placed vertically, rather than horizontally or at a gentle slope, is most unusual: TROGODITI PERSI (10B5) supplies an instance.

The name associated with a symbol is placed immediately above it wherever possible. This practice is maintained even along routes where there is a shore immediately above, so that viewers of the map may be left uncertain whether a settlement really is coastal or situated inland. Successive instances occur along the upper coast of Italy on Segment 4, for example: Arimino, Fano Fvrtvn(a)e, and Ancone for certain, perhaps even Ravenna. To be sure, along the African coast on the same segment (where there are fewer names and features to be accommodated) there is less scope for doubt. More generally, it is important to recognize that nowhere did the mapmaker demonstrate special concern to clarify which settlements were coastal; his engagement was primarily with the land, after all, rather than the sea.

(f) Numerals

Most distance figures are recorded as numerals rather than in words, using certain letters (alone or in combination) for the purpose in accordance with typical Roman practice. The few oddities to be found seem best regarded as uncorrected slips on the part of one or more copyists. Such are XIIIII for the Adnovas stretch (4B5), and a puzzling inverted V on the Lacenivm stretch (6B2).

Twenty-eight is written XXIIX once (Apamia, 9C5).[96] The number four is always written IIII, although XL is used for forty; 450 appears as CCCCL (Thimara, 11C5). Much greater variation occurs in the case of the number nine. The strong preference is for VIIII, although instances of IX are far from rare. Limited space is plainly the usual reason for the latter choice, as on the Cibistra stretch (9B2).[97] However, that choice is by no means automatically exercised. In the upper Vbaza Castellv stretch

(3C4), for example, the distance figure is LVIIII rather than LIX, despite the difficulty of accommodating the former to the little space available. Likewise for Sestias (4B3), it might have seemed preferable to choose XIV, but still the figure remains XIIII written in two tiers. Only two stretches later, by contrast, the logical choice of IX is made for Nvmana (4B3).[98] For two successive stretches of nine miles – Tvrris cesaris, Dertvm (5B5) – IX is the choice both times, even though there is ample space available for VIIII;[99] the same applies to the choice of XXIX for the two successive stretches Soloae and Tamiso (9B3).

Some higher, longer numerals are divided by a stop – such as XXX.III for Scarabantio (4A2) – but this format evidently signifies nothing more than a copyist's whim. There are comparable instances where such numerals are divided simply by a space (without a stop): for example, XX IIII for Pisandcs (5B5), and XX VII for Pompeiopolis (8A5), where division of the numeral in this way helps to fill the ample space available along the stretch.[100]

To record a distance of one mile, the map does not employ the numeral I. Instead, it resorts to the Roman circular or sideways figure-of-eight symbol for one thousand (the number of paces that one Roman mile represented), written as the letters "co": see, for example, the stretch for Cosa (3B4).[101] Although this was a standard Roman symbol, its use on the map has needlessly confused commentators.[102]

3. COMPONENTS OF THE MAP

(a) Coastlines

Without question, the coastlines as drawn do adequately define and separate the principal landmasses. Much minor variation occurs in this line work, but in all probability it has no significance beyond a wish on the part of mapmaker or copyist to offer a little embellishment, like the somewhat larger bays along the African coast in 2C4–2C5, for example, or the peninsula jutting out from India in 11A5. There are also plenty of instances, by contrast, where it is clear that departures from an otherwise generalized coastline are consciously made to fulfill a purpose, in particular to reflect the distinctive physical location of a settlement that the mapmaker wishes to mark, often with a symbol,[103] or to define and name a bay, gulf, or other notable stretch of open water.

In this latter connection, the mapmaker appears to have given the term *portvs* a wider and more puzzling connotation than its typical sense of haven or harbor in Latin usage.[104] There can be little doubt, for example, that Port(vs) Calovitanvs (5A3) names an entire gulf, and the same applies to P[– ? –] [– ? –] (6B2).[105] By contrast, Port(vs) Planaticvs (4B1) remains ambiguous: is it naming only the small bay where the initial **P** is placed, or the entire gulf at the head of which the name stands? The significance of Port(vs) Senia (4B2) is equally obscure when the city of Senia is marked and named just above it; Port(vs) Tvrris (5A5) creates similar uncertainty.

A different puzzle is created by instances where the mapmaker introduces a quite unmistakable departure from generalized coastline, but for no discernible purpose of the types just mentioned. Are these departures merely more pronounced embellishment? Or do they reflect, for instance, the more detailed presentation of coastline on some earlier map used selectively by the mapmaker? To be considered in this connection, for example, are the jagged coasts of England and Gaul that face one another in 1A1, together with the similar coast at the far end of Sardinia in 3C1; the bay created between vmbro Fl. and Hasta in 3B3; the bay likewise created on Crete below mountain range no. 84 in 7B5; and the narrow extended peninsula in 11A5–11B5.

(b) Rivers

Rivers – whether related to the route network or not – form an important component of the map, although the presentation of them (as of so much else on the map) seems a mix of the painstaking and the cavalier. Over 130 rivers are to be found, many with tributaries and branches in addition.[106] The Po (Padvs, no. 10) is by far the most complex river system. Its presentation with a total of thirty-five associated tributaries and branches serves as a further reflection of the prominence accorded to Italy. Pliny the Elder[107] associates as many as sixty tributaries with the Danube (no. 15A); but on the map, by contrast with the Po, it has a mere nine. River courses vary from immensely long – the Danube extends across almost five segments (3A1–7A5) – to extremely short.[108] There is little variation in the thickness of river line work. A few rivers rendered thinner than the norm can be observed,[109] but this treatment would appear to reflect no more than a copyist's lapse of concentration. Evidently the mapmaker was not intent upon varying line-work widths to differentiate rivers by size or significance; rather, such contrasts emerge only from the length of a river and the number of its tributaries or branches. Even then, serious misrepresentation or confusion is often evident, whether caused by lack of understanding, or the map's compressed shape, or both. Major tributaries of the Danube, for example, are drastically shrunk,[110] while the Savus (no. 27A) and Dravus (no. 27B) – neither of them named – eventually join and flow into the Adriatic rather than becoming separate Danube tributaries as they should. The Brintesia (no. 10jj), if correctly identified as the Brinta,[111] is made a branch of the Po rather than a tributary of the Medvacvs in a different river system. The Medvacvs, in turn (no. 10FF), appears as a tributary of the Po, as does the Afesia (no. 10CC), although in reality neither is one.

There is no knowing to what extent the mapmaker has added rivers that were missing from the maps he consulted; the same uncertainty attaches to some of the mountain ranges that serve as these rivers' sources. Even so, it seems natural to imagine that he may sometimes have taken such initiatives in the case of short rivers crossed by route stretches sharing the same name.[112] That said, there is also no lack of route stretches bearing a river's name where he might have added the corresponding river but did not.[113] Naturally, if the river concerned was known to be of some length and importance, he might hesitate to add it unless informed about its course. At least in some instances – the Inn (Latin Aenus) and Arno, for example, two major omissions – such information must have been readily enough accessible. Occasionally, there seems reason to wonder what purpose a succession of unnamed rivers serves beyond providing general confirmation that rivers were part of a region's landscape, as with the four tributaries of the Danube in Dacia (nos. 15G, 15H, 15I, 15J). Elsewhere, our difficulties in identifying certain unnamed rivers could suggest that, although they were taken over from one or more earlier maps, the reshaping of the surrounding landmass has served to obscure their place within it; consider, for example, rivers nos. 102, 103, 104, and 113 in Asia Minor.

It is a surprise that so many rivers lack a name on the map as it survives. These include even the Tiber (no. 26A) and its tributary the Anio (no. 26D), and elsewhere in Italy the Volturnus (no. 58). Further afield, rivers as major as the Dravus (no. 27B), Orontes (no. 119), and Euphrates (no. 126A) all go unnamed too; indeed, the Euphrates is not fully distinguished from the Fl. Tygris (no. 127). In addition, the names of the Rhône (no. 9A) and Danube (no. 15A) can only be inferred from the notices OSTIA FL. RODANI (1B5) and Hostia Fl. Danvbii (7A5) at the mouth of each river respectively. In the case of several lesser unnamed rivers, it is understandable that pressure of space caused a name to be dropped (assuming that it was marked on the original map);[114] but in many other instances the ample space available renders the repeated absence of river names a puzzle.[115]

In some instances there is cause to ponder whether viewers of the map are expected to infer that an unnamed river shares the "river" name of a route stretch that is either adjacent to the river or actually crosses it.[116] In this way, it might be inferred that unnamed river no. 41 is in fact Fl. Marta, no. 57 is Fl. Safe, no. 60 is Fl. Silarvm. However, while these (and other)[117] inferences do seem to be valid, it would evidently be misguided to assume that all such linkages are trustworthy. For example, unnamed river no. 58 is not the Calor, even though the route stretch Calor Fl. (5B5) is conspicuously close to its source; comparable mistaken inferences can be identified elsewhere too.[118]

The design permits rivers to range freely over the map in any direction; as a result, the direction of a river's flow may not be immediately apparent. Careful attention has been given both to marking the source (usually in a mountain range), and to ensuring that each river course, including tributaries and branches, is geographically credible. In consequence, it is rare for a river to be shown traversing a mountain range[119] or lacking a source[120] or an outlet,[121] or for the direction of flow to be ambiguous.[122]

(c) Open Water (including Lakes)

Although the proportion of open-water names more or less beyond recovery is distressingly high, I detect a total of over seventy marked across the map, including even one in the band of ocean that forms its topmost feature.[123] Of this total, around fifteen name lakes; in the case of seven other lakes, there is no visible trace of a name. It would seem that the earlier maps upon which the mapmaker drew offered an abundance of open-water names; he could only select some to mark, because it was open water that his own design so largely removed. If our copy does preserve his choices at all faithfully, then some large expanses are left without a name where one might have been expected – the Tyrrhenian Sea, for example, and the Indian Ocean. Elsewhere, however, he did not restrain himself from crowding compressed spaces with open-water names, especially (for whatever reason) the European side of the Black Sea from 7A3. In another area where space is limited, his determination to mark "Creticvm Pelagvs" as well as LYBICVM P[.]LAGVS below it (both 7B5) stands out. Similarly important to him were HADRIATICVM PELAGVS (6B2–7B5) and IGEVM MARE (6C1), although the placement of each is a puzzle. The former name only begins where the sea named by it should end, and it is then deftly extended as far as Crete; the latter is misplaced between the lower coastline of Sicily and the coast of Africa. Disorientation caused by the map's compression of the Mediterranean hardly seems a sufficient explanation in these instances. Equally, it seems unlikely that a mapmaker so concerned to name open water would exhibit such gross ignorance of geography here.[124]

Lakes would appear to be a landscape feature of minimal concern to the mapmaker; or, at best, he concluded that his compressed layout had to eliminate several of note. In Italy in particular, Lakes Trasumenus (*BAtlas* 42 C2), Volsiniensis (42 B3), Sabatinus (42 C4), and Fucinus (44 E2) are all omitted. Elsewhere, the two lakes in the Lychnidos area (49 C2–49 D3) are reduced to one (6B4); so also, the three immediately south of the Propontis (52 B4, D4, E4) are reduced to one (8B2). No lake is drawn with a notably distinctive shape.

(d) Islands

Islands always formed a vital component of Greek and Roman worldview.[125] In all probability, those shown on the Peutinger map were taken over, like the rivers, from earlier maps. There can be no question that the mapmaker considered them important, even though few are related to the route network.[126] In fact our copy marks well over one hundred islands, including some rendered very tiny, like Ins. Dyme (no. 55, 6B2), and a few clusters.[127] Islands appear across the entire map, four even situated off the coast of India at the map's extreme righthand edge (nos. 108–11). Fading of certain parts of our copy (especially the Aegean region on Segment 8), together with the poor definition of black lettering against the green open-water background, create major obstacles to the recovery of many island names. Even so, there seems little doubt that most islands were named, and that – surprisingly – far fewer of their names came to be omitted by successive copyists than were river names. Among the islands that are more than specks, Djerba is exceptional for being unnamed (no. 42), especially as there is ample space in which to fit its name.

To judge by our copy at least, the mapmaker felt no concern to give small islands any distinctive shape; they are rendered simply as a square or circle. In consequence, the rather more precise rendering of islands in the Gulf of Salona region stands out,[128] so much so that some initiative on the part of a copyist could even be suspected. The mapmaker can also seem lax in his placement of islands – disoriented perhaps by his draining of the Mediterranean and remolding of landmasses. Sason island[129] and Cephalania[130] are marked twice.[131] The islands of the Aegean appear especially jumbled. In 2B4–2C4 are to be found two islands that in fact lie off the west coast of Italy[132] placed on either side of an island whose real geographical position is far distant, off the coast of North Africa.[133] The difficulty of placing islands in the Mediterranean satisfactorily is only increased by the mapmaker's apparent wish to include all those of any consequence in the region, despite the removal of so much open water. Malta and Gozo remain notable omissions,[134] however, as does Euboea. Conceivably, the latter was let slip when the eastern seaboard of mainland Greece (in 6B5) was separated from the Aegean islands (in 8B1).[135]

(e) Mountains

The geographical and cultural importance of mountains must have been very evident on earlier maps, and the mapmaker seeks to convey it in turn, albeit in rather limited fashion. The map presents about 140 mountain ranges in total, uniformly rendered as bands of stunted height, but varying tremendously in length, and (like rivers) ranging in any direction as required. However, the open-jaw shape of the ranges (no. 138A–B) named MONS LYMODVS (11B4) is far from typical. Individual mountains or peaks are not singled out by the mapmaker; rather, except for the additions MONS OLIVETI (9C1) and MONS SYNA (8C4) made by Christian copyists, any named "Mons" in the singular is in fact a range. It is true that several road stations do seem to take their names from specific mountains, but none of them is marked.[136] Nor is any attempt made to distinguish a mountainous region, let alone differences in elevation. It has been imagined that the color, or lack of it, in which mountain ranges are variously rendered signifies differences in geology, say, or minerals.[137] More probably, however, such contrasts in color are mere embellishment either already present on the original map or introduced later by copyists.

The lack of names for mountain ranges is yet more striking than it is for rivers. Even the Alps (no. 14),[138] Apennines (no. 15), and Caucasus (nos. 88, 89)[139] go unnamed, while a notable proportion of the names that are marked appear in regions beyond Roman territory on Segments 10 and 11. Whether this lack of concern to name mountain ranges extends back to the original map – or even further to maps on which it was based – can only be a matter for speculation. Ptolemy's *Geography*, at least, betrays no lack of interest in offering names and coordinates for mountains. Just possibly the absence of names for them on the Peutinger map stems from conscious self-restraint determined by the mapmaker himself at the planning stage. His expectation may have been that the compression of landmasses that his design demanded would permit no more than a minimal representation of mountain ranges.[140] Only in the light of experience was this self-imposed limitation to seem too cautious, perhaps. That said, we might still expect the Alps and the Apennines to have been named, so the likelihood of omissions by copyists also needs to be taken into account.

(f) Peoples and Regions

There is no doubt that the mapmaker wished to mark the names of peoples and regions, and earlier maps – however they presented such names – presumably offered them in abundance. His handling of these, too, appears lax, although at the same time it surely reflects certain constraints imposed by the extreme shape of his frame. We may infer from his failure to differentiate the two types of name that he regarded them more or less as one. Hence he evidently did not regard the choice of the people name LVGDVNENSES (1A1–1B5) for one part of Gaul, in contrast to the regional ones [–?–] ITANIA (1B1–1B5) and BELGICA (1A1–2A2) for two others, as an inconsistency of more note than a variation of the case in which such names are marked.[141] He seems to have been unconcerned to complete "sets" in any case. In particular, the names of Italy's regions not only appear in very different sizes (see below), but they also lack at the least Aemilia, Latium, and Umbria. Likewise in Gaul, Narbonensis is missing, and among the names of provinces bordering the Danube, Dacia.

For viewers of the map, there is the likelihood of further confusion arising from its maker's evident lack of concern to differentiate between, on the one hand, the names of peoples or regions written in minuscules and, on the other, those of isolated settlements marked (again in minuscules) by name only and unrelated to the route network. Svani (9A2), for example, can with some confidence be reckoned the name of a people rather than of a settlement, especially when SVANISARMATAE (9A3) also came to be marked in capitals. Even so, in plenty of comparable instances, the viewer (and modern editor) can only guess whether a name is to be understood as that of a people, region, or settlement – insofar as such differentiation was meant to matter.[142] If the classifications in my database are followed (conjectural in many instances), then the total number of peoples named is approximately 140, and of regions approximately 90. Many people names are expanded variants on well-known peoples like the Sarmatae, just mentioned; others the mapmaker evidently relished expanding upon include the Getvli, Indi, and in particular the Scythae on Segment 11.

The lettering of each name for a people or region is sized and spaced, as already noted, to span the appropriate part of the map. Hence immense variations occur, from the tiny Osismi (1A2)[143] to GAETVLI (2C5–4C1) to PROVINCIA AFRICA (2C5–6C3), which spans three and a half segments. Such variations can prove considerable within a landmass too: CALABRIA (5B5–6B2), for example, is far less prominent than APVLIA (5B2–5B5), which immediately precedes it; the latter in turn dwarfs both LVCCANIA (5B5–6B1) and BRITTIVS (6B1–6B2).[144] Overlap – as of [– ? –]DIA (3C2–3C5) with PROVINCIA AFRICA – also occurs; so does occasional cramming within limited space.[145] It is the exception rather than the norm for the name of a people or region to be repeated when it has to cover a wide expanse.[146] A single occurrence is the mapmaker's preference – perhaps to eliminate the risk of confusing viewers, as well as boring them – even if the result has to be less than satisfactory. For all the skill with which EGYPTVS (8C3–8C5) is placed, therefore, the name still covers only the Nile Delta. ASIA (8B2–9B1) in its turn just cannot span the province satisfactorily, and PROVINCIA is not appended as a supplement in this instance. Elsewhere the regular abbreviated "Ins" is expanded to INSVLA on Crete and Cyprus in view of their size; PELAGVS is used in place of MARE for the same purpose. The need for mere repetition is overcome by varying the name of a people (such as Sarmatae or Scythae) with multiple different prefixes as mentioned above, or of a province (such as Pannonia or Syria) with qualifying adjectives like Superior/Inferior, Phoenix/Cole.

4. ROUTE NETWORK[147]

(a) Content and Planning

Scholars have consistently assumed that the route network was intended for use by travelers, administrators, even generals. However, in my opinion this assessment – so characteristic of the Western approach to cartography as science – is too generous. To be sure, the network is an ambitious, original creation, which reflects immense effort and some careful attention to detail. Even so, the notion of practical application on the ground as its primary function is to be rejected. The main purpose, rather, is to convey certain general impressions about Rome's power.[148] Interpretation of the network from this perspective can, in turn, provide the key to some otherwise puzzling characteristics.

The mapmaker envisioned that his design could provide a dynamic framework within which to demonstrate how Roman control and organization made possible an astonishing ease of movement overland everywhere across the *orbis terrarum*. For the purpose, he made the decision to exploit itinerary lists of a type familiar to Romans who had traveled long distances, especially if they had served as officials or soldiers.[149] This plan was sound in principle, but in all likelihood it proved a sterner challenge than anticipated to execute in practice. Contrary to expectation, a tidy, well-organized, comprehensive collection of routes and distances could be found for some regions only. Elsewhere the mapmaker faced the chores of first assembling the necessary material, then editing it for cartographic presentation, in particular by eliminating duplications, which must have been many.

However, the mapmaker lacked the data and motivation, not to mention the time perhaps, to do more than the minimum as editor. It was not his concern, for example, to determine the nominative of a place-name in the many instances where his source had only used an oblique case; in consequence, he evidently did not mind retaining a jumble of cases for names.[150] Whether his route data was all up-to-date seems another matter of indifference; some plainly was not current, and in other instances he may not have been able to judge.[151] He was equally unconcerned to distinguish between more important and less important routes, let alone to highlight a "most recommended" one – say, for traversing Asia Minor in order to reach Antioch in Syria. Hence the regular fourth-century "Pilgrim's Road" route there from Constantinople via Ancyra does not stand out.[152]

To achieve a degree of comprehensive coverage was essential for the mapmaker's purpose, because any extensive parts of the map where there were known to be routes could hardly be left with none shown. Even so, in many regions it would suffice if routes could be traced along the coastline and at least representatively through the landmass; there was certainly no need to ensure that all routes of importance were included.[153] In instances where a coastline could only be "covered" by resorting to a maritime itinerary, the mapmaker was quite willing to adopt this expedient, but without indicating that travelers would have to proceed by ship there.[154] More generally, the routes shown did not have to be the most direct. Indeed, if a direct route could hardly be padded out to fill the space available for it on the map, and a circuitous alternative with that capacity lay to hand, then the mapmaker would prefer the latter, as he did between Avgvsta vindelicv and Regino (3A1–3A4).[155] In the case of Lambese to Theveste (2C2–3C5) – for which two alternative routes are offered, running parallel and creating the visual impression of approximately equal length – attention to the distance figures is essential. Only once they are totaled for each route does the fact emerge that the lower of this pair is in fact very circuitous.[156]

Although the earlier maps at the mapmaker's disposal may well not have shown land routes,[157] the collation that he made of itineraries should have enabled him to identify with relative ease the necessary main junctions (normally settlements) for the network that he envisaged. These he then marked as accurately as the distortions of his own map could allow, so that they became the nodal points (marked by symbols) for its route network.

The reverse may also have occurred; an existing map may have led him to believe that a particular settlement was important even though he lacked an itinerary in which it was listed, and consequently he went in search of one. In any case, by some means or other he must have formed the conviction that certain settlements along a route (or at the end of one) merited a symbol, despite the fact that they do not serve as junctions on the map.[158] At least, whatever his criteria for considering a settlement worthy of a symbol, presentation of a more or less even spread of them to the viewer does not seem to have mattered to him.[159]

It was conceivably the mapmaker's own initiative to integrate baths and spas into the route network, marking some of them with especially prominent symbols.[160] How and why he made the choices that he did in this connection remain open questions. If nothing else, the information at his disposal – however it was obtained – is likely to have been patchy.[161] Baths may have held special appeal for him, or for a patron, or both; they also symbolized peace, leisure, and the recovery of health, as well as civilization and its command of technology.

Symbols aside, to the mapmaker the stopping points he could fit along a route were hardly more than just "filler," essential to his design, but without further intrinsic interest. In this respect they may be considered comparable to the components of flexible "stock" scenes on, say, the Column of Trajan, where fighting or marching or a siege fill whatever lengths the overall design requires. It is striking that on many routes the mapmaker nonetheless went to considerable trouble to accommodate more stopping points than he could fit comfortably there.[162] In such circumstances, merely to omit some might seem the most convenient expedient, but in practice perhaps it was not. The result was liable to appear slapdash, and the process of elimination called for invidious choices that were better avoided altogether. On other routes, by contrast, especially when high distance figures occur, the possibility remains open that the mapmaker did prove willing to risk omitting some stopping points.[163] Or it could simply be that no more were listed in the material at his disposal – welcome though they would have been to fill out the route – and a more detailed record never came to hand.[164]

To the mapmaker, distance figures were merely numbers. He recorded whatever figure was associated with a stopping point, without bothering about its accuracy, let alone the unit of measurement. He seems to have been equally indifferent to wide variations in the distance figures recorded along a route or adjacent routes. In this latter connection it may appear incongruous to us, but evidently not to him, that at the same time as he began to record huge figures (in an Indian unit?) on some routes from Segment 11B onward, by contrast the figures on six stretches from Paresaca (11B1) to Nicea Nialia (11C1) are all between a mere four and seven (Roman miles?).[165] Otherwise, as variable a sequence as 9–26–41–24–60–40, for example, would have scant practical value for the typical traveler, who could hardly expect to cover more than about twenty-five miles per day.[166]

The route network in certain regions proved extraordinarily difficult to present, but the mapmaker nonetheless persevered. The clearest examples are Italy in Segments 4 and 5, Asia Minor, and the lands to the east of the Roman Empire. Inevitably, on the surviving copy slips and shortcomings by successive copyists have only compounded any that already existed on the original map.[167] Even so, expedients attributable to the mapmaker himself can still be identified. Observe, for example, the resort to "vertical" routes, as from unnamed symbol no. 42 (5B4) and Venvsie (5B5). From Asia Minor onward, his collation of different itineraries and his ability to map the information from them satisfactorily both become less assured. Thus places appear twice; some of this duplication may be better explained differently, but the rest is most likely to be the mapmaker's. To the left of Asia Minor, duplication seems rare. Tivisco – shown once in 6A4 with a symbol, once without – is a striking example, the more puzzling insofar as it could easily have been eliminated.[168] Other instances mostly appear minor.[169]

From Asia Minor onward to the map's righthand end, however, serious confusion and duplication develop that can only be attributed to the mapmaker. Routes in the Amvrio (8B4) and Trallis (8B5) areas, for example, become badly muddled.[170] The distance figure of a mere xv for the stretch isaria to Animvrio (9B2) may be a copyist's slip, but the severe and misleading compression of this region must be the mapmaker's. It must be his error, too, to mark Pompeiopolis on one route without a symbol, and again on another route just below with a symbol, followed immediately by Soloe (the same city by another name in fact) without a symbol (all 9B3). Prvsias and Cio (both 8B2) are another such duplication of a single city – occupying successive stretches, the former with a symbol, the latter without. The same possibly applies to Piramvm and Mallo (both 9B4), the former marked above the latter, both without a symbol. Most egregious is the duplication of Amasia, which appears on two different routes, in both instances with a symbol (8A5, 9A1).[171] Five further such duplications – in three instances once with a symbol and the other time without – can be identified with more or less confidence across Segments 10 and 11.[172]

It is a surprise that the mapmaker's presentation of the route network declines so strikingly from Asia Minor onward, and an explanation is called for. If (as seems likely) he worked from the left, an improvement in quality as he proceeded might be expected, not a decline. Such a progression has been observed of Trajan's Column; its sculptors began at the bottom and made fewer mistakes as they carved upward, because their grasp of what was wanted grew with experience.[173] The production of the Peutinger map is clearly a different case. Here a variety of factors no doubt had a deleterious impact from Asia Minor onward. Most damaging perhaps was a struggle on the part of the mapmaker to integrate route information and distance figures in Roman sources with data in corresponding non-Roman material as he moved beyond the Roman Empire.[174] Quite apart from the unfamiliarity of Persia and India as landmasses, the severe compression of both that the layout required became a source of added difficulty. Further possible inducements to reduced rigor can be imagined too. By this stage the mapmaker may have found himself under pressure to meet an inflexible deadline for delivery of the map. Completeness and accuracy had never been his primary concerns. Moreover, he sensed that the lands east of the Roman Empire and the routes there would receive the least attention or scrutiny from viewers. He may also have anticipated that these lands would in any case lie outside most viewers' range of vision in the context for which the map was intended.[175] Altogether, therefore, at this end of the map he was prepared to lower his customary standard of work, shrewdly wagering that he would not be called to account for the lapses.

(b) Presentation

As argued above, the basis for laying out the route network is a set of principal settlements marked by symbols. These may well have been the next features to be marked on the original map, immediately following completion of its physical landscape base. As with the principal rivers and mountain ranges, it is impossible to identify confidently just which settlements the mapmaker marked thus before he developed the route network. The most likely are key nodal points such as Rome itself and Carthage immediately below it in Africa on Segment 4, and (to illustrate from Segment 6) Tarento, Regio, Messana, and Olympia. If the map's physical and cultural features are to relate at all satisfactorily, it is important that such settlements should be sited more or less in their correct locations; to place them thus would be in any event none too difficult once the physical landscape was adequately outlined. By the same token, initial placement of all the settlements along the African coast meriting a symbol was equally important, although in this instance it might have proven a greater challenge to site them at appropriate intervals. A major settlement that merited marking initially was not necessarily a junction on the route network. Neither Ipponte diarito nor Vtica Colonia, for example (both on Segment 4), was assigned that function, but both were major settlements nonetheless, and the place of each along the entire length of the African coast needed to be established. No doubt it was partly in relation to how major coastal settlements had been sited first that the mapmaker then proceeded to place certain major settlements inland. On this hypothesis, therefore, in Segment 1 the placement of inland Sitifi col. and Cvlchvl Colonia, for example, would have been influenced by the prior placement of coastal Rvsvccvrv colon and Saldas Colonia.

The instances just cited can be replicated across the map. As with rivers and mountains, the issue of whether a settlement was marked before the development of the route network or during it matters less than a recognition that there needed to be some settlements in the former category whose symbols could serve as "anchors." These were then linked by the names of settlements or road stations situated in between, each name accompanied by a figure for the distance to the next. Symbols aside, it is in fact the names with their associated figures that created the frame for the route network, not (as might appear at first glance) the red line work beneath the names and distance figures. The names and figures had to be positioned with care to allow for the insertion of chicanes,[176] but only after the names and figures were in position could the route line work be drawn.[177] This is not to deny that the route line work enhances the map and assists its viewers. In certain instances such assistance is vital. Without it, a short link like that between Clefantaria and Membrissa (4C3) would be overlooked (our copyist has indeed overlooked it), as might the long one between yconio (9B2) and Fines cilicie (9B3). In the absence of line work, it is no longer clear how the stretches for Haste (10C4) and Amostas (10B4) link to the network. The routes immediately beyond Aqvis Tatelis (2B4) could easily be misunderstood: the line work here clarifies that from Aqvis Tatelis it is only possible to reach Foro Fvlvi or Libarnvm through Dertona, and not directly in either case.

The potential for confusion in this latter instance is compounded by the surprising absence of a symbol for Dertona. The mapmaker's normal practice was to mark each place where travelers face a choice of onward routes with a symbol, although he refrained from doing this when two routes merely merge but do not intersect, especially in the case of short links between two routes.[178] An important consequence is that only those places marked by a symbol have their location established. Otherwise the mapmaker stopped short of marking any settlement or road station along a route with a specific location. He could hardly have been unaware of the cartographic convention of siting a place or feature with a simple dot or mark ("point symbol"),[179] but he resolutely refused to adopt it on this map, even where it could prove advantageous and avoid clumsiness – as, for example, at the start or finish of a route,[180] or for settlements marked in isolation from the route network,[181] or where pressure of space required a route to become more or less "vertical."[182]

The mapmaker's priority in this regard was presumably to maintain an unhindered sense of continuous movement to the right, as well as to keep the map free of distracting clutter. Such means also act to reduce the risk of viewers imagining the placement of intermediate settlements or road stations to be more accurate than it really is. The three considerations that determine these placements are in fact the amount of space available between two junction points, the number of intermediate settlements or road stations that the mapmaker opted to mark there, and the length of these names with their associated distance figures. The route stretch for a short name with a high distance figure, therefore, may well occupy visibly less space than that for a long one with a low distance figure: compare

Elvsa LXXI (9C1) with Tasinemeti VIIII (4A1), for example. In principle, the length of a route stretch (bounded by a chicane at either end) is just whatever length the name itself and the relevant distance figure happen to comprise. Ideally, therefore, after space has been made to insert the distance figure from the starting-point's symbol to the first intermediate settlement or road station, the remainder of the route should comprise a series of stretches neatly demarcated thus until the endpoint symbol is reached. Instances where this ideal is achieved can be found: Carnvnto to Brigantio with four intermediate settlements or road stations, for example (4A2–4A3).

However, because there is liable to be great variation in the lengths required for stretches, many routes inevitably depart from the ideal more or less. Either the mapmaker found that the names and distance figures at his disposal were fewer or shorter (or both) than the width available could accommodate; or they were too many and too long. The first case was easier for him to handle. He merely separated names and distance figures to make longer stretches than their letters strictly require. Even so, extreme instances occur where this expedient would not suffice. So here he resorted to spelling out the details of the stretch, perhaps with a second mention of the name, as in: "Si[lesv]a. A SILESVA AVIBVS MILIA XVIII" (5C2).[183] In the second case, where space is tight, the natural solution (as already noted above) was simply to omit one or more intermediate settlements or road stations altogether. By definition it is impossible to establish just how often the mapmaker deliberately resorted to this rash expedient, although any stretch with an unusually high distance figure (assuming the original numeral has been copied accurately) could give rise to suspicion.[184]

It is easier to identify contrasting instances where the mapmaker clearly might have made omissions on purpose but declined (or declined to be more drastically selective).[185] Instead, he often runs the end of one stretch over the start of the next. Or he slopes a route so that names and distance figures appear more beside it than along it (6B3, 11B2). Or he stacks names and distance figures above and below a route (2B1, 7C1). Such stacking is very much a last resort, however; it is so untidy, as well as potentially confusing for viewers. In those instances the route line work cannot run under every name, and the correct sequence of stretches may not be self-evident. Another drastic but clumsy expedient is to elongate a route and then swing it back, as from Amasia (8A5) to Sinope (9A1) for example, where the route continues below and beyond Sinope, and then makes a sharp reverse turn upward to enter it from the right.[186] In principle, one ingenious means of saving space on a route is to mark with a symbol a settlement otherwise not considered to merit one;[187] but again it is hard to establish whether the mapmaker allowed himself this expedient, or whether a copyist has introduced it.[188]

In principle, the mapmaker would seem to have been committed to stating the distance from every settlement or road station on the route network to the next onward place. For the inclusion of a place on the network, therefore, we might expect him to have had this distance figure at his disposal as well as the name (unless the place is a route's terminal point). It is understandable that oversight by successive copyists has led to the omission of many distance figures (stretches overlaid in orange on Map A). The possibility that some stretches lacked distance figures even on the original map should not be ruled out either. In an uncrowded area of North Africa, for example, where there is little to distract a copyist's attention, it does seem remarkable that all three of the final stretches of the remote route ending at Veri[189] should lack distance figures. One possible explanation is that even the mapmaker happened not to know them but chose to mark these stretches anyway, not least because they improved the coverage of a distinctly empty area.

The mapmaker was evidently not concerned to state the unit in which any distance figure was measured, except in those few instances cited above where his main purpose was to fill space by spelling out the details of an elongated stretch. These instances confirm the natural assumption that the Roman mile is the unit normally used.[190] Uniquely, the name Lvgdvno (1B5) is followed by an affirmation that it is "capvt Galliar(vm)" and that the unit of distance measurement used thus far is the (Gallic) league – "vsq(ve) hic legas."[191] Even so, this vague warning is hardly well placed to assist viewers who follow the route network from the left, nor does it inform them of how the two units relate to one another. It is perhaps best regarded as a copyist's addition.[192] To be sure, the map in its incomplete surviving state never specifies where on relevant routes the adoption of the Gallic league as the unit of distance measurement either begins or ends. Moreover, there is reason to think that even within Gaul the map's practice is inconsistent, recording some distances in leagues and others in Roman miles unpredictably.[193]

It has been claimed[194] that in regions to the east of the Roman Empire two more units for distances are used, the Persian parasang and an otherwise unknown Indian one; this latter prospect has more to recommend it than the former. A switch to some Indian unit might be inferred from the exceptionally high distance figures (ranging from 220 to 630) found on the seven stretches of the lower route from Tazora (11B3) through to an unnamed settlement symbol (no. 77, 11C5). However, if the original mapmaker did somehow signify use of a different unit here, all trace of such indication has disappeared. Otherwise, the fact is that both in this part of the map and elsewhere no sequence of distance figures is sufficiently out of the ordinary as to create the impression of a switch from Roman miles to another unit such as Gallic leagues or Persian parasangs. The point applies in particular to the upper route from Tazora itself and its continuations. It remains likely that the mapmaker needed to consult non-Roman sources for distance figures in Persian territory and beyond, but perhaps felt able to convert all of them to Roman miles except for one Indian unit.[195]

Use of the Greek stade is specified once, for a sea crossing, in a notice that may conceivably have been reproduced from an earlier map; even so, neither endpoint of the crossing is specified.[196] Otherwise, it seems, the mapmaker's intention was to dispense with all distances by sea.[197]

A well-prepared Roman itinerary would evidently include as a matter of course a figure for the total distance between its starting and finishing points. But such totals, too, are absent from the map as it survives. It is hard to see how they might be marked there neatly and meaningfully; a table of them to one side would not be so awkward to provide, however. Their absence from the map itself is perhaps no surprise for the further reason that its maker was plainly averse to promoting any one route above any other, or to highlighting his recommended route between two places when a choice was available. The line work of all routes is of equal weight, and at each junction the user is not prompted in any way to choose one onward route rather than another. Moreover, if totals were omitted altogether, the mapmaker thereby freed himself from the potentially tiresome obligation to ensure that the figures for successive stretches matched overall. Inaccuracy in this regard is not then immediately detectible, and there is no obstacle to the inclusion of stretches for which the distance happens to be lacking.

Another practical concern for travelers that the mapmaker treats with indifference is the need to proceed by ship at certain stages rather than by land. Such transfers are routinely indicated in the Antonine Itinerary, for example. As just noted, the mention of any distance by sea is the rarest of occurrences on the map, and only once is a stretch noted as requiring a ship, down a river as it happens: Hostilia to Ravenna "Per padvm" (3B4), with no distance figure. Elsewhere, however, the route in five stretches from Miletvm (9B1) to Patras (9B2) can in fact only be traversed by sea.[198] The same surely applies to the route in eleven stretches from Apsaro (9A5) – if not farther back to Trapezvnte (9A2) – all the way to Sebastoplis (10A2). In practice this route seems viable only by ship along the Black Sea coast; hence its appearance on the map separated from that coast is all the more unsatisfactory. A journey Gesogiaco – Gravinvm – Ivliobona (all in 1A2) as represented by the map would likewise seem to require a ship, but again the need is not indicated.[199]

A striking aspect of the map's design is a concern to demonstrate the availability of a route along almost all the 'edges' and coastlines that it presents. The map's upper edge is demarcated thus all the way from Lvgdvno (Batavorum) at the lefthand end of Segment 1 first below the Rhine, then below the Danube and even beyond it, as far as Tomis on the Black Sea at the far end of Segment 7. This "demarcation" resumes from Trapezvnte on Segment 9 and continues till the Caspian Sea is reached at Teleda (10A5). Again from the lefthand margin of Segment 1 where our copy begins, a corresponding route is already in progress close to the lower edge. This route continues into Segment 6. There is then only a route along the lower Mediterranean shore until Egypt is reached. Hereon, however, one route or another again runs close to the map's lower edge all the way to its end, except for a break (or detour) demanded by the marshes into which the Euphrates and Tigris drain (10C3). Within the map, too, no coastline is without its corresponding route, except for much of the upper shore of the Black Sea already mentioned, the upper left-facing shore of Gaul, the final part of the Peloponnese beyond Epitavro evidently (7B1–7C1), and the right-facing shore of India at the map's far end. While these shores of Gaul and India may lack a route along them, the mapmaker leaves viewers in no doubt that there was still access to them by this means, in fact ample access in the case of Gaul. Routes ring the only three islands – Sicily, Crete, and Cyprus – on which a network of routes is drawn.

(c) Pictorial Symbols

There can be no denying that the mapmaker intended the many pictorial symbols or "vignettes" (over 550 of them on our copy) to be a distinctive feature of the map, and that they do certainly enhance its appeal. They need to be appreciated both in the general context of classical mapmaking and more specifically in conjunction with the various principles that determine this particular map's presentation; how accurately they have been reproduced by copyists is an important related issue.

Without question, pictorial symbols as such are not a novel feature here. They are to be seen both on the Dura shield[200] and on the sixth-century Madaba mosaic map,[201] the former likely to predate the Peutinger map, the latter to be later work.[202] Illustrations featuring comparable symbols also appear in the earliest extant manuscript of technical treatises by Roman land surveyors (*agrimensores*). The manuscript probably dates to the sixth century, although the possibility remains open that these illustrations are a copyist's addition rather than a component of the treatises as originally written at the earliest around A.D. 100.[203] This said, there can be no doubt that viewers of a publicly displayed land-survey map, just as of Rome's Marble Plan,[204] were expected to grasp the significance of conventional representation of, say, centuriation, or (on the Plan) a column base or a staircase. It is impossible to say whether maps for public display ever incorporated an explanatory "key" or "legend." No surviving specimen of classical cartography shows any sign of one; but then no specimen (the Peutinger map included) is complete. If there never was a key in any instance, this should hardly surprise us. Ancient artists at least, if not surveyors too, expected viewers of their work to interpret images for themselves – as at a Roman triumphal procession, where the images of (say) conquered regions or cities were evidently not labeled.[205] No more are the Columns of Trajan or Marcus Aurelius accompanied by a "key."

Detailed analysis of the map's pictorial symbols forms the subject of an entire monograph published by Annalina and Mario Levi (1967). The interpretation that they advocate there may be disputed, but their differentiation and classification of the symbols are robust enough, and these are gratefully adopted here with minimal modification. The Levis create seven categories (A–G) of symbol. Typically, the size of the symbols in the (A) and (B) categories is smaller than all those in the other categories; the three elaborate symbols in category (F) are very large.

(A) occurs most often by far; its basis is a pair (always intended to be identical) of twin towers. In each tower there are usually one or more doors, or one or more windows;[206] roofs are mostly pointed, but sometimes domed, and even diamond-shaped. The pairs are presented, broadly speaking, in four styles:

(A)

> (Aa, with 53 variants): with each tower standing separately but linked both above, below, and even around, by a wall of some kind, either presumably a blank fortification, or some flat-roofed structure that incorporates a window, even a door or perhaps gate;[207]
>
> (Ab, with 20 variants): with the towers linked below, and even around too, but nowhere higher up;
>
> (Ac, with 7 variants): with the towers abutting one another directly, leaving no space or structure in between;
>
> (Ad, with 8 variants): with the space in between the two outer towers occupied by a third tower (sometimes smaller), making a three-tower symbol.

(B, with 36 variants): rectangular "temple" buildings, presented sideways on, with sloping roof, and always some combination of door(s) and windows.

(C, with 38 variants): rectangular "bath" buildings, presented obliquely from above so as to depict the entire open space, or pool, that most of these structures enclose; all roofs are pointed, and there are always window(s) or door(s) or both.

(D, with 5 variants): buildings (storehouses?) comprising two, three, or four elongated rectangular blocks, in some instances with open courtyards in between; doors, windows, pointed roofs.

(E, with 6 variants): cities defined by their circuit walls with towers and gates.

(F, with 3 variants): elaborate symbols for major cities, each individually designed, with an enthroned personification of the city as the centerpiece.

(G, with 7 variants): either symbols designed for an exceptional purpose, or extraordinary embellishments of category (A).

Altogether the mapmaker can be seen as deliberately limiting himself to the use of few categories of symbol, and even then he only uses one category very often, and two others often (see further below). He would surely have had no difficulty in devising additional symbols for forts, bridges, and mountain passes, for example,[208] not to mention line-work styles for routes along rivers or across open water, territorial boundaries, fortification lines, and aqueducts. Yet he preferred to exercise restraint in the interests of offering viewers an attractive, uncluttered presentation, and in order to accentuate certain features such as Rome itself and the category (C) symbols, which are made especially conspicuous.

It is notable that the great majority of symbols appearing on our copy of the map belong to category (A): 434 out of the 559 total. Moreover, within this category as many as 306 reflect no more than a mere five of the eighty-eight variants; four of these five are only minimally different from one another.[209] Otherwise in only two instances[210] does a variant in any category of symbol appear as many as nine times, and in a great number of instances – including almost the entire categories (D), (E), (F), (G) – a variant is actually unique. In category (C), with its thirty-eight variants, only two (C1, C2) appear more than three times.

In all likelihood the number of variants within the larger categories was far smaller on the original map, and it is successive copyings that have vastly increased their total. Often, it seems, copyists were unconcerned to reproduce individual symbols very fully or accurately. Most of them cannot be dashed off rapidly; rather, to draw them correctly requires time and care.[211] Perhaps inevitably, our copyist (not to mention his predecessors) failed to be as painstaking as he might in every case, so that in effect many of the variants separated out by the Levis amount to little more than trivial departures from a recognizable standard. Indeed, a purist could readily identify even more variants, in particular (for what little it would probably be worth) by adding the application of color to the criteria adopted by the Levis.[212] It is at least striking that in drawing the commonest type of symbol (Aa), from Segment 9 onward our copyist mostly ceased to bother with the triangles of black ink in the gable of each of the two towers, so that variant (Aa2) is rare before that point, and variant (Aa1) rare after it.

Most, if not all, symbols were presumably meant to require the use of both black and red inks. When both are not used, we can often be confident enough that this is a copyist's slip or oversight.[213] Occasionally, however, it is conceivable that only one color ink was intended.[214] The norm is for the frame of a symbol to be drawn in black, but in some instances it is partly red[215] and in others wholly red.[216] In addition, some or all of a symbol's "walls" may be colored brown.[217]

In practice even the three main categories of symbol (A, B, C) differentiated by the Levis seem less clear-cut than might be imagined from the drawings in their book, because many of these drawings are in fact "ideal forms" rather than exact reproductions. Thus, in my perception, those variants of the (D) category which have no more than two roofs separated by open space (their D2, 4, 7, 9, 10) are better classified as further variants of the (C) category, rather than as signifying a quite different type of structure. In particular, the Levis' C31 and D10 are very similar, and not sited so far apart from one another on the map. Equally, those variants of the (C) category where the building is fully roofed over would hardly lead viewers of the map to assume that a bath or spa is being represented, especially when the associated name has no such obvious connotation.[218]

Despite their lack of special concern for most symbols, copyists nonetheless evidently did devote time and trouble embellishing some for one reason or other. They even added several, while omitting others. For example, both the name AD SCM PETRVM and its symbol – comparable in style to category (B) – are surely subsequent additions to ROMA (4B5). The symbol for Tarso cilicie (9B4), by contrast, has been dropped, as has presumably that for the major junction Casarodvno (1B3).[219]

The case of Casarodvno raises the important issue of the mapmaker's criteria for determining which places should be marked with a symbol and why. On the route network one primary criterion is plainly the function of a place as more than just a T-junction.[220] On Segment 1, it is true, this justification for a symbol is neglected in several instances,[221] but thereafter failure to observe it is notably rare.[222] Given the mapmaker's determination not to employ simple "point symbols," the crossover of regular stretches can prove notably untidy and confusing.[223] So it is much to the benefit of viewers for every place that serves as more than just a T-junction to be marked with a symbol.

This said, a high proportion of places marked by a symbol are in fact situated either at a T-junction, or simply along a route, or are even isolated (off the route network). In each of these instances there needed to be some other reason – not necessarily self-evident from the map itself – that prompted the mapmaker to mark the name with a symbol and to choose its category. His sources for making these decisions elude us.[224]

It is tempting to suspect that places with certain forms of name are automatically marked with the associated category of symbol, so that in particular any name incorporating a divinity should be marked with category (B), and "Aqvae" or similar names with category (C). It is true that all six occurrences of Addiana(m) are marked by a symbol,[225] but by contrast instances of Adhercvle(m)[226] and Admercvriv(m)[227] are to be found both with and without a symbol, while neither occurrence of Admartis[228] is marked by one.[229] Again, many of the "Aqvae" names are marked by a symbol, but not all. It is presumably deliberate choice, therefore, not accident, that the two occurrences of Adaqvas at 5C1 and 5C3 should both be marked by a symbol while Aqvas Regias (5C1) in between them is not. Likewise Aqva viva (4B4) is marked by a symbol, but the same name in 4A3 is not, nor is Adaqvas in 4B3.[230]

Very deliberate selection of names for marking by a symbol is suggested by the fact that in some instances a route can proceed a considerable distance across the map without any name being so marked. On the route from Petavione (4A2) to the right, for example, not until Mvrsa maior (5A2) is another place marked by a symbol, after fifteen intervening stretches. The interval is even greater – over thirty intervening stretches – between Leptimagna col. (6C4) and Bernicide (7C4). Strikingly, however, there then at once follow three places marked by symbols: Hadrianopol(is), Tavchira col., and Ptolomaide.

Such indicators that the mapmaker's use of symbols was carefully considered are unimpeachable. At the same time, however, contrary indicators can be observed that are hard to account for. For example, some instances occur (already noted above), where a place is definitely or very probably marked twice on the map, one time with a symbol, the other without one,[231] thus suggesting that the mapmaker became prone to proceed arbitrarily in this regard. Equally, when a place is to be marked by a symbol, the category chosen may seem puzzling. A category (B) symbol hardly seems the obvious choice for Saldas Colonia (1C4), Aventicvm Heletiorvm (2A2), or (onward from the latter) Avgvsta Rvracvm (2A4); the possibility that one or more of these symbols represents a copyist's slip cannot be ruled out. Likewise it is odd to find Ad Pretorivm (4A5), Ad Horrea (5C2), and Aqva viva (4B4) all marked by category (C) symbols.[232] The intended significance of the category (D) symbol – occurring in only five instances, each a unique variant – is particularly difficult to determine.

It seems reasonable to infer that the mapmaker's category (A) symbol[233] was meant to distinguish places of administrative, commercial, military, or other well-known importance, and mostly it does fulfill this purpose. Even so, queries arise about certain choices, juxtapositions, and omissions. Unless the mapmaker was just reacting automatically to the first word of the name, it is a surprise to find Fano Fvgitivi (4B3), for example, marked by a symbol when the Bordeaux Itinerary[234] terms it only a *mutatio*, the most modest type of stopping point. Other places seemingly too modest to mark by a symbol are: Bitvriza (3B3); Indenea, Iovnaria (both 5A2); Inalperio, Siclis, Epetio (all 5A3); Inaronia (5A4), and possibly the unnamed symbol (no. 38) immediately beyond;[235] Adteglanvm (5B5); fons (7B3); Melena (8A2); Gargara (8B3); Bylae (9A3); and also several across Segments 10 and 11 that remain more or less impossible to evaluate for lack of information.[236]

Among unexpected juxtapositions are the appearance of Tvbvrbomaivs (4C4) without a symbol, but Admercvrivm (4C5) nearby with one; likewise Gravisca without a symbol, followed by Mindo Fl. with one (both 4B2); Adnonvm with a symbol, followed by Casilino without one (both 5B3); Haila without a symbol, followed by Addianam with one (both 8C5); Evropos without a symbol, followed by Nagae with one (both 11B2). Here, then, are five cities that the mapmaker might have been expected to mark by a symbol but chose not to, for whatever reasons. Others can be suggested too, with varying degrees of confidence.[237]

5. THE INTEGRATION OF CARTOGRAPHY AND ART

The lack of consistency that time and again may be suspected in the map-maker's marking of symbols did not deter the Levis[238] from maintaining that the great majority of them were designed to indicate at a glance to travelers the level of services and accommodation (on a scale from modest to extensive) available at the places thus identified. To be sure, the Levis forbear to elaborate upon this perspective in detail. It is in any case hard to credit, with its presumption of an extraordinary level of detailed knowl-edge on the mapmaker's part, not to mention a sophisticated coding of symbols faithfully reproduced by a long succession of copyists. Underpin-ning this perspective, too, is the broader assumption that the map truly was designed for practical use. The close examination of the mapmaker's design and practice attempted in the present chapter, however, leads me to conclude that this traditional view is no longer sustainable.

Even so, to propose alternative priorities on the part of the mapmaker is no reason to disparage his cartographic skills. On the contrary, his imagi-native remolding of the *orbis terrarum*, his studied choice of components for the map, his adherence to mature cartographic principles, and much else besides, are all masterly. Nonetheless, it needs to be recognized that overall he deployed such expertise for the accomplishment of primarily noncar-tographic ends; hence he remained unperturbed by levels of selectivity, inconsistency, and carelessness unacceptable in a map intended for serious consultation on the ground. The idiosyncratic integration of scientific data and artistic inspiration is precisely the quality that gives his creation its special force. This is not a map to be taken at face value for making journeys or planning campaigns. In their various ways, certain earlier maps and comparable images either produced by Romans or known to them had already idealized regions[239] or cities, especially Rome itself.[240] This map goes further by daring to idealize the entire world, and through a rad-ical refashioning it articulates fundamental contemporary concerns about Roman power and values, the subject of Chapter 5.

RECOVERY OF THE ORIGINAL MAP FROM
THE SURVIVING COPY

T HIS THIRD AND last of the chapters to examine the surviving copy
marks a transition to making the lost original map the primary focus
of attention. The issue addressed here – of how accurately our copy may
be reckoned to reproduce the original – has the greatest importance, but
in fact the confidence with which assessments can be offered must vary
considerably. If the danger were not already obvious enough by its very
nature, Ptolemy himself warns that repeated copying of a map leads to
the compounding of errors.[1] Moreover, even for the production of the
original, it may be unrealistic to assume that the data was uniformly correct
and complete as supplied or marked in the first instance.[2]

Thereafter, omissions, slips, and distortions are all too easily introduced
by copyists through oversight or inaccuracy, especially in the case of line
work. Copyists are also liable to make deliberate omissions, adjustments,
and additions. Where parchment is used – as in the case of our copy –
certain adjustments may patently be mere shifts in the placement of names
in order to avoid holes or cuts.[3] More generally, however, there will
often be no means for copyists' initiatives to be detected once made, let
alone reappraised. Some may reflect worthy intentions in the interests of
improving and updating the map. Others, by contrast, may at best be
decorative licence on the part of copyists keen to embroider it in some
way or other, and unconcerned that its integrity might suffer as a result.[4]

By definition, an assessment of the extent to which our surviving copy
is reckoned to depart from the lost original further depends upon the
impression formed of the latter's character and date. Due consideration of
these fundamental issues must await Chapter 5. Suffice it to state here my
view that the lost original is most likely to have been produced for display
in a ruler's public space during the Tetrarchic period around A.D. 300. If
our sole surviving copy is to be dated around 1200,[5] then nine hundred
years separate it from the original, through a line of successive copies –
no doubt varying in quality – which is beyond recall. Hence all efforts to

determine what is distinctive about our copy rather than taken over from its exemplar are thwarted. A key concern in this connection, and equally indeterminable, is the date of this exemplar. In particular, even if it was old enough to be Carolingian, there seems at best only a slim prospect that it still reproduced the lettering style of the original rather than using uncial, which our copy (and maybe its exemplar too) abandons in moving toward Gothic. More generally, the older the exemplar, the more likely it is to have suffered fading in the way that our copy has, causing some lettering to become illegible and even to vanish altogether.

1. COPYISTS' INITIATIVES

There need be no doubt that, along with contemporary features, the maker of the original map himself was content to include ones from the past. Two which never even coexisted stand out as integral components of the map: Campania before the eruption of Mount Vesuvius in A.D. 79 on Segment 5, and Dacia as a Roman province between the early second and late third centuries on Segments 6 and 7.

By contrast, I regard anything on the copy that is identifiably Christian (whether written or drawn) as post-original. I say the same about the conspicuous insertion of a new name Constantinopolis with new symbols where Byzantium had no doubt been marked (8B1); there are signs of matching changes at Chrisoppolis across the straits (8A1). Post-original too, in my view, is the creation of an exceptionally visible symbol for Antiochia (9B4), rendered larger than that for Rome itself in fact, the map's intended focal point. In all three of these instances it is very clear that there was minimal concern to integrate the new symbols neatly into the route network. Some modification of the symbol for nearby Tarso cilicie (9B4) may have been intended, too, when that for Antiochia was enlarged to dominate this part of the map. In the event, apparently the modification was not made (or at least not retained by our copyist), because there is now no symbol at all for Tarso cilicie. Also likely to be enlarged and embellished – but less clumsily – are the symbols for Aqvileia (3A5), Ravenna (4B1), Tessalonic(a)e (7B2), Nicomedia (8A2), Nicea (8B2), and unnamed symbol no. 53 (8B4 = Ancyra).[6] The stage in the map's history at which all these various alterations to well-known cities were introduced (together or piecemeal) is further cause for speculation – sooner after production of the original rather than later perhaps, but there is no means of knowing for certain.

Comparable conspicuous additions – perhaps made later rather than earlier – surely include the two elaborately decorated areas of forest named as SILVA VOSAGVS (2A2) and SILVA MARCIANA (2A5), as well as the learned "special notices" about geography, Alexander's exploits, and the like.[7] No doubt it was in part because they had undergone fewer successive copyings that such special notices reflect near-perfect accuracy in their presentation.[8] The curious decorative enlargement of the symbol for Admatricem (5A5) was perhaps made later rather than earlier;[9] the same may be imagined of the multiple lesser embellishments to other symbols.[10] Whether or not the "realistic" shapes of islands in the Gulf of Salona represent a copyist's improvement (given that otherwise all but the largest islands are typically rendered just as small squares or circles), it is impossible to say.[11] Even so, the unique clustering of symbols inland here (5A2–5A4) for otherwise insignificant places that elsewhere would not be so likely to merit them heightens suspicion.

Also visible are a few instances where notable changes either were initiated but then never completed, or were introduced by one copyist but later abandoned by a successor. Most striking, as already mentioned, is the ample space evidently left clear to insert an enlarged symbol for Tarso cilicie (9B4), which our copyist could not or would not add. Likewise puzzling on a more modest scale is the exceptional presentation of Casarodvno (1B3) as a major junction without a symbol. The natural assumption must be that there was a symbol here on the original map. Just conceivably, a copyist either altered this or at least cleared space to do so, and a successor displeased with the result – whatever form it took – chose merely to link the routes again, but without reinstating any symbol. Likewise, it was no doubt a copyist who began to add the supplementary red line work visible along some river courses in Segments 1–4; but this initiative demanded extra work which either the copyist himself perhaps, or his successors for certain, chose not to pursue systematically. A comparable economy, again by a copyist perhaps, is the simplification of the rendering of the commonest type of symbol (Aa) from Segment 9 onward by omission of the tiny triangles of black ink in the gables of the two towers.

Insofar as subjective impression is to be relied upon (our only possible guide in this instance), it would seem that the map has maintained its overall framework soundly enough despite successive copying over a nine-hundred-year span. If this favorable assessment is at all correct, then the preservation of the original's integrity is likely to stem from the choice of skillful artists, rather than scribes, to undertake the copying for the most part. These artists keenly appreciated how vital it was to reproduce the line work for coasts, principal mountain ranges, and principal rivers with precision, as well as to place the symbols accurately, if such a large, complex map was to remain meaningful and its mass of further detail incorporated satisfactorily.

2. NAMES AND FIGURES

Understandably enough perhaps, it was much of the detail that confused the artist copyists or failed to engage their attention. In the details, therefore, lie most of the shortcomings to be detected throughout the surviving copy. Perhaps because their skills and interests were above all artistic rather than scholarly, copyists were evidently never concerned to improve and update the map by substituting the post-antique name of a city for its Roman one,[12] or even (except in a mere two instances) by appending such a name after a Roman one.[13] Equally, there is no sign of any attempt to convert names marked in oblique cases to the nominative for the sake of consistency. The adjustments made to accommodate a Christian outlook are minimal: the area occupied by the heartland of the Bible remains restricted, and the Christian "special notices" are fitted into space that in all likelihood was otherwise empty on the original map.

Time and again, the surviving copy reflects incomprehension in the copyist's handling of names and words, as well as repeated disregard for spelling them correctly or dividing them meaningfully.[14] Observe the formulation "Hadreabhadre Bvrnomilia XIII" (4A4), and such spellings as PATAVIA (1A1–1A4), Media (twice, 3A2, 4A2 = Raetia), REGI OTRASPA (3B2–3A3), Parna (3B3), CAPANIA (5B1–5B5), Phinipopolis (7A1), TRHACIA (7B2–8A1), Adherbas Fl. (8A2), Patras (9B2 = Patara), Alexandria catisson (9B4 = Alexandria ad Issum), Damaspo (9C3), MONS DAROP+NISOS (11B3). The same disregard is to be found in the presentation of certain route stretches where the names of the two successive places are written along the stretch as well as at either end, but spelled differently in each instance.[15] Likewise, some names of peoples and regions that recur are spelled differently.[16]

Certain misspellings may derive from inability to interpret a predecessor's lettering – as with Parna and Phinipopolis, for example. There is no doubt that, at some stage in successive copying, a predecessor's **H** has more than once been misread for **N**, creating Nalata (6A1), Nibl(a)e (6C1), Nemesa (9C4).[17] In the case of Nalata, to write **H** does in fact seem to have been our copyist's first instinct, but he then altered the letter to **N**. Elsewhere, too, there is evidence that he could take the trouble to emend what he determined to be an incorrect spelling (either his own or on the exemplar).[18] We may imagine, therefore, that his spelling of certain other names incorporates the correction (now by definition no longer identifiable) of what he considered to be a slip on the exemplar. Even so, it is hard to believe that he made many such changes when egregious slips and omissions still abound in his own presentation of names. In six notable instances, capitalized names could not have been difficult to supplement if they had been left incomplete on the exemplar as they are on our copy: NITIOBRO (1A4); NAGMVS (1C4); REGI OTRASPA (3B2–3A3); [– ? –]DIA (3C2–3C5 = Numidia); MEDIA PROVI[– ? –] (4A2–5A1); BVR (4A3). By contrast, PAFLAGONIA (8A5) was evidently corrected at some stage; its lettering was widely spaced out as PAGONIA, and then FLA was crammed in between **A** and **G**.

Overall, the number of instances in our copy where a symbol or river lacks its name is substantial; the same may be said of the names or distance figures (or both) for many route stretches.[19] The great majority of these omissions, if not all of them, must surely be slips by copyists, which successors working from a flawed exemplar would hardly be able to restore. The progress of such losses is beyond recall, even though their cumulative effect is all too evident. The succession of three stretches without name or distance figure between Adsilanos (3A5) and Tasinemeti (4A1) stands out.[20] Hereabouts, too, either our copyist or a predecessor duly wrote "Fl." for river no. 27A near the righthand edge of Segment 3, but then overlooked completion of the name in 4A1. In many instances (though by no means all), pressure of space seems the most likely reason why a name or a figure is missing,[21] and distance figures emerge as the most dispensable component. To be sure, efforts were made to preserve these figures by presenting the numeral on two tiers,[22] or writing it above the place-name,[23] or permitting route line work[24] or a river to run through it.[25] Nonetheless, in other instances no such expedient was contrived, and the figure is missing.[26]

It is impossible to determine the degree of accuracy with which the distance figures that are marked have been copied. Reliable modern measurements may often act as a check, but still, allowance must made for miscalculation in the first instance, as well as for scribal errors embedded in the original map itself. It is no surprise to find a few distance figures that are manifest nonsense (for whatever reason).[27] Some others make numerical sense but are in fact undeniably far too high[28] or too low[29] for the route stretch where they appear. In several instances, too, uncertainty over the reading of a letter creates confusion.[30] Unfortunately, most slips in a distance figure, once committed, would have been very elusive to detect, let alone to correct, even had successive copyists wished to try. The length of a stretch on the map is no guide, because it is quite unrelated to distance on the ground. If recourse to attempting some calculation from the total figure for a route was considered in order to resolve an uncertainty, in all likelihood none was possible because the mapmaker evidently dispensed with such totals. Other source materials from which to check or restore figures can hardly have been at a copyist's disposal to serve as an alternative recourse except in the rarest of instances.

3. ROUTE LINE WORK

As was only to be expected, the route network posed the most formidable challenge to copyists, especially the need to match the names and distance figures along the routes with the corresponding line work and its chicanes. In the production of medieval illuminated manuscripts it was evidently routine procedure for the work to be divided between an artist (for the decoration) and a scribe (for the text). Alternatively, a single individual might act in both capacities, as Steinmann is inclined to think was the case for our copy of the map.[31] Whether or not the production of the original was divided is an even greater enigma. Such division is at least attested for a fifth-century world map (now lost),[32] and while the production of a map as complex as ours could certainly have benefited from it, it is impossible to say whether this was the arrangement adopted. What does emerge clearly from inspection of our copy, however, is that the integration of the written and line-work components of the route network has often slipped, no doubt as successive copies were made.

A common occurrence – and potential source of confusion – is for what was evidently intended as only one stretch to be drawn as two (or even three).[33] In these cases it is impossible to be sure whether the extra chicane that creates the seemingly redundant stretch[34] has been introduced by a copyist in error or whether it was already drawn by the mapmaker because his layout called for it. The instances most likely to extend back to the original map are those where a route has to be turned or lowered; an extra chicane unquestionably fulfills a useful function here.[35] Certain other instances – where the drawing of two stretches is understandable but hardly essential – can be identified as ambiguous;[36] at least some of these may have appeared thus on the original map. Change introduced by copyists, however, can be more widely suspected in further cases where no extra chicane would seem to be required if a name and its distance figure had been placed with greater care.[37]

A related shortcoming of our copy is that its placement of names does not invariably leave adequate space for the corresponding route line work to be run underneath,[38] or for a chicane to be drawn where it is needed.[39] For the most part, to be sure, concern to allow adequate space for these purposes is evident,[40] but by no means invariably. Examples can be found where a chicane is not created in the normal way,[41] or where a name and its distance figure are on different levels.[42] Line work that should match lettering has sometimes not been drawn. For example, a chicane and stretch could readily have been created for Catvalivm (1A4), as could chicanes for Ilio (8B2) and Tharsidarate (10B2); but the opportunities are missed. Equally, the chicane for Aeliae (5C2) should have preceded the name rather than following it, and that after Presididiolele (4C1) should have followed the distance figure rather than the name. The copyist who ran the route line work for the Ceserina stretch (6B1) up from the shoreline evidently failed to grasp that in fact it ought to proceed inward from the lefthand edge of the parchment.[43] It seems similarly slipshod to run route line work through a symbol rather than interrupting it in the regular way.[44] Elsewhere, confusion results both from this line work reaching a symbol that it should bypass,[45] and from the reverse – line work bypassing a symbol that it is intended to reach.[46]

Instances can be identified where a copyist's eye slipped, with the result that a name (and distance figure) is duplicated or loses its supposedly original placement and is shifted to a nearby route. Lvria and Cvria (both 3A1) appear to duplicate one another, and the first of two occurrences of the name Sallvnto on the same route (6A1) may be a careless substitution for Salthva. Similarly, a copyist's eye or mind must have wandered when he wrote the first of the two occurrences of Fines cilicie (8B4, 9B3) along routes: in all likelihood Fines galatie is meant here, since GALATIA appears immediately above. Lacvs et mons ciminvs (4B2) seems to have been shifted from the third route above its present placement, and the name Admartis (4B4) should perhaps belong on the route immediately below where it appears now (4B3, unnamed stretch no. 32). In a double shift, Fl. elevter should probably belong on the stretch immediately above (Ortosias–Demetri), while the second distance figure on that stretch should be moved in turn to the route still higher (all in 9C3).[47] Quite remarkable is the manner in which names and distance figures on the Ravgonia–Isvmbo route recur on the first part of the route down from Artaxata (both 10A4–10B5). There remains the possibility, however, that this duplication goes back to the original map rather than having been introduced by a copyist.[48] The same uncertainty surrounds the switching of the Bergomvm and Levceris stretches (both 3A2), which occur in reverse order on the ground.

Inevitably, the denser the route network becomes, the more challenging that part of the map is to copy, and the greater the chance of mistakes being introduced. Italy on Segment 4 illustrates the risk all too well. Even so, complexity alone can hardly account for the remarkable amount of route line work that should have been drawn here on our copy but never was: from Mindo Fl. to Centv cellis (4B2); on the entire route from ANCONE to Vrbesalvia and across to Asclopiceno (4B3); presumably from Foro Flamini to Spoletio (4B3, distance figure missing); presumably from ROMA to unnamed symbol no. 34 and on to Hostis (4B5, distance figures missing); and at the extreme edge of the parchment from Adaqvas Albvlas up to Tibori on the Via tybvrtina (4B5). How far our copyist was responsible for these omissions, and how far they were carried over from the exemplar, it is as usual impossible to say.

Omissions of route line work elsewhere are readily identifiable from the "Routes: conjectural restoration of missing line work (bright red)" overlay on Map A. Especially surprising is the sheer extent of omissions in 7B5 and 8B1, from Cenopvrio and Perintvs to Constantinopolis, and from Apris to Heraclea and Macrontecos, as well as to Aprodisia, Callipol[– ? –] and Se[– ? –]. It is a further puzzle that Chrisoppolis across the straits (8A1) should be left without distance figure or route line work either up to iovisvri(vs) or down to Calcedonia. Another route that it is a surprise to find without line work is Thelser to Albania (all in 10B5), especially as a thin, faint line with appropriate chicanes has been drawn from Fl.

Rhamma to Titana Fl.[49] In addition, it seems improbable that the original map should have shown no link to Babylonia and Selevcia (both 10C4) from the left; as it is, on our copy any route or connector to them that has been omitted is now beyond recovery.[50] Perhaps the difficulty of running line work through so much mountain range deterred copyists from drawing it for the Tyana (9B2) to Tarso cilicie (9B4) route; even so, this is another substantial omission.

A type of line work that was evidently all too prone to being overlooked by copyists is the short connector from one long route to another. Plenty of these omissions can at least be identified with confidence, because the relevant distance figure was copied, but not the associated line work. Such carelessness is particularly striking in the case of Nicomedia (8A2), where two connectors – one up to Artane, the other down to Eribvlo – each has a distance figure but no line work. Meantime, however, the copyist drew the onward extension from Eribvlo to Nicea (8B2), line work and all, with impeccable diligence. Elsewhere, short connectors for which the line work is missing are to be found across the map.[51] This repeated flaw could support a claim that, at some stage in the production of successive copies, the work had been divided between scribe and artist, with the latter performing unreliably. By contrast, if a single individual acted as sole copyist, it would seem extraordinarily inattentive to copy so many distance figures but overlook their associated line work. To be sure, in some of these instances it is conceivable that a copyist consciously chose not to run line work along stretches where the placement of lettering or other features made it more or less impossible to fit.[52] The presentation of the map suffers all the same.

Certain other connectors can only be conjectured as highly likely, as neither a distance figure nor line work remains to confirm any omission. However, Tavchira col. would surely have had a link to Ptolomaide (7B4) on the original map, as would helyacapitolina to Herichonte (9C1); Chrisoppolis (8A1) would not have been left isolated either, as mentioned above.[53] Altogether more troublesome is the reverse phenomenon, where it would seem that one or more copyists – were they slapdash, tidy-minded, or ill-informed – added connectors that in all likelihood are mistaken. Naturally, it remains possible that some or even all these appeared on the original map. Nonetheless, it is also easy to see how readily they might have been introduced in the course of copying only to continue undetected thereafter. At Sostra (7A2), for example, the presentation of the route from Melta to Ad radices is clumsy, with Sostra intended to serve as both "dead end" and turning point. It must have seemed such a trivial step to join Sostra and Nicopolistro with route line work, although in fact this link makes no sense at all on the ground and presumably was never intended by the mapmaker. With varying degrees of confidence, modern research can identify several other connectors that likewise seem mistaken.[54] Tetrapyrgia (9B3) furnishes an intriguing case where our own copyist evidently began a connector down to Selevcia, but then at once realized that this was an error and did not continue it.

Two further, less common types of error can be identified that tended to be introduced in the course of copying but could equally well have been embedded in the original map. The first type is to shift the branching of one route from another by a single stretch earlier or later than it occurs on the ground. Thus the route to Bobiano (5B3) from Teneapvlo ought rather to start from the previous Larinv stretch (both 5B2), just as the route to Psdio ought to start from Haila instead of from the next stretch on the map, Addianam (all 8C5). All it takes to introduce this latter slip is the merest shift of lettering and line work, but from a geographical perspective the consequences are dire, because on the ground Haila and Addianam lie in quite different directions from Psdio. The second type of error is to muddle the order or placement of stretches along a route. For example, it would seem that the order of the Vicinivm and Batva stretches on the map should in fact be reversed (both 6A1), and likewise those of Evvenos Fl. and Calidon Fl. (both 6B4); the placement of the Tegeas stretch (6B5) also seems mistaken.[55]

4. COPYISTS' FLAWS IN PERSPECTIVE

There should be little need to labor the observation that accurate copying of so complex a map constituted a formidably difficult task to accomplish in its entirety. If the challenge were not already self-evident enough from the multiple flaws that our copy exhibits, well-documented shortcomings in the performance of its engravers from the sixteenth through the nineteenth centuries only provide further confirmation.[56] Seldom at any stage during that period or earlier was the copying undertaken by adequately qualified individuals with an unwavering concern to reproduce all the map's elements faithfully, rather than just some. Less care, it seems, was typically devoted to lettering, symbols, and route line work than to coastlines, principal mountain ranges, and principal rivers. This said, there is also no question that certain symbols in particular must have been subjected to major alteration well before our copy was made; later, it is easy for us to see how boldly the first (1598) published engraving of the map "improves" names across the map.

In the end we can only be thankful that successive copyists were sufficiently motivated to undertake the challenge of reproducing the map at all, and that over a nine-hundred-year span they do seem to have maintained its overall framework soundly. It is a relief, however, that the unchecked introduction of yet more flaws and changes into other components did not continue beyond the point it had reached in our copy. To be sure, it is possible that some of the detail was flawed even in the original. Moreover, it is important to place the subsequent accumulation of flaws in perspective.

It may dismay those scholars who subject the map to close inspection and evaluation, but it is as well to remember that they form a minority, and a very demanding one. It is most unlikely that the map was designed to bear such detailed scrutiny. Rather, its maker's primary purpose was to convey a range of larger impressions, to be discussed in Chapter 5. The map still achieves this goal for a broad audience more or less as effectively in its current blemished state as its original must have done.

THE ORIGINAL MAP

From here on, my attention no longer focuses on the surviving copy of the map but turns to the lost original. This chapter addresses its fundamentals: authorship and date; sources; context and purpose. By their very nature these aspects are interrelated, and any conclusions drawn about them can only be tentative at best in view of the loss of the object itself. But the importance of the questions to be raised justifies the attempt to formulate responses, however imperfect. Taken together, those proposed here envisage the original map as a bold experiment in combining and developing established approaches to cartography. A novel form of map is the result, with the forceful ideology of Diocletian's Tetrarchy (c. A.D. 300) as its principal inspiration.

1. AUTHORSHIP AND DATE

In antiquity it was rare for products of technical or artistic expertise to carry their maker's name. Thus the absence of any such name on the surviving copy of the map is no surprise, and the likelihood is that none appeared on the original in the first place. The only scholar who has proposed a named individual as the maker of the original is Konrad Miller.[1] He dated it to the late fourth century and attributed it to Castorius. This identification derives from the fact that one Castorius happens to be the source most often cited in a *Cosmographia* (by an anonymous cleric claiming to be from Ravenna, c. 700) for information likely to be somehow derived from itineraries. In claiming that this Castorius was the maker of the Peutinger map's original, Miller makes two highly speculative inferences: first, that Castorius was a real person (otherwise unknown) active in the late fourth century rather than just one of the several undoubtedly fictitious individuals invented by the cosmographer; and second, that Castorius had been responsible for this very map rather than just a text. Few scholars have been persuaded by such an insecure sequence of reasoning, and Miller's rash identification of a fourth-century Castorius as the maker of the Peutinger map's original is rightly to be set aside.[2]

The basis for proposing any other named individual is absent. In fact a team or "workshop" is the most likely maker, headed by a highly paid artist of the type listed in the Tetrarchs' Edict on Maximum Prices of 301 as *pictor imaginarius* (figure painter).[3] He would serve as the principal (*conductor, redemptor*) who made a contract of *locatio operis faciendi* with a patron, stipulating in particular the work to be done and where, the price, payment arrangements, deadline for completion, and any penalties for lateness. Naturally, the patron (whoever he, she, or they were) had to be satisfied by the final result. Earlier, before the contract was agreed, the patron had in all likelihood prescribed certain features of the design and its intended context, but there is no knowing to what extent or how inflexibly.[4] The team (if such it was) responsible for producing the map must surely have included one or more members with cartographic experience or insight, because their achievement is such a mature and disciplined one. Despite the very different character (and, in all likelihood, earlier date) of the Severan Marble Plan of Rome, its cartographic design and presentation correspond to a surprising degree with those of the map; conceivably, their makers received some similar training.[5] Where that might have happened in the case of the map, however, and where indeed the original was made, it is impossible to say.

Predictably enough, the surviving copy of the map is as unforthcoming about the date of the original's production as it is about its maker's identity and location. Moreover − as Chapter 4 has shown − additions, embellishments, slips, and omissions that can only have been introduced over successive copyings are all readily identifiable. As observed there too, it is quite evident that the maker of the original in his turn was content to include features from the past that could never even have coexisted. In particular, the cities of Campania destroyed by the eruption of Vesuvius in A.D. 79 make a striking mismatch with the Roman route network in Dacia, a province north of the Danube only annexed by Trajan early in the second century. At least, however, this part of the route network does offer a vital marker in any attempt to establish a terminus post quem for the original, in other words the earliest period at which it could unquestionably have been produced. It does not follow, however, that the same feature can also furnish a terminus ante quem, a latest possible date for production of the original. The province we know to have been abandoned by the Romans during the 270s, but a record of its route network must have remained thereafter, and a mapmaker could still take the opportunity to use it, not only demonstrating how far Roman control had once stretched, but also reinforcing the commitment made by emperors to the eventual recovery of Dacia for Rome.[6]

A reliable terminus ante quem for production of the original map is indeed elusive, although two suggestive pointers merit consideration.

First, there is often a striking correspondence between the names within certain areas on the surviving copy of the map and those listed for it by the anonymous Ravenna cosmographer mentioned above, who wrote circa 700. It is equally clear that the cosmographer used a variety of sources. The inference seems inescapable that, by circa 700, Peutinger-type maps and related materials were available and in use. Hence it becomes hard to imagine that production of the original of the Peutinger map would postdate 700.[7] Second, it is striking that the only signs of Christian influence in the surviving copy are names and features not integral to the map's design and presentation. In particular, the layout accords no notable prominence to the Holy Land and other regions of special significance for Christians. Naturally, such a layout still remains a possibility once Rome's rulers had embraced Christianity from the early fourth century. But when the design of such a large and powerful map ignores Christian thinking so thoroughly, any dating from the fourth century onward seems less and less likely as time advances.

To be sure, these two pointers can merely serve as suggestive ones for consideration, and there remains no means to hand of irrefutably disproving the possibility that the production of the original map might even postdate antiquity altogether. In fact, Emily Albu argues that it was a Carolingian display piece of the ninth century.[8] This claim is difficult to credit, however.[9] It expects a Carolingian team to have commanded an array of materials concerning the route network that is impressive even in antiquity itself, as well as to have drafted the immense physical and cultural map base in all its complexity. At the same time, the team studiously excluded post-antique forms of place-names along with any sign of Christian influence. While it might be mistaken to deny that a Carolingian team would possess the capacity to make a success of a project framed in these demanding ways, credibility is nonetheless strained. Motive is a related puzzle. The map's shape is so extreme, its detail so dense and – for Carolingians – so uncharacteristically anachronistic. While the wish to create a new map of the ancient Roman Empire is readily understandable, the choice to do so in this manner seems extraordinary. Moreover, as amply demonstrated in Chapter 3, there seems no escaping the conclusion that an artist, not a scholar, controlled the map's presentation. During antiquity that was unexceptional. In the Carolingian period, by contrast, the impetus for this map might be expected to have come more from scholars, with greater influence on their part discernible in the presentation than it actually reflects. A development observed in two Carolingian geographical treatises – *De mensura orbis terrae* by Dicuil, and the anonymous *De situ orbis* – is the way in which they select from classical sources in order to establish northern Europe as the focus of their attention rather than the Mediterranean.[10]

While fully acknowledging the absence of sufficient unequivocal indicators, I prefer to regard the production of the original map as a Roman initiative that postdates the organization of Dacia as a province in the early second century and predates Constantine's sole rule, his confident promotion of Christianity, and his foundation of Constantinople in 324.[11] Within this span of two centuries, the map could be associated with, say, the emperor Philip's millennium celebrations at Rome in 247, or with Severan rule; but such linkages seem hardly compelling. Rather, in my estimation the map's design and presentation match best the preoccupations of Diocletian's Tetrarchy (c. 300); these are treated in the discussion of the map's context and purpose.[12] Granted, the connections identified can be no more than subjective, and hence this dating of the original map deserves to be treated with as much caution as any other.

2. SOURCES

The impressive and varied range of materials drawn upon for the making of the map is readily enough recognized, but the disappointment remains that no specific identification of a source can be made with any confidence. Altogether, in its choice of components and their presentation, the map does seem to be a highly original creation. At the same time it must surely derive from the adaptation and mosaicing of an indeterminate number of detailed maps (see Chapter 3), none of which survives or is even described with any precision in an extant text. It is a reasonable presumption that geographers rather than artists took the lead in producing these earlier maps, but still such fundamentals as their scope, orientation, and scale remain beyond recovery. The maker of the Peutinger map's original clearly also made extensive use of data likely to be derived only from texts of one kind or another. However, very few of the relevant type survive, so that again little can be said with confidence about exactly what these texts comprised, where they were obtained and assembled, or just how they were exploited for making the map.

Large "world" maps were unquestionably to be found on public display in Rome and elsewhere, and as such were of potential value for the making of the Peutinger map's original. Most famous of its type was the map of the *orbis terrarum* commissioned by M. Vipsanius Agrippa. It was only completed after his death in 12 B.C., and thereafter for an indefinite long period it remained on display in a portico in Rome.[13] Scholars have repeatedly imagined that this map formed the principal base for the Peutinger map's original, although in fact any such linkage can be no more than wishful thinking. Not only is Agrippa's map lost, but the paucity of ancient references to it has even prompted the claim that there was no image at all, instead just a monumental text displayed in much the same way that Augustus' record of his own achievements (*Res gestae*) is inscribed on a temple wall at Ancyra (modern Ankara).[14] In any case, Agrippa's map (if it were such, as still seems probable) would have needed supplementing later in some remoter regions – such as Britain – where Roman penetration postdated Augustus' rule, with corresponding subsequent advance in geographical knowledge. Equally, there was nowhere near an empire-wide route network in Agrippa's time.

At least there seems no doubting that both Agrippa's map and the text known to have been somehow associated with it demonstrated a concern for accuracy that can only derive from the geographic and cartographic learning developed by Greeks, especially Eratosthenes at Alexandria and his successors from the third century B.C. onward. Products of this unique expertise were vital to all Greek and Roman mapping of large areas thereafter, and the maker of the Peutinger map's original, too, must have drawn upon it. His presentation of the Taurus mountains (no. 109A) extending from Asia Minor all the way across to the farthest shore of India at the map's righthand edge surely reflects Dicaearchus' concept of an east–west axis (*diaphragma*) that ran from the Straits of Gibraltar, through the Mediterranean, and then along the line of the Taurus mountains, which were reckoned to extend to the Himalayas.[15] Even so, more generally, it is impossible to determine the degree to which the maker of the Peutinger map exploited such Greek expertise, let alone whether he used Agrippa's map specifically. At best, he is likely to have relied more upon manuscript maps as well as geographic writings that incorporated maps.

Description of a large map of the *orbis terrarum* valued in part for its capacity to improve students' grasp of geography happens to form the climax to a Latin panegyric delivered in the late 290s. This map, and possibly regional ones too, were on display at a rhetorical school named Maeniana at Augustodunum (modern Autun) in Gaul.[16] The school had suffered damage, and the speaker Eumenius, its highly paid new head, is seeking a provincial governor's permission to rebuild it at his own expense.[17] The map is apparently already in place, and has even been seen by the governor:

> Videat praeterea in illis porticibus iuventus et cotidie spectet omnes terras et cuncta maria et quidquid invictissimi principes urbium gentium nationum aut pietate restituunt aut virtute devincunt aut terrore devinciunt. Siquidem illic, ut ipse vidisti, credo, instruendae pueritiae causa, quo manifestius oculis discerentur quae difficilius percipiuntur auditu, omnium cum nominibus suis locorum situs spatia intervalla descripta sunt, quidquid ubique fluminum oritur et conditur, quacumque se litorum sinus flectunt, qua vel ambitu cingit orbem vel impetu inrumpit Oceanus.

> Ibi fortissimorum imperatorum pulcherrimae res gestae per diversa regionum argumenta recolantur, dum calentibus semperque venientibus victoriarum nuntiis revisuntur gemina Persidos flumina et Libyae arva sitientia et convexa Rheni cornua et Nili ora multifida; dumque sibi ad haec singula intuentium animus adfingit aut sub tua, Diocletiane Auguste, clementia Aegyptum furore posito quiescentem aut te, Maximiane invicte, perculsa Maurorum agmina fulminantem aut sub dextera tua, domine Constanti, Bataviam Britanniamque squalidum caput silvis et fluctibus

exserentem aut te, Maximiane Caesar, Persicos arcus pharetrasque cal-
cantem. Nunc enim, nunc demum iuvat orbem spectare depictum, cum
in illo nihil videmus alienum.

In [the school's] porticoes let the young men see and examine daily every
land and all the seas and whatever cities, peoples, nations, our most invin-
cible rulers either restore by affection or conquer by valor or restrain by
fear. Since for the purpose of instructing the youth, to have them learn
more clearly with their eyes what they comprehend less readily by their
ears, there are pictured in that spot – as I believe you have seen yourself –
the sites of all locations with their names, their extent, and the distance
between them, the sources and mouths of rivers everywhere, likewise the
curves of the coastline's indentations, and the Ocean, both where its circuit
girds the earth and where its pressure breaks into it.

There let the finest accomplishments of the bravest emperors be recalled
through different representations of regions, while the twin rivers of Persia
and the thirsty fields of Libya and the convex bends of the Rhine and the
fragmented mouths of the Nile are seen again as eager messengers constantly arrive. Meanwhile the minds of those who gaze upon each of these
places will imagine Egypt, its madness set aside, peacefully subject to your
clemency, Diocletian Augustus, or you, unconquered Maximian, hurling
lightning upon the smitten hordes of the Moors, or beneath your right
hand, Constantius, Batavia and Britannia raising up their grimy heads from
woods and waves, or you, Maximian Caesar [Galerius], trampling upon
Persian bows and quivers. For now, now at last it is a delight to examine
a picture of the world, since we see nothing in it which is not ours.[18]

While Eumenius clearly praised this map for more than just its instruc-
tional value, even his rhetorical outline of its character leaves no doubt
about the careful attention to geography that it reflected. It, too, was likely
to have been in the same Hellenistic cartographic tradition as Agrippa's
map displayed at Rome. The same may be suggested of a similarly ambitious map commissioned by the emperor Theodosius II in the year of
his fifteenth consulship (435) at Constantinople and now lost. The only
surviving testimony to it consists of dedicatory verses addressed to the
emperor by its pair of makers:

Hoc opus egregium, quo mundi summa tenetur,
Aequora quo, montes, fluvii, portus, freta et urbes
Signantur, cunctis ut sit cognoscere promptum
Quicquid ubique latet, clemens genus inclita proles
Ac per saecla pius, totus quem vix capit orbis,
Theodosius princeps venerando iussit ab ore
Confici, ter quinis aperit cum fascibus annum.
Supplices hoc famuli, dum scribit pingit et alter,
Mensibus exiguis, veterum monimenta secuti,

In melius reparamus opus culpamque priorum
Tollimus ac totum breviter comprendimus orbem.
Sed tamen hoc tua nos docuit sapientia, princeps.

The creation of this outstanding work – containing all the world, marking
its seas, mountains, rivers, harbors, straits, and cities, available for everyone
to discover whatever lies hidden anywhere – the emperor Theodosius
ordered in his own esteemed voice when he assumed the fasces at New
Year for the fifteenth time, a famous son of a merciful family, forever
godfearing, barely confined by the entire globe. Within a few months we
humble servants – one of us coloring, while the other writes – restore[d]
this work for the better, following memorials from the past, removing
previous imperfection, and covering the entire globe in miniature. But it
was your wisdom even so, emperor, that instructed us in this task.[19]

It is unclear whether this map was a wholly original creation (as the
opening lines could be seen to imply) or the revision of an earlier one (as
the closing lines imply). Beyond doubt, however, is the map's distinction
as a geographically detailed work commissioned by the emperor, which
occupied two skilled workers for months.[20]

Just as the maps exploited by the maker of the Peutinger map's original
cannot be identified for lack of surviving examples, so too it is impossible
to be sure of the texts and lists consulted by him. If his incorporation of
the complex network of land routes in particular was original work, as
seems credible,[21] he must have needed extensive data that was unlikely to
be already available in the required form. Authority to acquire this data,
and some assistance in organizing it, would both have been invaluable too.
It was bold to commit to showing the route network extending across
the entire empire, and even far beyond to the East, with no large region
overlooked. A standard "route book" for the empire seems not to have
existed. The surviving unofficial Antonine Itinerary collection (*ItAnt*)[22] –
in all likelihood compiled during the late third century, at much the same
period as the Peutinger map perhaps – leaves the impression that author-
itative listings were available at least for certain routes, and even for some
regions. Elsewhere, however, information would have had to be pieced
together laboriously from public and private sources,[23] and the level of
detail could vary unpredictably. Hence the mapmaker was even willing to
turn to maritime itineraries for coverage of certain coasts where he could
not secure information about a land route (because in fact there was
none).[24]

Minor differences abound between the presentation of a route and the
corresponding distance figures on the Peutinger map, in the Antonine
Itinerary, and in the so-called Bordeaux Itinerary (*ItBurd*).[25] For comparison, Table 1[26] (end of chapter) is an instructive sample, which aligns the
listings for routes in Italy covered in all three. The Bordeaux Itinerary, as
the meticulous record of actual journeys undertaken from Bordeaux to

Jerusalem and back in 333, is the fullest record here, with even the most minor stops (*mutationes*) recorded. This said, it is important to note that in Italy (and elsewhere too) the Peutinger map in some instances includes more stopping points than the Antonine Itinerary. In other instances too, as already observed in Chapter 3, there must surely have been additional stopping points known to the Peutinger mapmaker from his sources, which he nonetheless chose to omit for one reason or other.

Two categories of data important to the Peutinger mapmaker that itinerary lists (at least in their surviving form) would not supply are an identification of baths or spas and an indication of the relative importance of stopping points. It was clearly the mapmaker's standard practice to mark full junctions on the route network with a pictorial symbol, but there is no knowing what sources he used (including maps perhaps) to mark places thus at T-junctions, or along a route, or in isolation.[27] It seems improbable that he drew directly upon some separate catalog (if one existed) of "significant places,"[28] if only because the names for places on the map marked by a symbol appear in the same variety of cases to be found in itinerary lists rather than all in the nominative.[29] At least, therefore, whatever the unidentified further sources were that determined the mapmaker's disposition of symbols, the clear impression is that they did not cause him to depart from his practice of primarily relying upon itinerary lists to lay out routes. It may be noted that neither Pliny's *Natural History* nor Ptolemy's *Geography* would help him in the disposition of symbols,[30] nor in all likelihood would the official *formula* or *forma* (Greek τύπος), a document evidently drawn up for each province, listing those of its communities liable to Roman taxation.[31]

It is impressive, although perhaps hardly surprising, that the mapmaker was able to incorporate stopping points and distance figures for routes in Persian territory to the east of the Roman Empire. Persian – and before them Assyrian – routes had long been well organized; they had also been recorded by Greek writers.[32] Two distance markers inscribed in Greek on stone around 300 B.C. are known: one (with the stade as the unit of distance) from near Persepolis on the route through there from Susa to Ecbatana; the other, less well-preserved, found at Pasargadae and recording distances (the unit is unclear) from there, followed by a summary in Aramaic.[33] There also survives a summary narrative itinerary of a route extending as far east as Arachosia, written in Greek by Isidore of Charax around the end of the first century B.C.; his unit of distance is the *schoinos*.[34] Early in the second century the Roman historian Tacitus mentions a distance – in stades – covered by a fast-moving military force during Parthian civil strife in the 40s A.D.[35] Again, however, specific sources that the Peutinger mapmaker used for Persia cannot be identified.

We likewise cannot point to specific sources that the mapmaker used for India, even though – as in the case of Persia – it is no surprise that distance figures were obtainable, albeit perhaps several centuries old. Such data somehow gathered by Alexander's marshal Seleucus I Nicator is reproduced by Pliny the Elder, with the original figures converted into Roman miles.[36] Strabo cites Megasthenes, who served both Alexander and Seleucus I, for the claim that the Indians "make roads, and at every ten stades place a pillar showing the branches and the distances."[37] No such pillar has survived, and the unit of distance used on them is unknown. Reference to the *kos* by Asoka in his Seventh Pillar Edict (242 B.C.) may at least be noted: "On the roads I have had banyan trees planted, which will give shade to beasts and men, I have had mango groves planted, and I have had wells dug and rest houses built at every half-*kos* [or every eight *kos*]. And I have had many watering places made everywhere for the use of beasts and men."[38]

The very high figures appearing on certain of the Peutinger map's routes in India conceivably reflect those cases where the mapmaker was unable to find distances converted to Roman miles (or otherwise readily convertible) and instead had to rely upon an Indian unit which he – like modern scholars – felt unable to convert with confidence. In consequence, he merely reproduced the Indian figures found in his source without specifying the unit.[39]

A revealing example of the type of non-Roman itinerary data that the mapmaker might have attempted to exploit is perhaps to be found in the so-called Armenian Itinerary. This has survived with the *Geography* by Ananias of Sirak and (although certainty is impossible) is thought to have formed part of it, inserted immediately following his section on Asia.[40] Ananias' life span, which is reckoned to have been circa 610 to 685, extends far into the period of Arab domination of Armenia, although his text represents Armenia, Caucasia, and the Persian Empire as they were prior to 636.[41] The Itinerary offers distance figures in miles, evidently Arab ones, but is also concerned to provide the basis for conversion into several alternative units.[42] It takes the Armenian capital Dwin[43] as its nodal point and offers five routes that fan out from there, as well as three further ones that extend onward from two of the five. Of greatest interest for the Peutinger map is the first route of the five: "From Dwin to Karin – 200 miles, from Karin to the frontier ditch – 100, from there to Kolonia – 90, from there to Niksar – 100, from there to Amasia – 80, from there to Gangra – 105, from there to Angora – 80, from there to Constantinople – 120, from there to Rome – 3,000."

Here the reference to a demarcated frontier is notable, as is the mention of Amasia as a staging point, one of the settlements puzzlingly dupli-cated in error on the Peutinger map.[44] The Itinerary makes it easier to imagine how such duplication could occur, as the mapmaker had to place increasing reliance upon non-Roman data once his knowledge of routes from familiar sources diminished when they proceeded beyond the Roman Empire. The distance units, nomenclature, and direction of travel reflected in non-Roman sources were all liable to create confusion, which the map's severe compression of unfamiliar lands beyond Roman territory only compounded.

3. CONTEXT AND PURPOSE

The surviving copy of the map is not just incomplete; it is also without context. We can only be certain that it was placed on display somewhere for a period, as was a similar map at Padua in the late fifteenth century.[45] It is most important to consider in turn the context intended for the original of the Peutinger map, and the purpose for which it was produced.[46] Knowledge of the term by which the mapmaker and his intended audience typically referred to the map might prove an instructive pointer, but there is no clue. Ancient terminology for maps and related objects remained altogether loose in any case.[47] The term *itinerarium pictum* (in contrast to *perscriptum* or *adnotatum*) appears in an idealistic tract *Epitoma rei militaris* by Vegetius addressed to the emperor (probably in the late fourth century):[48]

> Primum itineraria omnium regionum in quibus bellum geritur plenissime debet habere perscripta, ita ut locorum intervalla non solum passuum numero sed etiam viarum qualitate perdiscat, compendia deverticula montes flumina ad fidem descripta consideret; usque adeo ut sollertiores duces itineraria provinciarum in quibus necessitas gerebatur non tantum adnotata sed etiam picta habuisse firmentur, ut non solum consilio mentis verum aspectu oculorum viam profecturus eligeret.

> In the first place a commander ought to have itineraries of all the regions in which war is waged written out very fully, so that he may gain a firm grasp of the distances between places (and not only the mere number of miles but also the condition of the routes), and may take into account shortcuts, byways, mountains, and rivers accurately recorded. Moreover, for those provinces where crises were occurring, we are assured that the more able commanders had itineraries that were not just noted down but also in picture form. Thus when setting out he would choose a route not only by a mental process but visually.

Whether the Peutinger map may fairly be termed an "itinerary in picture form" of the type credited (or imagined?) by Vegetius seems dubious, however. Some of the features mentioned by him are reflected in it, others are not, and its value on a military campaign – outside the Roman Empire especially – would surely have been very limited. The conspicuousness of the route network on the map might at least justify terming it more broadly an *itinerarium*, as it was by Celtis.[49] Without doubt, the weight of modern opinion has repeatedly chosen to classify it as a comprehensive way finder or route diagram. Comparisons have been made to modern transport diagrams, particularly those in the style inspired by Harry Beck's innovative London Tube diagram first issued in 1933.[50] Not surprisingly perhaps, the Publicity Department of the London Underground Group rejected Beck's design as "too 'revolutionary'"[51] when he first presented it in 1931, much as Häffelin in the 1780s had dismissed the Peutinger map as "si peu correcte et si bizarre."[52]

Even so, as observed in Chapter 3, the map consists of much more than just the route network. In fact, the network may not form the basis of the map as has been widely assumed, and its practical usefulness to travelers is diminished in a variety of ways. The original choice of frame for the map and the consequent compression of the vast area covered, the further skewing demanded by the central placement of the city of Rome, the inclusion of places and routes that do not cohere chronologically, the lack of concern for featuring direct routes or main ones – all these factors, and more, categorize the route network as only one distinctive component among several, still very important to be sure, but not in itself the primary purpose of the map. Rather, comprehensive control of the landscape across the entire known world is conveyed, both its main physical components (landmasses, islands, rivers, mountains, open water) and its cultural ones (peoples and man-made features, especially cities and routes).

Conceivably, the map's shape was intended in part to recall the familiar presentation of a text on papyrus[53] – that is, in a succession of short, vertical columns laid out along a strip that could be unfurled (and furled up again) bit by bit as the reader proceeded.[54] The material on which the original map was presented is a matter of pure speculation. Nonetheless, a papyrus strip to be unfurled bit by bit seems far from the most likely choice, particularly given the quantity of names in display capitals for regions, peoples, and open water, which can only be comprehended by unfurling a much wider section of the strip (up to several meters) than would be convenient for a reader when tackling a text. Hence there seems good reason to reckon that the map was designed to be spread out and viewed fully open. At the same time, its details can only be appreciated fully from close up. It does not follow, however, that the context for which the map was designed would necessarily allow viewers the opportunity to inspect the details any more than they could ever be inspected on the Columns of Trajan and Marcus Aurelius, say, or on Rome's Marble Plan, or possibly its *miliarium aureum* (golden milestone).[55]

Any map presented on pliable material like papyrus or parchment could well be intended as a portable item for travelers. But even if the Peutinger map is meant to convey that impression, it is hard to imagine a patron who could afford this masterpiece actually exposing it to the risks of practical use on journeys, the more so when it would be beneath such an exalted individual to take personal responsibility for day-to-day arrangements.[56] At the same time it would be a rash individual who kept this great map – with its stark demonstration of Roman might – for exclusively private

viewing. Such behavior had been known to provoke allegations of trea-
sonous imperial ambitions.[57]

Rather, in my view, the original map is likely to have been designed
for display by some recognized authority, and primarily for a celebratory,
propagandistic purpose. As far back as the third century B.C., paintings
were among the means by which Roman achievements were routinely
commemorated; they were placed on temple walls, for example, or carried
in triumphal processions.[58] Lactantius imagines the Persian king Sapor to
be aware of this Roman practice when he insults his captive the emperor
Valerian (c. 260):[59]

> Nam rex Persarum Sapor, is qui eum ceperat, si quando libuerat aut vehicu-
> lum ascendere aut equum, inclinare sibi Romanum iubebat ac terga prae-
> bere et imposito pede supra dorsum eius illud esse verum dicebat exprobans
> ei cum risu, non quod in tabulis aut parietibus Romani pingerent.

> For whenever the Persian king Sapor, his captor, wanted to mount either
> his carriage or his horse, he would order the Roman to bend down for
> him and to offer him his back, and then, planting his foot on the latter's
> spine he would say to him with an accusing laugh that *this* was how things
> truly were, not as Romans painted them in pictures or on walls.

Maps became familiar to Romans as one type of such art for commem-
orative display, and they could vary considerably in character, since few
cartographic norms ever developed. The Peutinger map is best understood
as artwork designed in this tradition, and for a specific type of location.
Paint seems the most likely medium – applied either directly to a wall
or to movable panels – although tapestry should not be ruled out.[60] A
portico with one or more colonnades would furnish a suitable setting, as
it is known to have done for Agrippa's world map at Rome as well as for
the maps at the rhetorical school in Augustodunum.

The fact is, however, that the deliberate placement of the city of Rome
at the center of the Peutinger map – its dominant symbol, unequalled as
a nodal point for routes extending in all directions – would gain added
force if the setting were the apse of an imperial reception hall (Latin
aula, Greek *basilica*). In architectural terms, neither such a space, nor the
apse as a component of it, was at all novel by the Tetrarchic period. But
both gained fresh importance from the new ceremonial style instituted
by Diocletian, which called for a ruler to hold solemn court seated on
a throne in the *aula* of his palace (Latin *palatium*, Greek *basileia*).[61] The
curved wall of an apse within which a throne was set would have made an
ideal setting for an extended map of the *orbis terrarum* under Roman sway
that was deliberately oriented north and centered on the city of Rome. In
addition, where (as often) there are spur walls on either side of the apse,[62]
these would act to block any view of such a map's outer limits from all
vantage points in the hall except the closest. The excellent preservation of

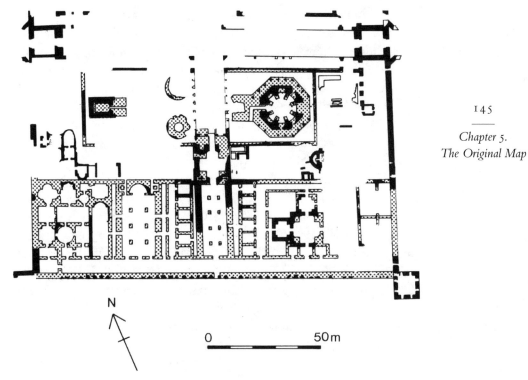

N

0   50m

FIGURE 4. Basement level of Diocletian's palace, Split: ground-plan detail. Line drawing
from J. J. Wilkes, *Diocletian's Palace, Split: Residence of a Retired Roman Emperor*, rev. ed.,
fig. 4. Oxford, 1993.

the basement level in the palace built by Diocletian at Split (Croatia) for
his retirement serves to illustrate this feature uniquely well – assuming that,
as seems likely, the architecture of the hall here does replicate the *aula* on
the lost main level above (see Figure 4 and Plate 17).[63] Hence the message
would be reinforced that Roman sway was infinite, literally extending out
of sight to both west and east. At the same time, the layout of the map
ensures that viewers in the body of the hall would miss nothing of primary
significance: on the far left there is only the open water of the western
Ocean, while to the right is India, typically of interest only as a symbol of
the distant and exotic.[64] A *tota farrago*[65] this far righthand end might well
appear to a cartographic expert, but in fact few viewers of the map would
recognize it as a "complete hotchpotch," let alone be concerned.

   In relation to the map's context and purpose, its squat height merits
consideration. In principle it is conceivable that the surviving copy represents an earlier copyist's reduction of a taller original. In practice, however,
so much adjustment would have been required (affecting far more than
just the height of the original) that such a taxing transformation is hard to
credit. Rather, the severe compression of the *orbis terrarum* that the map's
squatness calls for can only have been a conscious decision on the part of
the mapmaker. This squatness could make the map a suitable object for a
frieze along a wall, or even for presentation spirally, like the well-known

succession of scenes that wind their way up Trajan's Column. In normal circumstances, however, any such setting ought to be able to accommodate a taller map without difficulty. A possible explanation for such deliberate squatness, therefore, is that the original map formed only one component of artwork that was several times larger overall and is otherwise lost.

For example, the map's special attention to features and routes on land could have been matched in a corresponding map that privileged open water and routes there. Moreover, for there to have been a set of three completed by a celestial map would be entirely natural. It is in knowledge gained of the heavens and of everything on land and sea that the value of studying geography lies, proclaims Strabo in the opening sentences of his work.[66] In the monumental Julio-Claudian Sebasteion at Aphrodisias in western Asia Minor (mid first century A.D.), the upper of the two stories included a series of "universal allegories," of which two relief figures survive, Hemera (Day) and Okeanos (Ocean); to these there no doubt corresponded Night and Earth respectively, and other pairings can readily be imagined.[67] On the arch of the Tetrarch Galerius at Thessalonica (Plate 18), two of the emperors sit side-by-side, flanked by the other two standing. The busts below the seated emperors have been identified as Sky and Earth, and at either side of the scene appear reclining personifications

PLATE 17. *Aula* of Diocletian's palace, Split (basement level). Photo: Gregory Aldrete.

of Earth and Sea. Rees aptly sums up the impact upon viewers: "Whether or not specific identifications are upheld, the scene clearly projects the cosmic nature of Tetrarchic rule, imperial influence reaching far beyond the mundane concerns of government."[68]

Equally, the map could have formed one part of a design with even more components, in particular a globe image divided horizontally into zones (Greek *klimata*). The scheme – perhaps first devised by the fifth-century Greek thinker Parmenides – remained current in Late Antiquity.[69] Both the number of zones envisaged and their relative heights were prone to vary according to the visions of different thinkers, although at least five zones were to be expected, with the northern and southern habitable ones each bordered by a frigid zone (top and bottom of the globe) on one side and an equatorial torrid zone on the other (see Figure 5). If the map was designed to represent the northern habitable zone (*oikoumene* in Greek), and no other zone was less squat than it was, then the entire globe image must have been at least 1.65 meters tall or thereabouts (5 ft., 5 in.). When such an image was positioned at an appropriate height on the wall behind a throne placed in the center of an apse, not only would the map representing the northern habitable zone be very conspicuous, but also the map's center point – the city of Rome – could feature directly behind and above the throne, as Figure 6 envisages.

The quest to find compelling images for the zones beyond the *oikoumene* in either direction need hardly have posed an insuperable challenge to an

PLATE 18. Arch of Galerius (detail), Thessalonica. Photo: J. Matthew Harrington.

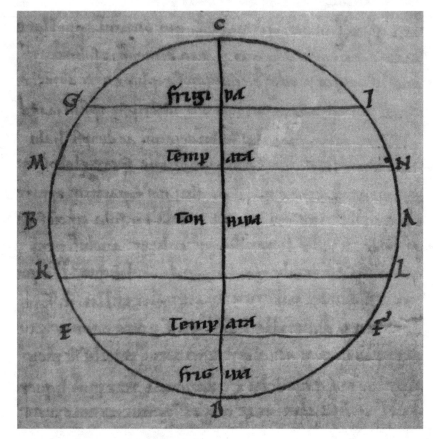

FIGURE 5. This diagram of the division of the globe into zones (Greek *klimata*) illustrates an eleventh-century manuscript of the *Commentary* by the fourth-century Latin author Macrobius on Cicero's *Dream of Scipio*. Both above and below a deep central "torrid" zone are a "temperate" (habitable) one and then a "frigid" one. The letters marked around the globe match references made by Macrobius in his discussion of this worldview. Photo: British Library, London. From Macrobius, *Commentarii in Somnium Scipionis*, MS Harley 2772, f. 67v.

imaginative artist. For example, Hyperboreans enjoying their extraordinary haven of ideal climate could be engagingly depicted within the topmost frigid zone.[70] Elsewhere on much of the globe, harsh extremes of climate and landscape could be sketched, along with monstrous creatures and pitiful peoples whose vulnerability, dispersion, and strife made a sharp contrast to the civilization, peace, and connectivity of the *oikoumene* under Roman sway. It was envoys of such poverty-stricken and unproductive peoples that the second-century historian, Appian, claimed to have seen begging the emperor in vain to extend Roman rule to them. Earlier in the same century Plutarch referred to the type of notice with which, he says, artists typically filled the remotest parts of their maps: "Beyond are waterless deserts infested by wild animals," "Murky bog," "Scythian cold," "Frozen sea."[71] Whatever the nature of the images elsewhere on the globe, it was essential that they be clearly subordinated to the map representing the *oikoumene*. During ceremonies, everything in the lower half or so of the globe would in any case become largely screened from view by the throne and by the array of emperor's associates standing on either side of it. Of all the zones, the *oikoumene* would then be the most visible.

Persistent claims that Rome dominated the *oikoumene* (land, sea, and even sky), and that the city's territory had come to span the world, go back in the surviving record at least to the Greek historian Polybius in the mid-second century B.C. They were further exploited by promoters and admirers of Augustus' rule in particular.[72] Earlier, both Pompey and Julius Caesar had also been hailed as world rulers,[73] and so were many of Augustus' successors. Claudius – uniquely among Roman emperors perhaps – would even describe himself thus (ὁ τῆς οἰκουμένης αὐτοκράτωρ).[74] Altogether it is no surprise, therefore, that the Peutinger map should project Roman world rule,[75] nor that this sway should be projected as far east as India and Sri Lanka. Augustan propaganda had developed the latter claim, which was maintained into the fourth century,[76] and perhaps even later to Justinian's time on the Barberini Diptych (Plate 19).[77]

It can seem more than coincidence that the choices made for the map's presentation should so effectively reinforce the ideals of Diocletian's Tetrarchy. As rulers, the Tetrarchs strove to demonstrate the special importance that they attached to the city of Rome itself. They commissioned a series of large construction projects there, although it was plain that the city was only a symbol now, no longer a uniquely privileged imperial residence and capital.[78] This was a painful change, for which the populace abused Diocletian when he and Maximian both attended the special celebration held in November 303 for their *vicennalia* as Augusti and for the *decennalia* of

FIGURE 6. Globe-map image imagined within the apse of a Late Roman *aula*. Sketch by Daniel Talbert.

PLATE 19. Barberini (sixth-century?) ivory diptych. Photo: Louvre, Paris / Art Resource, NY.

the two Caesars.[79] Later, in 306, it was the discontented populace's desire to have their own emperor in Rome, which led to the proclamation of Maximian's son, Maxentius. He did in fact make immense efforts to revive the city and its prestige during his residence there, but was eventually ousted by Constantine at the Battle of the Milvian Bridge in October 312. Even then, Constantine did not demolish Maxentius' grand structures, but rather adapted them to assert his own clemency, strength, and devotion to Rome. The central placement of Rome on the map asserts the city's symbolic value in the eyes of the Tetrarchs. So, too, by extension, the symbolic importance of Italy, Rome's heartland, is promoted by the generous amount of space it occupies on the map, while in reality under the Tetrarchy it, in turn, lost its privileged status and was divided into "regions" (regiones).[80]

Three recurrent themes articulated by the Tetrarchy and about it are the need for the four rulers to maintain a harmonious unity (Plate 20),

PLATE 20. Porphyry statue of the four Tetrarchs, Basilica San Marco, Venice. Photo: Elizabeth Robinson.

Mary T. Boatwright captures the essence of the statue: "This group portrait of the four Tetrarchs (ca. 300) was originally mounted on a column in Constantinople.... All four wear the identical military cloak (*paludamentum*) fastened at the right shoulder; abrasion suggests that a metal brooch or a stone of a different color was fixed here originally. Each man's breastplate is held in place by an elaborate military belt. Each also carries an eagle-headed sword in a rich scabbard, and wears a Pannonian cap, the front of which was originally ornamented with a jewel or stone in its center. In rendering all the Tetrarchs alike and positioning them so closely together, this group portrait embodies the unanimity that the four men were resolved to uphold. Their furrowed brows indicate their concern for the empire. But at the same time their elevation above their subjects is conveyed by the gems they wear, as well as by the use of porphyry – a rare, hard, reddish-purple stone reserved by this time exclusively for emperors and their families. During the Middle Ages, this statue was taken from Constantinople to Venice, where it now stands at the southwest corner of St. Mark's Basilica." (From Boatwright et al., *The Romans from Village to Empire*, p. 442. New York and Oxford, 2004.)

to repossess the entire empire from the usurpers and invaders who had fragmented it from within and without, and to devote themselves to the advancement of their subjects' well-being.[81] The map points to the fulfillment of these ideals, with its confident representation of the entire *orbis terrarum* (not merely the empire) under the sway of Rome at the center, the absence of overtly military features, and instead the conspicuous marking of cities, temples, and spas. These are repeated indicators that everyone may once again feel secure, free to recover and to enjoy the benefits of Roman civilization. The Tetrarchs' concern for their subjects is comprehensive and inclusive. Cities stand out as *lumina* (rays of light),[82] and great numbers of them are marked along with a profusion of lesser settlements; even the humblest viewers might have the satisfaction of finding their place of origin to be shown there. Meantime, the many peoples beyond the north, south, and east of the empire pose no threat. Realization that the map shows not a single boundary anywhere acts to impress – even shock – viewers in a society accustomed to the careful demarcation of territory at every level.[83]

Moreover, travel by land over great distances within the empire, and even far beyond it to the east, is presented as demonstrably feasible and safe. As contemporary viewers of the map would know well, the Tetrarchs prided themselves on their tireless traveling – most of it by land routes – in the course of duty to which their rhetoric at least set no geographical limit.[84] Hence the closing sentence of the lengthy preamble to their Edict on Maximum Prices of 301 takes pains to underscore that this statute applies "non civitatibus singulis ac populis adque provinciis, sed universo orbi" ("not [just] to individual cities and peoples and provinces, but to the entire world").[85] More broadly, the map reflects the empire's situation as the Tetrarchs represent it in the climax of the immense sentence that opens the same edict:

> . . . Fortunam rei publicae nostrae – cui iuxta inmortales deos bellorum memoria, quae feliciter gessimus, gratulari licet tranquillo orbis statu et in gremio altissimae quietis locato, etiam pacis bonis, p[r]opter quam sudore largo laboratum est – disponi fideliter adque ornari decenter honestum publicum et Romana dignitas maiestasque desiderant, ut nos, qui benigno favore numinum aestuantes de praeterito rapinas gentium barbararum ipsarum nationum clade conpressimus, in aeternum fundatam quietem debitis iustitiae munime[nti]s saepiamus.

> . . . Public decency and Roman dignity and majesty desire that the fortune of our state be organized in good faith and elegantly adorned, and that it be thanked – beside the immortal gods – as we recall the wars that we have fought successfully, at a time when the world is in tranquility, placed in the lap of a most profound calm, as well as benefiting from a peace that was toiled for with abundant sweat. Let us therefore, we who with the kind favor of the deities crushed the previous seething ravages of barbarian

peoples by destroying those very nations, protect the peace established for eternity with the appropriate defenses of justice.[86]

Rome's importance is upheld, and the unity of the empire's rule reinforced, by the map's giving no special prominence to the new Tetrarchic capitals. Equally, the bewildering proliferation of names for the new array of smaller provincial units[87] is ignored in favor of retaining the fewer, more familiar, and more reassuring old names for provinces. In addition, the exclusive use of Latin throughout may serve to reflect the Tetrarchs' deliberate concern to communicate in this language so far as possible, even in the east of the empire, where Greek might have been the more natural choice for their unprecedented stream of administrative and legal pronouncements.[88]

Beyond its promotion of the Tetrarchy as envisaged here, the map can also be seen to hold strong appeal for fourth-century intellectual taste in art, literature, and education. In whatever medium the original was presented, it surely reflected to the full the fourth century's love of bright colors.[89] The pictorial symbols may be compared to the jewels or precious stones (*segmenta*) with which the finest masterpieces of the time were studded for heightened brilliance – most obviously mosaics or monuments, but also (figuratively) poems, and (literally) dress. In this latter regard, the portraits of the two consuls that form part of the Codex-Calendar of 354 are particularly striking (Plates 21, 22).[90] Constantius II alone, as emperor, has jewels on his *toga picta*, but there are cameo vignettes on that of his colleague Gallus, and bands or stripes (*clavi*) on both men's togas. The map, in turn, resembles a long, colorful robe or frieze celebrating Rome and Roman rule, with its pictorial symbols as *segmenta* and its route line work as *clavi*. It is again characteristic of fourth-century artwork in its capacity to dazzle viewers so thoroughly on first impression that they became disoriented. Once recovered, they might turn their attention wherever they wished and appreciate the different elements of a work at their own pace.[91] Hence there should be no dominant element that would impose the adoption of a particular perspective. This is notably the case with the route network on the map; no one route is differentiated from another, and it is up to viewers themselves to determine where to start and then where to turn next at each junction as they proceed.

The map's drastic and seemingly unfamiliar compression of the *orbis terrarum* is calculated to provoke a range of reactions from intellectuals. Laughter at such absurdity[92] might be forthcoming from those who shared the quirky sense of humor in which the author of the *Historia Augusta* delights.[93] The audacity with which landmasses have been manipulated could serve to intrigue viewers familiar with those earlier Roman thinkers and poets who contemplated primeval conflicts between land and sea, and the consequences of rejoining separated landmasses.[94] The map could even

PLATE 21. Codex-Calendar of 354, Constantius II. Photo: © Biblioteca Apostolica Vaticana. Romanus 1 ms., Barb. lat. 2154, fol. 13. By permission of Biblioteca Apostolica Vaticana, with all rights reserved.

make fantasies of bridging the Adriatic Sea seem feasible.[95] At the same time, the sheer accumulation of details is a fashionable feature of fourth-century literature that the map amply indulges.[96] Each individual detail may be trivial and boring, but their great mass – an encyclopedic *ekphrasis* of empire – makes an arresting impression.[97] It is a delight, too, to realize that the place-names and distance figures typically derive from sources of a quite different type from the map, and are ingeniously reused in its fresh, more attractive setting – a cartographic match for the technique of "cento" verse composition. Plenty of names are deliciously exotic and "difficult" too.[98] The exquisite compactness of the map is also to be relished. Finally in this connection, it would not escape those well educated in geography that a thoroughly informed grasp of the map was their exclusive preserve. In

PLATE 22. Codex-Calendar of 354, Gallus. Photo: © Biblioteca Apostolica Vaticana.
Romanus I ms., Barb. lat. 2154, fol. 14. By permission of Biblioteca Apostolica Vaticana,
with all rights reserved.

fact, even they are liable to be teased and challenged by its remolding of the
world, which almost (but not quite) eliminates a north–south dimension,
and substantially (but deftly) varies the scales at which different regions
appear. By the same token, only the well-educated would be aware that
on the ground Pergamum and Alexandria, for example, were in nowhere
near such close proximity, nor Hippo Regius and Carthage so far distant;
any viewers who imagined otherwise from the map merely betrayed their
lamentable ignorance.

Ultimately there can be no proof of the Peutinger map's context or its
purpose; for lack of evidence, both must remain matters of conjecture.
Even so, in my estimation the long established view that regards the

PLATE 23a, b. *Signa imperii* (scepter and orbs) associated with the self-proclaimed Tetrarch Maxentius. Photos: Clementina Panella.

map as little more than a route diagram for use in making or planning journeys unduly reflects modern preoccupations rather than Roman ones. At the same time it fails to appreciate the relative significance of the map's principal elements as they would be most likely to strike Roman viewers. Seen through Roman eyes, the route network becomes only part of a cartographic reassertion of the long-standing claim to domination of the known world made by Rome's imperial rulers. To Romans, the map was designed to serve above all as a display piece, both celebratory and reassuring; the claims and ideals that it projects had special importance and resonance during the Tetrarchy.

Last but not least, the map may be associated, however loosely, with the remarkable group of *signa imperii* unearthed in 2005 in an official excavation on the northeast slope of Rome's Palatine hill, 230 meters from the Colosseum.[99] The recovery of such imperial emblems is unprecedented: these comprise scepters, tips of ceremonial lances, and four globes or orbs – three of glass and one of blue chalcedony (quartz; Plate 23a, b). With the blades protected by poplar-wood cases, all the items were wrapped in the silk and linen of imperial standards, and then carefully buried. The map furnishes pictorial reinforcement of a special kind for the emblems listed last, the orbs that a Roman ruler – quite possibly Maxentius in this instance – mounted on a scepter or held in his hand to symbolize world domination. The map with its enthroned ROMA figure holding a scepter and orb is a perfect fit for placement behind or above such a ruler as he sat on his throne. It forms either part of a larger artwork or a self-contained one, perhaps mounted on movable panels.[100]

Table 1. Comparative Listing of Routes in Italy by the Bordeaux Itinerary (*ItBurd*), Antonine Itinerary (*ItAnt*), and Peutinger Map

It. Burdigalense (555,11–557,10)	mil.	It. Antonini (339,7–341,5 *rovesciato*)	m.p.	T. Peutingeriana	mil.
mansio Byrigante		Brigantione		Brigantio	
inde ascendis Matronam				In Alpe Cottia	...v
mutatio Gesdaone	X			Sadaone	VIII
mansio Ad Marte	VIIII	Ad Martis	XVIII	Martis	
civitas Segussione	XVI	Segusione	XVI	Segusione	XVII
inde incipit Italia					
mutatio Ad Duodecimum	XII				
mansio Ad Fines	XII	Fines	XXXIII	Finibus	XXII
mutatio Ad Octavum	VIII				
civitas Taurinis	VIII	Taurinis	XVIII	Augusta Taurinorum	XIIII
mutatio Ad Decimum	X				
mansio Quadratis	XII	Quadratis	XXIII		
mutatio Ceste	XI				
mansio Rigomago	VIII	Rigomago	XIII		
mutatio Ad Medias	X	Carbantia	XII		
mutatio Ad Cottias	XIII	Cottiae	XII	Cutias	
mansio Laumello	XII	Laumellum	XII	Laumellum	XII
mutatio Duriis	VIIII				
civitas Ticino	VII	Ticinum	XXII	Ticeno	XXI
mutatio Ad Decimum	X				
civitas Mediolanum	X	Mediolanum	XXII	Mediolanum	

[tronco Milano–Aquileia]

It. Burdigalense (557,10–559,11)	mil.	It. Antonini (127,9–128,6)	m.p.	T. Peutingeriana	mil.
civitas Mediolanum		Mediolanum civitas			
mutatio Argentea	X				
mutatio Ponte Aureoli	X				
civitas Bergamo	XIII	Bergome civitas	XXXIII	[Bergomum]	
mutatio Tellegate	XII				
mutatio Tetellus	X				
civitas Brixia	X	Brixia civitas	XXXVIII	Brixia	XXXV
mansio Ad Flexum	XI	Sermione mansio	XXII	Ariolica	XXXII
mutatio Beneventum	X				
civitas Verona	X	Verona civitas	XXII	Verona	XIII
mutatio Cadiano	X				
mutatio Aureos	X				
civitas Vincentia	XI	Vicetia civitas	XXXIII	Vicentia	XXXIII
mutatio Ad Finem	XI				
civitas Patavi	X	Patavis civitas	XXII	Patavis	XXII
mutatio Ad Duodecimum	XII				
mutatio Ad Nonum	XI				
civitas Altino	VIIII	Altinum civitas	XXXIII	Altino	XXX
mutatio Sanos	X				
civitas Concordia	VIIII	Concordia civitas	XXXI	Concordia	XXX
mutatio Apicilia					
(o Ad Pacilia)	VIIII				
mutatio Ad Undecimum	XI				
civitas Aquileia	XI	Aquileia civitas	XXXI	Aquileia	XXX

Table I (continued)

[tronco Aquileia–Atrante (confine con il Norico)]

It. Burdigalense (559,11–560,10)	mil.	It. Antonini (128,6–129,3)	m.p.	T. Peutingeriana	mil.
civitas Aquileia		Aquileia		Aquileia	
mutatio Ad Undecimum	XI			Ponte Sonti	XIIII
mutatio Ad Fornolus	XII				
mansio Fluvio Frigido	XII	Fluvio Frigido	XXXVI		
mutatio Castra	XII				
inde surgunt Alpes Iuliae				In Alpe Iulia	XV
Ad Pirum summas Alpes	VIIII				
mansio Longatico	X	Longatico mansio	XXII	Longatico	V
mutatio Ad Nonum	VIIII			Nauporto	VI
civitas Emona	XIIII	Hennoma civitas	XVIII	Emona	XII
mutatio Ad Quartodecimo	X			Savo fluvius	VIIII
				Ad Publicanos	XI
mansio Hadrante fines Italiae et Norici	XIII	Adrante mansio	XXV	Adrante	VI

[tronco Aulona/Otranto–Capua]

It. Burdigalense (609,3–610,14)	mil.	It. Antonini (111,7–112,1 e 115,7–118,4 rovesciati)	m.p.	T. Peutingeriana	mil.
mansio Aulona, transis mare stadia mille, quod facit milia centum, et venis Odronto mansio mille passus		Hydrunto		Ydrunte	
mutatio Ad Duodecimum	XIII				
mansio <Lu>peas	XII	Lupias	XXV	Luppia	XXV
mutatio Valentia	XIII			Balentium	XV
civitas Brindisi	XI	Brundisium	XXV	Brindisi	X
mansio Speluncas	XIIII	Speluncas	XVIIII	Speluncis	XXVIII
mutatio Ad Decimum	XI				
civitas <E>gnatiae	X	Egnatiae	XX	Gnatiae	XXI
mutatio Turres Aurilianas	XV	Turribus	XVI	Turris Caesaris	IX
mutatio Turres Iuliana	VIIII				
civitas B<a>r<i>s	XI	Varia	XXI	Barium	XX
mutatio Butuntones	XI	Butruntus	XII	Butuntos	
civitas Rubos	XI	Rubos	XI	Rubos	XIIII
mutatio Ad Quintumdecimum	XV				
civitas Canusio	XV	Canusio	XXIII		
mutatio Undecimum	XI				
civitas <H>erdonis	XV	Erdonias	XXVI		
civitas Aecas	XVIII	Ecas	XVIIII	Aecas	
mutatio Aquilonis	X				
fines Apuliae et Campaniae					
mansio Ad Aequum Magnum	VIIII	Equo Tutico	XVIII	Aequo Tutico	XVIII
mutatio vicus Forno Novo	XII			Foro Novo	XII
civitas Benevento	X	Benevento	XXI	Benevento	X
civitas et mansio Claudiis	XII	Caudis	XI	Caudio	XI
mutatio Novas	VIIII			Ad Novas	VIIII
				Calave?	VI
civitas Capua	XII	Capua	XXI	Capuae	V

(continued)

Table 1 (continued)

[tronco Capua–Roma]

It. Burdigalense (610,14–612,4)	mil.	It. Antonini (106,5–109,1 rovesciato)	m.p.	T. Peutingeriana	mil.
Capua		Capua		Capuae	
				Casilino	III
mutatio Ad Octavum	VIII			Ad Nonum	VI
				Urbanis	III
mutatio Ponte Campano	VIIII			Ad Ponte Campano	III
civitas S<i>nuessa	VIIII	Sinuessa	XXVI	Sinuessa	...
civitas Menturnas	VIIII	Minturnis	VIIII	Menturnis	VIIII
civitas Formis	VIIII	Formis	VIIII	Formis	VIIII
civitas Fundis	XII	Fundis	XIII	Fundis	XIII
civitas Tarracina	XIII	Tarracina	XIIII	Terracina	XIII
mutatio Ad Medias	X			...	X
mutatio Appi Foro	XIIII	Api Foro	XVII		
mutatio Sponsas	VII	Tribus Tabernis	X	Tres Tabernas	...
				Sub Lanubio	...
civitas Aricia et Alb<a>n<o>	XIIII	Aricia	XVII	Aricia	...
mutatio Ad Nono	VII			Rosellas	III
in urbe Roma	VIIII	Urbe	XVI	Roma	X

[tronco Roma–Milano]

It. Burdigalense (612,10–617,5)	mil.	It. Antonini (124,8–127,9)	m.p.	T. Peutingeriana	mil.
Ab urbe		Ab urbe		Roma	
				Ad Pontem Iulii	III
mutatio Rubras	VIIII			Ad Rubras	VI
mutatio Ad Vicensimum	XI	Rostrata villa	XXIIII	Ad Vicesimum	XI
mutatio Aqua Viva	XII			Aqua Viva	VII
civitas Ucriculo	XII	Ocriculi civitas	XXI	...	
civitas Narniae	XII	Narnia civitas	XII		
civitas Interamna	VIIII	Interamnia civitas	VIII	Interamnio	
mutatio Tribus Tabernis	III			Ad Fine	X
mutatio Fani Fugitivi	X			Fano Fugitivi	II
civitas Spolitio	VII	Spoletio civitas	XVII	Spoletio	...
mutatio Sacraria	VIII			...	
civitas Trevis	IIII				
civitas Fulginis	V				
civitas Foro Flamini	III	Foro Flamini vicus	XVIII	Foro Flamini	
civitas Noceria	XII			Nuceria Camellaria	XII
civitas Ptanias	VIII				
mansio Herbello	VII	Helvillo vicus	XXVII	Helvillo	XV
mutatio Ad Hesis	X			Ad Ensem	V
mutatio Ad Cale	XIII	Cale vicus	XXIII	Ad Calem	VII
mutatio Intercisa	VIIII			Ad Intercisa	VIIII
civitas Foro Semproni	VIIII	Foro Semproni	XVIII	Foro Semproni	XII
mutatio Ad Octavo	VIIII				
civitas Fano Furtunae	VIII	Fano Fortunae	XVI	Fano Fortune	XVIII
civitas Pisauro	<VIII>	Pisauro civitas	VIII	Pisauro	VIII
<civitas> Ariminum	<XXIIII>	Arimino	XXIIII	Arimino	XXIII
mutatio Conpetu	XII			Ad Confluentes	XII
civitas Cesena	VI	Caesena civitas	XX	Curva Cesena	VIII
civitas Foro Populi	VI			Foro Populi	VII
civitas Foro Livi	VI			Foro Livi	VII
civitas Faventia	X	Faventia civitas	XXIIII	Faventia	X
				Sinnum fluvius	III

Table 1 (continued)

civitas Foro Corneli	X	Foro Corneli civitas	X	Foro Corneli	VI
				Silarum fluvius	VII
civitas Claterno	XIII			Claterna	VII
				Idex fluvius	VI
civitas Bononia	X	Bononia civitas	XXIIII	Bononia	IIII
mutatio Ad Medias	XV				
mutatio Victoriolas	X			Foro Gallorum	XVII
civitas Mutena	III	Mutina civitas	XXV	Mutina	VIII
mutatio Ponte Secies	V				
civitas Regio	VIII	Regio civitas	XVII	Lepido Regio	XVII
mutatio <T>annero	X			Tannetum	XI
civitas Parme	VIII	Parmae civitas	XVIII	Parma	II
mutatio Ad Tarum	VII				
mansio Fidentiae	VIII	Fidentiola vicus	XV	Fidentia	XV
mutatio Ad Fonteclos	VIII			Florentia	X
civitas Placentia	XIII	Placentia civitas	XXIIII	Placentia	XV
mutatio Ad Rota	XI				
mutatio Tribus Tabernis	V				
civitas Laude	VIII	Laude civitas	XXIIII	Laude Pompeia	XX
mutatio Ad Nonum	VII				
civitas Mediolanum	VII	Mediolanum civitas	XVI	Mediolanum	XVI

From M. Calzolari, "Ricerche sugli itinerari romani. L'Itinerarium Burdigalense," in *Studi in onore di Nereo Alfieri* (*Atti dell'Accademia delle Scienze di Ferrara* 74 Supplemento, 1997), 127–89, at 147–51.

CONCLUSION

THE MAP'S PLACE IN CLASSICAL AND MEDIEVAL
CARTOGRAPHY

1. THE MAP IN RELATION TO CLASSICAL
CARTOGRAPHY

Our ignorance of large Greek and Roman maps in general,[1] and of the Peutinger map's original in particular, is so profound that it remains impossible to determine with confidence just how creative a work the latter really was. It is at least conceivable, however, that no previous mapmaker had been so bold as to take a frame of such extreme dimensions and then to set the entire *orbis terrarum* within it, with the city of Rome as the center point – all of which required that the landscape be remolded on an epic scale. There seems no reason to doubt that the large maps of which we are dimly aware reflect, by contrast, the scientific tradition of Hellenistic Alexandria with its concern for accurate representation of the world.[2] To be sure, such cartography still offered ample scope for parading Roman achievements, and it was undoubtedly exploited for this purpose, as Eumenius illustrated at Augustodunum in the late 290s.[3]

Naturally enough, it had been the Romans' traditional habit to envisage their surroundings from the vantage point of Rome and Italy at the center.[4] This outlook was reflected in the so-called *miliarium aureum* or "golden milestone," evidently a pillar (now lost) that Augustus set up in the forum at Rome in 20 B.C.; it recorded distances between Rome and communities throughout Italy.[5] But once the Romans' empire dominated the Mediterranean and beyond, this inland sea evidently became the central feature in their mind's eye, and the various surviving descriptions of provinces, say, or listings of legionary bases, typically proceed anticlockwise starting from some point at the fringe, not from Rome itself.[6] So it is in fact unusually original of C. Julius Solinus, in his text *Collectanea Rerum Memorabilium* –[7] written around 300 perhaps but heavily dependent upon first-century A.D. predecessors – to begin from Rome; thereafter throughout he maintains Rome (and Italy) as his principal frame of reference. In cartography, the Peutinger map risks yet more inventiveness by drastically refashioning the world in subordination to Rome at its center, with results that can only be appreciated to the full by viewers already familiar with a more accurate rendering of geography.

The comprehensive featuring of land routes is an associated component of the Peutinger map that may also be original. Testimony confirming their appearance on other Greek or Roman maps (with the exception of localized plans) is all but nonexistent,[8] and it is certainly understandable that cartographers who strove to produce accurate maps of large regions would hesitate to introduce such complex and challenging line work. Moreover, it would seem that the emperors of the first two and a half centuries A.D. were unconcerned – for a variety of possible reasons – to make widespread claims about their control of land routes over a vast area. In practice, maintenance of routes was divided among local communities everywhere, and they may hardly have been visualized as an integrated empire-wide "network" even by emperors.[9]

It could have been the new ideology of the Tetrarchy, however, that gave the mapmaker inspiration to think in these terms. The Tetrarchs were committed to coordinating tighter control at the local level across the empire, and mobility was vital to them and to their troops. Although the routes as represented by the map are barely adequate for making or planning actual journeys, and any specifically military reference is absent, nonetheless the range and value of the network are brilliantly conveyed. The manner in which the routes forge horizontally and purposefully across the landscape infuses the map with a lively sense of cohesion and dynamism not to be found in any map compiled from Ptolemy's coordinates. For all their dedication to accuracy, such products of the Hellenistic tradition seem static by comparison.

The imaginative artistic idea of making the route network such an energizing and unifying component of the Peutinger map may well have proven a sterner challenge to execute than anticipated, because so much of the extensive data required had to be assembled, organized, and plotted from scratch. Even so, altogether the mapmaker's novel set of bold choices led him to combine elements that the cartographic tradition represented by Ptolemy mostly kept separate for use either on small-scale world maps or on larger-scale regional ones.[10]

2. LOST COPIES OF THE MAP

If only because a single copy of the Peutinger map survives, it is natural to view it as simply the last in a succession of copies that extended back in a direct line to a single original. In hope of penetrating this undocumented succession, two vague records have been wishfully interpreted as relevant references. Each remains a possibility in principle, but still far from certain.

First, a catalog made of the holdings in the monastic library at Reichenau on Lake Constance in 821/822 includes the entry "mappa mundi in rotulis II."[11] Second, centuries later, at the Dominican house of Colmar, the author of *Annales Colmarienses* states: "Anno 1265 mappam mundi descripsi in pelles duodecim pergameni" ("In the year 1265 I drew a map of the world onto twelve skins of parchment"). However, the sheer vagueness of both records should firmly discourage claims that the Peutinger map is being referred to in either instance, rather than some other "world map" of any type or shape.[12]

(a) Ravenna Cosmography

Better documented, by contrast, is the likelihood that the surviving copy in fact represents only one line of succession among several significantly similar in character. The relevant testimony is both textual and cartographic. Earliest is that of the *Cosmographia* in five books compiled by an unnamed cleric claiming to be from Ravenna, probably around A.D. 700,[13] in my view about four centuries after the original map was produced. The cosmographer's purpose of seeking to preserve a vision of the world once known to the Romans prompted him to list, region by region, the names of settlements, rivers, islands, peoples, around five thousand in all.[14] Among his various sources were clearly either maps such as the Peutinger map or lists of names along routes derived from such maps.[15] Regardless of whether it was he who took over names directly from maps himself, or whether this was done by previous compilers that he drew upon, it is obvious that the work was done in the most slapdash manner. There is failure to distinguish between types of name, let alone between the relative significance of settlements. There is also near-total omission of distance figures, as well as repeated jumbling of the names within an area rather than reproduction of correct sequences of them route by route.[16]

Even so, for present purposes two related observations seem beyond dispute. First, the frequency with which the names offered by the cosmographer for any given area match those on the Peutinger map is striking.[17] At the same time, second, there are also certain clear instances where the listing of names is entirely comparable in character but cannot in fact derive from the Peutinger map. The map, for example, marks no more than a handful of isolated settlements on Sardinia and Corsica, whereas the cosmographer (5.26–27) lists a total of thirty-three. Moreover, in the West generally he uses some contemporary place-names rather than earlier Roman equivalents,[18] and elsewhere there is reason to believe that he took over certain names directly from Greek sources.[19] He also covered regions beyond the scope of the Peutinger map, such as Arabia and Ethiopia.

Altogether it is evident that the cosmographer's work was only made possible by maps incorporating the level of detail that the Peutinger map offers, as well as by itineraries and other lists that both underlay such maps and were compiled from them. Whether the Peutinger map itself was among the cosmographer's sources at first or second hand must remain uncertain, and matters little. Far more significant is the realization that well before circa 700 there existed various maps – differing in scope and, no doubt, shape – of the same type.

(b) Beatus, *Commentary on the Apocalypse*

Similar engagement with such maps is evident in the commentary on the Apocalypse completed in the first instance in 776 by Beatus at the Benedictine monastery of Liébana in northern Spain; he issued a revised version later. A substantial number of illustrations form an integral part of this work,[20] and there can be no question that a map was always included among them in Book Two, where the prologue specifically refers to a *pictura* designed to illustrate the mission of the Apostles.[21] Because Beatus in effect merely assembled excerpts from previous writers on the Apocalypse, it is possible that he took over a map too, either from the commentator upon whom he relied most heavily, the late fourth-century Donatist theologian Tyconius, or one added to Tyconius' work later by a copyist. Equally, Beatus could have drawn his own map; in this event it is impressive that satisfactory source materials for the purpose were available at remote Liébana.

Uncertainty surrounds not just the Beatus map's ultimate authorship but also its appearance as it originally accompanied the commentary in 776. The long-standing argument over which of the fourteen maps that survive in the manuscripts is the most authentic has focused recently upon three.[22] Even the oldest of these postdates the completion of Beatus' commentary by a century and a half. It is in the manuscript probably produced at the monastery of Tábara in Léon for the monastery of San Miguel de Escalada around 940, now in the Pierpont Morgan Library, New York (M. 644); this map is rectangular in shape and contains ninety-six place-names.[23] The second possibly most authentic Beatus map – in a manuscript dated 1086, now in the cathedral of Burgo de Osma – is almost circular in shape, and has 120 place-names.[24] The third possibility – produced at the abbey of Saint-Sever in Gascony (southwestern France) around 1050, today in the Bibliothèque Nationale, Paris – is a notably larger map than the other two[25] and richer in names (270) than all other Beatus maps. However, before siding with those scholars who have been persuaded that this richness is decisive in rendering the Saint-Sever map closest to Beatus' original, it is as well to reflect that many of its names are relatively recent (fifty of them marked within an enlarged Gascony), and that no declaration of greater or lesser authenticity can escape recourse to subjective criteria. The fact is that we cannot be sure of even the shape or size of Beatus' original map.

Unmistakable nonetheless, as well as significant for present purposes, is the degree to which names and even several notices on the Saint-Sever map correspond to ones on the Peutinger map. The two notices *In his locis scorpiones nascvuntvr* and *In his locis elefanti nascvuntvr* appear on both maps in India, for example, not to mention elsewhere such names of minimal resonance in the medieval West as Megara and Mot(h)one.[26] To be sure, it remains possible that the notices were added to a forerunner of our surviving copy of the Peutinger map only after the mid-eleventh century rather than earlier; but the place-names that the Peutinger and Saint-Sever maps have in common again point to the latter having drawn upon the kinds of maps and records of names that the former represents.[27] The Saint-Sever map amply attests to the circulation and use of such material in a tradition that must extend back to the seventh century at least – as seen above with reference to the Ravenna cosmography – and in all likelihood earlier too. Continuation of the tradition is apparent in the lost map known only from the detailed treatise *Descriptio Mappe Mundi* written in Paris by Hugh of St-Victor around 1130–1140,[28] as well as in the surviving Hereford Cathedral Mappamundi produced around 1300.[29]

(c) A Version Sketched by Prisciani

Striking testimony to the existence of a map very similar to the Peutinger map, but not identical to it, derives from a sketch probably made in 1495. Gautier Dalché[30] first drew attention to its significance in 2003. This sketch is a map occupying a double spread (42.2 cm wide × 30 [$16\frac{1}{2}$ × $11\frac{3}{4}$ in.]) in the *Historiae Ferrarienses* (History of Ferrara) handwritten by a learned and cartographically aware humanist in the service of the Este family, Pellegrino Prisciani (c. 1435–1518; Plate 24). The sketch spans the Lower Po valley from Verona to Ravenna with a layout and multiple details that the Peutinger map's presentation matches. There are obvious differences too, however, in particular the marking of Forum Alieni, an obscure Roman town (somewhere northeast of Hostilia), which the Peutinger map omits.[31] Below his sketch, Prisciani notes that the *cosmographia quaddam antiquissima* from which he derived it was difficult to read, because its mix of Greek and Latin lettering had suffered from aging.

Prisciani further notes that he had seen this *cosmographia* (world map?) displayed on a wall of an *anticamera* (anteroom) in the bishop's residence at Padua (a city ruled by Venice). When he enquired about its origin, Taddeo Quirini[32] – Venetian nobleman and *archipresbyterus* (a minor position) of the cathedral at Padua – told him that, at the time of the Council of Basle, Venetian *oratores* (spokesmen?) had obtained the map as a gift through the authority and mediation of the pope; that later Jacopo Zeno,[33] bishop of Padua (from 1460), had it as a gift; and that he left it to the episcopal see on his death (in 1481).[34]

The reliability of Quirini's account is hard to gauge. The celebrated church council held at Basle only functioned meaningfully between February 1432 and (at the latest) July 1440. If the map had belonged to Zeno – who never went to Basle and was only twenty-two in 1440 – it may simply have become "his" along with the bishopric of Padua, and he in turn passed it on to his successor. The claim that it was originally acquired through the authority and mediation of the pope is unexpected, if the implication is that this occurred at the council; the proceedings were in fact notorious for the extreme hostility shown toward the papacy in the person of Pope Eugenius IV (a Venetian by origin, elected in 1431). The council even voted to suspend him in January 1438, and then to depose him in June 1439.[35] The Venetian Republic, however, supported the pope and repeatedly sent diplomatic delegations to lobby in their joint interest.[36] It remains credible, therefore, that the map was somehow brought back by such a delegation, even if perhaps not with papal help.

167

Conclusion: The
Map's Place in
Classical and
Medieval
Cartography

This said, note may be taken of a neglected coincidence – drawn to my attention by Martin Steinmann – concerning one Venetian who occupied a prominent position at the council for a period. Pietro Donato (born c. 1390) became bishop of Padua in 1428 and was subsequently commissioned by Eugenius IV to serve as cochairman of the council.[37] In this unenviable capacity he resided in Basle from October 1433 until May 1436. Nonetheless, the move afforded him – in common with others attending the council – opportunities to pursue his passion for scholarship and book collecting. This he did, not only in Basle itself, but also by visiting Reichenau[38] and traveling up the Rhine valley, as well as possibly even farther afield.[39] Of special note for present purposes is his initiative in borrowing a precious volume from the library at Speyer, which he then had copied in Basle. The copy still survives in the Bodleian Library, Oxford (the Speyer exemplar has been lost),[40] with Donato's autograph record:

Exemplata est hec cosmographia que Scoti dicitur cum picturis ex vetustis-simo codice quem habui ex Spirensi bibliotheca a. D. M.CCCC.XXXVI. mense Ianuario, dum ego Petrus Donatus, Dei pacientia episcopus Padu-anus, vice sanctissimi domini Eugenii pape IIII. generali Basiliensi concilio praesiderem.

This so-called *Cosmographia Scoti* has been copied with its illustrations from a most ancient volume that I obtained from the library at Speyer in the month of January of the year of our Lord 1436, while I, Petrus Donatus, by God's grace bishop of Padua, was presiding at the general council of Basle on behalf of his Holiness Pope Eugenius IV.

The majority of the volume's thirteen Latin works, ranging in date from Late Roman to Carolingian, may be broadly described as geographical, with content often comparable to that of the Peutinger map.[41] The volume is included in the inventory (not necessarily complete) that Donato compiled of his remarkable library near the end of his life, probably in 1445;[42] he died in 1447. There is no mention of any map in the inventory,[43] and of course still no further testimony as to how the map that Prisciani saw reached Padua, other than Quirini's account half a century or so after the

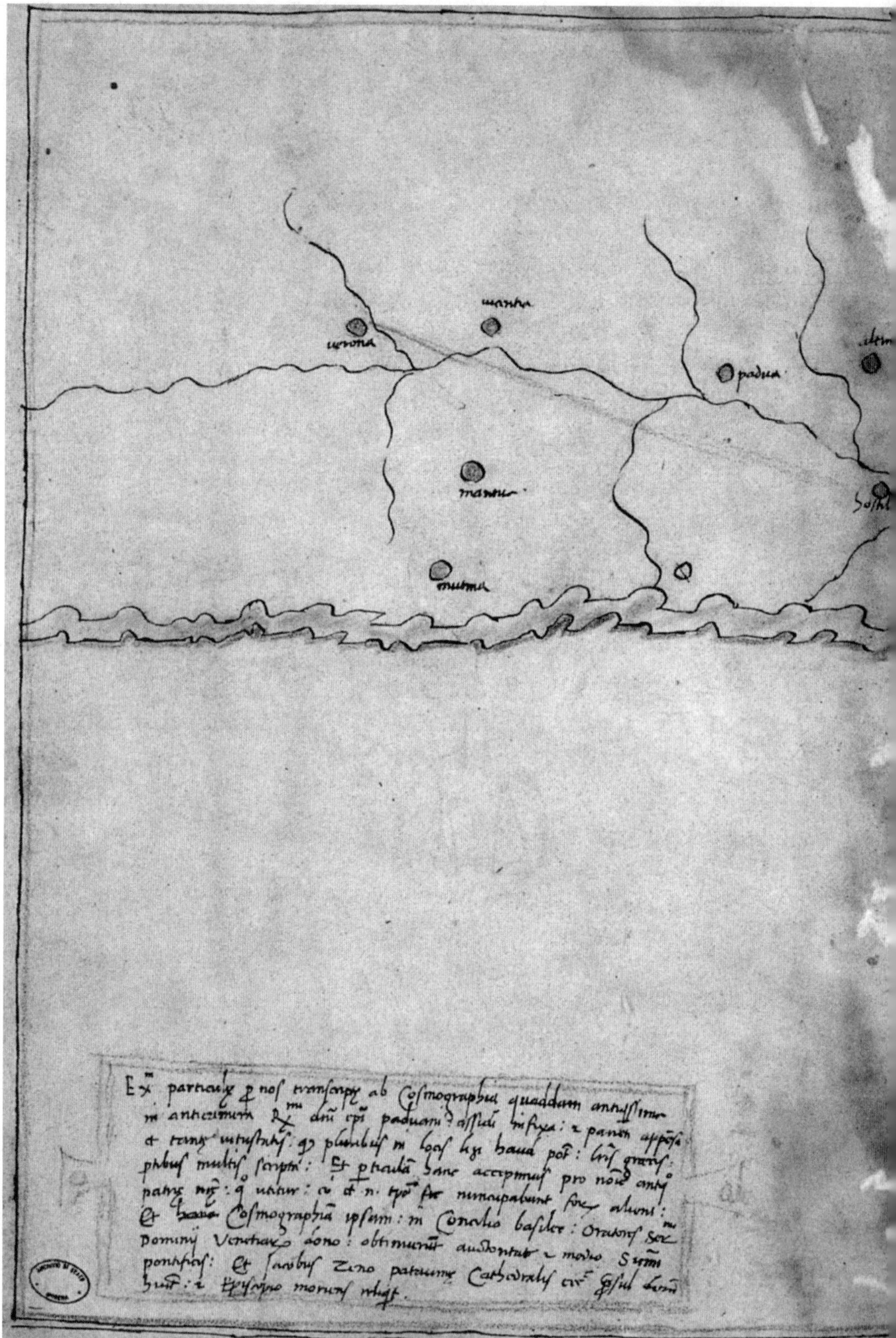

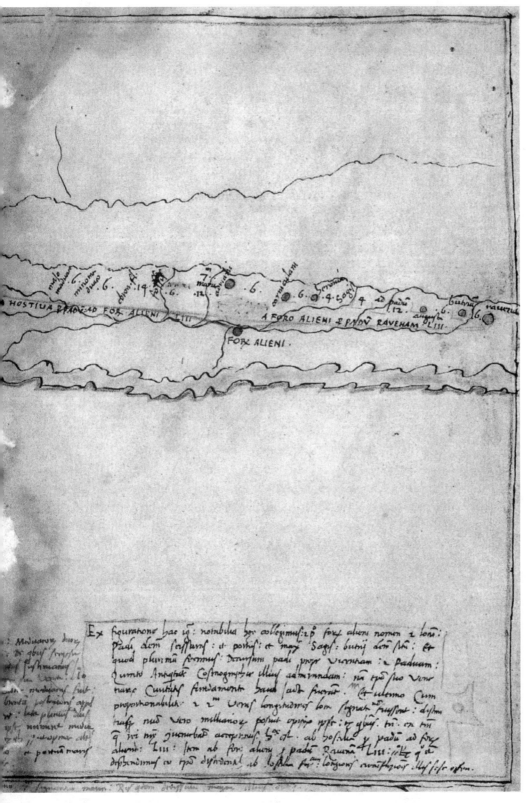

PLATE 24. Prisciani's sketch made at Padua, probably in 1495. Photo: Archivio di Stato, Modena. MS 129, f. 44v–45r.

Council of Basle. Even so, that Donato, the pope's cochairman, brought it back with him to Italy should at least be recognized as a uniquely attractive and fitting possibility.[44] At the same time it is important to remember that Donato's successors in Padua – Fantino Dandolo (bishop 1448–1459),[45] Zeno, Foscari, and Barozzi – were also all learned humanists and bibliophiles.

Prisciani's testimony aside, nothing further is known of the scope, prior history, or ultimate fate of the map that he saw and sketched; nor, it seems, can the *anticamera* where it was displayed be identified.[46] Above all, the precise nature of its relationship to our Peutinger map remains beyond recovery. Even so, the confirmation that at least one other map closely comparable in content and character survived through the late fifteenth century is a most revealing new insight. It is conceivable that Celtis became aware of this map in Padua, and that its supposed arrival there through Basle alerted him to be on the lookout in Germany for the exemplar from which it was copied, or another copy.[47] In the event, it was a variant version that he stumbled across. As to the exemplar of the map that reached Padua, there is no knowing where it had been located, and how long it survived.

(d) Misidentification in Trier

The prospect that another copy – either of the Peutinger map or of one closely comparable to it – was to be found in Trier arose from a claim attributed to a reputable scholar, Johann Wyttenbach, and published in 1835.[48] According to this unsigned newspaper report, the fragment of the map that Wyttenbach had discovered showed part of Spain, which only made his claim more tantalizing, given the absence of this region in our surviving copy. Wyttenbach himself is the only possible source for the report, but in all likelihood it was published prematurely, and he no doubt came to regret his identification as overly hasty. At least, no further word about it was ever forthcoming from him, and only after his death in 1848 did it emerge from an inspection of the fragment that it could not possibly be from the Peutinger map or from a variant of it (such as Prisciani saw).[49] Rather, it is a Ptolemaic map on a conic projection that was perhaps drawn around the mid-fifteenth century.

3. MEDIEVAL CARTOGRAPHY IN RELATION TO THE MAP

Because so many medieval maps, like their classical forerunners, are lost, conclusions formulated about the influence of the Peutinger map's original can be no more than tentative at best. Any sign of close imitation is lacking, but that is hardly a surprise given the map's extraordinary size and extreme shape. One medieval map, however, appears sufficiently comparable in

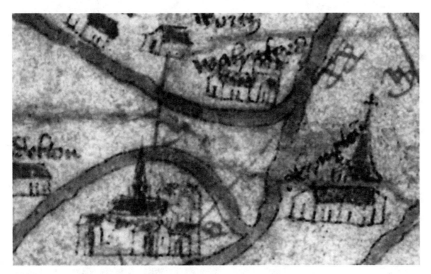

171

Conclusion: The
Map's Place in
Classical and
Medieval
Cartography

PLATE 25. Settlements, routes, and rivers on the Gough map (MS. Gough Gen. Top 16, detail, Oxfordshire). Photo: © Bodleian Library, University of Oxford.

design and presentation to invite speculation that its anonymous maker might have been influenced by an opportunity to inspect and ponder the Peutinger map, or a version of it. This so-called Gough map survives only as a copy made on vellum in the 1350s or 1360s,[50] but the lost original is reckoned to date to early in the reign of King Edward I of England (1272–1307). Measuring 55.3 cm tall by 116.4 (22 × 45 in.), the surviving copy represents Great Britain with a recognizable coastline at a scale of approximately 1:1,000,000 overall, although within the map the "scale" at which different regions are shown in fact varies considerably.

The character and quality of the Gough map make it a distinctive piece of creative cartography. It has no known contemporary counterpart, but does bear some striking resemblances to the Peutinger map in certain respects. The orientation is east, the color palette is similar, and there is the same preoccupation with rivers and islands (the latter mostly rendered without recognizable coastlines). The mapmaker was also very concerned to show settlements, and in many instances in England (but not Scotland) the distance from one to the next. Each settlement is marked by a red-roofed pictorial vignette of six or so different sizes. Distance figures are given in Latin numerals (without any unit of distance), and these figures are placed beside or across a straight red line that links two settlements without continuing through a vignette (Plate 25).[51] Meantime, in order to present such a mass of detail clearly, the mapmaker exercised obvious restraint in introducing such other features as regional names, special notices, mountains, forests, and animals; equally, a figure for the total distance between a pair of principal settlements is never noted. The only boundary line is Hadrian's Wall.

Clear differences remain to be sure; in particular, routes appear on the Gough map in a puzzlingly selective manner rather than comprehensively, as on the Peutinger map. Even so, there is good reason to regard it as uncannily similar to the Peutinger map in its general presentation (and it, too, was nailed up for display at some stage). Moreover, a familiar controversy has arisen about its purpose. To what degree, if at all, was it created to be a traveler's guide, an ongoing debate asks; or were deeper levels of political and cultural meaning intended? Altogether, it seems plausible, and by no means surprising, that a talented thirteenth-century mapmaker in Britain might somewhere have seen a version of the Peutinger map (perhaps even including more of Britain than our copy preserves), and that both the presentation and the goals of his own map were influenced by it.[52] So far as is known, however, his initiative remained exceptional; other maps of Britain comparable to the Gough map were not to be produced for another three centuries.

More broadly, there seems justifiable cause to claim that the Peutinger map and others like it were to achieve lasting influence in both their design and their content. They demonstrated not only how large maps could be designed to serve more forcefully than ever as compelling emblems of power, but also how such maps could present an extraordinary number of settlements to the viewer, relating them to one another meaningfully through a network of routes without any need for their coordinates to be known. It could have been such features as the central placement of Rome in the Peutinger map's frame, together with the drastic, selective reshaping of the world, which encouraged Late Antique and medieval mapmakers to devise further creative ways of giving their own work its intended impact. At the same time, the success of the Peutinger mapmaker's effort to assemble, organize, and present itinerary data aroused a lasting preoccupation with this previously neglected jumble of material. Hence, not just mapmakers, but also compilers of handbooks and other scholarly texts, became eager to acquire such data and to adapt it for their own purposes.

To imagine that *mappaemundi* have their origin in the Peutinger map would be too sweeping and simplistic,[53] but the map's radical cartography can be reckoned to have made a formative contribution that has not been appreciated to date. *Mappaemundi*, in turn, exploit both texts and images to convey Christian history and belief within a geographical framework that need be no more than schematic. Altogether, the Peutinger map can be seen to embody a pivotal transition from classical cartography to medieval – a creative advance in the former, a stimulus for the latter to develop its own distinctiveness. In short, the Peutinger map merits long overdue recognition as a work of lasting cartographic and cultural inspiration. It has always been much more than a mere route diagram.

LATIN TEXT APPENDED TO THE 1598 ENGRAVING OF THE MAP

SPECTATORI S.

TABVLAM damus, ex qua MARCVS VELSERVS Augustanae Reip. VII. Vir, perpauca olim quae tum comparebant schidia, magno eorum applausu vulgavit quibus interiores litterae serio cordi. Integram pollicitus, si autographum aliquando in manus venisset: latebat enim, et periisse erat suspicio. Audiit FORTVNA OBSEQVENS, Velserus voti damnatus est. Ad quem nuncium ABRAHAMVS ORTELIVS laetitia exiliens, quod per annos amplius viginti omnibus vestigiis frustra indagasset, sibi editionis provinciam depoposcit. Et vero aequum bonum visum tanto candidato reliquos petitores concedere; primus se Velserus facilem praebuit, fidem quam publico obstrinxerat curasse interpretatus, si per Ortelium solveret. Cum homo septuagenario maior, cui plus animi plusque in rem communem studij, quam vitae superfuit, operi ad finem decurrenti immoritur. Moriens – *non ille oblitus amorum*, Ioanni Moreto veteri amico testamento legat, qui perficiendo, pietatem quam defuncti iudicio debuit, praestitit.

Velserus de tabulae auctore, aetate, vsu, aliis, ad schedas praefatus est, quae nobis probantur. Addimus: Auctorem Christianum fuisse, id vero ex S. Petri nomine, et iis quae de Moise Israelitisque tradidit, intelligi. Magnitudinem tabulae, praeter Occidentis imperium tum aestimari non potuisse, nunc constare hoc amplius, complexam orbem vniversum, qua illo nimirum aeuo cognitus, inter HERCVLIS COLVMNAS & ALEXANDRI ARAS, ab extremo Occidente in Orientis vltima. Et apparere sane omnia, nisi quod initio Columnas versus, pauxilla quaedam Britanniae, Aquitaniae, Hispaniae, Africae exciderint. Circumcirca MARE ire, olim ATLANTICVM nomine. De Itinerariis tabulis, esse apud Vegetium lib. 3. c. 6. quae legi etiam mereantur, et cogitandum videri, an prouinciarum memoria, cuius P. Victor in Basilica Antoniniana regione circi Flaminij meminit, eo pertineat. De viarum stratura, apud Galenum esse Methodi lib. 9. c. 8.

Explicando, Velserum imitari erat animus, sed vastum sese et longum ostendit negotium, non vnius tantum hominis industriam exercere natum, neque protrahenda per eum colorem doctorum desideria.

Porro si haec quoque scire referat: Autographum latum est pedem Augustanum vnum circiter, longum vltra viginti duos: scalptori ad istam mensuram contrahere visum commodius. Litterae in eo charactere Langobardico, quem caelo difficulter efformes: scalptor Romanas reddidit. Cetera fidem coluit, sancte integre, vt in permultis, quantumuis certis testatisque erroribus corrigendis, sibi nunquam quidquam permiserit, ab exemplari sciens volens nusquam abiuerit. Nec scienti nec volenti, quin oculos ingeniumque maxime intendenti, id interdum vsu venire potuisse, neque ego dubito, neque quisquam cui hoc genus mediae aetatis scriptiones cognitae, in quibus litteras vi et pronunciatione diuersas omnino, figura plerumque non est internoscere. Tu vale bone Spectator boneque Lector, et fruere monumento, cui vtvt crebris naevis resperso, nihil par et nihil secundum ex antiquitate reliquum superest.

ENGLISH TRANSLATION OF
J. KASTELIC, "VODNIKOVA KOPIJA
TABULE PEUTINGERIANE"*

Translated by Gerald Stone

N.B.: Citation styles, etc. have been left as in the original article.

VODNIK'S COPY OF THE TABULA PEUTINGERIANA
Jože Kastelic

A particularly interesting item, kept in the Archaeological Department of the National Museum, is an 1809 copy of the Tabula Peutingeriana. The first available edition of the Tabula from the Vienna original was produced by F. C. Scheyb in Vienna in 1753. In 1809 the French military commissar Étienne Marie Siauve, a well-known archaeologist, who at that time perhaps was preparing *De antiquis Norici viis, urbibus et finibus epistola* (published Verona 1811), tried to get hold of Scheyb's edition from Zois.[1] Siauve gave a new impetus to Slovene archaeology, which at that time was represented by Vodnik; he trained Vodnik in epigraphy and numismatics, and acquainted him with the archaeology of ancient Emona. Zois sent the order for Scheyb's edition to Kopitar in Vienna, but in Vienna the famous book was out of print. Only with difficulty, and after a long search, Kopitar borrowed a copy from the Library of the Discalceate Carmelites, on condition that it was returned by New Year 1810, and he sent it to Ljubljana on October 10, 1809. At the same time he sent, in addition, a critical study of Scheyb's edition, a manuscript written in German by the Court Librarian, the ex-Jesuit Josef Benedikt Heyrenbach (1738–1779).[2] But Zois returned the book with Heyrenbach's essay only at the end of January 1810. By February 16, 1810 it had already been in Vienna for several days, having arrived there, owing to the journey and to rough handling, in such a condition that Kopitar in embarrassment gave the good father a tenner for a mass for a good cause.[3] So in the last months

* *Glasnik Muzejskega društva za Slovenijo* 23 (1942): 98–100.

of 1809 the Scheyb edition of the Tabula was lying in Ljubljana at the disposal of Siauve, Zois, and Vodnik.

Because Siauve knew no German, Vodnik translated Heyrenbach's essay into Latin, abbreviating it a little. On March 1, 1810 he wrote to Kopitar:[4] 'For Siauve and other non-Germans I have summarized into Latin Heyrenbach's rod, with which he beat Scheyb.' The manuscript of Vodnik's translation was found in September 1942 in the University Library. It was lying in Scheyb's edition, which later after all had come back to Ljubljana as a purchase probably soon after February 1810 and at all events before Zois's death in 1819. In an agent's catalog of Zois's library, dated March 30, 1823, it is mentioned under the addenda: '1 [copy]. Peutingeriana tabula itineraria, quae in Augusta bibliotheca Vindob. nunc asservatur. Vind. 1753. groß Fol. 16 [Guld]. 51 [Kreutz.]'; the book was cataloged by Čop with shelf-mark IV 10581. Vodnik's manuscript contains the Latin translation of the critical study in duplicate on twelve quarto leaves written on both sides. In the first version the text has been corrected slightly, then it has been written out carefully. The title of the manuscript is: 'Censura Tabulae Peutingerianae adservatae in Bibliotheca augusta Vindobonensi; auctore Josepho Heurenbach custode ejusdem Bibliothecae; latine brevius reddita opera Valentini Vodnik lectore publico Poëticae, Geographiae et Historiae in Lyceo Labacensi, in Carniolia Provincia Illyrici, anno 1809'. Having been found, the manuscript is now kept in the University Library in a collection of manuscripts.

More important in 1809, however, was another work. Vodnik writes in the same letter to Kopitar: 'I have copied out the entire Peutinger Table and two grammatists have colored it; now we have arranged it so that it is as similar to its old face as was possible.' It is this very copy by Vodnik of the Tabula that is now kept in the National Museum. It is 6.42 m long, that is, 40 cm shorter than the original. The difference is because the Ljubljana copy is torn off roughly at the boundary between the fourth and fifth Miller zone of the twelfth segment. The copy is 0.37 m wide, 3 cm wider, that is, than the original. The difference is due to the white base on which the map has been drawn afterwards in its true width of 0.34 m. The map is drawn on separate sheets of thin paper. The sheets are stuck together without regard to the length of the segments in either the original or Scheyb's edition. In addition, the map is firmly stuck onto thin white linen – Vodnik drew the map from Scheyb's plates, which are not colored. But because Scheyb in his plates uses hatching, as is the convention in sphragistics, and on page x gives instructions for the coloring, it was possible also to color the map, after it had been drawn. The greatest difference in color between the original and Vodnik's copy is in the roads, which in the original are red and in Scheyb designated as red, but in Vodnik's version are black. Vodnik only partly attempted to imitate the writing, generally he distinctly modernized the style of the letters. According to Vodnik's statement two 'grammatists' (i.e. pupils of the gymnasium) introduced the colors, and quite skilfully. Yet we cannot claim to see an approximation of style to the original in the pictures of buildings, mountains, flora, and particularly of the four figures of the main cities, despite a considerable artistic dexterity. On the other hand, in this respect even Scheyb himself is not exactly outstanding. In the first segment at the bottom Vodnik has written: *Descripta Lublanae mense Decembri 1809.* In 1815 Vodnik travelled to Vienna.[5] On that occasion in the Court Library he collated the original Tabula with Scheyb and his own copy, which he had brought with him from Ljubljana. He made corrections in pencil to his own copy. They relate, for example, to different divisions of the segments in the original and in Scheyb, inexact shades of color, but especially of course to badly recorded names. Vodnik carried out the work with the assistance of a certain Nemitz. In the twelfth segment he wrote at the bottom: *Nemitz et Vodnik contulerunt cum Orig[inali] 4 tum. 5. 6. 7. 9. 10. 12. [..] Octobris 1815.* Vodnik's work, however, was of importance not only for his own copy. Vodnik left in the Library for Kopitar a list of his comparisons, whence they were removed to Bratislava and then to Munich, where C. Mannert used them in his Leipzig edition of the Tabula in 1824. Mannert marked Vodnik's comparisons with an asterisk in the alphabetical list of places on pp. 45–63. Vodnik corrected Scheyb in 77 places. Where the manuscript is held I do not know. Probably the place to look for it would be the Munich Academy of Sciences.[6]

The question arises: where was the Tabula before it arrived in the National Museum and when did it arrive in the Museum? It is impossible to say whether before 1819 it was with Zois, with Vodnik, or in the Lyceum building. For a time it was stretched on a board or something similar, because vestiges of tacks can be seen on the top and bottom edges. It may have come into the Museum with the legacy of either Zois, or Vodnik, or on some other occasion. In the lists of Vodnik's legacy the Tabula is not mentioned, which means it did not come to the National Museum through Metelko's legacy or with Zupan's gifts.[7] At all events, A. Dimitz did not know it in 1859.[8] Nor did P. Hitzinger know anything about it in 1864.[9] But it certainly came into the Museum before 1903, because on the verso there is a note in Müllner's hand.

Vodnik's work on the Tabula is of importance for the history of Slovene cartography. Its cultural and historical significance is even greater. After Valvasor, Schönleben, and Dolničar it was Zois's circle which, with Linhart's book 'Versuch einer Geschichte von Krain und der übrigen südlichen Slaven Oesterreichs,' gave the first comprehensive and independent history of Slovenia's ancient times. Vodnik pursued his studies in the spirit of Linhart, and Siauve even gave him methodological impulses.[10] As in the spiritual world of German classicism, so in Zois's enlightening circle there prevails a view of a happy golden age of primitive man, when man, in close touch with nature, was a naive artist of life, just as nature itself is an artist. The theory of the golden age of antiquity among such latecomers as the Slovenes was bound to meet with a great response. Ancient times were a golden age. The older the nation, the closer it was to that age and so much the more were its original beauties able to contribute to the general development of humanity. In the face of the unique cultural maturity of Greece and Rome, which was beyond attainment and could only be admired, only one counter-value could be put forward – ancient cultural originality. That is the thought expressed by Vodnik in his 'Illyria Reborn', when he assessed the antiquity of the Illyrians and the Romans. The poem was a panegyric to the rationalistically conceived continuity of Slovene territory – it is the land that is important, not the people. His archaeological work too served the same purpose. Just as Kopitar was interested in the helmets of Negova because of the question of Hanka's manuscripts in the context of the Pannonian theory as to the source of Old Church Slavonic, so Vodnik too busied himself with archaeology mainly as a national historian and Slavist. It is interesting that Prešeren in his 'Elegy to my Countrymen' of 1832[11] is still an adherent of the rationalistically conceived cultural continuity of Slovene territory – in a note he even refers to Dolničar – but in 'The Baptism on the Savica' of 1836 like a true Romantic he is no longer concerned with autochthony and continuity but with the proper historical function of the Slovenes, which begins only with their arrival in the Christian, western, cultural sphere. In between lies the 'Wreath of Sonnets', love for Julia Primic, which triggered in Prešeren, along with new feelings, a new deepened view of life in its entirety. In the context of these two concepts of national history – the Classical and the Romantic – Vodnik's copy of the Peutinger Tabula occupies an interesting and significant place.

REFLECTIONS ON VODNIK'S COPY
OF VON SCHEYB'S ENGRAVING

The copy of von Scheyb's engraving of the Peutinger map that Valentin Vodnik and two unnamed pupils drew and colored during the winter of 1809–10 has been part of the National Museum's collection in Ljubljana since the late nineteenth century (see Plate 8). The copy is attached to a wooden roller and kept in a sturdy cylindrical carton. It remains complete but for the final 14–18 cm ($5\frac{1}{2}$–7 in.), which have been torn off and lost.[1] The map is drawn on fifteen thin sheets of paper laid side by side with minimal overlap and then backed with linen; adhesion of the paper to the linen has led to some slight creasing. The first two sheets are each 37.5 cm ($14\frac{3}{4}$ in.) tall, the remainder 38 cm (15 in.); each sheet is 46 cm (18 in.) wide. Because von Scheyb's twelve plates are each wider than this, and the eleven parchments wider still, Vodnik marks the breaks between both in pencilled figures at top and bottom; he records likewise von Scheyb's six internal divisions of each plate (letters A–F). Also along the top and bottom margins holes occur at irregular intervals, suggesting either that the map was pinned up for display at some stage, or that by this means tracing paper had been held in place from which line work and lettering were inscribed on the paper of the copy. It is equally possible that the holes served both purposes. At any rate, the paper of the copy itself is not transparent, so it seems unlikely that von Scheyb's line work and lettering were transferred to it direct.

It would appear that the first two sheets served an experimental function, and that a set of practices incorporating adjustments was then determined and observed thereafter. In particular, the initial intention was evidently to leave the copy uncolored, like the engraving itself, while painstakingly reproducing most of von Scheyb's indicators of color (by stippling, braiding, etc.). Most notably, all the route line work on these two sheets is black. Thereafter, however, this line work is drawn in red, and von Scheyb's indicators of color are omitted; instead, the features are actually colored. Presumably it had come to seem no more laborious to proceed in this way than to reproduce the indicators of color, and certainly the result is more distinctive.

Two different hands seem to have been responsible for drawing and coloring alternate sheets or pairs of them. They share some characteristics, such as the addition of upper-window slits to symbols (reminiscent of those added in the 1598 engraving);[2] these slits are even added along the roof of the Ad Dianam symbol (2C1), and its front and rear gables are – uniquely – surmounted by a cross. The two hands can be distinguished, however, by the first one's use of a thicker nib for lettering, and very notably by its addition of stippling below most symbols, creating the impression that the place is situated on a mound. The second hand, by contrast, never adds this stippling. In consequence, the Aqv(a)e Popvlani(a)e symbol (3B2), which happens to straddle the third and fourth sheets, lacks the stippling bottom left, but has it bottom right.

Open water and river courses are consistently colored in light brown. From the third sheet onward, as already mentioned, route line work is red and actually drawn in that color; there is no black line to which a red underlay is added, as in the reproduction of von Scheyb's engraving published by Katancsich.[3] For some red display capitals, both hands drew a framework in black and then colored it in with red; for others, by contrast, they drew the entire letter just in red. Brown (both light and dark) was frequently used for mountain ranges, as was pale gold. In other instances, however, the two hands seemed not to have coordinated their color choices. The first hand liked blue (both light and dark) sufficiently to use it for the SILVA VOSAGVS (2A2) and some mountain ranges; but the second hand rendered the SILVA MARCIANA (2A5) in light-brown. In general, the first hand used color more freely and flamboyantly than the second.

The symbol for Antioch is rendered with special care, those for Rome and Constantinople less so. Nowhere was an attempt made to reproduce the style of lettering in von Scheyb's engraving; rather, names are written in a regular early nineteenth-century style. In addition, both hands appear not to have made erasures. Instead, a slip was either adjusted or left abandoned but still visible: observe in this connection the rendering of the stretch that links Thisdro Col. with Svllecti (5C3).

It remains a puzzle that the two hands (that is, the two pupils?), while observing uniformity of presentation in many respects, declined to reconcile their practice in others, and that they were evidently permitted to maintain several conspicuous differences across the entire map.

VODNIK'S LATIN SUMMARY
OF HEYRENBACH'S ESSAY

(NATIONAL LIBRARY OF SLOVENIA, LJUBLJANA, MS 1443)

Vodnik wrote out his Latin summary of Heyrenbach's German twice on both sides of three pairs of pages (approx. size 19 cm wide × 23 [$7\frac{1}{2}$ × 9 in.]), that is, covering a total of twelve sides. For the version followed here (Plate 9), the sheets have narrow margins at lefthand and right; the other version likewise has a narrow lefthand margin, but a wider one to the right. The lettering of this other version is rather less florid.

It is hard to be sure which version Vodnik wrote first, and the minimal degree of difference between the two renders the question unimportant. There are some minor variations in punctuation. In both versions, plenty of small slips have been corrected. Occasionally an apparent slip remains in one version but has been corrected in the other; in the handful of such instances where the version I follow is faulty, I have taken over the correction.

Where the ms. underlines once, I italicize; where it underlines twice, I add an underline to my italic.

Censura

Tabulae Peutingerianae adservatae in Bibliotheca augusta Vindobonensi; auctore Josepho Heurenbach custode ejusdem Bibliothecae; latine brevius reddita opera Valentini Vodnik lectore publico Poëticae, Geographiae et Historiae, in Lyceo Labacensi, in Carniolia Provincia Illyrici, anno 1809.

Heurenbach succincte redditus e Germanico, ita de hac tabula judicat:

Veritatis amore ductus de Tabula Peutingeriana dicam, quod sentio. – Primo hujus tabulae intuitu quisque aequus rerum aestimator facile videt, ipsam aevo Imperatorum Suevicorum scriptam fuisse, tantumque a temporibus Theodosii, quod quidam persuadere conantur, abesse, ut nongentis circiter annis serius sit exarata. – Quodsi vero opus ipsum adtentius contemplor, tria in illo mihi videor detegere. Primo tabulam esse

apographon antiquioris autographi; tum additamenta ei inesse aevo autographi juniora; tertio demum, adjunctas fuisse accessiones bene meditatae
imposturae, quibus multo antiquioris aetatis sucum apographus operi suo,
quam par erat, allinere studuit. – Omnibus autem adcurate consideratis
patebit, hanc tabulam non esse primum apographon originarii autographi,
sed apographon alterius alicujus apographi sequioris, adeo, ut Tabula nostra *decimo tertio* aërae nostrae seculo sit adcensenda. *Haec sunt, quae spatio
temporis angusti ad scribendum coarctatus, paucis expediam,* pauca dein observaturus.

[page 2]

Tabula Peutingeriana est apographon antiqui autographi

Quum enim scriptor hujus Tabulae sit sequioris aevi, haud credi potest,
hominem adeo rudis seculi, nomina Romana tam concinnato ordine
digessisse, uti ipsum fecisse videmus, nisi antiquum quodpiam exemplar
prae oculis habuisset. Etsi quidem concederemus, atque diceremus, eum ex
Geographis, Historicis aliisque ejusmodi adminiculis rem totam conjectura
aliqua adsequutum esse, unde quaeso distantias locorum adeo justas, uti
re ipsa sunt, hausisset? – Quin quod Martyrologi et Geographi sequioris,
seu medii aevi vix nomina locorum noverunt. – Sed neque Martyrologia
nostra hodierna, etsi jam exactiora, huic operae conficiendae sufficiunt,
quanto ergo minus sufficere poterant Martirologia Adonis et Bedae, quae
sola medio aevo praesto fuerant, et nota. Neque acta conciliorum, aut historia ecclesiastica, nec tabulae episcopatuum adeo erant, exactae, uti nunc
sunt. Peutingeriana vero tabula nuspiam continet lacunam, verum ubique
continua est, et aeque dives locorum. Neutiquam ergo fructus fragmen-
tarii studii dici unquam poterit. Nam topographia ubique sibi constat; est
itaque opus, quod jussu et instituto imperationis cujuspiam, mensuras per
universum imperium Romanum fieri curantis, fuit confectum. – Quis,
amabo stationes, et distantias nominaque Romana locorum, insularum,
urbium et ceterarum fere minatiarum tempore illo sequiori migrationis
barbarorum, aut serius medio aevo tam adcurate novisset, etquidem tum,
quum pleraque loca Asiae interioris et Africae in tenebris latuerunt? –
Itaque autographum nostri apographi nequivit esse serius temporibus
Theodosii, seu anno aerae nostrae 393.

[page 3]

Tabula nostra exhibet additamenta juniora

Dea Roma/: ΘΕΑ ΡΩΜΗ: non est eadem pictura reddita, qua in antiquis
numismatibus; deest laurus, deest corona radiata, deest etiam diadema
Theodosianum duplici serie Margaritarum comam prementium. Adest
vero corona Barbara seculi XIII et XIV, adest umbo, sed non Romanus;
verum lapidi molendinario similior. Quum descriptor noster umbonem

non noverit, quo Ottones Saxonici in sigillis usi sunt, profecto serior Ottonibus vixit, et ruditer ea, quorum nullam habuit notitiam, in apographo suo depinxit. Pulvinar certe, throno impositum, Barbaries mera est, quae in sigillis XII et XIII seculi exhiberi coepta est. – Architectura urbium antiquior quidem, quam Gothica est, attamen junior multo, quam Romana. Tectorum forma, et portae angulares vix aevum XI seculi adsequuntur. Non desunt item argumenta, quod solaria fuerint usitata aevo Carolingorum. Throni urbium medium aevum sapiunt. – Donativa in monetis romanis plane alias nobis exhibent sellas, seu sedes, Romanorum. – Adde nomina coloris multo posterioris, qualia sunt, Tibori, ad Ioglandem, Garonna, hii montes etc. – /: *in transenna memineris*, penes Romam, legere: *via Triumphalis, loco: viatrium talis*: / Magnitudo Ravennae, quam turres indicant, et muri, signat tempora posteriora seu tempora Exarcharum, ante quos haec urbs numquam splenduit.

*Adjunctae sunt accessiones meditatae imposturae majorem antiquitatis sucum
Tabulae huic adlinientis*
De Hierosolymis apographus Tabulae haec ait: "Antea dicta Herusalem, modo Helya Capitolina." – Latet hic fraus. – Quid haec adnotatio ad mappam militarem faciat, quaerere supervacaneum arbitror; id solum quaero: estne isthaec nota loco suo facta, quantum chronologiam adtinet? . . . Haud quaquam. . . . Hierusalem enim retinuit nomen suum usque ad annum Chr: 134. Ad hunc annum vero Zonaras in vita Hadriani scribit: *"Urbem in*

[page 4]

Palaestina pro eversis Hierosolymis conditam Aeliam Capitolinam nominavit, et quo in loco DEI *templum olim fuerat, eo in loco post Iovis lucum condidit."* Novum istud nomen haud diuturno tempore urbs retinuit, paucis enim annis post mortem Imperatoris idololatris aeque ac Christianis iterum Hierusalem vocabatur. Quomodo nomen Aeliae Capitolinae congruit cum cetero statu occidentis? Eodem nimirum tempore Ravenna magnificentia exarchali praecelluisset? Franzi et Galli supra Lutetiam Parisiorum sedissent? Divi Petri templum extra Romae muros stetisset? Integer adhuc mundus idolorum cultui deditus, simulque res illae, quae dominante Christianismo serius vigebant, jam pridem obtinuissent? Iovis templo et luco integro licuisset, in mappa iussu 'imperatoris confecta, verba sequentia inserere: *"Desertum, ubi 40 annis erraverunt filii Israel ducente Moyse?"* – Quis itaque prohibebit dubitare, an non apographus noster, quum Hierusalem modo, id est aevo suo, Aeliam vocari dixisset, posteris imponere voluerit, ut crederent, opus suum multo antiquius esse, quam re ipsa sit?

Diximus hactenus, quid Tabula Peutingeriana non sit, dicamus jam, quid ipsa forsitan sit. – Scaliger autumat, eam esse opus cujuspiam Christicolae. – Esto! Quid hoc? – Alii Critici autumarunt, eam esse eandem ipsam, de qua Annalium Scriptor Colmariensis/: apud Ursticium Tomo I. p. 2 ad ann: Chri: 126/ meminit hisce verbis. *"Anno MCCLXV mappam mundi descripsi in pelles duodecim pergameni."* Quibus verbis innixus, editor Tabulae Peutingerianae, Dominus de Scheyb, ita enuntiat: *"Quasi lata sic esset sententia et auctorem et aetatem Authentici nostri Peutingeriani in hisce vocabulis latere. Non nego quidem pellibus conglutinatis quoque constare Tabulam Peutingerianam, quum tamen haec in fasciae longissimae, illa vero mappae fortassis quadratae formam*

[page 5]

concinnatae fuerint, praeterquam, quod Augusta hac tabula nostra undecim fere aequalibus et integris pellibus conglutinatis nullibi deficiente termino vel limbo compacta sit, uti ex consilio destinato ad explorandam hujus rei veritatem eas diligenter inspexi et observavi, idcirco necessaria consequutione concludo mappam illam Colmariensis Anonymi a nostra Peutingeriana infinitis parasangis distare ac distingui."

Commentator itaque fatetur, hanc mappam cum Colmariensi convenire in eo, quod ambae pellibus conglutinatis constent; intercedere vero inter eas hoc solum discrimen, quod Colmariensis duodecim, Peutingeriana vero undecim pellibus constet: deinde quod illa fortasse quadratae sit formae, haec vero voluminis. – *Fortasse?* quid hoc? num hae minutiae infinitae sunt parasangae? Qui scis Colmariensem fuisse formae quadratae? – Iam vero Colmariensis duodecim constabat pellibus, nostra vero undecim: quid ad haec respondebimus? Nil aliud, quam quod nostra non sit integra, et quod forsitan pellis una desit, quae Colmariensi non deerat. – At editor noster ait, "Vindobonensi nil *deesse* etc: *nullibi dificiente – limbo.*" Sane res se habet infinitis parasangis aliter, quam Scheyb dixit, nam evidens est, nostrae pellem deesse unam, etquidem Hispaniae Romanae, Lusitaniae, atque potioris partis Britaniae, Hadriani temporis notissimae, et jam dudum confectae provinciae Romanae, viis stratis haud carentis. Dices forsitan: consilio omissas! Non omissas, dicam, sed pellem amissam. Vide, amabo, segmentum primum! Lineae, fluvii et nomina ad partem occidentalem non sunt integra, sed anteriora quaepiam desiderantur. *Icampenses* putat, errans editor, novum esse, et hactenus eidem incognitum populum. Si hoc valeat, habebimus item *Aquitaniae* loco novam provinciam *Itaniam.* Ergo nostrae deest pellis et quidem una: nostraque totidem constitit pel

[page 6]

libus, quot Colmariensis. Estne igitur nostra eadem cum Colmariensi? Non ausim adfirmare, quum et apographon ejus esse queat. Siquidem errores descriptoris consideramus non restat nobis dubium, hunc fuisse hominem rudem, etquidem adeo, ut ejus aberrationes nequaquam auctori queant imputari. Errores 12 et 13 seculi, et discrimen inter literas H et N in eo erant posita, quod N ab H nil differet, nisi quod N cauda deorsum descendente ab H distinguebatur. Si itaque I-J loco H invenio, id est N loco H, facile vel modicum latinae linguae gnarus conjicies, descriptorem nostrum non fuisse auctorem Tabulae. Ut hoc animadvertas, vide Segm. VIII. D. *Hic lacus Tritonum. Hij montes subjacent paludi simili meotidi perquem nilus transit.* Viden H loco N? – Ibidem (: litera E:) exemplo sit descriptio, in qua hariolo tibi opus sit, ut dijudices, an *in* sit, an *nc*, aut *nt*, aut *m*, quod quidem *m* re ipsa est. Sic item *ad Scrofulas* fere *ad Scroficlas* facile leges, et *Bolodurum* facile *Bolodunum*; sic *Evandria* facile *Evathia* tibi legetur. Saepe descriptor signum obbreviationis transcurrit, ceu *Augusta Viromaduorum* loco *Viromanduorum* /: Mad: Mād/: Loco *Stanaco* invenis *Stailuco*; *vapineum* loco *vapincum*; jam *Ritumagus*, mox supra *Ratumagus*, loco *Rotomagus*; *Nudionum* loco *Noviomum*. Ob interjeta flumina haud bene legit descriptor nominum, fluminis cursu, discretas literas; *exemplum* habes in vocibus *Viatrium Talis*, loco Via Triumphalis; saepe vero voces discretas ob nimiam vicinitatem literarum in unam vocem conjunxit, ceu *Colcisindor/*, quod est: *colchis Indorum*, vel *Colchis Indica:* Quid quod loco *Ponte Scaldis* scripserit *Pontes Caldis?* et *Persepoliscon*, loco: Persepolisconmercium Persarum; ubi infra linea secunda addidit: *mercium Persarum;* loco *aequofalisco* vel *aequi falisci*, scribit: *aequo falsico*; et alibi mixtim invenimus confusas voces: *ad Speluncas Scinaloas XIII judeorum augusti.* – Verum et editorem nostrum insuper audiamus, qui inter cete

[page 7]

ra haec scribit: "*Non obscura divinatione conjectandum esse puto, quod auctor tabulae nomina gentium trans Rhenum, et trans Danubium, non vero situs et habitationes illorum noverit, adeoque earundem denominationes consulto, et dedita opera perturbato characterum, et literarum ordine, quasi calamo rerum ignaro in tabula conjecerit. Siquidem id luculente patet ex initio primi segmenti ad ostia Rheni, ubi varii populi hoc modo designantur* HACI, VAPLI VARII, CRHPSTINI, CHAMAVI, QUIEL, PRANCI *et circa Vindobonam ad Danubium ex vocibus* QUADI, *et* IUIVCI, *quas hoc modo scribit: Qi Vu Ac Dv IGI.*" – Si haec sententia valeret, neque nostri hodierni Geographi scirent, ubi sint Germania, Stiria et Carinthia; in nostris enim modernis mappis itidem haec nomina eodem fere modo invicem intermista sunt, sicut in Peutingeriana, e. gr: Quadi et Jutugi. Certe quidem distinctio illorum supra dictorum nominum erronea et portentosa est, verum non calliditati auctoris, sed ignorantiae descriptoris est tribuenda. Nonne commentator noster ipse fatetur, *quod nomina Chamavi quiel pranci, potius Chamavi, qui et Franci legenda sint? Procul dubio namque descriptor l* loco *t* et *p* loco *f* legit. Haec et alia plurima sphalmata commonstrant, tabulam nostram non autographon, sed apographon esse. Quaeritur solum, an ipsa haec tabula tam juvenis sit, ut apographon Colmariensis illius, quae anno Chr: 1265 conscripta fuit, jure dici posset. Solutio hujus quaestionis nullinde, nisi ex modo literas exarandi peti posse videtur. Commentator quidem in hac disquisitione exceptionem a foro quaeritat; ait enim: "*Superesset in praesentia veteris examen*

scripturae, formarum scilicet, quibus characteres vocabulorum in his nostris membra-
nis Peutingerianis

[page 8]

expressi conspiciuntur. Verum quemadmodum calami perpetuo mutantur, tantaque est manuum sensuumque varietas, quanta hominum /: ut Baringius ex Bartholino sapienter opinatur /: quare quilibet suo genio litat, suo modo docet, et scribit, ita certe, si temporum regionumque ratio habeatur, non facile in controversiam revocabitur, quod eadem regio varios characterum ductus semper produxerit." Ego vero supervacaneum esse arbitror, nos probare debere, quod characteres variarum aetatum distingui facile queant. Antiquitatum scrutatoribus istud non est ignotum; tales itaque haud difficulter dignoscent, an Tabula Peutingeriana fructus IV an XIII seculi sit. Commentator :/ Scheyb :/ vero omnem viam id distinguendi praecludere velle videtur; quaerit enim: *"quid si dicam, quod hae membranae penicillo, qui ex natura sua formas longe alias, quam calamus eadem quoque manu ductus efformat, quin immo a variis pictoribus, et scribis, sint exaratae et adumbratae?"* Respondeo, eum falli. Libeat inspicere tabulam ipsam! Flumina et aliae picturae fors penicillo sunt adumbratae, literae vero omnes calamo sunt exaratae, non pictae. Quod vero variae manus rem elaboraverint, non est veritati consentaneum; commentator id quidem nunquam demostrare poterit, quamquam theoriam literarum statuere conetur, quum ait: *"verumtamen si tabulam, cum quibuslibet seculi IV aut V scriptionibus comparemus, etiam ex eo nihil contra illius antiquitatem adstrui posse existimo, siquidem i sine puncto, s longum, m lunatum, x caudatum, um obbreviatum inveniemus."* At exstat in Roma subteranea inscriptio duas literas *i* cum punctis exhibens. Est quidem haec punctatio antiquis insolita; sed simul quaero: cur in commentatoris

[page 9]

nostri delineatione virgula supra *i*, fere ubique in Tabula adhibita plerumque ommissa fuit? – *s* longum quidem Tabulam argueret esse valde antiquam, sed, ut id valeat, oportet, ut in minuta scriptura omnia *s* longa essent: rotunda vero et longa mistim adhibita sunt, certissimum indicum discriminis inter XII et XIII seculum; itaquidem, ut quo plures rotundae literae sunt immixtae, tanto evidentius scriptura in XIII seculum sit rejicienda. An *m* lunatum tempore Theodosii obtinuerit, non disquiram; noverit solummodo commentator in nostra tabula nulla *m* lunata reperiri, sed partim intorta partim annularia. *x* quidem caudatum, sed variarum figurarum. Figura caudati *x*, quae in Tabula exstat, adscribenda est seculo XII vel XIIItio. In *um* obbreviato est adtendendum, quomodo facta sit obbreviatio. Timuit hac in re commentator multum immorari, quaerens potius viam, qua objectionibus diplomaticis effugeret; post quae tandem effatur: *"quidquid porro aequi rerum diplomaticarum aestimatores statuant, ego certe ausim heic adferre meam opinionem, quod nimirum perspectis argumentis in Cap: II allatis Scriptura tabulae nostrae itinerariae non ex M.SS. codicibus, quorum vix ullus ex primis aerae nostrae seculis uspiam deprehenditur, verum ipsimet codices M.SS., sitam vetusti ullibi reperirentur, ex ipsa nostra Theodosiana tabula sint dijudicandi.*" O bellum exemplar egregiae artis criticae! Tabulae Peutingerianae judicis partes tribuuntur, adeoque nulli subest ipsa disquisitioni. Parum quidem abest, quin tribunal conscendisset; nam pronum nobis est videre, argumentum commentatoris eo tendere, ut adserat: *demonstrandum quidem esset tabulam esse opus aevi Theodosiani, demonstro tamen; eam esse opus ejus aevi, quia ipsa opus est ejusdem aevi.* Jam videamus quid prosint argumenta – Cap. II. Adlata! Concedamus ea valere, nil tamen aliud inde sequetur,

[page 10]

quam autographon Theodosiani esse seculi; an vero haec tabula sit istud idem autographon, an ejus apographon; an hoc apographon itidem Theodosiano aevo sit confectum, an alio, semper erit quaestio, quam sola theoria literarum dirimere poterit. Diremta hac quaestione alios codices dubios ad hoc exemplar exigemus. At dicis: non exstant tam antiqua exemplaria, ad quae scriptura Tabulae nostrae exigi posset. Ajo, hanc curam me suscipere. Quo anno? anno Chr: 393 dicis. Quae ratio scribendi literas hoc aevo fuit? Dicam: unciales literae, et minusculae currentes fingebantur. – Anno 393 ais? Ergo scripturae ratio inter epitaphium Gaudentiae, et interdiplomata Ravennatica est reponenda. Quod si ita est, commentator rem est orsus, cui nunquam operam prius navaverat. Figura literarum, quae in nostra tabula reperiuntur, sunt inter alias hae: [six characters are illustrated (see Plate 9), with equivalents noted: *in, ih, ac, et, uu, us*]. Observa hic commentatorem figuras *in* et *ih* plane non novisse. Urbs Interamnium hac obbreviatione scripta est; verum nomen ei erat cetera notum, hanc ob rem indici suo id nomen inseruit, citavit illud tamen ad literam N. Alibi, credens I in Tabula esse deletum, nobis illud I signo deletionis adposito ante *n* adposuit. – IH, aut Hi ei eosdem peperit manes; legit enim Herusalem loco Hierusalem vel Therusalem; figuram alio loco eandem N esse credidit; hoc pacto loco Hiericho legit Nericho. Omnes istas figuras infinitis locis seculi XIII visere licet. Ante tempora Caroli Magni eas ego nuspiam vidi, neque puto me unquam visurum; primo quidem, quia adversantur formae singularum literarum illius aevi; tum quia non respondent rationi illo aevo usitatarum figurarum, quia illis temporibus literae inviam innectebantur ita, ut ultima pars literae

[page 11]

prioris efficeret initium sequentis. Hoc idem reperire fas est in epitaphio Gaudentiae, id est sexaginta annis ante praetextos natales nostrae Tabulae.

Hoc idem reperies in diplomate Ravennati et Longobardico. In figuris *ih* et *in* plane litera posterior intexta est priori, ita ut, nisi rem diplomatariam calleas, et aliis notis non commonearis, facile illas figuras unicam esse literam credas. Figura *in* commentatorem induxit, ut diceret, etiam Graecas inesse literas Tabulae nostrae; nam ubi NSVLA scriptum est, legit ipse ΝΗΣΟΣ, et quidem obbreviatum. De figura ξ novimus ex testamento Julii Caesaris, eam ad haec tempora non pertinere. Siglae 7 vix exemplum ante XI seculum reperire licebit. Hisce enim diebus scriptor diligens Walther edidit primarias substantiales formas characterum, unde subsequis temporibus tot variae formae enatae sunt. Sigla *UU* Tabulam nostram penitus in XIV seculum cogeret; animadverti tamen, eam ibi adparere, ubi *u*, priori *u* subjunctum, litera vocalis est; quo loco istud teutonicum W novissimo aevo notum fuit, vixque seculo XIII tribui poterit tempus ejus natale. Figura *9* hodiedum usitata, est antiqua; non adsequitur tamen aevum Theodosii, necque ei congruit. Argumento sit, quod in Codice Hilariano et in Livio Augustae Bibliothecae Vindobonesis illo demum seculo primum haec sigla comparet, quae hoc modo 4 efficta est. Tantum abest, ut sigla *9* sit antiquior, quam sigla 4, unde illa ortum duxit.

Dubitamus tandem, utrum Tabula nostra encomiis digna sit, quae ipsi Cap. IV tribuuntur. In hac editione omnes errores correcti fuisse dicuntur; at forsitan novi fuerunt commissi. Jam ideo timere licet, quod commentator scriptu

[page 12]

ram penitus non noverit; quod medio aevo usitatissimum z sit ipsi ignotum :/ Fol: I Index:/ quod esse putat aut Hispanicum, Anglicum et Orientale Th, aut italum ch, aut Anglicum Sh, Dz vel zh. Maxime triste vero est, quod quum discrimen inter *h* et *z* non noverit, eorum nullum item fecerit discrimen atque *h* loco *z* posuerit. Quae hinc etymologis nascuntur difficultates, facile quisque conjicit. Id quod de sigla *z* certe scimus, est, quod nomina ipsam continentia non sint Romana, sed Barbara. Quum vero in editione Tabulae nostrae, haec sigla male sit tractata, nil aliud restat, nisi, ut editor nomina, quae *h* vel *z* continent, denuo ad exemplar suum exigat, et in lucem edat; atque malo, cui auctor fuerat, ipse medeatur.

MILLER'S RECONSTRUCTION OF THE MAP'S WESTERN END[1]

In 1887 Konrad Miller published his book *Die Weltkarte des Castorius genannt die Peutingersche Tafel*, following it the next year with a lithograph of the map *Die Peutingersche Tafel*, a single piece in color at approximately two-thirds of the original map's size. Miller next devoted his efforts to medieval *mappaemundi*, issuing facsimiles (with transcriptions and comments) that appeared in five fascicles during 1895 and 1896. A sixth and final fascicle followed in 1898, in which he boldly reconstructed Roman maps or worldviews of the first to seventh centuries A.D. Among these is what he terms "Das 1. Segment der Tabula Peutingeriana (Castori)," the lost western end of the Peutinger map (Plate 16 above). The dimensions (40 cm wide × 22 [$15\frac{3}{4} \times 8\frac{3}{4}$ in.]) of this reconstruction were intended to match the format of *Die Peutingersche Tafel*, although – for whatever reason – its color palette (blue, light-brown, black) did not.

Miller undertook the reconstruction with his customary energy and self-confidence, believing that it presented "keine grossen Schwierigkeiten" ("no great difficulties").[2] In some respects his optimistic assessment was justified. For the principal regions missing – Britain, North Africa, Spain – ample data were readily available from such varied sources as the Antonine Itinerary, the Ravenna Cosmographer, and Roman milestones, and he exploited all these with skill. This aspect of his reconstruction is set aside here. Rather, the focus is upon his flawed regard for the map's design and presentation.

If Rome belongs at the center of the map,[3] then at the western end it is essential to restore more than the single parchment segment claimed by Miller. A single segment would in any case seem to offer too little space for accommodating the western end of the Mediterranean at a scale at all comparable to what is found on the surviving Segment 1. Consider [AQV]ITANIA (1B1–1B5), the sole regional name in display capitals continuing into that segment from the left. If Miller's reconstruction of its first three letters were enlarged to full size, his AQV would stand approximately

3.375 cm ($1\frac{1}{3}$ in.) from one another (and likewise this **V** from the first surviving letter, **I**). In fact, however, no two adjacent letters in the surviving part of the name stand less than approximately 5 cm (2 in.) apart, and the two most widely separated (NI) stand 14 cm ($5\frac{1}{2}$ in.) apart. Undeniably there is variation here, therefore, but the mapmaker's typical practice in placing the lettering of such names[4] confirms that AQV are most unlikely to have been bunched as close together as Miller's reconstruction requires. Instead, these three letters would have stood at least twice as far apart, and quite probably farther still; thus the name they begin would extend back deeper into the missing western end than Miller allows. In the same way, BRITANNIA – a regional name reasonably imagined by Miller, although not even its final letter is preserved in the part of England that survives – is likely to have spanned a much greater width than his reconstruction can accommodate.

There were, to be sure, major challenges for the mapmaker to overcome in manipulating the landmasses of Britain and the Iberian peninsula to fit a format that almost eliminates a north–south dimension. Miller must have been right into imagining that both landmasses would have been tilted leftward. Thus Britain's east coast duly faces the top margin of the map in his reconstruction, and its north coast faces leftward. We can observe[5] from Segment 1 how Gaul is similarly manipulated, with its north coast turned left to face southern Britain, and then, after a long narrow inlet for the Sinvs Aqvitanicvs (1B1–1B2), its west coast facing southwest Britain above. Even so, Britain is likely to have been made a considerably more elongated landmass than the one Miller reconstructed, and the same must be suggested for the Iberian Peninsula. Its north coast – continuing from southwest Gaul on the first surviving fragment – no doubt faced the top margin of the map, as Miller imagined. Whether his disposition for the other coasts (west, south, east) was accurate, however, must by definition remain uncertain. The one readily comparable case in the surviving part of the map is Asia Minor, where its north coast (on the Black Sea) also faces the top margin of the map, but the mapmaker minimized the west coast, instead making, first, most of it and then the entire south coast successively face the bottom margin of the map in a single line (on the Mediterranean). The possibility remains, therefore, that the Iberian Peninsula was not presented with nearly as tall a west coast as Miller reconstructed.

This claim may sound extreme; it could imply that the mapmaker thereby created an additional obstacle for himself in his already difficult task of manipulating the principal landmasses. But the fact is that in the surviving part of the map he can be seen to have avoided laying out routes "vertically" for any great distance.[6] Rather, so far as possible, he wanted to present routes running "horizontally." Hence doubt has to be cast on the frequency with which Miller's reconstruction opts for vertical routes comprising numerous stretches – most conspicuously below "Hadrian's

Wall,"[7] and along the lefthand coasts of the Iberian Peninsula and North Africa. In the likely event that the mapmaker laid out his design from left to right, the frequency of such vertical routes here implies that he felt pressed for space as soon as he began. This is an altogether improbable outlook for the initial stage; even across the entire surviving sweep of the map up to the Euphrates the mapmaker reflected it only in limited minor instances.

Other features of Miller's route layout seem questionable too. Ostensibly, he did have good reason not to run any route along the upper righthand coast of the Iberian Peninsula or along the upper lefthand coast of North Africa; in neither instance is there ancient testimony for one.[8] On the other hand, account needs to be taken of the mapmaker's visible concern in the surviving part of the map to run a route almost everywhere along the coasts of the principal internal bodies of water. This he accomplished around the entire Mediterranean and Adriatic, notably even between Miletus and Patara without any indication that the journey here would have to be made by sea.[9] With regard to Miller's reconstruction, therefore, the balance of probability is surely that the mapmaker would have continued routes along the two stretches of coastline where Miller omits them.

A routine concern on the part of the mapmaker was to ensure that the place-name on each onward route stretch be accompanied by a figure for the distance to the next place.[10] Miller duly acknowledged that in his reconstruction all the distance figures along routes are missing; lack of information is the justifiable cause. Inclusion of the figures would also require more space (as again he realized). Moreover, the absence of these figures perhaps too often led him to ignore the mapmaker's principle that to the right of each place marked by a symbol along a route there had to be an onward stretch for every continuation, with a distance figure placed above the line work, followed by a chicane that signifies the start of the next stretch. Cartenna (4 low),[11] for example, is presented well in this respect,[12] but more typically Miller leaves little or no space to the right of a symbol before inserting the next name; and when he does leave space, he is prone to omit any intervening chicane. Observe, for example, his continuations from Lix col. (1 low), Malaca (2 middle), Bricantia (3 high), Toleton (3 middle), Seguntio (4 high), Tingi (4 low), and Cesarea col. (5 low). Undeniably, lapses in these respects can be found in the surviving part of the map,[13] but still the principles of the mapmaker's practice are not in doubt, and it may be felt that any reconstruction departs from them so freely at its peril.

By the same token, the reconstruction's route layout exhibits an excess of untypical configurations. Attention has already been drawn to routes that for a considerable distance proceed vertically or at a pronounced slope. Note should now be taken of the frequency with which chicanes turn upward as a route moves to the right in the reconstruction,[14] rather than turning downward. Instances of such upturns do occur in the surviving part of the map,[15] but they are far more the exception there than in the reconstruction, because the mapmaker was determined to ensure that only a minimum of routes climb from left to right. Equally, the expedient of accommodating a route's length by bulging it out and around as it proceeds up (or down) remains much rarer in the map as it survives[16] than in the reconstruction. While the crossroads without a symbol at Intercatia (3 high) can be paralleled in the surviving part of the map,[17] it too should be recognized as most unusual.

In the same vein, the reconstruction's predilection for setting the name of a place marked with a symbol below the symbol or beside it seems to overlook the mapmaker's firm preference for setting a name above its symbol wherever possible.[18] A comparable concern that seems overlooked, although to a lesser degree, is the mapmaker's reluctance to set any name along a route below the route line work. In my view, he did this so seldom in the surviving part of the map[19] because he viewed the line work as little more than the confirmation and reinforcement of routes defined by names (each followed by a distance figure) and their placement. He laid out the names before the route line work, and not vice versa as, for example, several of Miller's routes in Britain could imply.[20]

Miller's decision to include both Ireland[21] and the Fortunate Islands[22] within the scope of the reconstruction seems well judged. The appearance of Thule,[23] by contrast, remains a rather more speculative choice, but by no means out of the question.

Finally, certain omissions on Miller's part (whether or not they represent a conscious choice) merit brief mention:

- open-water names (a notable concern of the mapmaker's elsewhere,[24] which he surely would not have neglected at the outset);
- rivers in Britain beyond the Thames, the only river to appear there in the surviving part of the map;
- names for both regions and peoples in the Iberian Peninsula;
- names for regions in North Africa (three peoples are marked by Miller);
- bath/spa symbols in both Britain and the Iberian Peninsula (featured twice in North Africa by Miller).

Altogether, Miller's flawed reconstruction of the map's lost western end can at least serve to promote a keener appreciation of the mapmaker's design skills and his cartographic principles. Otherwise, however, it should be set aside. It should certainly no longer be reckoned to convey a plausible impression of the missing part of the map.

WYTTENBACH'S CLAIM: A LOST PIECE OF
THE MAP DISCOVERED

The sole testimony to the claim that Johann Hugo Wyttenbach (1767–1848) had discovered a lost piece of the map is a notice published in the *Trier'sche Zeitung* on March 24, 1835:[1]

Herr Gymnasial-Direktor und Professor Wyttenbach hat abermals eine für die ältere Geschichte und Bibliographie höchst wichtige Entdeckung gemacht. Man weiss, das von der sogennanten Peutinger'schen Charte, welche die Militärstrassen durch das Weströmische Reich unter Theodosius dem Grossen bezeichnet, nur eilf Blätter bis jetzt bekannt waren. Es fehlte von den ganzen, aus zwölf Blättern bestandenen, römisch-kaiserlichen Reise-Charte das zwölfte Blatt, welches aber in der Reihe das erste ist. Auf diesem begann die Charte mit Britanien, Hispanien und Mauritanien. Von diesem bishieher unbekannten Blatte ist ein Theil, nämlich Spanien, vom Hrn. Direktor Wyttenbach glücklich entdeckt worden. Das Pergament-blatt war als Schmutzblatt einer Incunabel auf der hiesigen Stadtbibliothek angeklebt. Das Nähere darüber wird später bemerkt werden können.

Früher schon, im Jahr 1803, hatte Hr. Direktor Wyttenbach durch Auffindung der zwei letzten Blätter des 35zeiligen, von Peter Schöffer zu Mainz gedruckten Donat, eine für die Geschichte der Buchdruck-erkunst eben so wichtige als interessante Entdeckung gemacht. (s. darüber Geschichte der Erfindung der Buchdruckerkunst von Dr. Schaab, Mainz 1830).

Gymnasium Principal and Professor Wyttenbach has once again made an extremely important discovery for ancient history and bibliography. It is common knowledge that up to the present only eleven sheets were known of the so-called Peutinger's map, which shows the military roads throughout the Roman Empire of the West under Theodosius the Great. This Roman imperial travel map consisted of twelve sheets altogether, but the twelfth – which is, however, the first in the sequence – is missing. On it, the map began with Britain, Spain, and Mauretania. It is a part of this previously unknown sheet, namely Spain, that Principal Wyttenbach has had the good fortune to discover. The sheet of parchment was glued onto an incunable in the local city library as a wrapper. It will be possible to comment further on this later.

Earlier already, in the year 1803, Principal Wyttenbach had made a discovery that was both important and interesting for the history of the art of printing, when he found the last two sheets of the 35-line Donatus printed by Peter Schöffer in Mainz (on this, see *Geschichte der Erfindung des Buchdruckerkunst* by Dr. Schaab, Mainz 1830).[2]

This notice is anonymous, but it can only have derived from information supplied by Wyttenbach himself. The sheet that he saw formed part of a book wrapper in much the same way as two discoveries made in England during the 1980s, the so-called Aslake[3] and Duchy of Cornwall[4] maps. The discovery that the report mentions Wyttenbach as making in 1803 was certainly genuine, as was another (not mentioned) that he had made in 1828.[5] The claim that more of the Peutinger map had been found failed to create as much stir as had the announcement three years earlier (1832, also in a newspaper) of the discovery of the Ebstorf map.[6] Even so, the news was circulated widely in learned journals,[7] and the Real Academia de la Historia in Madrid wrote to Wyttenbach expressing interest and offering support.[8] Thereafter, even though he remained silent about his claim, it was remembered and credited for some time. Murray's guide for travelers to Vienna – revised in 1850 – states, of the imperial library: "Among its curiosities may be mentioned. . . . the celebrated *Tabula Peutingeriana*. . . . A part of it, containing England, Spain, and a portion of Africa, is wanting; but a fragment of this was recently found in the binding of a book in the library at Treves."[9]

Only after Wyttenbach's death in 1848 was a report published by Johannes Freudenberg demonstrating the falsity of the claim made in 1835.[10] He relied upon a tracing of Wyttenbach's find supplied by a colleague in Trier, Dr. Montigny. From it, Freudenberg reckoned that this map derives mainly from Ptolemy's *Geography* and dates to around 1500. Further discoveries and more recent scholarship can offer additional insight, although much still remains obscure. The map fragment – which Wyttenbach recovered from an "incunabulum of 1503" that remains unidentified – in fact comprises the two halves of a mutilated parchment sheet measuring 56 cm high by 40 (22 × 15¾ in.); today it bears the shelfmark V 1 (Kartenfragmente von ca. 1440) in the Trier Stadtbibliothek (Plate 26).[11] The map in its fragmentary (and unfinished) state covers the center of the Iberian Peninsula from top to bottom,[12] but notably with no mountains or routes shown, and only mouths for rivers – their courses have still to be drawn. Settlements are numbered in accordance with Ptolemy's listing and are marked by "point symbols," except in a few instances where a metal stamp in the form of a castle with twin towers has been applied. Boundaries between peoples and regions are drawn in red, and their names have been written but then crossed out. Longitude figures associated with a grid appear across the top and bottom, reflecting a Ptolemaic conic projection.

The notice published in 1835 omits to mention that on the verso of the sheet discovered by Wyttenbach appears a map of the same type showing part of Gaul. Subsequently, a fragment was discovered in Koblenz (first published in 1910) with a comparable Ptolemaic conic projection map of eastern Europe on the recto, and one of Europe in its entirety in trapezoidal projection on the verso. The identity of the mapmaker in all these instances – evidently a scholar ready to experiment – continues to be a matter for speculation, as does the date of this work (perhaps mid-fifteenth century?).[13]

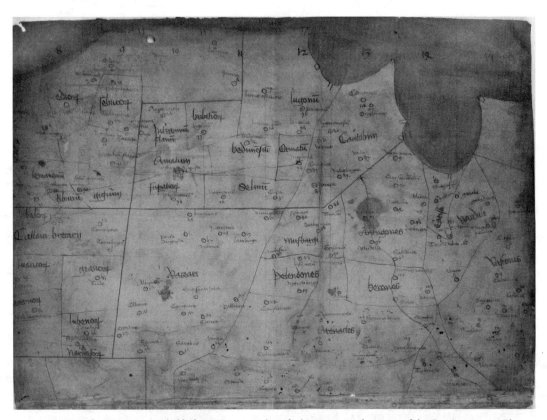

PLATE 26. Map fragment (upper half) from Trier misidentified in 1835 as a lost part of the Peutinger map. Photo: Stadtbibliothek Trier. Fragm V 1 (Kartenfragmente von ca. 1440).

USER'S GUIDE TO THE DATABASE
AND COMMENTARY

The database provides an entry, with brief commentary, for every name and for every feature *except* those mountain ranges which the map does not name. An illustration of the relevant part of the map in color heads each entry. For the entire map as a seamless whole, see Map A. The scope of the commentary is explained in the Introduction.

Where a better reading can be gained from the monochrome photographs taken in 1888, an illustration from these is included; for the complete set of these photographs, see Map B (i). In addition, occasional reference is made to the set of color photographs published by Weber (1976).

The rivers on the Peutinger map are outlined on a *Barrington Atlas* base in Map C (however, no farther east than the Euphrates and Tigris). The routes on the map are outlined similarly in Map D (however, no farther east than Maps 87 and 89). For guidance, see Appendix 9.

The database indexes names and features in multiple ways: see the Database Contents.

Feature Type

For the full range, see the listing in the Database Contents.

Symbol Type

For the full range, see Symbol Classification in the Database Contents, together with Chapter 3, section 4 (c) for discussion.

Grid

Grid figures have three components: the number of a map segment (1–11), followed by the numbers of a square within it determined vertically

(A,B,C) and horizontally (1,2,3,4,5). Normally, the figure for a name or feature specifies the "lowest-numbered" square that any part of it occupies (1A1–1A5 the "lowest" squares of all, 11C1–11C5 the "highest").

Numbering of Features

Certain groups of features are numbered for ease of reference and for secure identification on the map. For each group there is a separate number sequence (always beginning at 1) that extends across the entire map segment by segment:

Islands (all, whether named or not);
Isolated unnamed symbols (i.e., that do *not* form part of the route network);
Lakes and marshes (all, whether named or not);
Mountain ranges (all; however, those that are unnamed have no entry in the Database);
Rivers (all, whether named or not). In the case of a river with tributaries, the "main" river carries the letter A in addition, and its tributaries the same number with a capital letter B–Z–AA–onward; when a "main" river branches, each branch carries its number with lower-case letter b-onward. Arrow(s) indicate a river's direction of flow;
Unnamed route stretches; these include unnamed symbols that form part of the route network.

Name Forms

Each word is recorded as I am best able to read it on the map, without restoration. Lettering in red ink on the map appears in red. For the transcription of lettering, see Introduction, "Presentation of the Map."

The following conventions are used in recording incomplete names:

[– ? –] The presence of lettering is not in doubt, but no letter can be identified, nor the number of them determined;
[...] The presence of as many letters as there are dots here is not in doubt, but there is no means to identify any of these letters;
+ signifies a letter whose presence is not in doubt and to whose identity there is some clue (because the letter is partially preserved, for example).

Abbreviations on the map are transliterated as supplementary lettering in parentheses: thus Catorigomag' is written Catorigomag(o). See further Chap. 2, sec. 2 (b) (ii).

Stops marked before or after words and numbers, as well as dots above **y**, are normally ignored.

A period not enclosed in parentheses simply signifies a stop.

Route Stretch Data

The Roman numeral for a distance figure is recorded as best I can read it, followed by its Arabic numeral equivalent. The unit (league, mile, etc.) is not mentioned unless the map specifically records it.

Where two or more stretches of route are associated with a name or symbol, they are presented in order from the highest to appear on the map downward.

River crossing(s) in the course of a stretch (from left to right on the map), if any, are recorded by the number(s) of the river(s) in the order they are crossed.

References

Where possible, each entry offers a brief indication of where to begin a search for possible further information and analysis, especially of local issues. Notes appended to an entry may discuss such matters as difficulty in reading a name or figure, style of presentation, or the apparent marking of a place more than once. Local issues, however, such as the accuracy of the map or of its distance figures in relation to conditions on the ground, are seldom addressed.

BAtlas

If the corresponding name or feature can be identified in the *Barrington Atlas of the Greek and Roman World* (*BAtlas*), reference to it there is made. Use of a question mark (?) indicates a notably doubtful identification. For further information in every instance, it is vital to consult the *Map-by-Map Directory* that accompanies *BAtlas*. By definition, names or features termed "unlocated" (because there is insufficient information to mark them) appear only in the Directory. Certain names or features on the Peutinger map are missing from both *BAtlas* and its Directory because they are, for example, hopelessly garbled (note the comment in *BAtlas Directory*, p. 1355) or simply unknown beyond the name itself. In these instances, where possible, the entry in another reference work is cited (especially *RE*). Inevitably, however, many such entries add little beyond confirming our lack of knowledge.

In instances where *BAtlas* shows and names a river but does not mark the river crossing featured on the Peutinger map, reference is made to the river nonetheless. In comparable instances, too, where the Peutinger map marks a region name, and *BAtlas* marks only the identically named people of the region, reference is made to the latter.

ItMiller

Reference is made to the column number(s) where K. Miller, *Itineraria Romana* (*ItMiller*), provides an entry for the name or feature, and for any route stretch(es) associated with it. Where there is more than one such stretch, the order in which the column numbers are cited matches so far as possible the order in which the Database entry presents these stretches. Note, however, that where a name or feature occurs more than once in *ItMiller*, its principal entry is normally to be found at its first appearance. If the Database and *ItMiller* read a name differently, the latter's spelling of it is added here; otherwise the name is not repeated.

Caution when consulting *ItMiller*: the eleven parchment segments are numbered 2–12 (*not* 1–11), on the assumption that a single segment is missing at the lefthand end of the map.

ItAnt, ItBurd, ItMarit, *etc.*

A single representative reference (only) is cited where a name on the Peutinger map's route network occurs in earlier or contemporary *itineraries* (only). If the Database and the itinerary read a name differently, the latter's spelling of it is added here; otherwise the name is not repeated.

First choice for a citation is the land portion of *Itinerarium Antonini Augusti* (*ItAnt*): see further Map E and Appendix 9. Otherwise citations are drawn from:

> *Itinerarium Maritimum* (*ItMarit*, associated with *ItAnt*), in occasional instances relevant to a land route;
>
> *Itinerarium Burdigalense* (*ItBurd*; see further Map F and Appendix 9);
>
> Isidore of Charax, *Parthian Stations* (*FGH*, 781);
>
> "Vicarello cups," *CIL*, XI, 3281–84 = J. M. Roldán Hervás, *Itineraria Hispana: Fuentes antiguas para el estudio de las vías romanas en la Península Ibérica* (Valladolid, 1975), 154–56;
>
> Inscriptions from Rome (*CIL*, VI, 5076), Alichamps (*CIL*, XVII.2, 489), Autun (ibid., 490a), Junglinster (ibid., 676), Tongeren (ibid., 675).

TECHNICAL NOTE
Tom Elliott

Together, the database entries provide a record for every name and most features on the map.* Each entry is stored as an XML file, encoded according to the Guidelines of the Text Encoding Initiative (TEI), version P4;[†] the Contents list, Works Cited, and all indexes are also encoded thus. These XML files provide a robust format for communicating all aspects of the reference information about the map, as well as an unrivalled basis for further computational analysis of its content. Because TEI is in wide use

---

* For discussion of context, background, and design considerations, note T. Elliott, "Constructing a Digital Edition for the Peutinger Map," 99–110 in Talbert and Unger (2008).

[†] C. M. Sperberg-McQueen and L. Burnard (eds.), *TEI P4: Guidelines for Electronic Encoding and Interchange* (XML-compatible edition), 2004, http://www.tei-c.org/release/doc/tei-p4-doc/html/.

across humanities fields for the encoding of digitized primary sources, it furnishes an excellent basis for the long-term digital preservation of this data. For ready consultation, a corresponding HTML page is also provided for each XML component.*

Both the XML and the corresponding HTML files reference one or more "inset images." All such images are encoded as 72 dpi JPEG files (version 1.01). They are referenced in the XML using the TEI-standard <figure> element, extended by the addition of an "href" attribute used to provide the relative path to the desired image file.

---

* Hypertext Markup Language (HTML) is the "language of the Web," used to encode the information formatted and displayed by Web-browsing software. The present work employs XHTML (Extensible Hypertext Markup Language), conformant with the provisions of S. Pemberton et al., *XHTML™ 1.0 The Extensible HyperText Markup Language (Second Edition): A Reformulation of HTML 4 in XML 1.0*, W3C Recommendation 26 January 2000, revised 1 August 2002, http://www.w3.org/TR/xhtml1.

USER'S GUIDE TO THE MAP (A)
AND OVERLAID LAYERS

Map A presents the Peutinger map as a seamless whole, full size, in color. Its eleven segments, photographed in 2000, are rejoined as precisely as the parchment sheets' various small imperfections permit. The grids shown for reference are ones overlaid in the first instance on each segment individually. Hence, as is plainly visible, their horizontal divisions do not invariably quite match.

This display of the map permits a viewer to pan the map view (move up/down, left/right) and zoom in and out. For reference and study, a number of thematic layers are overlaid on the map. These may be turned "on" and "off" at will. Detailed instructions for users are included in the map application itself.

Layers

N.B.: Where there are different strengths or shades of color to be found for a feature on the map (e.g., red for route line work, red fill for mountains), there is no attempt to reproduce the variations in these layers.

Coastline (blue)
Grid framework
Grid labels (4A1, 4A2, etc. on each segment)
Island numbers (blue)
Lakes, area (blue fill)
Lake and marsh numbers (blue)
Map
Mountains, brown outline (no fill)
Mountains, brown fill
Mountains, pink fill
Mountains, red fill
Mountain numbers (pink)

Names of mountains, peoples, regions, display capitals (black and red)

Open water, lettering (violet)

River courses (blue)

River courses: numbers and flow direction arrows (both green)

River courses: restoration of partial erasures (blue dots)

River courses: supplementary line work (red dots)

Route linework (red)

Routes: conjectural restoration of missing line work (bright red)

> *Caution:* Normally, where no indication remains of what is missing, no restoration is made; likewise, there is no restoration where the placement of the stretch is unclear, as for Tranvpara (6A5).

Route stretches with no distance figure (orange)

Route stretches with no start marked (yellow)

Routes: one stretch drawn as two or more (black)

Symbols

Symbols: numbers for isolated unnamed symbols (light-blue)

Unnamed route stretches (purple)

Unnamed route stretch numbers (purple).

TECHNICAL NOTE

Map A is a web application, developed using open-source software components and hosted cooperatively at New York University by the Institute for the Study of the Ancient World (ISAW) and the Digital Library Services Team. The Djakota JPEG 2000 Image Server is used to provide multiresolution tiles of the rasterized Peutinger map images to the web application running in a user's browser.* In the browser, the OpenLayers JavaScript map display library combines these images with the vector overlays (in Scalable Vector Graphics format) together with simple controls for layer manipulation, panning, and zooming.† Map A was initially developed for Internet Explorer only by David O'Brien at the Ancient World Mapping Center using plain Javascript and the now defunct Adobe SVG Viewer. The subsequent production implementation (described here) has been developed on an entirely new, cross-browser code base by Sean Gillies at ISAW, reusing the original raster and vector imagery.

* http://sourceforge.net/projects/djakota/

† OpenLayers: http://openlayers.org/; SVG: http://www.w3.org/Graphics/SVG/

USER'S GUIDE TO THE OUTLINING OF RIVERS AND ROUTES ON *BARRINGTON ATLAS* BASES (C–F)

WITH ASSOCIATED TEXTS: (a) ANTONINE ITINERARY (*ItAnt*) TEXT WITH JOURNEYS NUMBERED AS ON MAP E, AND (b) BORDEAUX ITINERARY (*ItBurd*) TEXT WITH JOURNEYS LETTERED AS ON MAP F

Map C outlines the Peutinger map's rivers eastward as far as the Euphrates and Tigris on *BAtlas* bases;

Map D outlines the Peutinger map's routes on *BAtlas* bases – but not beyond Maps 87 and 89, because too little is known for certain hereon;

Map E outlines the Antonine Itinerary's routes (*ItAnt*) on *BAtlas* bases;

Map F outlines the Bordeaux Itinerary's routes (*ItBurd*) on *BAtlas* bases.

Maps C–F may be overlaid upon one another. Each has the same "mosaic" of bases, which allows the user to proceed seamlessly through *BAtlas*. A Locator Outline (Fig. 7) of the *BAtlas* maps comprising the mosaic forms part of this Appendix. Each individual *BAtlas* map can be brought into the mosaic, or removed, as the user wishes. Be aware that, where two or more overlap, the upper map may need to be removed in order for certain data marked on the lower to be seen.

   The mosaic presents these *BAtlas* maps at a consistent scale, which the user may enlarge or reduce freely. *Caution:* These maps were all produced for presentation at either 1:1,000,000 or 1:500,000 scale (shown on the Locator Outline); as with any map, the results are liable to prove unsatisfactory if an enlargement is attempted far in excess of the original scale. The lack of high definition in the maps' presentation reflects their intended role as no more than background here.

   The rivers shown on the Peutinger map eastward as far as the Euphrates and Tigris are outlined (no more precisely than that) on Map C in blue in order to identify them and their courses. Each is numbered as in the Database.

The routes shown on the Peutinger map are outlined on Map D stretch by stretch, with each stretch normally indicated by an unbroken straight line drawn in blue between the stopping points at either end; the name of each of these points is added as it appears on the Peutinger map. Even where it would seem likely that a stretch shown on the Peutinger map does match a route shown in *BAtlas*, the outline still does not consciously attempt to adopt the exact course of that route. Whether to credit such a match or not is left for users to judge (the relevant *BAtlas Directory* is recommended for reference); the outline merely remains neutral on this issue. The outline also takes no account of how accurate any distance figure appearing on the Peutinger map should be considered to be. However, the outline does adhere to the identifications and locations for stopping points that *BAtlas* marks, *including* ones where *BAtlas* registers uncertainty in one respect or another; see further its Map Key and Guidelines for Reference.

In instances where *BAtlas* ignores a stopping point, or notes it only in the *Directory* as an Unlocated Toponym, usually the outline too does not mark that stopping point, except in one special circumstance explained immediately below. Normal practice is that when two or more unlocated stopping points occur between two that *can* be marked, then a single straight line is drawn (wavy, dashed) in pink, and above it is written a number ("two," "five," etc.) specifying the requisite number of unlocated stopping points traversed here between the two that can be marked.

The *special circumstance* arises when just a single unlocated stopping point occurs between two that can be marked. In that event, the unlocated stopping point is assigned a *hypothetical* location signified by a red point symbol, and the route line work either side of it is dashed and pink. The location typically reflects the relative distance stated by the Peutinger map *from* the previous stopping point and *to* the next (where these figures are preserved), but it is otherwise an entirely hypothetical location made solely for the purpose of this outline. It is not based on appraisal of relevant scholarship and means no disrespect to that scholarship. In rare instances where none of a succession of unlocated stopping points would otherwise be marked, it can become necessary to mark one even so, because it serves, say, as a fork. In consequence, exceptionally, at least one other in the same succession is marked, too, with a red point symbol. See, for example, Zaras–Svvaddvrvsi psidivm–Adcentenarivm–Lamasbva (*BAtlas* 34 D2), where the middle two of these four are both unlocated, but a fork in the route occurs at Adcentenarivm; hence both Svvaddvrvsi psidivm and Adcentenarivm are marked with a red point symbol rather than being left unmarked.

The Antonine and Bordeaux Itineraries both present predetermined "journeys" of widely varying length as self-contained units (unlike the Peutinger map, where users are left to develop their own journeys along the routes stretch by stretch). Accordingly, each journey is outlined on

204

Appendix 9: User's
Guide to the
Outlining of Rivers
and Routes on
Barrington Atlas
Bases (C–F), with
Associated Texts

Maps E and F (in red for *ItAnt*; in green for *ItBurd*) as a single unbroken "string" of stretches (*not* as a series of individual stretches), with its own number (1–251) in the case of *ItAnt*, or letter in the case of *ItBurd* (A–E). The user can introduce, or remove, each individual route at will. The user is also able to observe where two or more journeys (or Peutinger map routes) evidently duplicate one another. *BAtlas* and its *Directory* are relied upon in the same way as for Maps C–D. Likewise the occurrence of two or more unlocated stopping points between two that can be marked is signified according to the principles already explained, using red wavy line work for *ItAnt* and green wavy line work for *ItBurd*, with the number written above. Single unlocated stopping points are marked by a red point symbol.

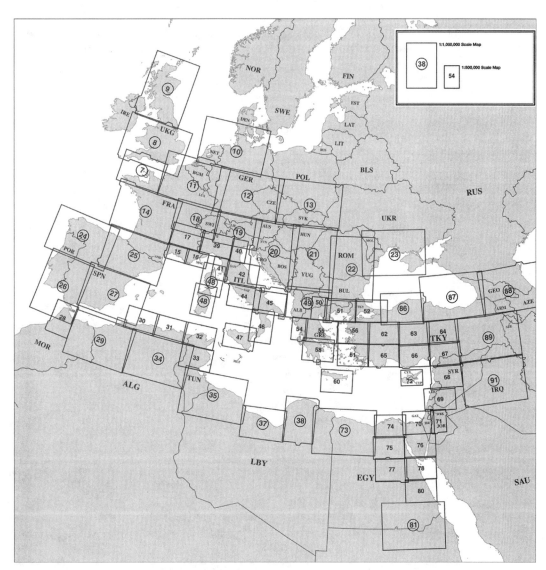

FIGURE 7. Locator Outline of *Barrington Atlas* maps forming the bases for Maps C–F. From R. J. A. Talbert (ed.), *Barrington Atlas of the Greek and Roman World*. Princeton [NJ] and Oxford, 2000. Adapted with permission of Princeton University Press.

The edition followed is O. Cuntz, *Itineraria Romana*, vol. 1 (Leipzig: Teubner, 1929). However, the distance unit *m.p.* (*milia passuum*, for Roman miles) is omitted. Any distance figure with no distance unit attached can therefore be taken to be in Roman miles.

	1,1	INCIPIT ITENERARIUM PROVINCIARUM		
	1,2	ANTONI AUGUSTI.		
	2,1	PROVINCIAE AFRICAE.		
	2,2	A TINGI MAURETANIA, id est ubi Bacuates et Mace-		
	2,3	nites barbari morantur, per maritima		
	3,1	loca Cartaginem usque:		
	3,2	Ab exploratione, quod Mercurios dicitur,		
	4,1	Tingi usque	CLXXIIII,	174
	4,2	Rusadder	CCCXVIII,	318
	5,1	Cesarea Mauretanie	CCCCXXIII,	423
	5,2	Saldis	CCXVIII,	218
	5,3	Rusiccade	CCXVIII,	218
	6,1	Hippone Regio	CXV,	115
	6,2	Cartagine	CXCIII,	193
	6,3	mansionibus his:		
I	6,4	A Mercurios	CLXXIIII	174
	6,5	Sala colonia	XVI	16
	7,1	Thamusida	XXXII	32
	7,2	Banasa	XXXII	32
	7,3	Frigidis	XXIIII	24
	7,4	Lix colonia	XVI	16
	8,1	Tabernis	XVI	16
	8,2	Zili	XIIII	14
	8,3	Ad Mercurios	VI	6
	8,4	Tingi colonia	XVIII	18
	9,1	A Tingi litoribus navigatur usque		
	9,2	ad Portus Divinos:		
	9,3	Ad Septem Fratres	LX	60
	9,4	Ad Abilem	XIIII	14
	9,5	Ad Aquilam Minorem	XIIII	14
	10,1	Ad Aquilam Maiorem	XIIII	14
	10,2	Ad promunturium Barbiti	XII	12
	10,3	Tenia Longa	XXIIII	24
	10,4	Cubucla	XXIIII	24
	10,5	Parietina	XXIIII	24
	10,6	Promunturium	XXV	25
	11,1	Ad Sex Insulas	XII	12
	11,2	Promunturio Cannarum	XXX	30
	11,3	Promunturio Rusaddi	L	50
	11,4	Rusadder colonia	XV	15
	11,5	Ad Tres Insulas	LXV	65
	11,6	Flumen Malva	XII	12

12,1	Flumen Malva dirimit Mauretanias		
12,2	duas, incipit Caesariensis:		
12,3	Lemnis	XXII	22
12,4	Popleto flumen	XXX	30
12,5	Ad Fratres	VI	6
12,6	Artisiga	XXV	25
12,7	Portu Caecili	XII	12
12,8	Siga municipium	XV	15
13,1	Portu Sigensi	III	3
13,2	Camarata	XII	12
13,3	Ad Salsum flumen	XII	12
13,4	Ad Crispas	XXV	25
13,5	Silva colonia	VI	6
13,6	Castra Puerorum	VI	6
13,7	Portus Divinos	XVIII	18
13,8	Portus Magnos	XXXVI	36
13,9	Quiza municipium	XL	40
14,1	Arsenaria	XL	40
14,2	Cartenna colonia	XVIII	18
14,3	Iar castellum	XIIII	14
14,4	Cartili	XII	12
15,1	Gunugus	XII	12
15,2	Caesarea colonia	XII	12
15,3	Tipasa colonia	XVI	16
15,4	Casae Calventi	XV	15
15,5	Icosium colonia	XXXII	32
16,1	Rusguniae colonia	XV	15
16,2	Rusubbicari	XXIIII	24
16,3	Cisi municipium	XII	12
16,4	Rusuccuru colonia	XII	12
17,1	Iomnio municipio	XVIII	18
17,2	Rusazis municipium	XXXVIII	38
17,3	Saldis colonia	XXXV	35
18,1	Musulubio	XXVII	27
18,2	Coba municipium	XXVIII	28
18,3	Igilgili colonia	XXXVIIII	39
18,4	Paccianis Matidie	XXIIII	24
19,1	Chulli municipium	LX	60
19,2	Rusiccade	L	50
19,3	Paratianis	XXV	25
19,4	Culucitanis	XVIII	18
20,1	Tacatua	XXII	22
20,2	Sullucu	XVIII	18
20,3	Hippone Regio colonia	XXXII	32
21,1	Ad Dianam	XXXII	32
21,2	Tuniza	XV	15
21,3	Thabraca	XXIIII	24
21,4	Hippone Zarito	LX	60
22,1	Tuneiza	XX	20
22,2	Membrone	X	10
22,3	Utica	VI	6

Appendix 9: User's Guide to the Outlining of Rivers and Routes on Barrington Atlas *Bases (C–F), with Associated Texts: Antonine Itinerary*

208

Appendix 9: User's
Guide to the
Outlining of Rivers
and Routes on
Barrington Atlas
Bases (C–F), with
Associated Texts:
Antonine Itinerary

	22,4	Ad Gallum Gallinacium	XII	12
	22,5	Cartagine	XV.	15
2	23,1	Item ab Tocolosida Tingi	CXLVIII:	148
	23,2	Volubilis colonia	IIII	4
	23,3	Aquis Dacicis	XVI	16
	23,4	Gilda	XII	12
	23,5	Vopiscianis	XXIII	23
	24,1	Tremulis	XVIIII	19
	24,2	Oppido Novo	XII	12
	24,3	Ad Novas	XXXII	32
	24,4	Ad Mercurios	XII	12
	24,5	Tingi colonia	XVIII.	18
3	24,6	A Cartagine Cirta	CCCXXI,	321
	24,7	Sitifi	C,	100
	25,1	Caesarea	m.p.?, sic:	
	25,2	A Carthagine Unuca	XXII	22
	25,3	Sicilibra	VII	7
	25,4	Vallis	XV	15
	26,1	Coreba	XX	20
	26,2	Musti	XXVIII	28
	26,3	Laribus colonia	XXX	30
	26,4	Altieuros	XVI	16
	26,5	Admedera colonia	XXXII	32
	27,1	Thebeste colonia	XXV	25
	27,2	Altaba	XVIII	18
	27,3	Iusti	XVIII	18
	27,4	Marcimeni	XXIIII	24
	27,5	Macomadibus	XXIIII	24
	28,1	Sigus	XXVIII	28
	28,2	Cirta colonia	XXV	25
	28,3	Mileum	XXV	25
	28,4	Idicra	XXV	25
	29,1	Cuiculi	XXV	25
	29,2	Sitifi	XXV	25
	29,3	Perdices	XXV	25
	30,1	Cellas	XXVIII	28
	30,2	Macri	XXV	25
	30,3	Zabi	XXV	25
	30,4	Aras	XXX	30
	30,5	Tatilti	XVIII	18
	30,6	Auza	XLIIII	44
	30,7	Rapidi	XVI	16
	31,1	Tirinadi	XXV	25
	31,2	Caput Cilani	XXV	25
	31,3	Sufasar	XVI	16
	31,4	Aquis	XVI	16
	31,5	Caesarea	XXV.	25
4	31,6	Item a Sitifi Saldas	LXXVIIIIS:	79.5
	31,7	Orrea	XVIII	18
	32,1	Lesbi	XVIII	18

	32,2	Tubusuptus	XXV	25
	32,3	Saldis	XVIII.	18
5	32,4	Item a Lambese Sitifi	CIIS:	102.5
	32,5	Tadutti	XVIII	18
	32,6	Nova Sparsa	XXXII	32
	32,7	Gemellas	XXVIIS	27.5
	33,1	Sitifi	XXV.	25
6	33,2	Item a Theveste per Lam–		
	33,3	besem Sitifi	CCXII:	212
	33,4	Tinfadi	XXII	22
	33,5	Vegesela	XX	20
	33,6	Mascula	XVIIII	19
	33,7	Claudi	XXII	22
	34,1	Tamugadi	XXII	22
	34,2	Lambese	XIIII	14
	34,3	Diana	XXXII	32
	34,4	Nova Petra	XIIII	14
	34,5	Gemellas	XXII	22
	34,6	Sitifi	XXV.	25
7	34,7	Item a Turres Caesaris Cirta	XL:	40
	34,8	Sigus	XV	15
	35,1	Cirta	XXV.	25
8	35,2	Item a Tamugadi Lamasba	LXII:	62
	35,3	Tadutti	XXVIII	28
	35,4	Diana Veteranorum	XVI	16
	35,5	Lamasba	XVIII.	18
9	35,6	Item a Lamasba Sitifi	LXII, sic:	62
	35,7	Zarai	XXV	25
	36,1	Perdicibus	XII	12
	36,2	Sitifi	XXV.	25
10	36,3	Item a Calama Rusuccurru	CCCXCIIII:	394
	36,4	Ad Rubras	XX	20
	36,5	Ad Albulas	XXX	30
	36,6	Ad Dracones	XIIII	14
	36,7	Ad Regias	XXIIII	24
	37,1	Tasaccora	XXV	25
	37,2	Castra Nova	XVIII	18
	37,3	Ballene praesidio	XX	20
	37,4	Mina	XVI	16
	37,5	Gadaum castra	XXV	25
	37,6	Vaga	XVIII	18
	37,7	castellum Tingitanum	XVIII	18
	38,1	Tigaua municipio	XXII	22
	38,2	Oppido Novo colonia	XXXII	32
	38,3	Tigaua castra	II	2
	38,4	Maliana	XVI	16
	38,5	Sufasar	XVIIII	19
	38,6	Velisci	XV	15
	38,7	Tanaramusa castra	XVI	16

209

Appendix 9: User's Guide to the Outlining of Rivers and Routes on Barrington Atlas Bases (C–F), with *Associated Texts: Antonine Itinerary*

*Appendix 9: User's
Guide to the
Outlining of Rivers
and Routes on*
Barrington Atlas
*Bases (C–F), with
Associated Texts:
Antonine Itinerary*

	38,8	Tamariceto praesidio	XVI	16
	38,9	Rapido castra	XVI	16
	39,1	Rusuccurru colonia	XII.	12
11	39,2	Item Rusuccuro Saldis	XCVII:	97
	39,3	Tigisi	XII	12
	39,4	Bida municipium	XXVII	27
	39,5	Tubusuptus	XL	40
	39,6	Saldis colonia	XVIII.	18
12	39,7	Item a Saldis Igilgili	CLVIIII:	159
	39,8	Ad Olivam	XXX	30
	39,9	Ad Sava municipium	XXV	25
	40,1	Sitifi colonia	XXIIII	24
	40,2	Satafi	XVI	16
	40,3	Ad Basilicam	XVI	16
	40,4	Ad Ficum	XV	15
	40,5	Igilgili	XXXIII.	33
13	40,6	Item a Lambese Cirta	LXXXIIIS:	83.5
	40,7	Tamugadi	XIIII	14
	40,8	Ad Rotam	XXX	30
	41,1	Ad lacum Regium	XX	20
	41,2	Cirta colonia	XX.	20
14	41,3	Item a Musti Cirta	CXCVIIIIS:	199.5
	41,4	Sicca	XXXII	32
	41,5	Naraggara	XXX	30
	41,6	Tagora	XX	20
	41,7	Tipasa	XXIIII	24
	42,1	Gazaufula	XXXV	35
	42,2	Sigus	XXXIII	33
	42,3	Cirta	XXV.	25
15	42,4	Item a Cirta Hippone Regio	XCIIII:	94
	42,5	Aquis Tibilitanis	LIIII	54
	42,6	Ad villam Servilianam	XV	15
	42,7	Hippone Regio	XXV.	25
16	42,8	Item ab Hippone Regio Carta-		
	42,9	gine	CCXVIII:	218
	43,1	Onellaba	L	50
	43,2	Ad Aquas	XXV	25
	43,3	Simittu colonia	V	5
	43,4	Bulla Regia	VII	7
	43,5	Novis Aquilianis	XXIIII	24
	43,6	Vico Augusti	XVI	16
	43,7	Cluacaria	XXX	30
	44,1	Tuburbo Minus	XV	15
	44,2	Cigisa	XXVIII	28
	44,3	Cartagine	XVIII.	18
17	44,4	Item alio itinere ab Hippone Regio Carta-		
	44,5	gine	CCXXVIII:	228
	44,6	Tagaste	LIII	53
	44,7	Naraggara	XXV	25

	45,1	Sicca Veneria	XXXII	32
	45,2	Musti	XXXIIII	34
	45,3	Membressa	XXXV	35
	45,4	Sicilibra	XVII	17
	45,5	Unuca	XIII	13
	45,6	Pertusa	VII	7
	46,1	Cartagine	XIIII.	14
18	46,2	Item a Thenis Teveste	CLXXV:	175
	46,3	Oviscae	XXV	25
	46,4	Amudarsa	XXV	25
	46,5	Autenti	XXV	25
	46,6	Sufetula	XXX	30
	46,7	Vegesela	XXX	30
	47,1	Menegesem	XX	20
	47,2	Teveste	XX.	20
19	47,3	Item ab Aquis Regis Sufibus	XLIII:	43
	47,4	Marazania	XV	15
	47,5	Sufibus	XXVIII.	28
20	47,6	Item ab Assuras Thenas	CXCII:	192
	47,7	Tucca Terebentina	XV	15
	48,1	Sufibus	XXV	25
	48,2	Sufetula	XXV	25
	48,3	Nara	XV	15
	48,4	Madasuma	XXV	25
	48,5	Septiminicia	XXV	25
	48,6	Tabalta	XX	20
	48,7	Macomadibus	XV	15
	48,8	Thenis	XVII.	17
21	48,9	Item a Tuburbo per Valos Ta-		
	48,10	capas	CCCVIII:	308
	49,1	Vallis	XVIII	18
	49,2	Coreva	XX	20
	49,3	Musti	XXVI	26
	49,4	Assuras	XXX	30
	49,5	Tucca Terebentina	XII	12
	49,6	Sufibus	XXV	25
	49,7	Sufetula	XXV	25
	49,8	Nara	XV	15
	49,9	Madassuma	XXXII	32
	50,1	Septiminicia	XXV	25
	50,2	Tabalta	XX	20
	50,3	Cellis Picentinis	XXX	30
	50,4	Tacapis	XXX.	30
22	50,5	Item a Cartagine in Bizancio Sufetula us-		
	50,6	que	CLXXII:	172
	50,7	Unuca	XXII	22
	51,1	Vallis	XXII	22
	51,2	Coreva	XX	20
	51,3	Musti	XXVI	26
	51,4	Assuras	XX	20

*Appendix 9: User's
Guide to the
Outlining of Rivers
and Routes on
Barrington Atlas
Bases (C–F), with
Associated Texts:
Antonine Itinerary*

212

*Appendix 9: User's
Guide to the
Outlining of Rivers
and Routes on*
Barrington Atlas
*Bases (C–F), with
Associated Texts:
Antonine Itinerary*

	51,5	Tucca Terebentina	XII	12
	51,6	Sufibus	XXV	25
	51,7	Sufetula	XXV.	25
23	52,1	Item a Cartagine per Adrumetum Sufetula		
	52,2	usque	CCX:	210
	52,3	Vina	XXXIII	33
	52,4	Pupput	X	10
	52,5	Horrea Caelia	XXXIII	33
	52,6	Adrumeto	X	10
	53,1	Vico Augusti	XXV	25
	53,2	Aquis Regis	XXV	25
	53,3	Masclianis	XVIII	18
	53,4	Sufetula	XXXVI.	36
24	53,5	Item a Thusdro Teveste	CXCV:	195
	54,1	Vico Augusti	XXXI	31
	54,2	Aquis Regis	XXXV	35
	54,3	Masclianis	XVIII	18
	54,4	Sufetula	XXXVI	36
	54,5	Cilio	XXV	25
	54,6	Menegere	XXV	25
	54,7	Teveste	XXV.	25
25	54,8	Item alio itinere a Theveste Thus-		
	54,9	dro	CLXXXV:	185
	54,10	Meneggere	XXV	25
	54,11	Cilio	XXV	25
	54,12	Sufetula	XXV	25
	55,1	Masclianis	XXXVI	36
	55,2	Aquis Regis	XVIII	18
	55,3	Germaniciana	XXII	22
	55,4	Aeliae	XVI	16
	55,5	Tusdro	XVIII.	18
26	55,6	Item a Sufibus Adrumetu	CVIII:	108
	55,7	Marazanis	XXVIII	28
	55,8	Aquis Regis	XX	20
	55,9	Vico Augusti	XXXV	35
	55,10	Adrumeto	XXV.	25
27	55,11	Item a Sufetula Clipea	CCXVI:	216
	56,1	Masclianis	XXXVI	36
	56,2	Aquis Regis	XVII	17
	56,3	Vico Augusti	XXXII	32
	56,4	Adrumetu	XXV	25
	56,5	Horrea	XVIII	18
	56,6	Pupput	XXX	30
	56,7	Curubi	XXVI	26
	56,8	vel Neapoli	XII	12
	57,1	Clipeis	XX.	20
28	57,2	Item a Cartagine Clipeis	LXXXV:	85
	57,3	Maxula Prates	X	10
	57,4	Casula	XX	20

	57,5	Curubi	XXV	25
	57,6	Clipeis	XXX.	30
29	57,7	Item a Cartagine Thenis	CCXVII,	217
	57,8	inde Lepti Magna	CCCCXXII,	422
	57,9	in Alexandria	DCCCCII:	902
	58,1	A Cartagine Maxula civitate	XVIII	18
	58,2	Vina civitate	XXVIII	28
	58,3	Pupput vicus	XII	12
	58,4	Horrea Caelia vicus	XXX	30
	58,5	Adrumetum colonia	XVIII	18
	58,6	Lepti Minus civitas	XVIII	18
	59,1	Thusdro colonia	XXXIII	33
	59,2	Usula civitas	XXXII	32
	59,3	Thenis colonia	XXVIII	28
	59,4	Macomadibus municipium	XXVIII	28
	59,5	Cellas vicus	XXVI	26
	59,6	Tacapas colonia	XXX	30
	59,7	Agma sive Fulgurita villa	XXV	25
	60,1	Giti municipium	XXV	25
	60,2	Ponte Zita municipium	XXXV	35
	60,3	Villa Magna, villa Privata	XXX	30
	61,1	Fisida vicus	XXXI	31
	61,2	Casas villa Aniciorum	XXVI	26
	61,3	Sabrata colonia	XXVIII	28
	62,1	Vax villa Repentina	XXVII	27
	62,2	Ocea colonia	XXVIII	28
	62,3	Megradi villa Aniciorum	XXV	25
	63,1	Minna villa Marsi	XXVVIII	29
	63,2	Lepti Magna colonia	XXVVIII	29
	63,3	Seggera	XX	20
	64,1	Berge	XXIIII	24
	64,2	Base	XXV	25
	64,3	Thebunte	XXX	30
	64,4	Auxiqua	XXX	30
	64,5	Annesel	XXX	30
	64,6	Auxiu	XVIII	18
	64,7	Stixgi	XXV	25
	64,8	Macomadibus Sirtis	XX	20
	65,1	Iscina	XXX	30
	65,2	Tramaricio	XXXI	31
	65,3	Aubereo	XXV	25
	65,4	Digdica	XXIIII	24
	65,5	Tugulus	XXIIII	24
	65,6	Banadedari	XXV	25
	65,7	Anabucis	XXV	25
	65,8	Tiniodiri	XXV	25
	66,1	Boreo	XII	12
	66,2	Tincausari	XXIII	23
	66,3	Attici	XXV	25
	66,4	Chorotus	XXV	25
	66,5	Chaminos	XXII	22

Appendix 9: User's Guide to the Outlining of Rivers and Routes on Barrington Atlas *Bases (C–F), with Associated Texts: Antonine Itinerary*

214

Appendix 9: User's Guide to the Outlining of Rivers and Routes on Barrington Atlas Bases (C–F), with Associated Texts: Antonine Itinerary

	67,1	Beronice	XXX	30
	67,2	Adriane	XXVIII	28
	67,3	Theucira	XVIII	18
	67,4	Ptholemais	XXVI	26
	67,5	Semeros	XXXII	32
	67,6	Lasamices	XXVI	26
	68,1	Cyrene	XXV	25
	68,2	Limniade	XXI	21
	68,3	Darnis	XXIIII	24
	68,4	Hippon	XXVIII	28
	69,1	Michera sive Elene	XXX	30
	69,2	Badrin	XXV	25
	69,3	Ausufal	XX	20
	69,4	Catabathmon	XXV	25
	70,1	Alexandria	VIIII.	9
30	70,2	Item alio itinere ab Ptholomaida in Alexan-		
	70,3	dria:		
	70,4	Semeros	XXXII	32
	70,5	Lasamices	XXVI	26
	70,6	Cyrene	XXV	25
	70,7	fines Marmariae		
	70,8	Limniade	XXI	21
	70,9	Darnis	XXIIII	24
	71,1	Hippon	XXVIII	28
	71,2	Papi	XIIII	14
	71,3	Paniuros	XXX	30
	71,4	Micera	XX	20
	71,5	Iucundiu	XL	40
	71,6	Gereatis	XXXII	32
	71,7	Catabathmos	XXXV	35
	71,8	fines Alexandriae		
	71,9	Geras	XVIII	18
	72,1	Zagilis	XXXII	32
	72,2	Aristeu	XX	20
	72,3	Thabrasta	XXXII	32
	72,4	Parecomo	XXVI	26
	73,1	Euticu	XL	40
	73,2	Pedone	XXVI	26
	73,3	Caportis	XVI.	16
31	73,4	Item iter quod limitem Tripolitanum per Tur-		
	73,5	rem Tamalleni a Tacapas Lepti Magna du-		
	73,6	cit	DCV:	605
	74,1	A Tacapis ad Aquas	XVIII	18
	74,2	Agariabas	XXX	30
	74,3	Turre Tamalleni	XXX	30
	74,4	Ad Templum	XII	12
	74,5	Bezereos	XXX	30
	74,6	Ausilimdi	XXXII	32
	75,1	Agma	XXX	30
	75,2	Auzemmi	XXX	30

	75,3	Tabalati	XXX	30
	75,4	Thebelami	XXV	25
	75,5	Tillabari	XX	20
	75,6	Ad Amadum	XXX	30
	76,1	Tabuinati	XXV	25
	76,2	Thramusdusim	XXV	25
	76,3	Thamascaltin	XXX	30
	76,4	Thenteos	XXX	30
	76,5	Auru	XXX	30
	76,6	Vinaza	XXXV	35
	76,7	Thalatati	XVI	16
	77,1	Thenadassa	XXVI	26
	77,2	Mesphe	XXX	30
	77,3	Lepti Magna	XL.	40
32	77,4	Item a Thelepte Tacapas	CLII:	152
	77,5	Gemellas	XXII	22
	77,6	Gremellas	XXV	25
	77,7	Capsae	XXIIII	24
	78,1	Thasarte	XXXV	35
	78,2	Aquas Tacapitanas	XXVIII	28
	78,3	Tacapas	XVIII.	18
	78,4	SARDINIA.		
33	78,5	ITER SARDINIAE a portu Tibulas Caralis	CCXLVI:	246
	79,1	Turublo Minore	XIIII	14
	79,2	Elefantaria	XV	15
	79,3	Longone	XII	12
	79,4	Ulbia	XXXVIII	38
	79,5	Coclearia	XV	15
	79,6	Portu Liguidonis	XII	12
	80,1	Fano Carisi	XV	15
	80,2	Viniolis	XII	12
	80,3	Sulcis	XXXV	35
	80,4	Porticenses	XXIIII	24
	80,5	Sarcapos	XX	20
	80,6	Ferraria	XX	20
	80,7	Caralis	XIII.	13
34	80,8	Alio itinere ab Ulbia Caralis	CLXXII:	172
	81,1	Caput Tyrsi	XL	40
	81,2	Sorabile	XLV	45
	81,3	Biora	XLV	45
	81,4	Caralis	XLII.	42
35	81,5	A Tibulas Caralis	CCXIII:	213
	81,6	Gemellas	XXV	25
	81,7	Luguidunec	XXV	25
	82,1	Hafa	XXIIII	24
	82,2	Molaria	XXIIII	24
	82,3	Ad Medias	XII	12
	82,4	Foro Traiani	XV	15
	82,5	Othoca	XVI	16

215

Appendix 9: User's Guide to the Outlining of Rivers and Routes on Barrington Atlas *Bases (C–F), with Associated Texts: Antonine Itinerary*

216

———

*Appendix 9: User's
Guide to the
Outlining of Rivers
and Routes on*
Barrington Atlas
*Bases (C–F), with
Associated Texts:
Antonine Itinerary*

	82,6	Aquis Neapolotanis	XXXVI	36
	82,7	Caralis	XXXVI.	36
36	82,8	A portu Tibulas per conpen-		
	82,9	dium Ulbia	XVI.	16
37	83,1	Item a Tibulas Sulcis	CCLX:	260
	83,2	Viniolas	XII	12
	83,3	Erucio	XXIIII	24
	83,4	Ad Herculem	XXII	22
	83,5	Ad Turrem	XVIII	18
	83,6	Nure	XVII	17
	83,7	Carbia	XVI	16
	83,8	Bosa	XXV	25
	84,1	Cornos	XVIII	18
	84,2	Tharros	XVIII	18
	84,3	Othoca	XII	12
	84,4	Neapolis	XVIII	18
	84,5	Metalla	XXX	30
	84,6	Sulcis	XXX.	30
38	84,7	Item a Sulcis Nura	LXVIIII:	69
	85,1	Tegula	XXXIIII	34
	85,2	Nura	XXXV.	35
39	85,3	A Caralis Nura	XXII.	22
	85,4	CORSICAE.		
40	85,5	A Mariana Palmas	CXXVI:	126
	85,6	Aleria	XL	40
	85,7	Praesidio	XXX	30
	85,8	Portu Favoni	XXX	30
	86,1	Plalas	XXV.	25
	86,2	SICILIAE.		
41	86,3	A Traiecto Lilybeo	CCLVII:	257
	86,4	Messana	XII	12
	87,1	Tamaricios sive Palmas	XX	20
	87,2	Per Tauromenium Naxo	XV	15
	87,3	Acio	XXIIII	24
	87,4	Catina	VIIII	9
	88,1	Capitonianibus	XXIIII	24
	88,2	Gela sive Filosofianis	XXI	21
	88,3	Petilianis	XXVII	27
	88,4	Agrigentum	XVIII	18
	88,5	Cena	XVIII	18
	88,6	Allava	XII	12
	88,7	Ad Aquas	XII	12
	88,8	Ad fluvium Lanaricum	XXIII	23
	89,1	Mazaris	X	10
	89,2	Lilybeum	XII.	12
42	89,3	Alio itinere a Lilybeo Messana	CCCXXXVI:	336
	89,4	Aquis Larodes	XLVI	46
	89,5	Agrigento	XL	40
	89,6	Calvisiana	XL	40

	89,7	Hible	XXIIII	24
	89,8	Agris	XVIII	18
	90,1	Syracusis	XXIIII	24
	90,2	Catina	XLIIII	44
	90,3	Tauromenio	XXXII	32
	90,4	Messana	XXXII.	32
43	90,5	A Messana Tindaride	XXXVI.	36
44	90,6	Item a Lilybeo per maritima loca Tindaride		
	90,7	usque	CCVIII:	208
	91,1	Drepanis	XVIII	18
	91,2	Aquis Segestanis sive Pincianis	XIIII	14
	91,3	Parthenico	XII	12
	91,4	Hyccara	VIII	8
	91,5	Panormo	XVI	16
	91,6	Solunto	XII	12
	92,1	Thermis	XII	12
	92,2	Cefalodo	XXIIII	24
	92,3	Haleso	XXVIII	28
	92,4	Caleate	XXVI	26
	92,5	[A Caliate Solusapre	VIIII]	9
	92,6	Agatinno	XX	20
	93,1	Tindaride	XXVIII.	28
45	93,2	Item a Thermis Catina	XCI:	91
	93,3	Enna	LII	52
	93,4	Agurio	III	3
	93,5	Centuripa	XII	12
	93,6	Aethna	XII	12
	94,1	Catina	XII.	12
46	94,2	Item a Catina Agrigentum mansionibus nunc		
	94,3	institutis	XCII:	92
	94,4	Capitonianis	XXIIII	24
	94,5	Philosophianis	XXI	21
	94,6	Gallonianis	XXI	21
	94,7	Cosconianis	XII	12
	95,1	Agrigentum	XIII.	13
47	95,2	Item ab Agrigentum per maritima loca Sira-		
	95,3	cusas	CXXXVII:	137
	95,4	Dedalio	XVIII	18
	95,5	Plintis	V [refugio]	5
	95,6	Chalis	XVIII [plaga]	18
	95,7	Calvisianis	VIII [plaga]	8
	96,1	Mesopotamio	XII [plaga]	12
	96,2	Hereo [sive Cymbe]	XXIIII [refugium]	24
	96,3	Apolline	XX [plaga]	20
	96,4	Siracusis	XXXII.	32
48	96,5	Item ab Agrigento Lilybeo	CLXXV:	175
	96,6	Pitinianis	VIIII	9
	96,7	Comicianis	XXIIII	24
	96,8	Petrine	IIII	4
	97,1	Pirama	XXIIII	24

*Appendix 9: User's
Guide to the
Outlining of Rivers
and Routes on*
Barrington Atlas
*Bases (C–F), with
Associated Texts:
Antonine Itinerary*

	97,2	Panoruo	XXIIII	24
	97,3	Hyccaris	XVIII	18
	97,4	Longarico	XXIIII	24
	97,5	Ad Olivam	XXIIII	24
	97,6	Lilybeum	XXIIII.	24

218
―――
*Appendix 9: User's
Guide to the
Outlining of Rivers
and Routes on
Barrington Atlas
Bases (C–F), with
Associated Texts:
Antonine Itinerary*

49	97,7	Item ab Yccaris maritima:		
	97,8			
	97,9	Parthenico	XII	12
	97,10	Ad Aquas Perticianenses	XV	15
	98,1	Drepanis	XVIII.	18

	98,2	ITALIAE.		
50	98,3	Iter quod a Mediolano per Picenum et Cam-		
	98,4	paniam ad Columnam, id est Traiectum		
	98,5	Siciliae, ducit	DCCCCS:	900.5
	98,6	A Mediolano Laude civitas	XVI	16
	98,7	Placentia civitas	XXIIII	24
	99,1	Fidentiola vicus	XXIIII	24
	99,2	Parme civitas	XV	15
	99,3	Regio civitas	XVIII	18
	99,4	Mutina civitas	XVII	17
	99,5	Bononia civitas	XXV	25
	100,1	Foro Corneli civitas	XXIIII	24
	100,2	Faventia civitas	X	10
	100,3	Cesena civitas	XXIIII	24
	100,4	Ariminum civitas	XX .	20
	100,5	Pisauro civitas	XXIIII	24
	100,6	Senagallia civitas	XXVI	26
	100,7	Ultra Anconam m.p. IIII	XXVI	26
	101,1	Potentia civitas	XVI	16
	101,2	Castello Firmano	XX	20
	101,3	Troento civitas	XXVI	26
	101,4	Castro	XII	12
	101,5	Aterno vicus	XXII	22
	102,1	Iterpromium vicus	XXV	25
	102,2	Sulmone civitas	XXVIII	28
	102,3	Aufidena civitas	XXIIII	24
	102,4	Serni civitas	XVIII	18
	102,5	Bononiano civitas	XVIII	18
	103,1	Super [Tha]mari fluvium	XVI	16
	103,2	Ad Equum Tuticum	XXI	21
	103,3	Ad Matrem Magnam	XVI	16
	103,4	In Honoratianum	XX	20
	104,1	Venusium civitas	XVIII	18
	104,2	Opino	XV	15
	104,3	Ad fluvium Bradanum	XXVIII	28
	104,4	Potentia	XXIIII	24
	104,5	Acidios	XXIIII	24
	104,6	Grumento	XVIII	18
	104,7	Semucla	XVII	17
	105,1	Nerulo	XVI	16

219

*Appendix 9: User's
Guide to the
Outlining of Rivers
and Routes on
Barrington Atlas
Bases (C–F), with
Associated Texts:
Antonine Itinerary*

	105,2	Summurano	XVI	16
	105,3	Caprasis	XXI	21
	105,4	Cosentia	XXVIII	28
	105,5	Ad fluvium Sabutum	XVIII	18
	105,6	Ad Turres	XVIII	18
	106,1	Ad fluvium Angitulam	XIII	13
	106,2	Nicotera	XXV	25
	106,3	Ad Mallias	XXIIII	24
	106,4	Ad Columnam	XIIII.	14
		Appia.		
51	106,5	Item ab Urbe recto itinere ad Co-		
	107,1	lumnam	CCCCLV:	455
	107,2	Aricia	XVI	16
	107,3	Tribus Tabernis	XVII	17
	107,4	Api Foro	X	10
	107,5	Tarracina	XVIII	18
	108,1	Fundis	XIIII	14
	108,2	Formis	XIII	13
	108,3	Minturnis	VIIII	9
	108,4	Sinuessa	VIIII	9
	109,1	Capua	XXVI	26
	109,2	Nola	XXI	21
	109,3	Nuceria	XV	15
	109,4	in medio Salerno		
	109,5	Ad Tanarum	XXVIII	28
	110,1	Ad Calorem	XXIIII	24
	110,2	In Marcelliana	XXV	25
	110,3	Caesariana	XXI	21
	110,4	Nerulo	XXIII	23
	110,5	Summurano	XIII	13
	110,6	Caprasis	XXI	21
	110,7	Cosentia	XXVI	26
	110,8	Ad Sabutum fluvium	XVIII	18
	111,1	Ad Turres	XVIII	18
	111,2	Vibona	XXI	21
	111,3	Nicotera	XVIII	18
	111,4	Ad Mallias	XXIIII	24
	111,5	Ad Columnam	XIIII.	14
52	111,6	A Capua Benevento	XXXIII.	33
53	111,7	Item a Capua Equo Tutico	LIII, sic:	53
	111,8	ubi Campania limitem habet		
	111,9	Caudis	XXI	21
	112,1	Benevento	XI	11
	112,2	Equo Tutico	XXI.	21
54	112,3	Ab Equo Tutico per Roscia-		
	112,4	num Regio	CCCCLXXVIII, sic:	478
	112,5	Sentianum	XXXIII	33
	112,6	Beleianum	XXXIIII	34
	113,1	Venusia	XII	12

	113,2	Ad Pinum	XII	12
	113,3	Ipnum	XII	12
	113,4	Caelianum	XL	40
	113,5	Heraclia	XXVIII	28
	113,6	Ad Vicesimum	XXIIII	24
	114,1	Turios	XX	20
	114,2	Roscianum	XII	12
	114,3	Paternum	XXVII	27
	114,4	Meto	XXXII	32
	114,5	Tacina	XXIIII	24
	114,6	Scilacio	XXII	22
	114,7	Cocinto	XII	12
	115,1	Succeiano	XX	20
	115,2	Subsicivo	XXIIII	24
	115,3	Altanum	XX	20
	115,4	Hipporum	XXIIII	24
	115,5	Decastadium	XXII	22
	115,6	Regio	XX.	20
55	115,7	Item ab Equo Tutico Hydrunto ad		
	115,8	Traiectum	CCXXXV:	235
	116,1	Ecas	XVIII	18
	116,2	Erdonias	XVIIII	19
	116,3	Canusio	XXVI	26
	116,4	Rubos	XXIII	23
	117,1	Butruntus	XI	11
	117,2	Varia	XII	12
	117,3	Turribus	XXI	21
	117,4	Egnatiae	XVI	16
	118,1	Speluncas	XX	20
	118,2	Brundisium	XVIIII	19
	118,3	Lupias	XXV	25
	118,4	Hydrunto	XXV.	25
56	119,1	A Brundisio Tarentum ad latus	XLIIII.	44
57	119,2	A Varis per conpendium Tarentum	LX.	60
58	120,1	A Benevento Tarentum	CLVII:	157
	120,2	Aeclano	XV	15
	120,3	Sub Romula	XXII	22
	121,1	Ponte Aufidi	XXII	22
	121,2	Venusia	XVIIII	19
	121,3	Silvium	XX	20
	121,4	Blera	XIII	13
	121,5	Sub Lupatia	XIIII	14
	121,6	Canales	XIII	13
	121,7	Tarento	XX.	20
59	121,8	A Terracina Benevento	CXIII:	113
	121,9	Fundis	XIII	13
	121,10	Furmis	XIII	13
	121,11	Minturnis	VIIII	9
	121,12	Theano	XVIII	18
	122,1	Alifas	XVII	17

	122,2	Telesia	XXV	25
	122,3	Benevento	XVIII.	18
60	122,4	Item a Terracina Neapolim	LXXXVII:	87
	122,5	Sinuessa	XLIIII	44
	122,6	Literno	XXIIII	24
	122,7	Cumis	VI	6
	123,1	Puteolis	III	3
	123,2	Neapoli	X.	10
61	123,3	A Neapoli Nuceria Constantia	XXXI.	31
62	123,4	A Litirno Miseno	XII, sic:	12
	123,5	Cumis	VI	6
	123,6	Bais	III	3
	123,7	Miseno	III.	3
63	123,8	Ab Urbe		
	123,9	Mediolanum	CCCCXXXIII,	433
	124,1	inde Aquileia	CCLX,	260
	124,2	inde Sirmium	CCCCI,	401
	124,3	inde Nicomedia	DCCLXXXII,	782
	124,4	inde Antiocia	DCCLV,	755
	124,5	inde Alexandria	DCCCII,	802
	124,6	inde in Aegypto Hiera Sicaminos		
	124,7	usque	DCCLXIII:	763
	124,8	Ab Urbe Rostrata Villa	XXIIII	24
	125,1	Ocriculi civitas	XXI	21
	125,2	Narnia civitas	XII	12
	125,3	Interamnia civitas	VIII	8
	125,4	Spoletio civitas	XVII	17
	125,5	Foro Flaminis vicus	XVIII	18
	125,6	Helvillo vicus	XXVII	27
	125,7	Cale vicus	XXIII	23
	126,1	Foro Semproni	XVIII	18
	126,2	Fano Fortunae	XVI	16
	126,3	Pisauro civitas	VIII	8
	126,4	Arimino	XXIIII	24
63.1	126,5	[ab Arimino recto itinere Ravenna	XXXIII,	33
63.1	126,6	inde navigatur Septem Maria Altinum us-		
63.1	126,7	que,		
63.1	126,8	inde Concordia	XXXI	31
63.1	126,9	Aquileia	XXXI]	31
63	126,10	item ab Arimino Caesena civitas	XX	20
	126,11	Faventia civitas	XXIIII	24
	127,1	Foro Corneli civitas	X	10
	127,2	Bononia civitas	XXIIII	24
	127,3	Mutina civitas	XXV	25
	127,4	Regio civitas	XVII	17
	127,5	Parmae civitas	XVIII	18
	127,6	Fidentiola vicus	XV	15
	127,7	Placentia civitas	XXIIII	24
	127,8	Laude civitas	XXIIII	24

222

Appendix 9: User's Guide to the Outlining of Rivers and Routes on Barrington Atlas *Bases (C–F), with Associated Texts: Antonine Itinerary*

63	127,9	Mediolanum civitas	XVI	16
	127,10	Bergome civitas	XXXIII	33
	127,11	Brixia civitas	XXXVIII	38
	127,12	Sermione mansio	XXII	22
	128,1	Verona civitas	XXII	22
	128,2	Vicetia civitas	XXXIII	33
	128,3	Patavis civitas	XXII	22
	128,4	Altinum civitas	XXXIII	33
	128,5	Concordia civitas	XXXI	31
	128,6	Aquileia civitas	XXXI	31
	128,7	Fluvio Frigido	XXXVI	36
	129,1	Longatico mansio	XXII	22
	129,2	Hennoma civitas	XVIII	18
	129,3	Adrante mansio	XXV	25
	129,4	Caleia civitas	XXIIII	24
	129,5	Ragundone	XVIII	18
	129,6	Patavione civitas	XVIII	18
	130,1	Aqua Viva	XX	20
	130,2	Iovia hic Sinista	XVIII	18
	130,3	Lentulis	XXXII	32
	130,4	Sirota	XXXI	31
	130,5	Marinianis	XX	20
	130,6	Vereis	XXII	22
	131,1	Mursa civitas	XXVI	26
	131,2	Cibalas civitas	XXIII	23
	131,3	Ulmos vicus	XXII	22
	131,4	Sirmi civitas	XXVI	26
	131,5	Bassianis civitas	XVIII	18
	131,6	Tauruno classis	XXX	30
	132,1	Singiduno castra	IIII	4
	132,2	Aureo Monte	XXIIII	24
	132,3	Ab Aureo Monte Vinceia	VI	6
	132,4	Margo	VIII	8
	133,1	et leg. m. p. VIII		
	133,2	inde Euminacio	X	10
	133,3	Viminacio	XXIIII	24
	134,1	Municipio	XVIII	18
	134,2	Idimo	XXVII	27
	134,3	Horreo Margi	XVI	16
	134,4	Pompeis	XXXIIII	34
	134,5	Naissi	XXIIII	24
	135,1	Remisiana	XXV	25
	135,2	Turribus	XVIII	18
	135,3	Meldia	XXX	30
	135,4	Serdica	XXIIII	24
	135,5	Burgaraca	XVIII	18
	136,1	Helice	XXI	21
	136,2	Lissas	XXI	21
	136,3	Bessapara	XXII	22
	136,4	Philippopoli	XXII	22
	136,5	Cillis	XXXI	31

136,6	Pizo	XX	20
136,7	Arso	XVIII	18
137,1	Subzupara	XVIII	18
137,2	Burdipta	XXII	22
137,3	Hadrianopoli	XXIIII	24
137,4	Ostudizo	XVIII	18
137,5	Burtudizo	XVIII	18
137,6	Bergule	XVIII	18
137,7	Drizipara	XIIII	14
138,1	Izirallo	XVI	16
138,2	Heraclia	XVII	17
138,3	Cenofrurio	XVIII	18
138,4	Melantiada	XXVIII	28
138,5	Bizantio [qui et Constantinopoli]	XVIII	18
139,1.2	Calcedonia, traiectus in Bithinia	IIII	4
139,3	Panticio	XV	15
140,1	Libissa	XXIIII	24
140,2	Nicomedia	XXII	22
140,3	Libo	XXI	21
141,1	Nicia	XXIII	23
141,2	Moedo Orientis	XVI	16
141,3	Tottaio	XXVIII	28
141,4	Dablis	XXVIII	28
141,5	Cenon Gallicanon	XVIII	18
142,1	Dabastana	XXI	21
142,2	Iuliopolim	XXVI	26
142,3	Laganeos	XXIIII	24
142,4	Minizo	XXIII	23
142,5	Manegordo	XXVIII	28
143,1	Ancira	XXIIII	24
143,2	Corbeunca	XX	20
143,3	Rosolatiaco	XII	12
143,4	Aspona	XXXI	31
144,1	Parnasso	XXIIII	24
144,2	Ozzala	XVII	17
144,3	Nitazi	XVIII	18
144,4	Coloniam Arcilaida	XXVII	27
144,5	Nandianulus	XXV	25
144,6	Sasima	XXIIII	24
145,1	Andabalis	XVI	16
145,2	Tiana	XVI	16
145,3	Faustinopolim	XVIII	18
145,4	Podando	XXVI	26
145,5	Nampsucrone	XXVII	27
145,6	Aegeas	XXI	21
146,1	Catabolo	XXIIII	24
146,2	Bais	XVI	16
146,3	Alexandria	XVI	16
146,4	Pagris	XVI	16
147,1	Antiochia	XVI	16
147,2	Platanos	XXV	25

223

*Appendix 9: User's
Guide to the
Outlining of Rivers
and Routes on
Barrington Atlas
Bases (C–F), with
Associated Texts:
Antonine Itinerary*

224

*Appendix 9: User's
Guide to the
Outlining of Rivers
and Routes on
Barrington Atlas
Bases (C–F), with
Associated Texts:
Antonine Itinerary*

147,3	Catela	XXIIII	24
147,4	Laudicia	XVI	16
148,1	Gabala	XVIII	18
148,2	Balanea	XIIII	14
148,3	Antarado	XXIIII	24
148,4	Arcas	XXXII	32
148,5	Tripoli	XVIII	18
148,6	Biblo	XXXII	32
149,1	Berito	XXIIII	24
149,2	Sidona	XXX	30
149,3	Tyro	XXIIII	24
149,4	Ptolomaidam	XXXII	32
149,5	Sycamina	XXIIII	24
150,1	Caesarea	XX	20
150,2	Betaro	XVIII	18
150,3	Diospoli	XXII	22
150,4	Iamnia	XII	12
151,1	Ascalona	XX	20
151,2	Gaza	XVI	16
151,3	Rafia	XXII	22
151,4	Rinocorura	XXII	22
152,1	Ostracena	XXIIII	24
152,2	Cassio	XXVI	26
152,3	Pentascino	XX	20
152,4	Pelusio	XX	20
152,5	Heracleus	XXII	22
153,1	Tanis	XXII	22
153,2	Thumuis	XXII	22
153,3	Cyno	XXV	25
153,4	Taba	XXX	30
154,1	Andro	XII	12
154,2	Nitine	XII	12
154,3	Hermupoli	XXIIII	24
154,4	Chereu	XXIIII	24
154,5	Alexandriam	XX	20
155,1	Chereu	XXIIII	24
155,2	Hermupoli	XX	20
155,3	Andro	XXI	21
155,4	Niciu	XXXI	31
156,1	Letus	XXVIIII	29
156,2	Memphi	XX	20
156,3	Peme	XX	20
156,4	Isiu	XX	20
156,5	Caene	XX	20
157,1	Tacona	XX	20
157,2	Oxirincho	XXIIII	24
157,3	Ibiu	XXX	30
157,4	Hermupoli	XXIIII	24
157,5	Chusis	XXIIII	24
157,6	Lyco	XXXV	35
158,1	Apollinos Minore	XVIII	18

	158,2	Hisopis	XXVIII	28
	158,3	Ptolomaida	XXII	22
	158,4	Abydo	XXII	22
	159,1	Diospoli	XXVIII	28
	159,2	Tentira	XXVII	27
	159,3	Contra Copto	XII	12
	159,4	Papa	VIII	8
	160,1	Hermunti	XXX	30
	160,2	Lato	XXIIII	24
	160,3	Apollonos Superiore	XXXII	32
	160,4	Contra Tumuis	XVIIII	19
	160,5	Contra Ombos	XXIIII	24
	161,1	Contra Suenem	XXIIII	24
	161,2	Parembole	XVI	16
	161,3	Tzitzi	II	2
	161,4	Tafis	XIIII	14
	161,5	Talmis	VIII	8
	162,1	Tutzis	XX	20
	162,2	Pselcis	XII	12
	162,3	Corte	IIII	4
	162,4	Hiera Sicamino	IIII.	4
64	162,5	Item a Pelusio Memphi	CXXIII:	123
	162,6	Dafno	XVI	16
	163,1	Tacasarta	XVIII	18
	163,2	Thou	XIIII	14
	163,3	Scenas Veteranorum	XXVI	26
	163,4	Helius	XIIII	14
	163,5	Memphi	XXIIII.	24
65	164,1	Item per partem Arabicam trans Nilum:		
	164,2	Contra Pselcis	X	10
	164,3	Contra Talmis	XXIIII	24
	164,4	Contra Tafis	X	10
	164,5	Filas	XXIIII	24
	164,6	Siene	III	3
	165,1	Ambos	XXX	30
	165,2	Contra Apollonos	XL	40
	165,3	Contra Lato	XL	40
	165,4	Thebas	XL	40
	165,5	Vico Apollonos	XXII	22
	165,6	Copton	XXII	22
	166,1	Cenoboscio	XL	40
	166,2	Thomu	L	50
	166,3	Pano	IIII	4
	166,4	Selino	XVI	16
	166,5	Anteu	XVI	16
	166,6	Muthi	VIII	8
	167,1	Isiu	XXIIII	24
	167,2	Hieracon	XX	20
	167,3	Pesla	XXVIII	28
	167,4	Antenou	XXIIII	24

225

*Appendix 9: User's
Guide to the
Outlining of Rivers
and Routes on*
Barrington Atlas
*Bases (C–F), with
Associated Texts:
Antonine Itinerary*

	167,5	Poes Artemidos	VIII	8
	168,1	Musae	XXXIIII	34
	168,2	Hipponon	XXX	30
	168,3	Alyi	XVI	16
	168,4	Thimonepsi	XVI	16
	168,5	Afrodito	XXIIII	24
	169,1	Scenas Mandras	XX	20
	169,2	Babylona	XII	12
	169,3	Heliu	XII	12
	169,4	Scenas Veteranorum	XVIII	18
	169,5	Vico Iudaeorum	XII	12
	170,1	Thou	XII	12
	170,2	Hero	XXIIII	24
	170,3	Serapiu	XVIII	18
	170,4	Clysmo	L.	50
66	170,5	Item a Serapiu Pelusio	LX, sic:	60
	171,1	Thaubasio	VIII	8
	171,2	Sile	XXVIII	28
	171,3	Magdolo	XII	12
	171,4	Pelusio	XII.	12
67	171,5	Item a Copton Beronicen usque	CCLVIII, sic:	258
	172,1	Poeniconon	XXIIII	24
	172,2	Dydime	XXIIII	24
	172,3	Afrodito	XX	20
	172,4	Compasi	XXII	22
	172,5	Iovis	XXIII	23
	172,6	Aristonis	XXV	25
	172,7	Falacro	XXV	25
	173,1	Apollonos	XXIII	23
	173,2	Cabalsi	XXVII	27
	173,3	Cenon Hidreuma	XXVII	27
	173,4	Beronicen	XVIII.	18
	175,1	ITER TRACIAE.		
68	175,2	A Cabile per conpendium Adrianopoli us-		
	175,3	que	LXXVIIII:	79
	175,4	Orudisza ad Burgum	XXX	30
	175,5	In Medio	XXV	25
	175,6	Adrianopoli	XXIIII.	24
69	175,7	A Plotinopolim Heraclea	XXV	25
	175,8	Traianopolim	XXII	22
	175,9	Apris	XXIII	23
	176,1	Resisto	XXII	22
	176,2	Heraclea	XXV.	25
70	176,3	A Sebastia Cocuso per Meli-		
	176,4	tenam	CCXCIIIS, sic:	293.5
	176,5	Blandos	XXIIII	24
	177,1	Euspena	XXVIII	28
	177,2	Aranis	XXIIII	24
	177,3	Ad Praetorium	XXVIII	28
	177,4	Pisonos	XXXII	32

	177,5	Meletena	XXII	22
	178,1	Arcas	XXVI	26
	178,2	Dandaxina	XXIIII	24
	178,3	Osdara	XXIIII	24
	178,4	Ptandari	XXIIII	24
	178,5	Cocuso	XXXVIII.	38
71	178,6	Item a Sebastia Cocuso per		
	178,7	Caesaream	CCLVIII:	258
	179,1	Scanatu	XXVIII	28
	179,2	Malandara	XXX	30
	179,3	Armaxa	XXVIII	28
	179,4	Eulepa	XXIIII	24
	179,5	Caesarea	XVI	16
	180,1	Artaxata	XXVII	27
	180,2	Coduzalaba	XVIIII	19
	180,3	Comana	XXIIII	24
	180,4	Ptandari	XXIIII	24
	180,5	Cocuso	XXXVIII.	38
72	180,6	Item a Sebastia Cocuso per		
	180,7	conpendium	CCVI:	206
	181,1	Tonosa	L	50
	181,2	Ariarathia	L	50
	181,3	Coduzalaba	XX	20
	181,4	Comana	XXIIII	24
	181,5	Ptandari	XXIIII	24
	181,6	Cocuso	XXXVIII.	38
73	181,7	Item ab Arabisso per conpendium		
	181,8	Satalam	CCXXIII:	223
	182,1	Tonosa	XXVIII	28
	182,2	Zoana	XXV	25
	182,3	Gundusa	XXIII	23
	182,4	Eumeis	XXX	30
	182,5	Sara	XVIII	18
	182,6	Dagalasso	XX	20
	183,1	Nicopoli	XXIIII	24
	183,2	Olotoaelariza	XXIIII	24
	183,3	Ad Dracones	XXVI	26
	183,4	Haza	XXIIII	24
	183,5	Satala leg. XV Apollinans	XXVI.	26
74	184,1	A Germanicia per Dolicum et Zeuma		
	184,2	Aedissam usque	LXXXVII:	87
	184,3	Sicos Basilisses	XX	20
	184,4	Dolica	X	10
	185,1	Zeuma	XII	12
	185,2	Bemmaris	XX	20
	185,3	Edissa	XXV.	25
75	186,1	Item a Germanicia per Samosatam		
	186,2	Edissam	XC:	90
	186,3	In Catabana	XV	15
	186,4	Nisus	XVI	16

227

*Appendix 9: User's
Guide to the
Outlining of Rivers
and Routes on
Barrington Atlas
Bases (C–F), with
Associated Texts:
Antonine Itinerary*

228

———

*Appendix 9: User's
Guide to the
Outlining of Rivers
and Routes on*
Barrington Atlas
*Bases (C–F), with
Associated Texts:
Antonine Itinerary*

	186,5	Tharse	XIIII	14
	186,6	Samosata leg. VII	XIII	13
	187,1	Edissa	XII.	12
76	187,2	Item ab Antiochia Hemesa	CXXXIIII, sic:	134
	187,3	Niaccaba	XXVI	26
	187,4	Caperturi	XXIIII	24
	187,5	Apamia	XX	20
	187,6	Larissa	XVI	16
	188,1	Epitania	XVI	16
	188,2	Arethusa	XVI	16
	188,3	Hemesa	XVI.	16
omitted	188,4	Item ab Arbalisso Muzana	XLVIII:	48
	188,5	In Medio	XXII	22
	188,6	Muzana	XXVI.	26
77	188,7	Item a Germanicia Edissa	LXXXIIII:	84
	188,8	Sico Basilisses	XV	15
	189,1	Dolica	XV	15
	189,2	Zeuma	XIIII	14
	189,3	Cannaba	XIII	13
	189,4	In Medio	XII	12
	189,5	Aedissa	XV.	15
78	189,6	Item a Cyrro Edissa	XCII:	92
	189,7	Ciliza sive Urmagiganti	XII	12
	190,1	Abarara	X	10
	190,2	Zeugma	XXII	22
	190,3	Bemmari Canna	XL	40
	190,4	Bathenas Meri	VIII	8
	190,5	Aedissa	X.	10
79	190,6	Item a Nicopoli Edissa	CXXXVII:	137
	190,7	Aliaria	XIII	13
	190,8	Gerbedisso	XV	15
	191,1	Dolicha	XX	20
	191,2	Zeuma	XXIIII	24
	191,3	Canaba	XXV	25
	191,4	In Medio	XXII	22
	191,5	Aedissa	XVIII.	18
80	191,6	Item a Callecoma Edissa	LXXXV:	85
	191,7	Bathnas	XXIIII	24
	191,8	Hierapoli	XXI	21
	192,1	Thilaticomum	X	10
	192,2	Bathanas	XV	15
	192,3	Aedissa	XV.	15
81	192,4	Item a Carris Hierapoli	LXXXIII:	83
	192,5	Bathnas	XXX	30
	192,6	Thilaticomum	XXII	22
	193,1	Hierapoli	XXXI.	31
82	193,2	Item a Cyrro Hemesa	CLI:	151
	193,3	Minnicam	XX	20
	193,4	Beroa	XXII	22

	194,1	Calcida	XVIII	18
	194,2	Arra	XX	20
	194,3	Capareas	XXIII	23
	194,4	Epifania	XVI	16
	194,5	Aretusa	XVI	16
	194,6	Hemesa	XVI.	16
83	194,7	Item a Dolica Seriane	CXXVIII:	128
	194,8	Hanunea		
	194,9	Cyrro	XXIIII	24
	194,10	Minnica	XXIIII	24
	194,11	Borea	XX	20
	195,1	Calcida	XV	15
	195,2	Androna	XXVII	27
	195,3	Seriane	XVIII.	18
84	195,4	Item a Callicome Larissa	LXXVIIII:	79
	195,5	Calcida	XVIII	18
	195,6	Temmeliso	XX	20
	195,7	Apamia	XXV	25
	195,8	Larissa	XVI.	16
85	195,9	Item ab Eumari Neapolim	CCXXVII:	227
	196,1	Geroda	XL	40
	196,2	Thelsee	XVI	16
	196,3	Damasco	XXIIII	24
	196,4	Aere	XXXII	32
	196,5	Neve	XXX	30
	196,6	Capitoliada	XXXVI	36
	197,1	Gadara	XVI	16
	197,2	Scytopoli	XVI	16
	197,3	In Medio	X	10
	197,4	Neapoli	VII.	7
86	197,5	Item a Seriane Scytopoli Occara	CCCXVIII:	318
	197,6	Salaminiada	XXXII	32
	198,1	Hemisa	XVIII	18
	198,2	Laudicia	XVIII	18
	198,3	Libo	XXXII	32
	198,4	Heliupoli	XXXII	32
	198,5	Abila	XXXVIII	38
	198,6	Damasco	XVIII	18
	198,7	Aere	XXXII	32
	198,8	Neve	XXX	30
	198,9	Capitoliada	XXXVI	36
	198,10	Gadara	XVI	16
	198,11	Scytopoli	XVI.	16
87	199,1	Item a Caesarea Eleuteropoli	LXXVII:	77
	199,2	Betaro	XXXI	31
	199,3	Diospoli	XXVIII	28
	199,4	Eleuteropoli	XVIII.	18
88	199,5	Item a Damasco Hemesam	CLII:	152
	199,6	Abila	XXXVIII	38

229

Appendix 9: User's Guide to the Outlining of Rivers and Routes on Barrington Atlas Bases (C–F), with Associated Texts: Antonine Itinerary

230

————

Appendix 9: User's Guide to the Outlining of Rivers and Routes on Barrington Atlas *Bases (C–F), with Associated Texts: Antonine Itinerary*

	199,7	Heliupoli	XXXII	32
	199,8	Conna	XXXII	32
	199,9	Laudicia	XXXII	32
	199,10	Hemesa	XVIII.	18
89	199,11	Item a Neapoli Ascalona	LXXIIII:	74
	200,1	Elia	XXX	30
	200,2	Eleuteropoli	XX	20
	200,3	Ascalona	XXIIII.	24
90	200,4	Item a Claudiopoli Ancyra	CXXXIIII:	134
	200,5	Gratia	XXIIII	24
	200,6	Garus vicus	XXX	30
	200,7	Legna	XXIIII	24
	201,1	Grentius	XXXII	32
	201,2	Ancyra	XXIIII.	24
91	201,3	Item a Pessinunto Ancyra	XCVIIII:	99
	201,4	Germa	XVI	16
	201,5	Vinda	XXIIII	24
	201,6	Papyra	XXXII	32
	201,7	Ancyra	XXVII.	27
92	201,8	Item a Tavia Caesarea usque	CVIIII:	109
	202,1	Therma	XVIII	18
	202,2	Soanda	XVIII	18
	202,3	Sacoena	XXXII	32
	202,4	Ochras	XVI	16
	202,5	Caesarea	XXIIII.	24
93	202,6	Item a Dorilao Ancyra	CXLI:	141
	202,7	Arcelaio	XXX	30
	202,8	Germa	XX	20
	202,9	Vindia	XXXII	32
	203,1	Papyra	XXXII	32
	203,2	Ancyra	XXVII.	27
94	203,3	Item ab Ancyra Tabiam	CXVI:	116
	203,4	Bolecasgus	XXIIII	24
	203,5	Sarmalius	XXIIII	24
	203,6	Ecobrogis	XX	20
	203,7	Adapera	XXIIII	24
	203,8	Tavia	XXIIII.	24
95	203,9	Item a Tavia Sebastiam	CLXI:	161
	204,1	Corniaspa	XXI	21
	204,2	Pardosena	XXV	25
	204,3	Sibora	XXV	25
	204,4	Agriane	XX	20
	204,5	Simos	XXX	30
	204,6	Sebastia	XL.	40
96	204,7	Item a Tavia per Sebastopolin Sebastiam us-		
	204,8	que	CLXVI:	166
	205,1	Mogaro	XXX	30
	205,2	Daorano	XXIIII	24
	205,3	Sebastopoli	XL	40

	205,4	Verisa	XXIIII	24
	205,5	Fiarasi	XII	12
	205,6	Sebastia	XXXVI.	36
97	205,7	Item ab Ancyra per Nisam Caesaream		
	205,8		CXCVIII:	198
	205,9	Gorbeus	XXIIII	24
	206,1	Orsologiaco	XVIII	18
	206,2	Aspona	XX	20
	206,3	Parnasso	XXII	22
	206,4	Nisa	XXIIII	24
	206,5	Asiana	XXXII	32
	206,6	Saccasena	XXVIII	28
	206,7	Caesarea	XXX.	30
98	206,8	Item a Caesarea Satala	CCCXX:	320
	206,9	Eulepa	XVI	16
	206,10	Armaxa	XXIIII	24
	206,11	Marandara	XXVIII	28
	206,12	Scanatus	XXXVIIII	39
	207,1	Sebastia	XXVIII	28
	207,2	Camisa	XXVII	27
	207,3	Zara	XVIII	18
	207,4	Dagolasso	XX	20
	207,5	Nicopoli	XXIIII	24
	207,6	Olotedariza	XXIIII	24
	207,7	Dracontes	XXVI	26
	207,8	Haia	XXVI	26
	207,9	Satala	XXVI.	26
99	207,10	Item a Satala Melitena per ripam Samosa-		
	207,11	tam usque	CCCXLI:	341
	207,12	Suisa	XVII	17
	208,1	Arauracos	XXVIII	28
	208,2	Carsagis	XXIIII	24
	208,3	Sinervas	XXVIII	28
	208,4	Analiba	XXVIII	28
	208,5	Zimara	XVI	16
	209,1	Teucila	XVI	16
	209,2	Sabus	XXVIII	28
	209,3	Dascusa	XVI	16
	209,4	Chiaca	XXXII	32
	209,5	Melitena	XVIII	18
	210,1	Miasena	XII	12
	210,2	Lacotina	XXVIII	28
	210,3	Perre	XXVI	26
	210,4	Samosata	XXIIII.	24
100	210,5	Item a Caesarea Melitena	CCXXVIII:	228
	210,6	Artaxata	XXIIII	24
	210,7	Codozalaba	XXIIII	24
	210,8	Comana	XXVI	26
	210,9	Siricis	XXIIII	24
	210,10	Ptandaris	XVI	16

231

*Appendix 9: User's
Guide to the
Outlining of Rivers
and Routes on
Barrington Atlas
Bases (C–F), with
Associated Texts:
Antonine Itinerary*

232

*Appendix 9: User's
Guide to the
Outlining of Rivers
and Routes on*
Barrington Atlas
*Bases (C–F), with
Associated Texts:
Antonine Itinerary*

	210,11	Arabiso	XII	12
	211,1	Osdara	XXVIII	28
	211,2	Dandexena	XXIIII	24
	211,3	Arcas	XXII	22
	211,4	Melitena	XXVIII.	28
101	211,5	Item a Caesarea Anazarbo	CCXI:	211
	211,6	Arassaxa	XXIIII	24
	211,7	Codozalaba	XXIIII	24
	211,8	Comana	XXVI	26
	211,9	Siricis	XXIIII	24
	211,10	Cocuso	XV	15
	211,11	Laranda	XVIII	18
	212,1	Badimo	XVIII	18
	212,2	Praetorio	XXII	22
	212,3	Flaviada	XXII	22
	212,4	Anazarbo	XVIII.	18
102	212,5	Item a Sebastia Cocuso	CCVI:	206
	212,6	In Medio	XXV	25
	212,7	Tonosa	XXV	25
	212,8	In Medio	XXV	25
	212,9	Ariarathia	XXV	25
	212,10	Doduzalaba	XX	20
	212,11	Comana	XXIIII	24
	212,12	Tandari	XXIIII	24
	213,1	Cocuso	XXXVIII.	38
103	213,2	Item a Nicopoli Arabisso	CCXXVI:	226
	213,3	Dagalasso	XXIIII	24
	213,4	Zara	XX	20
	213,5	Camisa	XVIII	18
	213,6	Sebastia	XXIIII	24
	213,7	In Medio	XXV	25
	213,8	Ariarathia	XXV	25
	213,9	Coduzalaba	XX	20
	213,10	Comana	XXIIII	24
	213,11	Tandari	XXIIII	24
	213,12	Arabisso	XXII.	22
104	214,1	Item a Sebastopoli Caesaream		
	214,2	usque	CCVII:	207
	214,3	Verisa	XXIIII	24
	214,4	Siara	XII	12
	214,5	Sebastia	XXXVI	36
	214,6	Scanatus	XXVIII	28
	214,7	Maiandara	XXXVIIII	39
	214,8	Armaxa	XXVIII	28
	214,9	Eulepa	XXIIII	24
	214,10	Caesarea	XXVI.	26
105	214,11	Item a Cocuso Arabisso usque	LII:	52
	214,12	Ptandari	XXVIII	28
	214,13	Arabisso	XXIIII.	24

106	214,14	Item a Cocuso Melitenam	CXLII:	142
	215,1	Ptandari	XXVIII	28
	215,2	Arabisso	XII	12
	215,3	Asdara	XXVIII	28
	215,4	Dandexena	XXIIII	24
	215,5	Arcas	XXII	22
	215,6	Melitena	XXVIII.	28
107	215,7	Item a Meletena Samosata	XCI:	91
	215,8	Mesena	XII	12
	215,9	Lacotena	XXVIII	28
	215,10	Perre	XXVI	26
	215,11	Samosata	XXIIII.	24
108	215,12	Item a Nicopoli Satalam	CXXII:	122
	215,13	Olotoedariza	XXIIII	24
	215,14	Carsais	XXIIII	24
	216,1	Arauracos	XXIIII	24
	216,2	Soissa	XXIIII	24
	216,3	Satala	XXVI.	26
109	216,4	Item a Trepezunta Satalam	CXXX:	130
	216,5	Ad Vicensimum	XX	20
	216,6	Zigana	XXII	22
	217,1	Thia	XXIIII	24
	217,2	Sedisca, fi. Ponti	XVII	17
	217,3	Domana	XXIIII	24
	217,4	Satala	XVIII.	18
110	217,5	Item per ripam a Viminacio Nico-		
	217,6	mediam	X̅I LXII, sic:	
	217,7	Cuppe	XXIIII	24
	218,1	Novas	XXIIII	24
	218,2	Talia	XII	12
	218,3	Egeta	XXI	21
	218,4	Aquis	XVI	16
	219,1	Dortico	X	10
	219,2	Bononia	XVII	17
	219,3	Ratiaria leg. XIIII GG.	XVIII	18
	219,4	Almo	XVIII	18
	220,1	Cebro	XVIII	18
	220,2	Augustis	XVIII	18
	220,3	Variana	XII	12
	220,4	Valeriana	XII	12
	220,5	Oesco leg. V Mac.	XII	12
	221,1	Uto	XIIII	14
	221,2	Securisca	XII	12
	221,3	Dimo	XII	12
	221,4	Novas leg. I Ital.	XVI	16
	222,1	Scaidava	XVIII	18
	222,2	Trimammio	VII	7
	222,3	Sexantapristis	XII	12

Appendix 9: User's
Guide to the
Outlining of Rivers
and Routes on
Barrington Atlas
Bases (C–F), with
Associated Texts:
Antonine Itinerary

222,4	Tigra	VIIII	9
222,5	Appiaria	XIII	13
223,1	Transmariscam	XVI	16
223,2	Candidiana	XIII	13
223,3	Teclicio	XII	12
223,4	Dorostoro leg. XI Cl.	XII	12
224,1	Sucidava	XVIII	18
224,2	Axiupoli	XII	12
224,3	Capidava	XVIII	18
224,4	Carso	XVIII	18
224,5	Cio	X	10
225,1	Biroe	XIII	14
225,2	Trosmis leg. I Iovia	XVIII	18
225,3	Scytica		
225,4	Arrubio	VIIII	9
225,5	Diniguttia	VIIII	9
226,1	Novioduno leg. II Herculea	XX	20
226,2	Aegiso	XXIIII	24
226,3	Salsovia	XVII	17
226,4	Salmorude	VIIII	9
226,5	Vale Domitiana	XVII	17
227,1	Ad Salices	XXVI	26
227,2	Historio	XXV	25
227,3	Tomos	XXXVI	36
227,4	Callacis	XXX	30
228,1	Timogitia	XVIII	18
228,2	Dionisopoli	XXIIII	24
228,3	Odisso	XXIIII	24
228,4	Marcianopoli	XVIII	18
229,1	Scatris	XXVI	26
229,2	Ancialis	XXIIII	24
229,3	Debelco	XXIIII	24
230,1	Sadame	XVIII	18
230,2	Tarpodizo	XVIII	18
230,3	Ostodizo	XXXII	32
230,4	Burtudizo	XVIII	18
230,5	Bergule	XVIII	18
230,6	Drizipara	XIIII	14
230,7	Tzirallo	XVI	16
230,8	Heraclia	XVIII	18
230,9	Cenofrurio	XVIII	18
230,10	Melantiada	XXVII	27
230,11	Bizantio	XVIII	18
231,1	Pantecio	XV	15
231,2	Lybissa	XXIIII	24
231,3	Nicomedia	XXII.	22
III	231,4	A Beroa Adrianopolim	LXXXVII:	87
	231,5	Castra Iarba	XXX	30
	231,6	Burdipta	XXV	25
	231,7	Hadrianopolim	XXXII.	32

	231,8	ITEM DE PANNONIIS IN		
		GALLIAS per mediterranea		
	231,9	loca, id est a Sirmi per Sopianas		
	231,10	Treveros usque:		
112	231,11	A Sirmi Lauriaco	CCCCXXXVII,	437
	232,1	Augusta Vindelicum	CCXVI,	216
	232,2	Ad Fines	CXXXVI,	136
	232,3	Treveros	leugas, non m.p., CCXXI:	221
	232,4	Ulmos	XXVI	26
	232,5	Civalis	XXIII	23
	232,6	Mursa	XXII	22
	232,7	Antianis	XXIIII	24
	232,8	Suppianis	XXX	30
	233,1	Limusa	XXII	22
	233,2	Silicenis	XVI	16
	233,3	Valco	XXIIII	24
	233,4	Mogetiana	XXX	30
	233,5	Sabaria	XXXVI	36
	233,6	Scarabantia	XXXIIII	34
	233,7	Muteno	XII	12
	233,8	Vindomona	XXII	22
	234,1	Comagenis	XXIIII	24
	234,2	Cetio	XXIIII	24
	234,3	Arlape	XXII	22
	234,4	Loco Felicis	XXVI	26
	235,1	Lauriaco	XX	20
	235,2	Ovilavis	XXVI	26
	235,3	Laciaco	XXXII	32
	235,4	Iovavi	XXVIII	28
	236,1	Bidaio	XXXIII	33
	236,2	Ponte Aeni	XVIII	18
	236,3	Isinisca	XX	20
	236,4	Ambre	XXXII	32
	236,5	Augusta Vindelicum	XXVII	27
	237,1	Rostro Nemaviae	XXV	25
	237,2	Campoduno	XXXII	32
	237,3	Vemania	XV	15
	237,4	Brigantia	XXIIII	24
	237,5	Arbore Felice	XX	20
	238,1	Ad Fines	XX	20
	238,2	Vindonissa	leugas m.p. XXX	30
	238,3	Arialbino	XXIII	23
	239,1	Monte Brisiaco	XXX	30
	239,2	Argentorato	XXXVIII	38
	240,1	Tabernis	XIIII	14
	240,2	Decem Pagis	XX	20
	240,3	Divodoro	XXXVIII	38
	240,4		XII	12
	240,5	Triveros	XVI.	16

235
———

*Appendix 9: User's
Guide to the
Outlining of Rivers
and Routes on*
Barrington Atlas
Bases (C–F), with
*Associated Texts:
Antonine Itinerary*

	241,1	Item per ripam PANNONIAE a Daurono in		
	241,2	GALLIS ad leg. XXX usque:		
113	241,3	A Taurino Lauriaco	DLXXXVII,	587
	241,4	inde Augusta Vindelicum	XL,	40
	241,5	Argentorato	XXXVIII,	38
	241,6	ad leg. XXX	m.p., sic:	
	242,1	A Laurino	XXV	25
		Ritti	XXXIII	33
		in medio		
	242,2	Aciminci	CXIII	113
	242,3	Cusi	XXXIII	33
	243,1	Bononia	XVI	16
	243,2	Cucci	XVI	16
	243,3	Cornaco	XVI	16
	243,4	Teutiburgio	XVI	16
	243,5	Mursa	XVI	16
	243,6	Ad Novas et Aureo Monte		
	243,7	Antianis	XXIIII	24
	244,1	Altino in medio		
	244,2	Lugione	XXV	25
	244,3	Ad Statuas in medio		
	244,4	Alisca ad latus		
	244,5	Ripa Alta	XXVIIII	29
	245,1	Lussunio	XVIII	18
	245,2	Annamatia in medio		
	245,3	Intercisa	XXIIII	24
	245,4	Vetus Salinas in medio		
	245,5	Matrica	XXVI	26
	245,6	Campona in medio		
	245,7	Aquinquo leg. II Adiut.	XX	20
	246,1	A laco Felicis in medio		
	246,2	Crumero	XXXIII	33
	246,3	Azao in medio		
	246,4	Bregetione leg. I Adiut.	XVIII	18
	246,5	Ad Mures et ad Statuas in medio		
	246,6	Arabona	XXX	30
	247,1	Quadratis in medio		
	247,2	Flexo	XXII	22
	247,3	Gerulata in medio		
	247,4	Carnunto	XXX	30
			leg. XIIII G.G.	
	248,1	Aequinoctio et Ala Nova in medio		
	248,2	Vindobona	XXVII	27
			leg. X Gem.	
	248,3	Comagenis	XX	20
	248,4	Cetio	XXX	30
	248,5	Arlape	XX	20
	248,6	Loco Felicis	XXV	25
	249,1	Lauriaco	XX	20
			leg. III	
	249,2	Ovilatus	XVI	16

249,3	Ioviaco	XXVII	27
249,4	Stanago	XVIII	18
249,5	Bolodoro	XX	20
249,6	Quintianis	XXIIII	24
249,7	Augustis	XX	20
250,1	Regino	XXIIII	24
250,2	Abusina	XX	20
250,3	Vallato	XVIII	18
250,4	Summunturio	XVI	16
250,5	Augusta Vindelicum	XX	20
250,6	Guntia	XXII	22
250,7	Celio Monte	XVI	16
250,8	Camboduno	XIIII	14
251,1	Vemania	XV	15
251,2	Brigantia	XXIIII	24
251,3	Arbore Felice	XX	20
251,4	Finibus	XX	20
251,5	Vitudoro	XXII leg.	22
251,6	Vindonissa	XXIIII leg.	24
251,7	Rauracis	XXVII leg.	27
252,1	Arialbino	XVII leg.	17
252,2	Uruncis	XXII	22/10
		leugas X	
252,3	Monte Brisiaco	XXIII	23/15
		leugas XV	
252,4	Helueto	XXVIII	28/19
		leugas XVIIII	
252,5	Argentorato	XXVIIII	29/19
		leugas XVIIII	
253,1	Brocomago	XX	20
253,2	Concordia	XVIII	18
253,3	Noviomago	XX	20
253,4	Bingio	XXV	25
254,1	Antunnaco	XVII	17
254,2	Boudobrica	XVIIII	19
254,3	Bonna	XXII	22
254,4	Colonia Agrippina	leugas	
254,5	Durnomago	leugas VII ala	7
255,1	Burungo	leugas V ala	5
255,2	Nevensio	leugas V ala	5
255,3	Gelduba	leugas VIIII ala	9
255,4	Calone	leugas VIIII ala	9
255,5	Veteris	leugas XXI ca-	21
256,1		stra leg. XXX Ulpia.	
256,2	Burginacio	leugas VI ala	6
256,3	Harenatio	leugas X ala.	10
114	256,4	Item a Lauriaco Veldidena:		
	256,5	Ovilavis	XXVI	26
	256,6	Iaciaco	XXXII	32
	256,7	Iovavi	XXVIII	28
	257,1	Bidaio	XXXIII	33

237

Appendix 9: User's Guide to the Outlining of Rivers and Routes on Barrington Atlas *Bases (C–F), with Associated Texts: Antonine Itinerary*

238
___
Appendix 9: User's
Guide to the
Outlining of Rivers
and Routes on
Barrington Atlas
Bases (C–F), with
Associated Texts:
Antonine Itinerary

	257,2	Ponte Aeni	XVIII	18
	257,3	Isinisco	XX	20
	257,4	Ambrae	XXXII	32
	257,5	Ad pontes Tesseninos	XL	40
	257,6	Parthano	XX	20
	258,1	Veldidena	XXIII.	23
115	258,2	Item a Lauriaco per medium		
	258,3	Augusta Vindelicum sive Brigantia	CCCXI, sic:	311
	258,4	Ovilavis	XXVI	26
	258,5	Laciaco	XXXII	32
	258,6	Iovavi	XXVIII	28
	258,7	Bidaio	XXXII	32
	258,8	Ponte Aeni	XVIII	18
	258,9	Isinisco	XX	20
	258,10	Ambrae	XXXII	32
	258,11	Augusta Vindelicum	XXVII	27
	258,12	Rostro Nemaviae	XXV	25
	258,13	Camboduno	XXXII	32
	259,1	Vemania	XV	15
	259,2	Brigantia	XXIIII.	24
116	259,3	Item a Ponte Aeni ad Castra	CL:	150
	259,4	Turo	XLIIII	44
	259,5	Iovisura	LXIIII	64
	259,6	Ad Castra	XLII.	42
117	259,7	Item a Ponte Aeni Veldidena:		
	259,8	Albiano	XXVIII	28
	259,9	Mastiaco	XXVI	26
	259,10	Veldidena	XXVI.	26
118	259,11	Item ab Hemona per Sisciam Sirmi		
	259,12		CCCXI, sic:	311
	259,13	Praetorio Latovicorum	XXXIIII	34
	259,14	Novioduno	XXXI	31
	260,1	Quadrato	XXVIII	28
	260,2	Siscia	XXVIIII	29
	260,3	Varianis	XXIII	23
	260,4	Manneianis	XXVI	26
	260,5	Incero	XXVIII	28
	260,6	sed mansio Augusti in praetorio est		
	260,7	Picentino	XXV	25
	260,8	Leucono	XXVI	26
	260,9	Cirtisa	XV	15
	261,1	Cibalis	XXII	22
	261,2	Ulmos	XXII	22
	261,3	Sirmi	XXVI.	26
119	261,4	Item a Vindobona Poetovione	CLXXXIIII:	184
	261,5	Aquis	XXVIII	28
	261,6	Scarabantia	XXXI	31
	261,7	Sabaria	XXXIIII	34
	261,8	Arrabone	XX	20

	261,9	Alicano	XL	40
	262,1	In medio Curta		
	262,2	Poetovione	XXXI.	31
120	262,3	Item a Poetovione Carnunto	CLXIIII, sic:	164
	262,4	Halicano	XXXI	31
	262,5	Salle	XXX	30
	262,6	Savaria	XXXI	31
	262,7	Scarabantia	XXXIIII	34
	262,8	Carnunto	XXXVIII.	38
121	262,9	A Sabaria Bregetione	CII, sic:	102
	262,10	Bassiana	XVIII	18
	262,11	Mursella	XXXIIII	34
	263,1	Arrabona	XX	20
	263,2	Bregetione	XXX.	30
122	263,3	A Sabaria Aquinco	CLXVIIII:	169
	263,4	Mestrianis	XXX	30
	263,5	Mogentianis	XXV	25
	263,6	Caesariana	XXX	30
	263,7	Osonibus	XXVIII	28
	263,8	Floriana	XXVI	26
	263,9	Acinquo	XXX.	30
123	264,1	A Sopianas Acinquo	CXXXV, sic:	135
	264,2	Ponte Sociorum	XXV	25
	264,3	Valle Cariniana	XXX	30
	264,4	Gorsio sive Hercule	XXX	30
	264,5	Iasulonibus	XXV	25
	264,6	Acinquo	XXV.	25
124	264,7	Item a Sopianas Bregetione	CXS:	110.5
	264,8	Iovia	XXXII	32
	264,9	Fortiana	XXV	25
	265,1	Herculia	XX	20
	265,2	Floriana	XV	15
	265,3	Bregetione	VIII.	8
	265,4	De Italia per Histriam in Dalmatia.		
125	265,5	Item a Siscia Mursam	CXXXIIII, sic:	134
	265,6	Varianis	XXIII	23
	265,7	Aquis Balissis	XXX	30
	265,8	Incero	XXV	25
	265,9	Stravianis	XXIIII	24
	265,10	Mursa	XXX.	30
126	265,11	A Poetavione Siscia	C:	100
	265,12	Aqua Viva	XVIIII	19
	266,1	Pyrri	XXX	30
	266,2	Dautonia	XXIIII	24
	266,3	Siscia	XXVII.	27
127	266,4	A Sabaria Vindobona	LXXXVIII, sic:	88
	266,5	Scarabantia	XXXIIII	34
	266,6	Muteno	XVIII	18
	266,7	Vindobona	XXXVI.	36

240

*Appendix 9: User's
Guide to the
Outlining of Rivers
and Routes on
Barrington Atlas
Bases (C–F), with
Associated Texts:
Antonine Itinerary*

128	266,8	Item ab Acinquo Crumero que castra		
	266,9	constituta sint	XLII:	42
	266,10	Ulcisia castra	VIIII	9
	266,11	Cirpi mansio	XII	12
	266,12	Ad Herculem castra	XII	12
	266,13	Solva mansio	VIIII.	9
129	266,14	Item a Sirmio Carnunto	CCCXI:	311
	267,1	Ulmo	XXVI	26
	267,2	Cibalis	XXIIII	24
	267,3	Mursa	XXII	22
	267,4	Antianis	XXIIII	24
	267,5	Sopianis	XXX	30
	267,6	Ponte Mansuetiana	XXV	25
	267,7	Tricciana	XXX	30
	267,8	Cimbrianis	XXV	25
	267,9	Crispiana	XXV	25
	267,10	Arrabona	XXV	25
	267,11	Flexo	XXV	25
	267,12	Carnunto	XXX.	30
130	267,13	Item a Sirmio Salonas	CCLXXXIIII:	284
	268,1	Budalia	VIII	8
	268,2	Hispaneta	VIII	8
	268,3	Ulmo	X	10
	268,4	Cibalis	XXII	22
	268,5	Cirtisia	XXIIII	24
	268,6	Urbate	XXV	25
	268,7	Servitti	XXIIII	24
	268,8	Ad Ladios	XXIIII	24
	269,1	Aemate	XVIII	18
	269,2	Leusaba	XIII	13
	269,3	Sarnade	XVIII	18
	269,4	Salviae	XXIIII	24
	269,5	Pelva	XVIII	18
	269,6	Aequo	XVII	17
	269,7	Salonas	XXI.	21
131	270,1	Item ab Aquileia per Istriam Sa-		
	270,2	lonas	CXCVIIII:	199
	270,3	Fonte Timavi	XII	12
	270,4	Tergeste	XII	12
	271,1	Ningum	XXVIII	28
	271,2	Parentium	XVIII	18
	271,3	Pola	XXXI	31
	272,1	traiectus sinus Liburnici Iader us-		
	272,2	que	stadia CCCCL	450
	272,3	Blandona	XX	20
	272,4	Arausa	XX	20
	272,5	Praetorio	XXX	30
	272,6	Tragurio	XV	15
	272,7	Salonas	XIII.	13

132	272,8	Ab Aquileia per Liburniam		
	272,9	Sisciam	CCXIII:	213
	273,1	Fonte Timavi	XII	12
	273,2	Avesica	XII	12
	273,3	Ad Malum	XVIII	18
	273,4	Ad Titulos	XVII	17
	273,5	Tharsatico	XVII	17
	273,6	Ad Turres	XX	20
	273,7	Senia	XX	20
	274,1	Avendone	XVIII	18
	274,2	Arupio	X	10
	274,3	Bibium	X	10
	274,4	Romula	X	10
	274,5	Quadranta	XIIII	14
	274,6	Ad Fines	XIIII	14
	274,7	Sisciae	XXI.	21
133	274,8	Item ab Augusta Vindelicum		
	274,9	Verona	CCLXXII:	272
	275,1	Abuzaco	XXXVI	36
	275,2	Parthano	XXX	30
	275,3	Veldidena	XXX	30
	275,4	Vipiteno	XXXVI	36
	275,5	Sublavione	XXXII	32
	275,6	Endidae	XXIIII	24
	275,7	Tridento	XXIIII	24
	275,8	Ad Palatium	XXIIII	24
	275,9	Verona	XXXVI.	36
134	276,1	Ab Aquileia Lauriaco	CCLXXII:	272
	276,2	viam Belloio	XXX	30
	276,3	Larice	XXIIII	24
	276,4	Santico	XXIIII	24
	276,5	Viruno	XXX	30
	276,6	Candalicas	XX	20
	276,7	Monate	XXX	30
	276,8	Sabatinca	XVIII	18
	276,9	Gabromago	XXX	30
	277,1	Tutatione	XX	20
	277,2	Ovilavis	XX	20
	277,3	Lauriaco	XXVI.	26
135	277,4	A Brigantia per lacum Mediolanium		
	277,5		CXXXVIII:	138
	277,6	Curia	L	50
	277,7	Tinnetione	XX	20
	277,8	Muro	XV	15
	277,9	Summo Laco	XX	20
	278,1	Como	XV	15
	278,2	Mediolano	XVIII.	18
136	278,3	Alio itinere a Brigantia Comum	CXCV, sic:	195
	278,4	Curia	L	50

241

*Appendix 9: User's
Guide to the
Outlining of Rivers
and Routes on*
Barrington Atlas
*Bases (C–F), with
Associated Texts:
Antonine Itinerary*

242

Appendix 9: User's
Guide to the
Outlining of Rivers
and Routes on
Barrington Atlas
Bases (C–F), with
Associated Texts:
Antonine Itinerary

	278,5	Tarvesede	LX	60
	278,6	Clavenna	XV	15
	278,7	Ad lacum Comacinum	X	10
	279,1	Per lacum Comum usque	LX.	60
137	279,2	Item ab Aquileia per conpendium		
	279,3	Veldidena	CCXV, sic:	215
	279,4	Ad Tricensimum	XXX	30
	279,5	Iulio Carnico	XXX	30
	279,6	Longio	XXII	22
	279,7	Agunto	XVIII	18
	280,1	Littamo	XXIII	23
	280,2	Sebato	XXIII	23
	280,3	Vipiteno	XXXIII	33
	280,4	Veldidena	XXXVI.	36
138	280,5	Ab Opitergio Tridento	CX, sic:	110
	280,6	Ad Cerasias	XXVIII	28
	280,7	Feltria	XXVIII	28
	280,8	Ausuco	XXX	30
	281,1	Tridento	XXIIII.	24
139	281,2	Item ab Aquileia Bononiam	?:	
	281,3	Concordia	XXXI	31
	281,4	Altino	XXXI	31
	281,5	Patavis	XXXII	32
	281,6	Ateste	XXV	25
	281,7	Anneiano	XX	20
	281,8	Vico Variano	XVIII	18
	281,9	Vico Sernino	XX	20
	282,1	Mutina	XIII	13
	282,2	Bononia	XVIII.	18
140	282,3	A Verona Bononia	CV:	105
	282,4	Hostilia	XXX	30
	282,5	Colicaria	XXV	25
	282,6	Mutina	XXV	25
	282,7	Bononia	XXV.	25
141	282,8	A Vercellas Laude	LXX:	70
	282,9	Laumello	XXV	25
	283,1	Ticino	XXII	22
	283,2	Laude	XXIII.	23
142	283,3	A Cremona Bononia	?:	
	283,4	Brixello	XXXII	32
	283,5	Regio	XII	12
	283,6	Mutina	XVII	17
	283,7	Bononia	XXV.	25
143	283,8	Item a Faventia Luca	CXX:	120
	283,9	In Castello	XXV	25
	284,1	Anneiano	XXV	25
	284,2	Florentia	XX	20
	284,3	Pistoris	XXV	25
	284,4	Luca	XXV.	25

144	284,5	Item a Perme Laca	C.	100
	284,6	Via Clodia.		
145	284,7	Item a Luca Romam per Clo-		
	284,8	diam	CCXXXVIII:	238
	285,1	Pistoris	XXV	25
	285,2	Florentia	XXV	25
	285,3	Ad Fines sive Casas Caesarianas	XXV	25
	285,4	Arretio	XXV	25
	285,5	Ad Statuas	XXV	25
	285,6	Clusio	XII	12
	286,1	Vulsinis	XXX	30
	286,2	Foro Cassi	XXVIII	28
	286,3	Sutrio	XI	11
	286,4	Baccanas	XII	12
	286,5	Roma	XXI.	21
146	286,6	Item a Roma Foro Clodi	XXXII.	32
147	286,7	Item ab Arimino Dertonam	CCXXVIII:	228
	286,8	Curva Caesena	XX	20
	287,1	Foro Livi	XIII	13
	287,2	Faventia	X	10
	287,3	Foro Corneli	X	10
	287,4	Claterna	XIII	13
	287,5	Bononia	X	10
	287,6	Mutina	XXV	25
	287,7	Regio	XVIII	18
	287,8	Tannetum	X	10
	287,9	Parma	VIII	8
	288,1	Fidentia	XV	15
	288,2	Florentia	X	10
	288,3	Placentia	XV	15
	288,4	Comillomago	XXV	25
	288,5	Iria	XVI	16
	288,6	Dertona	X.	10
148	289,1	Item a Luca Pisis	XII.	12
149	289,2	Item a Luca Lune	XXXIII.	33
	289,3	Via Aurelia.		
150	289,4	A Roma per Tusciam et Alpes Maritimas		
	289,5	Arelatum usque	DCCXCVI:	796
	290,1	Loria	XII	12
	290,2	Ad Turres	X	10
	290,3	Pyrgos	XII	12
	291,1	Castro Novo	VIII	8
	291,2	Centum Cellis	V	5
	291,3	Martha	X	10
	291,4	Forum Aureli	XIIII	14
	292,1	Cosam	XXV	25
	292,2	Ad lacum Aprilem	XXII	22
	292,3	Salebrone	XII	12
	292,4	Manliana	VIIII	9
	292,5	Populonium	XII	12

243

*Appendix 9: User's
Guide to the
Outlining of Rivers
and Routes on
Barrington Atlas
Bases (C–F), with
Associated Texts:
Antonine Itinerary*

244

Appendix 9: User's Guide to the Outlining of Rivers and Routes on Barrington Atlas Bases (C–F), with Associated Texts: Antonine Itinerary

	292,6	Vadis Volaterranis	XXV	25
	293,1	Ad Herculem	XVII	17
	293,2	Pise	XII	12
	293,3	Papiriana	XI	11
	293,4	Lune	XII	12
	293,5	Boacias	XII	12
	294,1	Bodetia	XXVII	27
	294,2	Tegulata	XII	12
	294,3	Delphinis	XXI	21
	294,4	Genua	XII	12
	294,5	Libanum	XXXVI	36
	294,6	Dertona	XXXV	35
	294,7	Aquis	XXVIII	28
	295,1	Crixia	XX	20
	295,2	Canalico	X	10
	295,3	Vadis Sabatis	XII	12
	295,4	Pullopice	XII	12
	295,5	Albingauno	VIII	8
	295,6	Luco Bormani	XV	15
	295,7	Costa Ballene	XVI	16
	296,1	Albintimilio	XVI	16
	296,2	Lumone	X	10
	296,3	Alpe Summa	VI	6
	296,4.5	Cemenelo	VIIII	9
	297,1	Varum flumen	VI	6
	297,2	Antipoli	X	10
	297,3	Ad Horrea	XII	12
	297,4	Forum Iuli	XVIII	18
	298,1	Forum Voconi	XII	12
	298,2	Matavonio	XII	12
	298,3	Ad Turrem	XIIII	14
	298,4	Tegulata	XVI	16
	298,5	Aquis Sextis	XV	15
	299,1	Massilia	XVIII	18
	299,2	Calcaria	XIIII	14
	299,3	Fossis Marianis	XXXIIII	34
	299,4	Arelate	XXXIII.	33
151	300,1	Aliter a Roma Cosa	LXI:	61
	300,2	Careias	XV	15
	300,3	Aquis Apollinaribus	XVIIII	19
	300,4	Tarquinios	XII	12
	300,5	Cosam	XV.	15
152	300,6	Item a Roma per Portum Centum		
	300,7	Cellis	LXVIIII:	69
	300,8	In Portum	XVIIII	19
	300,9	Fregenas	VIIII	9
	301,1	Alsio	VIIII	9
	301,2	Ad Turres	IIII	4
	301,3	Pirgos	XII	12
	301,4	Castro Novo	VIII	8
	301,5	Centum Cellis	VIII.	8

153	301,6	Ab Urbe Hostis	XVI,	16
	301,7	Laurento	XVI,	16
	301,8	Lanuvio	XVI.	16
	302,1	Praenestina.		
154	302,2	Ab Urbe Benevento usque	CLXXXVIII:	188
	302,3	Gabios	XII	12
	302,4	Praeneste	XI	11
	302,5	Sub Anagniae	XXIIII	24
	302,6	Ferentino	VIII	8
	303,1	Frusinone	VII	7
	303,2	Fregellano	XIIII	14
	303,3	Fabrateria	III	3
	303,4	Aquino	VIII	8
	303,5	Casino	VII	7
	303,6	Venafro	XVI	16
	304,1	Theano	XVIII	18
	304,2	Alifas	XVII	17
	304,3	Telesia	XXV	25
	304,4	Benevento	XVIII.	18
	304,5	Lavicana.		
155	304,6	Ab Urbe Benevento usque	CLXX:	170
	304,7	Ad Quintanas	XV	15
	304,8	Ad Pictas	X	10
	305,1	Compitum	XV	15
	305,2	Ferentino	VIII	8
	305,3	Frusinone	VII	7
	305,4	Fregellano	XIIII	14
	305,5	Benevento mansionibus quibus et in		
	305,6	Prenestina	CI.	101
	305,7	Latina.		
156	305,8	Ab Urbe ad Decimum	X	10
	305,9	Roboraria	III	3
	305,10	Ad Pictas	XVII	17
	306,1	Compitum	XV	15
	306,2	intrat in Lavicanam.		
	306,3	Salaria.		
157	306,4	Ab Urbe Adriae usque	CLVI, sic:	156
	306,5	Ereto	XVIII	18
	306,6	Vico Novo	XIIII	14
	306,7	Reate	XVI	16
	307,1	Cutilias	VIII	8
	307,2	Interocrio	VI	6
	307,3	Falacrino	XVI	16
	307,4	Vico Badies	VIIII	9
	307,5	Ad Centesimum	X	10
	307,6	Asclo	XII	12
	308,1	Castro Truentino	XX	20
	308,2	Castro Novo	XII	12
	308,3	Hadriae	XV.	15

245

*Appendix 9: User's
Guide to the
Outlining of Rivers
and Routes on
Barrington Atlas
Bases (C–F), with
Associated Texts:
Antonine Itinerary*

Appendix 9: User's
Guide to the
Outlining of Rivers
and Routes on
Barrington Atlas
Bases (C–F), with
Associated Texts:
Antonine Itinerary

	308,4	Valeria.		
158	308,5	Ab Urbe Hadriae usque	CXLVIII, sic:	148
	309,1	Tiburi	XX	20
	309,2	Carsiolos	XXII	22
	309,3	Alba Tucentia	XXV	25
	309,4	Cerfennia	XIII	13
	310,1	Corfinio	XVI	16
	310,2	Interbromio	XI	11
	310,3	Theate Marrucino	XVII	17
	310,4	Hadriae	XXIIII.	24
	310,5	Flaminia.		
159	310,6	Ab Urbe per Picenum Anconam et inde		
	310,7	Brindisium usque	DCXXVII:	627
	311,1	Ocriculi	XLIIII	44
	311,2	Narniae	XII	12
	311,3	Ad Martis	XVIII	18
	311,4	Vemaniae	XVI	16
	311,5	Nuceriae	XVIII	18
	312,1	Dubios	VIII	8
	312,2	Prolaque	VIII	8
	312,3	Septempeda	XVI	16
	312,4	Trea	VIIII	9
	312,5	Auximum	XVIII	18
	312,6	Ancona	XII	12
	312,7	Numana	VIII	8
	313,1	Potentia	X	10
	313,2	Castello Firmano	XXII	22
	313,3	Castro Truentino	XXIIII	24
	313,4	Castro Novo	XII	12
	313,5	Hadriae	XV	15
	313,6	Ostia Aeterni	XVI	16
	313,7	Angelum	X	10
	313,8	Ortona	XI	11
	313,9	Auxano	XIII	13
	314,1	Histonios	XXV	25
	314,2	Uscosio	XV	15
	314,3	Arenio	XIIII	14
	314,4	Corneli	XXVI	26
	314,5	Ponte Longo	XXX	30
	314,6	Sipunto	XXX	30
	314,7	Salinis	XV	15
	314,8	Aufidena	XL	40
	315,1	Respa	XXIII	23
	315,2	Barium	XIII	13
	315,3	Ernesto	XXII	22
	315,4	Gnatiae	XV	15
	315,5	Speluncis	XXI	21
	315,6	Brundisium	XVIII.	18

160	315,7	Ab Helvillo Anconam	L:	50
	316,1	Ad Calem	XIIII	14
	316,2	Ad Pirum	VIII	8
	316,3	Senagallia	VIII	8
	316,4	Ad Aesim	XII	12
	316,5	Ancona	VIII.	8
161	316,6	A Septempeda Castro Truentino	LXXIII:	73
	316,7	Urbe Salvia	XII	12
	316,8	Firmum	XVIII	18
	317,1	Asclo	XXIIII	24
	317,2	Castro Truentino	XX.	20
	317,3	Iter quod ducit a Durrachio PER MACEDO-		
	317,4	NIAM ET TRACHIAM Bizantium usque:		
	317,5	A Brundisio traiectus Durachium us-		
	317,6	que	stadia num. Ī CCCC	
162	317,7	A Dyrrachio Bizantium	DCCLIIII, sic:	754
	318,1	Clodiana	XXXIII	33
	318,2	Scampis	XX	20
	318,3	Tres Tabernas	XXVIII	28
	318,4	Licnido	XXVII	27
	318,5	Nicia	XXXIIII	34
	319,1	Heraclea	XI	11
	319,2	Cellis	XXXIIII	34
	319,3	Edessa	XXVIII	28
	319,4	Pella	XXVIII	28
	320,1	Thessalonice	XXVII	27
	320,2	Mellissurgin	XX	20
	320,3	Apollonia	XVII	17
	320,4	Amphipoli	XXX	30
	320,5	Philippis	XXXIII	33
	321,1	Neapoli	XII	12
	321,2	Acontisma	VIIII	9
	321,3	Topiro	XVII	17
	321,4	Cosinto	XIII	13
	321,5	Porsulis	XXIII	23
	322,1	Brendice	XXI	21
	322,2	Milolito	XII	12
	322,3	Timpiro	XVI	16
	322,4	Traianopoli	VIIII	9
	322,5	Dimis	XVI	16
	322,6	Zervis	XXIIII	24
	322,7	Plotinopolim	XXIIII	24
	322,8	Hadrianopolim	XXI	21
	322,9	Ostidizo	XVIIII	19
	323,1	Burdidizo	XVIIII	19
	323,2	Bergule	XVII	17
	323,3	Drusiparo	XIIII	14
	323,4	Thirallo	XVI	16
	323,5	Perintho Erac.	XVIII	18
	323,6	Cenofrurio	XVIII	18

248

*Appendix 9: User's
Guide to the
Outlining of Rivers
and Routes on
Barrington Atlas
Bases (C–F), with
Associated Texts:
Antonine Itinerary*

	323,7	Melantrada	XXVII	27
	323,8	Bizantio	XVIIII.	19
163	323,9	Item a Brundisio sive ab Hydrunto traiec-		
	323,10	tus Aulonam	stadia num. Ī.	
	324,1	Inde per loca maritima IN EPIRUM ET THES-		
	324,2	SALIAM ET IN MACEDONIAM, sic:		
	324,3	Acroceraunia	XXXIII	33
	324,4	Phoenice	XLI	41
	324,5	Butroto	LVI	56
	325,1	Clycis Limen	XXX	30
	325,2	Actia Nicopoli	XX	20
	325,3	Acheloo	XXV	25
	325,4	Euenno	XX	20
	325,5	Delphis	XL	40
	326,1	Phocide	XL	40
	326,2	Thestias	XL	40
	326,3	Megara	XL	40
	326,4	Eleusina	XIII	13
	326,5	Athenis	XIII	13
	327,1	Oropo	XLIIII	44
	327,2	Thebis	XXXVI	36
	327,3	Calcide	XXIIII	24
	327,4	Opunte	XLVIII	48
	327,5	Demetriade	XIIII	14
	328,1	Larissa	XLIIII	44
	328,2	Dio	XXIIII	24
	328,3	Pudaia	XVIIII	19
	328,4	Berea	XVII	17
	328,5	Thessalia	LI	51
	328,6	Mellissurgin	XX.	20
	329,1	Item recto itinere ab Hydrunti Aulo-		
	329,2	nam	stadia Ī.	
164	329,3.4	Inde PER MACEDONIAM:		
	329,5	Apollonia	XXV	25
	329,6	Ad Novas	XXIIII	24
	329,7	Clodianis	XXV	25
	329,8	Scampis	XXII	22
	329,9	Tribus Tabernis	XXX	30
	329,10	Lignido	XXVII	27
	330,1	Scirtiana	XXVII	27
	330,2	Castra	VI	6
	330,3	Heraclia	XII	12
	330,4	Cellis	XXXIII	33
	330,5	Edessa	XXXIII	33
	330,6	Dioclitianopolis	XXX	30
	330,7	Thessalonica	XXVIIII	29
	330,8	Apollonia	XXXVI	36
	331,1	Amphipoli	XXXII	32
	331,2	Philippis	XXXII	32
	331,3	Acontisma	XXI	21

	331,4	Otopiso	XVIII	18
	331,5	Stabulo Diomedis	XXII	22
	331,6.7	Inipara sive Pyrsoali	XVIII	18
	331,8	Brizice	XX	20
	332,1	Traianopoli	XXXVII	37
	332,2	Gypsala	XXVIIII	29
	332,3	Syracella	XXV	25
	332,4	Apris	XXI	21
	332,5	Risisto	XXVI	26
	332,6	Heraclia	XXVI	26
	332,7	Cenofrurio	XXIIII	24
	332,8	Melantiada	XXVII	27
	332,9	Bizantio	XVIIII.	19
	333,1	DE TRACHIA IN ASIAM:		
165	333,2	A Traianopoli Callipoli ad traiectum		
	333,3	Asiae	CXXVIIII:	129
	333,4	A Traianopoli Dimis	XIII	13
	333,5	Syrascele	XXXVIII	38
	333,6	Arris	XXI	21
	333,7	Afrodisiade	XXXIIII	34
	333,8	Callipoli	XXIIII.	24
166	333,9	A Callipoli traiectum IN ASIA Lamsacum		
	333,10	usque	stadia LX.	60
	334,1	Inde Abydo	XXIIII	24
	334,2	Dardano	VIIII	9
	334,3	Ilio	XII	12
	334,4	Troas	XVI	16
	335,1	Antandro	XXXV	35
	335,2	Adramitio	XXXI	31
	335,3	Pergamo	LIII	53
	335,4	Germe	XXV	25
	336,1	Thyatira	XXXIII	33
	336,2	Sardis	XXXVI	36
	336,3	Philadelphia	XXVIII	28
	336,4	Tripoli	XXXIIII	34
	337,1	Hierapoli	XII	12
	337,2	Laudicia	VI.	6
167	337,3	Item DE DALMATIA IN MACEDONIAM,		
	337,4	id est a Salonis Durrachium	CCCIII, sic:	303
	337,5	Ponte Tiluri	XVI	16
	338,1	Trono	XII	12
	338,2	Bilubio	XIII	13
	338,3	Aufustianis	XVIII	18
	338,4	Narona	XXV	25
	338,5	Dallunto	XXV	25
	338,6	Leusinio	XL	40
	338,7	Andarva	XXVIIII	29
	338,8	Sallunto	XVIII	18
	339,1	Alata	XVII	17
	339,2	Birziminio	X	10

249

Appendix 9: User's Guide to the Outlining of Rivers and Routes on Barrington Atlas *Bases (C–F), with* Associated Texts: Antonine Itinerary

250
___

Appendix 9: User's
Guide to the
Outlining of Rivers
and Routes on
Barrington Atlas
Bases (C–F), with
Associated Texts:
Antonine Itinerary

	339,3	Cinna	XVIII	18
	339,4	Scodra	XII	12
	339,5	Durrachio	L.	50
	339,6	DE ITALIA IN GALLIAS:		
168	339,7	A Mediolano Arelate per Alpes		
	339,8	Gottias	CCCCXI:	411
	340,1	Ticinum	XXII	22
	340,2	Laumellum	XXII	22
	340,3	Cottiae	XII	12
	340,4	Carbantia	XII	12
	340,5	Rigomago	XII	12
	340,6	Quadratis	XIII	13
	341,1	Taurinis	XXIII	23
	341,2	Fines	XVIII	18
	341,3	Segusione	XXXIII	33
	341,4	Ad Martis	XVI	16
	341,5	Brigantione	XVIII	18
	341,6	Rame	XVIIII	19
	342,1	Eburoduno	XVIII	18
	342,2	Caturrigas	XVII	17
	342,3	Vapincum	XII	12
	342,4	Alabonte	XVIII	18
	342,5	Segusterone	XVI	16
	343,1	Alaunio	XXIIII	24
	343,2	Catuiaca	XVI	16
	343,3	Apta Iulia	XII	12
	343,4	Fines	X	10
	343,5	Cabellione	XII	12
	343,6	Glano	XVI	16
	344,1	Ernagino	XII	12
	344,2	Arelate	VII.	7
169	344,3	Item a Mediolano per Alpes		
	344,4	Graias Vienna	CCCVIII, sic:	308
	344,5	Novaria	XXXIII	33
	344,6	Vercellas	XVI	16
	345,1	Eporedia	XXXIII	33
	345,2	Vitricium	XXI	21
	345,3	Augusta Praetoria	XXV	25
	345,4	Arebrigium	XXV	25
	345,5	Bergintrum	XXIIII	24
	346,1	Darantasia	XVIIII	19
	346,2	Obilunnum	XIII	13
	346,3	Ad Publicanos	III	3
	346,4	Mantala	XVI	16
	346,5	Lemincum	XVI	16
	346,6	Labiscone	XIIII	14
	346,7	Augustum	XIIII	14
	346,8	Bergusia	XVI	16
	346,9	Vienna	XX.	20

170	346,10	Item a Mediolano per Alpes Graias		
	346,11	Argentorato	DLXXVII, sic:	577
	347,1	Ticinum	XXII	22
	347,2	Laumellum	XXII	22
	347,3	Vercellas	XXVI	26
	347,4	Eporedia	XXXIII	33
	347,5	Vitricium	XXI	21
	347,6	Augusta Pretoria	XXV	25
	347,7	Arebrigium	XXV	25
	347,8	Bergintrum	XXIIII	24
	347,9	Darantasia	XVIIII	19
	347,10	Casuaria	XVIIII	19
	347,11	Bautas	XXX	30
	347,12	Genava	XXV	25
	348,1	Equestribus	XVI	16
	348,2	Lacu Lausonio	XX	20
	348,3	Urba	XVIII	18
	348,4	Ariorica	XV	15
	348,5	Visontione	XVI	16
	349,1	Vetatuduro	XXII	22
	349,2	Epamantuduro	XII	12
	349,3	Gramato	XVIIII	19
	349,4	Larga	XXV	25
	349,5	Virincis	XVIII	18
	350,1	Monte Brisiaco	XXIIII	24
	350,2	Helveto	XX	20
	350,3	Argentorato	XXX.	30
171	350,4	Item a Mediolano per Alpes Penninas		
	350,5	Mogontiacum	CCCCXVIIII, sic:	419
	350,6	Novaria	XXXIII	33
	350,7	Vercellas	XVI	16
	351,1	Eporedia	XXXIII	33
	351,2	Vitricio	XXI	21
	351,3	Augusta Pretoria	XXV	25
	351,4	Summo Penino	XXV	25
	351,5	Octoduro	XXV	25
	351,6	Tarnaias	XII	12
	351,7	Penne Locos	XIII	13
	352,1	Vibisco	VIIII	9
	352,2	Uromago	VIIII	9
	352,3	Minnodunum	VI	6
	352,4	Aventiculum Helvetiorum	XIII	13
	353,1	Petinesca	XIIII	14
	353,2	Salodurum	X	10
	353,3	Augusta Rauracum	XXII	22
	354,1	Cambete	XII	12
	354,2	Stabulis	VI	6
	354,3	Argantovaria	XVIII	18
	354,4	Helvetum	XVI	16
	354,5	Argentorato	XII	12

251

*Appendix 9: User's
Guide to the
Outlining of Rivers
and Routes on*
Barrington Atlas
*Bases (C–F), with
Associated Texts:
Antonine Itinerary*

	354,6	Saletione	VII	7
	355,1	Tabernis	XIII	13
	355,2	Noviomago	XI	11
	355,3	Bormitomago	XIIII	14
	355,4	Bouconica	XIII	13
	355,5	Mogontiacum	XI.	11
172	356,1	A Mediolano per Alpes Cottias		
	356,2	Vienna	m.p. CCCCVIIII,	409
	356,3	inde Durocortoro	m.p. CCCXXXII	332
	356,4		quae fiunt	221
			leug. CCXXI,	
	356,5	Gesoriaco	m.p. CLXXIIII	174
	356,6.7		quae fiunt leug. CXVI:	116
	356,8	Ticinum	XXII	22
	356,9	Laumello	XXII	22
	356,10	Rigomago	XXXVI	36
	356,11	Quadratis	XVI	16
	356,12	Taurinis	XXI	21
	356,13	Ad Fines	XVI	16
	357,1	Segusione	XXIIII	24
	357,2	Ad Martis	XVI	16
	357,3	Brigantione	XVIIII	19
	357,4	Ramae	XVIII	18
	357,5	Ebreduno	XVII	17
	357,6	Caturricas	XVI	16
	357,7	Vapinquo	XII	12
	357,8	Monte Seleuco	XXIII	23
	357,9	Luco	XXVI	26
	357,10	Dea Bocontiorum	XII	12
	358,1	Augusta	XXIII	23
	358,2	Valentia	XXII	22
	358,3	Ursinis	XXII	22
	358,4	Vienna	XXVI	26
	358,5	Lugdunum	XXIII	23
	359,1	aut per conpendium	XVI	16
	359,2	Asa Paulini	m.p. XV leug. X	15/10
	359,3	Lunna	m.p. XV leug. X	15/10
	359,4	Matiscone	m.p. XV leug. X	15/10
	359,5	Tinurtium	m.p. XVIIII leug. XIII	19/13
	360,1	Gabilunnum	m.p. XXI leug. XIIII	21/14
	360,2	Augustodunum	m.p. XXXIII leug. XXII	33/22
	360,3	Sidoloucum	m.p. XXVII leug. XVIII	27/18
	360,4	Aballone	m.p. XXIIII leug. XVI	24/16
	361,1	Autesiodor	m.p. XXXIII leug. XXII	33/22
	361,2	Eburobrica	m.p. XVIII leug. XII	18/12
	361,3	Tricasis	m.p. XXXIII leug. XXII	33/22
	361,4	Artiaca	m.p. XVIII leug. XII	18/12
	361,5	Durocatelaunos	m.p. XXXIII leug. XXII	33/22
	362,1	Durocortoro	m.p. XXVII leug. XVIII	27/18
	362,2	Suessonas	m.p. XXXVII leug. XXV	37/25
	362,3	Noviomago	m.p. XXVII leug. XVIII	27/18

*Appendix 9: User's
Guide to the
Outlining of Rivers
and Routes on
Barrington Atlas
Bases (C–F), with
Associated Texts:
Antonine Itinerary*

	362,4	Ambianis	m.p. XXXIIII leug. XXIII	34/23
	363,1	Pontibus	m.p. XXXVI leug. XXIIII	36/24
	363,2	Gesoriaco	m.p. XXXVIIII leug. XXVI.	39/26
omitted	363,3	Item a Cavilunno Triveros.		
173	363,4	Item a Durocortoro Divodorum		
	363,5	usque	LXXIIII:	74
	364,1	Basilia	X	10
	364,2	Axuena	XII	12
	364,3	Virodunum	XVII	17
	364,4	Fines	VIIII	9
	364,5	Ibliodurum	VI	6
	364,6	Divodurum	VIII.	8
174	364,7	Alio itinere a Durocortoro		
	364,8	Divodorum usque	LXXXVII, sic:	87
	364,9	Fano Minervae	XIIII	14
	365,1	Ariola	XVI	16
	365,2	Caturicis	VIIII	9
	365,3	Nasium	VIIII	9
	365,4	Tullum	XVI	16
	365,5	Scarponna	X	10
	365,6	Divodorum	XII.	12
175	365,7	Item a Durocortoro Treveros		
	365,8	usque:		
	365,9	Vongo vicus	leug. XXII	22
	366,1	Epoisso vicus	leug. XXII	22
	366,2	Orolauno vicus	leug. XX	20
	366,3	Andethannale vicus	leug. XV	15
	366,4	Treveros civitas	leug. XV.	15
176	366,5	Ab Augustoduno Luticia Parisio-		
	366,6	rum	CLXXXVII:	187
	366,7	Alisincum	XXII	22
	367,1	Decetia	XXIIII	24
	367,2	Nevirnum	XVI	16
	367,3	Condate	XXIIII	24
	367,4	Bribodorum	XVI	16
	367,5	Belca	XV	15
	367,6	Canabum	XXII	22
	368,1	Salioclita	XXIIII	24
	368,2	Luticia	XXIIII.	24
177	368,3.4	A Lugduno, caput Germaniarum, Argentorato:		
	369,1	Albanianis	X	10
	369,2	Traiecto	XVII	17
	369,3	Mannaricio	XV	15
	369,4	Carvone	XXII	22
	369,5	Harenatio	XXII	22
	370,1	Burginatio	VI	6
	370,2	Colonia Traiana	V	5
	370,3	Veteribus	CO	1
	370,4	Calone	XVIII	18
	370,5	Novesiae	XVIII	18

254

Appendix 9: User's Guide to the Outlining of Rivers and Routes on Barrington Atlas *Bases (C–F), with Associated Texts: Antonine Itinerary*

	370,6	Colonia Agrippina	XVI	16
	370,7	Bonna	XI	11
	371,1	Antunnaco	XVII	17
	371,2	Confluentibus	VIII	8
	371,3	Vinco	XXVI	26
	371,4	Noviomago	XXXIIII	34
	371,5	Treveros	XIII	13
	371,6	Divodorum	XXXIIII	34
	372,1	Ponte Sarvix	XXIIII	24
	372,2	Argentorato	XXII.	22
178	372,3	A Treveros Agrippinam	leug. LXVII, sic:	67
	372,4	Beda vicus	leug. XII	12
	372,5	Ausava vicus	leug. XII	12
	373,1	Egorigio vicus	leug. XII	12
	373,2	Marcomago vicus	leug. VIII	8
	373,3	Belgica	leug. VIII	8
	373,4	Tolbiaco vicus Sopenorum	leug. X	10
	373,5	Agrippina civitas	leug. XVI.	16
179	374,1	Item a Treveris Argentorato	CXXVIII:	128
	374,2	Baudobrica	XVIII	18
	374,3	Salisione	XXII	22
	374,4	Vingio	XXIII	23
	374,5	Mogontiaco	XII	12
	374,6	Bormitomago	XVI	16
	374,7	Noviomago	XVIII	18
	374,8	Argentorato	XVIIII.	19
180	375,1	Item a Colonia Traiana Coloniam Agrippi-		
	375,2	nam	LXXI:	71
	375,3	Mediolano	VIII	8
	375,4	Sablonibus	VIII	8
	375,5	Mederiacum	X	10
	375,6	Teudurum	VIII	8
	375,7	Coriovallum	VII	7
	375,8	Iuliaco	XII	12
	375,9	Tiberiacum	VIII	8
	376,1	Colonia Agrippina	X.	10
181	376,2	Item a portu Gesoricensi Baga-		
	376,3	cum usque	LXXXIII:	83
	376,4	Tarvenna	XVIII	18
	376,5	Castello	VIIII	9
	376,6	Viroviacum	XVI	16
	376,7	Turnacum	XVI	16
	376,8	Pontes Caldis	XII	12
	377,1	Bagacum	XII.	12
182	377,2	A Castello per conpendium Tur- nacum		
	377,3	usque	XXXVIII:	38
	377,4	Minariacum	XI	11
	377,5	Turnacum	XXVII.	27

183	377,6	A Castello Colonia	CLXXII:	172
	377,7	Minariacum	XI	11
	377,8	Nemetacum	XVIIII	19
	377,9	Camaracum	XIIII	14
	378,1	Bagacum	XVIII	18
	378,2	Vodgoriacum	XII	12
	378,3	Geminicum	X	10
	378,4	Perniciacum	XXII	22
	378,5	Aduaga Tungrorum	XIIII	14
	378,6	Coriovallum	XVI	16
	378,7	Iuliacum	XVIII	18
	378,8	Colonia	XVIII.	18
184	378,9	Item a Tarvenna Turnacum	XLVIIII:	49
	378,10	Nemetacum	XXII	22
	378,11	Turnacum	XXVII.	27
185	379,1	Item a Tarvenna Durocortoro	CIII:	103
	379,2	Nemetacum	XXII	22
	379,3	Camaracum	XIIII	14
	379,4	Augusta Veromandorum	XVIII	18
	379,5	Contra Aginnum	XIII	13
	379,6	Augusta Suessonum	XII	12
	379,7	Fines	XIII	13
	379,8	Durocortoro	XII.	12
186	379,9	Per conpendium a Nemetaco Samara-		
	379,10	brivas	XVI.	16
187	380,1	A Samarobrivas Suessonas usque	LXXXVIIII:	89
	380,2	Curmiliaca	XII	12
	380,3	Caesaromago	XIII	13
	380,4	Litanobriga	XVIII	18
	380,5	Augustomago	IIII	4
	380,6	Suessonas	XXII.	22
188	380,7	Item a Bagaco Nerviorum Durocortoro Re-		
	380,8	morum usque	LIII:	53
	381,1	Duronum	XII	12
	381,2	Verbino	X	10
	381,3	Catusiacum	VI	6
	381,4	Minatiacum	VII	7
	381,5	Muenna	VIII	8
	381,6	Durocortoro	X.	10
189	381,7	Item a Caracotino Augustobonam usque	CLIII:	153
	382,1	Iuliobona	X	10
	382,2	Loium	VI	6
	382,3	Ratomago	XIIII	14
	382,4	Ritumago	VIIII	9
	382,5	Petromantalum	XVI	16
	383,1	Luticiam	XVIIII	19
	383,2	Metledo	XVIII	18
	383,3	Condate	XV	15
	383,4	Agedincum	XIII	13

255

*Appendix 9: User's
Guide to the
Outlining of Rivers
and Routes on*
Barrington Atlas
*Bases (C–F), with
Associated Texts:
Antonine Itinerary*

256

Appendix 9: User's
Guide to the
Outlining of Rivers
and Routes on
Barrington Atlas
Bases (C–F), with
Associated Texts:
Antonine Itinerary

	383,5	Glano	XVII	17
	383,6	Augustobona	XVI.	16
190	384,1	Item a Ratomago Luticiam		
	384,2	usque	LXXVII:	77
	384,3	Uggate	VIIII	9
	384,4	Mediolano Aulercorum	XIIII	14
	384,5	Durocasis	XVII	17
	384,6	Dioduro	XXII	22
	384,7	Luticia	XV.	15
191	384,8	Item a Caesaromago Luticiam		
	384,9	usque	XLVI:	46
	384,10	Petromantalium	XVII	17
	384,11	Brivaisare	XIIII	14
	384,12	Luticia	XV.	15
192	384,13	Item a Iuliobona Mediolanum	XXXIIII.	34
193	385,1	Item a Iuliobona Durocasis	LXXVIII:	78
	385,2	Brevodorum	XVII	17
	385,3	Noviomago	XVII	17
	385,4	Condate	XXIIII	24
	385,5	Durocasis	X.	10
194	385,6	Item ab Andemantunno Tullo Leucorum		
	385,7	usque	XLIII:	43
	385,8	Mosa	XII	12
	385,9	Solimariaca	XVI	16
	385,10	Tullum	XV.	15
195	386,1	Item ab Antemantunno Cambatem	CII:	102
	386,2	Varcia	XVI	16
	386,3	Vesentione	XXIIII	24
	386,4	Epamanduoduro	XXXI	31
	386,5	Cambate	XXXI.	31
196	386,6	Item ab Alauna Condate	LXXVII:	77
	386,7	Cosedia	XX	20
	387,1	Fano Martis	XXXII	32
	387,2	Ad Fines	VII	7
	387,3	Condate	XVIII.	18
	387,4	DE ITALIA IN HISPANIAS.		
197	387,5	A Mediolano Vapinco trans Alpes Cottias		
	387,6	mansionibus supra scriptis	CCLV,	255
	387,7	inde in Galleciam ad Leug. VII Ge–		
	387,8	minam	DCCCCLXXV:	975
	388,1	Alamonte	XVII	17
	388,2	Segustorone	XVI	16
	388,3	Alaunio	XXIIII	24
	388,4	Apte Iulia	XXVIII	28
	388,5	Cavellione	XXII	22
	388,6	Arelate	XXX	30
	388,7	Nemausum	XVIIII	19
	389,1	Ambrussum	XV	15
	389,2	Sextatione	XV	15

	389,3	Foro Domiti	XV	15
	389,4	Araura sive Cesserone	XVIII	18
	389,5	Beterras	XII	12
	389,6	Narbone	XVI	16
	389,7	Salsulis	XXX	30
	390,1	Ad Stabulum	XLVIIII	49
	390,2	Ad Pireneum	XVI	16
	390,3	Iuncaria	XVI	16
	390,4	Gerunda	XXVII	27
	390,5	Barcenone	LXVII	67
	390,6	Stabulo Novo	LI	51
	391,1	Tarracone	XXIIII	24
	391,2	Ilerda	LXII	62
	391,3	Tolous	XXXII	32
	391,4	Pertusa	XVIII	18
	391,5	Osca	XVIIII	19
	392,1	Caesaraugusta	XLVI	46
	392,2	Cascanto	L	50
	393,1	Calagorra	XXVIIII	29
	393,2	Vereia	XXVIII	28
	394,1	Tritio	XVIII	18
	394,2	Lybia	XVIII	18
	394,3	Segesamunclo	VII	7
	394,4	Verovesca	XI	11
	394,5	Segesamone	XLVII	47
	395,1	Lacobrica	XXX	30
	395,2	Camala	XXIIII	24
	395,3	Lance	XXVIIII	29
	395,4	Ad Leg. VII Geminam	VIIII.	9
198	396,1	Item ab Arelato Narbone	CI,	101
	396,2	inde Tarracone	CCXXXIIII,	234
	396,3	Karthagine Spartaria	CCCLX,	360
	396,4	Castulone	CCCIII, sic:	303
	396,5	Nemausum	XIIII	14
	396,6	Ambrussum	XV	15
	396,7	Sextantione	XV	15
	396,8	Foro Domiti	XV	15
	396,9	Cesserone	XVIII	18
	397,1	Beterris	XII	12
	397,2	Narbone	XII	12
	397,3	Ad Vicensimum	XX	20
	397,4	Combusta	XIIII	14
	397,5	Ruscione	VI	6
	397,6	Ad Centuriones	XX	20
	397,7	Summo Pyreneo	V	5
	397,8	Iuncaria	XVI	16
	397,9	Cinniana	XV	15
	398,1	Aquis Voconis	XXIIII	24
	398,2	Seterras	XV	15
	398,3	Praetorio	XV	15
	398,4	Barcenone	XVII	17

258

*Appendix 9: User's
Guide to the
Outlining of Rivers
and Routes on
Barrington Atlas
Bases (C–F), with
Associated Texts:
Antonine Itinerary*

	398,5	Fines	XX	20
	398,6	Antistiana	XVII	17
	398,7	Palfuriana	XIII	13
	399,1	Terracone	XVII	17
	399,2	Oleastrum	XXI	21
	399,3	Traia Capita	XXIIII	24
	399,4	Dertosa	XVII	17
	399,5	Intibili	XXVII	27
	399,6	Ildum	XXIIII	24
	400,1	Sebelaci	XXIIII	24
	400,2	Saguntum	XXII	22
	400,3	Valentia	XVI	16
	400,4	Sucronem	XX	20
	400,5	Ad Statuas	XXXII	32
	400,6	Ad Turres	VIIII	9
	401,1	Adello	XXIIII	24
	401,2	Aspis	XXIIII	24
	401,3	Ilici	XXIIII	24
	401,4	Thiar	XXVII	27
	401,5	Karthagine Spartaria	XXV	25
	401,6	Eliocroca	XLIIII	44
	401,7	Ad Morum	XXIIII	24
	401,8	Basti	XVI	16
	402,1	Acci	XXV	25
	402,2	Agatucci	XXVIII	28
	402,3	Viniolis	XXIIII	24
	402,4	Mentesa Bastiam	XX	20
	402,5	Castulone	XXII.	22
199	402,6	Item a Corduba Castulone	XCVIIII:	99
	402,7	Calpurniana	XXV	25
	403,1	Vircaone	XX	20
	403,2	Iliturgis	XXXIIII	34
	403,3	Castulone	XX.	20
200	403,4	Alio itinere a Corduba Castu-		
	403,5	lone	LXXVIII:	78
	403,6	Epora	XXVIII	28
	403,7	Uciense	XVIII	18
	404,1	Castulone	XXXII.	32
201	404,2	Item a Castulone Malacam	CCLXXVI, sic:	276
	404,3	Tugia	XXXV	35
	404,4	Fraxinum	XVI	16
	404,5	Bactara	XXIIII	24
	404,6	Acci	XXXII	32
	404,7	Alba	XXXII	32
	404,8	Urci	XXIIII	24
	405,1	Turaniana	XVI	16
	405,2	Murgi	XII	12
	405,3	Saxetanum	XXXVIII	38
	405,4	Caviclum	XVI	16

	405,5	Menova	XXXIIII	34
	405,6	Malaca	XII.	12
202	405,7	Item a Malaca Gadis	CLV, sic:	155
	405,8	Suel	XXI	21
	406,1	Cilniana	XXIIII	24
	406,2	Barbariana	XXIIII	24
	406,3	Calpe Carteiam	X	10
	407,1	Porto Albo	VI	6
	407,2	Mellaria	XII	12
	407,3	Belone Claudia	VI	6
	408,1	Besippone	XII	12
	408,2	Mercablo	XVI	16
	408,3	Ad Herculem	XII	12
	408,4	Gadis	XII.	12
203	409,1	Item a Gadis Corduba	CCXCV, sic:	295
	409,2	Ad Pontem	XII	12
	409,3	Portu Gaditano	XIIII	14
	409,4	Hasta	XVI	16
	410,1	Ugia	XXVII	27
	410,2	Orippo	XXIIII	24
	410,3	Hispali	VIIII	9
	410,4	Basilippo	XXI	21
	411,1	Carula	XXIIII	24
	411,2	Ilipa	XVIII	18
	411,3	Ostippo	XIIII	14
	412,1	Barba	XX	20
	412,2	Anticaria	XXIIII	24
	412,3	Ad Gemellas	XXIII	23
	412,4	Ipagro	XX	20
	412,5	Ulia	X	10
	412,6	Corduba	XVIII.	18
204	413,1	Item ab Hispali Corduba	XCIII, sic:	93
	413,2	Obucula	XLII	42
	413,3	Astigi	XV	15
	413,4	Ad Aras	XII	12
	413,5	Corduba	XXIIII.	24
205	413,6	Ab Hispali Italicam	VI.	6
206	414,1	Item ab Hispali Emeritam	CLXII, sic:	162
	414,2	Carmone	XXII	22
	414,3	Obucula	XX	20
	414,4	Astigi	XV	15
	414,5	Celti	XXXVII	37
	415,1	Regiana	XLIIII	44
	415,2	Emerita	XXIIII.	24
207	415,3	Item a Corduba Emeritam	CXLIIII, sic:	144
	415,4	Mellaria	LII	52
	416,1	Artigi	XXXVI	36
	416,2	Metellinum	XXXII	32
	416,3	Emerita	XXIIII.	24

259

Appendix 9: User's Guide to the Outlining of Rivers and Routes on Barrington Atlas Bases (C–F), with Associated Texts: Antonine Itinerary

260

*Appendix 9: User's
Guide to the
Outlining of Rivers
and Routes on*
Barrington Atlas
*Bases (C–F), with
Associated Texts:
Antonine Itinerary*

208	416,4	Item ab Olisippone Emeritam	CLXI, sic:	161
	416,5	Aquabona	XII	12
	417,1	Catobrica	XII	12
	417,2	Caeciliana	VIII	8
	417,3	Malateca	XXVI	26
	417,4	Salacia	XII	12
	418,1	Ebora	XLIIII	44
	418,2	Ad Atrum flumen	VIIII	9
	418,3	Dipone	XII	12
	418,4	Euandriana	XVII	17
	418,5	Emerita	VIIII.	9
209	418,6	A Salacia Ossonoba	XVI.	16
210	418,7	Alio itinere ab Olisippone Emeritam	CLIIII, sic:	154
	418,8	Aritio Praetorio	XXXVIII	38
	419,1	Abelterio	XXVIII	28
	419,2	Matusaro	XXIIII	24
	419,3	Ad Septem Aras	LX+?	60+?
	419,4	Budua	XII	12
	419,5	Plagiaria	VIII	8
	419,6	Emerita	XXX.	30
211	419,7	Item alio itinere ab Olisippone		
	419,8	Emeritam	CCXX, sic:	220
	419,9	Ierabrica	XXX	30
	420,1	Scallabin	XXXII	32
	420,2	Tabucci	XXXII	32
	420,3	Fraxinum	XXXII	32
	420,4	Montobrica	XXX	30
	420,5	Ad Septem Aras	XIIII	14
	420,6	Plagiaria	XX	20
	420,7	Emerita	XXX.	30
212	420,8	Item ab Olisippone Bracaram Augus-		
	420,9	tam	CCXLIIII, sic:	244
	421,1	Ierabriga	XXX	30
	421,2	Scallabin	XXXII	32
	421,3	Sellium	XXXII	32
	421,4	Conembriga	XXXIIII	34
	421,5	Aeminio	X	10
	421,6	Talabrica	XL	40
	421,7	Langobriga	XVIII	18
	421,8	Calem	XIII	13
	422,1	Bragara	XXXV.	35
213	422,2	Item a Bracara Asturicam	CCXLVII:	247
	422,3	Salacia	XX	20
	422,4	Praesidio	XXVI	26
	422,5	Caladuno	XVI	16
	422,6	Ad Aquas	XVIII	18
	422,7	Pinetum	XX	20
	422,8	Roboretum	XXXVI	36
	423,1	Compleutica	XXVIIII	29

	423,2	Veniatia	XV	15
	423,3	Petavonium	XXVIII	28
	423,4	Argentiolum	XV	15
	423,5	Asturica	XXIIII.	24
214	427,4	Item alio itinere a Bracara Astu-		
	427,5	rica	CCXV, sic:	215
	427,6	Salaniana	XXI	21
	428,1	Aquis Oreginis	XVIII	18
	428,2	Aquis Querquennis	XIIII	14
	428,3	Geminis	XVI	16
	428,4	Salientibus	XVIII	18
	428,5	Praesidio	XVIII	18
	428,6	Nemetobrica	XIII	13
	428,7	Foro	XVIIII	19
	429,1	Gemestario	XVIII	18
	429,2	Belgido	XIII	13
	429,3	Intereraconio Flavio	XX	20
	429,4	Asturica	XXX.	30
215	429,5	Item a Bracara Asturicam	CCXCVIIII, sic:	299
	429,6	Limia	XVIIII	19
	429,7	Tude	XXIIII	24
	430,1	Burbida	XVI	16
	430,2	Turoqua	XVI	16
	430,3	Aquis Celenis	XXIIII	24
	430,4	Tria	XII	12
	430,5	Assegonia	XIII	13
	430,6	Brevis	XXII	22
	430,7	Marcie	XX	20
	430,8	Luco Augusti	XIII	13
	430,9	Timalino	XXII	22
	430,10	Ponte Neviae	XII	12
	430,11	Uttaris	XX	20
	431,1	Bergido	XVI	16
	431,2	Interamnio Fluvio	XX	20
	431,3	Asturica	XXX.	30
216	423,6	Item per loca maritima a Bracara		
	423,7	Asturicam usque:		
	423,8	Aquis Celenis	CLXV	165
	424,1	Vico Spacorum	stadia CXCV	195
	424,2	Ad Duos Pontes	stadia CL	150
	424,3	Glandimiro	stadia CLXXX	180
	424,4	Atricondo	XXII	22
	424,5	Brigantium	XXX	30
	424,6	Caranico	XVIII	18
	424,7	Luco Augusti	XVII	17
	425,1	Timalino	XXII	22
	425,2	Ponte Neviae	XII	12
	425,3	Uttaris	XX	20
	425,4	Bergido	XVI	16
	425,5	Asturica	L.	50

*Appendix 9: User's
Guide to the
Outlining of Rivers
and Routes on*
Barrington Atlas
Bases (C–F), with
*Associated Texts:
Antonine Itinerary*

262

Appendix 9: User's
Guide to the
Outlining of Rivers
and Routes on
Barrington Atlas
Bases (C–F), with
Associated Texts:
Antonine Itinerary

217	425,6	Item de Esuri Pace Iulia	CCLXVII, sic:	267
	426,1	Balsa	XXIIII	24
	426,2	Ossonoba	XVI	16
	426,3	Aranni	LX	60
	426,4	Salacia	XXXV	35
	426,5	Eboram	XLIIII	44
	426,6	Serpa	XIII	13
	427,1	Fines	XX	20
	427,2	Arucci	XXV	25
	427,3	Pace Iulia	XXX.	30
218	431,4	Item ab Esuri per conpendium Pace		
	431,5	Iulia	LXXVI:	76
	431,6	Myrtili	XL	40
	431,7	Pace Iulia	XXXVI.	36
219	431,8	Item ab ostio fluminis Anae Emeri-		
	431,9	tam usque	CCCXIII:	313
	431,10	Praesidio	XXIIII	24
	431,11	Ad Rubras	XXVIII	28
	431,12	Onoba	XXVIII	28
	432,1	Ilipla	XXX	30
	432,2	Tucci	XXII	22
	432,3	Italica	XVIII	18
	432,4	Monte Mariorum	XLVI	46
	432,5	Curica	XLVIIII	49
	432,6	Contributa	XXIIII	24
	432,7	Perceiana	XX	20
	432,8	Emerita	XXIIII.	24
220	433,1	Item ab Emerita Caesaraugus-		
	433,2	ta	DCXXXII:	632
	433,3	Ad Sorores	XXVI	26
	433,4	Castris Caecili	XX	20
	433,5	Turmulos	XX	20
	433,6	Rusticiana	XXII	22
	433,7	Capara	XXII	22
	434,1	Caelionicco	XXII	22
	434,2	Ad Lippos	XII	12
	434,3	Sentice	XV	15
	434,4	Salmatice	XXIIII	24
	434,5	Sibarim	XXI	21
	434,6	Ocelo Duri	XXI	21
	434,7	Albocela	XXII	22
	435,1	Amallobriga	XXVII	27
	435,2	Septimanca	XXIIII	24
	435,3	Nivaria	XXII	22
	435,4	Cauca	XXII	22
	435,5	Segovia	XXVIIII	29
	435,6	Miaccum	XXIIII	24
	436,1	Titulciam	XXIIII	24
	436,2	Conplutum	XXX	30
	436,3	Arriaca	XXII	22

	436,4	Caesada	XXIIII	24
	436,5	Segontia	XXIII	23
	437,1	Arcobriga	XXIII	23
	437,2	Aquae Bilbitanorum	XVI	16
	437,3	Bilbili	XXIIII	24
	437,4	Netorbriga	XXI	21
	437,5	Secontia	XIIII	14
	438,1	Caesaraugusta	XVI.	16
221	438,2	Alio itinere ab Emerita Caesarea Au-		
	438,3	gusta	CCCXLVIII, sic:	348
	438,4	Lacipea	XX	20
	438,5	Leuciana	XXIIII	24
	438,6	Augustobriga	XII	12
	438,7	Toletum	LV	55
	438,8	Titulciam	XXIIII	24
	438,9	Conplutum	XXX	30
	438,10	Arriaca	XXII	22
	438,11	Caesada	XXIIII	24
	438,12	Segontia	XXIII	23
	438,13	Arcobriga	XXIII	23
	438,14	Aquae Bilbitanorum	XVI	16
	439,1	Bilbili	XXIIII	24
	439,2	Nertobriga	XXI	21
	439,3	Segontia	XIIII	14
	439,4	Caesaraugusta	XVI.	16
222	439,5	Item ab Asturica Caesaraugus-		
	439,6	tam	CCCCXCVII, sic:	497
	439,7	Bedunia	XX	20
	439,8	Briceco	XX	20
	439,9	Vico Aquario	XXXII	32
	439,10	Ocelo Duri	XVI	16
	439,11	Titulciam mansionibus supra scrip-		
	439,12	tis	CXCIIII	194
	439,13	Caesaraugusta mansionibus supra		
	439,14	scriptis	CCXV.	215
223	439,15	Item ab Asturica per Cantabria		
	439,16	Caesaraugusta	CCCI:	301
	440,1	Brigeco	XL	40
	440,2	Intercatia	XX	20
	440,3	Tela	XXII	22
	440,4	Pintiam	XXIIII	24
	440,5	Rauda		
	441,1	Cluniam	XXVI	26
	441,2	Vasamam	XXIIII	24
	442,1	Voluce	XXV	25
	442,2	Numantia	XXV	25
	442,3	Augustobriga	XXIII	23
	442,4	Turiassone	XVII	17
	443,1	Caravi	XVIII	18
	443,2	Caesaraugusta	XXXVII.	37

*Appendix 9: User's
Guide to the
Outlining of Rivers
and Routes on
Barrington Atlas
Bases (C–F), with
Associated Texts:
Antonine Itinerary*

264
———
Appendix 9: User's
Guide to the
Outlining of Rivers
and Routes on
Barrington Atlas
Bases (C–F), with
Associated Texts:
Antonine Itinerary

224	443,3	Item a Turassone Caesaraugustam	LVI	56
	443,4	Balsione	XX	20
	444,1	Allobone	XX	20
	444,2	Caesaraugusta	XVI.	16
225	444,3	Per Lusitaniam ab Emerita Caesarea		
	444,4	Augusta	CCCCLVIII, sic:	458
	444,5	Contosolia	XII	12
	444,6	Mirobriga	XXXVI	36
	444,7	Sisalone	XIII	13
	445,1	Carcuvium	XX	20
	445,2	Ad Turres	XXVI	26
	445,3	Mariana	XXIIII	24
	445,4	Lamini	XXX	30
	445,5	Alces	XL	40
	445,6	Vico Cuminario	XXIIII	24
	446,1	Titulciam	XVIII	18
	446,2	Caesaraugusta mansionibus supra		
	446,3	scriptis	CCXV.	215
226	446,4	Item a Liminio Toletum	XCV, sic:	95
	446,5	Murum	XXVII	27
	446,6	Consabro	XXIIII	24
	446,7	Toletum	XLIIII.	44
227	446,8	Item a Laminio alio itinere Caesarea		
	446,9	Augusta	CCXLVIIII, sic:	249
	446,10	Caput fluminis Anae	VII	7
	446,11	Libisosia	XIIII	14
	447,1	Parietinis	XXII	22
	447,2	Saltici	XVI	16
	447,3	Ad Putea	XXXII	32
	447,4	Valebonga	XL	40
	447,5	Urbiaca	XX	20
	447,6	Albonica	XXV	25
	447,7	Agiria	VI	6
	447,8	Carae	X	10
	447,9	Sermonae	XXVIIII	29
	448,1	Caesarea Augusta	XXVIII.	28
228	448,2	Item ab Asturica Terracone	CCCCLXXXII,	482
	448,3		sic:	
	448,4	Vallata	XVI	16
	448,5	Interamnio	XIII	13
	449,1	Palantia	XIIII	14
	449,2	Viminacio	XXXI	31
	449,3	Lacobrigam	X	10
	449,4	Dessobriga	XV	15
	449,5	Legisamone	XV	15
	449,6	Deobrigula	XV	15
	450,1	Tritium	XXI	21
	450,2	Virovenna	XI	11

	450,3	Atiliana	XXX	30
	450,4	Barbariana	XXXII	32
	450,5	Craccuris	XXXII	32
	451,1	Bellisone	XXVIII	28
	451,2	Caesarea Augusta	XXXVI	36
	451,3	Gallicum	XV	15
	451,4	Bortinae	XVIII	18
	451,5	Oscam	XII	12
	451,6	Caum	XXVIIII	29
	452,1	Mendiculeia	XVIIII	19
	452,2	Ilerda	XXII	22
	452,3	Ad Novas	XVIII	18
	452,4	Ad Septimum Decimum	XIII	13
	452,5	Tarracone	XVII.	17
229	452,6	Item a Caesarea Augusta Beneharno	CXII, sic:	112
	452,7	Foro Gallorum	XXX	30
	452,8	Ebelino	XXII	22
	452,9	Summo Pyreneo	XXIIII	24
	452,10	Foro Ligneo	V	5
	453,1	Aspalluga	VII	7
	453,2	Ilurone	XII	12
	453,3	Benearnum	XII.	12
	453,4	DE HISPANIA IN AEQUITANIA.		
230	453,5	Ab Asturica Burdicalam	CCCCXXI:	421
	453,6	Vallata	XVI	16
	453,7	Interamnio	XIII	13
	453,8	Palantia	XIIII	14
	453,9	Viminacio	XXXI	31
	454,1	Lacobrigam	XV	15
	454,2	Legisamone	XV	15
	454,3	Teobrigula	XV	15
	454,4	Tritium	XXI	21
	454,5	Virovesca	XI	11
	454,6	Vindeleia	XII	12
	454,7	Deobriga	XIIII	14
	454,8	Beleia	XV	15
	454,9	Suessatio	VII	7
	455,1	Tullonio	VII	7
	455,2	Alba	XII	12
	455,3	Aracaeli	XXI	21
	455,4	Alantone	XVI	16
	455,5	Pompelone	VIII	8
	455,6	Turissa	XXII	22
	455,7	Summo Pyreneo	XVIII	18
	455,8	Imo Pyreneo	V	5
	455,9	Carasa	XII	12
	455,10	Aquis Terebellicis	XXXVIIII	39
	456,1	Mosconnum	XVI	16
	456,2	Segosa	XII	12
	456,3	Losa	XII	12

265

Appendix 9: User's Guide to the Outlining of Rivers and Routes on Barrington Atlas *Bases (C–F), with Associated Texts: Antonine Itinerary*

266
____

*Appendix 9: User's
Guide to the
Outlining of Rivers
and Routes on*
Barrington Atlas
*Bases (C–F), with
Associated Texts:
Antonine Itinerary*

	456,4	Boios	VII	7
	456,5	Burdigalam	XVI.	16
231	456,6	Item ab Aquis Terebellicis Bur-		
	456,7	digalam	LXIIII, sic:	64
	456,8	Coequosa	XVI	16
	456,9	Telonnum	XVIII	18
	457,1	Salomaco	XII	12
	457,2	Burdigala	XVIII.	18
232	457,3	Item ab Aquis Terebellicis To-		
	457,4	losam	CXXX:	130
	457,5	Benearnum	XVIIII	19
	457,6	Oppido Novo	XVIII	18
	457,7	Aquis Convenarum	VIII	8
	457,8	Lugudunum	XVI	16
	457,9	Calagorris	XXVI	26
	458,1	Aquis Siccis	XVI	16
	458,2	Verno Sole	XII	12
	458,3	Tolosa	XV.	15
	458,4	DE AQUITANICA IN GALLIAS.		
233	458,5	Item a Burdigala Augustodu-		
	458,6	num	CCLXXIIII:	274
	458,7	Blauto	XVIIII	19
	459,1	Tannum	XVI	16
	459,2	Novioregum	XII	12
	459,3	Mediolanum Santonum	XV	15
	459,4	Aunedonnacum	XVI	16
	459,5	Rauranum	XX	20
	459,6	Lomounum	XXI	21
	460,1	Fines	XXI	21
	460,2	Agrantomago	XXI	21
	460,3	Ernodorum	XXVII	27
	460,4	Avaricum	XIII	13
	460,5	Tincontium	XX	20
	460,6	Deccidae	XXII	22
	460,7	Alisincum	XIIII	14
	460,8	Augustoduno	XXII.	22
	461,1	DE AQUITANIA IN GALLIAS.		
234	461,2	Item a Burdigala Argantoma-		
	461,3	go	CXCVII:	197
	461,4	Sirione	XV	15
	461,5	Ussubium	XX	20
	461,6	Fines	XXIIII	24
	461,7	Aginnum	XV	15
	461,8	Excisum	XIII	13
	461,9	Travectus	XXI	21
	461,10	Vesunna	XVIII	18
	462,1	Fines	XXI	21
	462,2	Augustoritum	XXVIII	28
	462,3	Argantomago	XXI.	21

235	462,4	Item ab Aginno Lugdunum	LXV:	65
	462,5	Lactura	XV	15
	462,6	Climberrum	XV	15
	463,1	Belsino	XII	12
	463,2	Lugdunum	XXIII.	23
	463,3	ITER BRITTANIARUM.		
236	463,4	A Gessoriaco de Gallis Ritupis in portu Britt-		
	463,5	taniarum	stadia numero CCCCL.	450
237	464,1	A limite, id est a vallo, Praetorio		
	464,2		CLVI:	156
	464,3	a Bremenio Corstopitum	XX	20
	464,4	Vindomora	VIIII	9
	465,1	Vinovia	XVIIII	19
	465,2	Cataractoni	XXII	22
	465,3	Isurium	XXIIII	24
	466,1	Eburacum leug. VI Victrix	XVII	17
	466,2	Derventione	VII	7
	466,3	Delgovicia	XIII	13
	466,4	Praetorio	XXV.	25
238	466,5	Item a vallo ad portum Ritu-		
	466,6	pis	CCCCLXXXI, sic:	481
	467,1	a Blatobulgio Castra Exploratorum	XII	12
	467,2	Luguvallo	XII	12
	467,3	Voreda	XIIII	14
	467,4	Brovonacis	XIII	13
	467,5	Verteris	XIII	13
	468,1	Lavatris	XIIII	14
	468,2	Cataractone	XVI	16
	468,3	Isuriam	XXIIII	24
	468,4	Eburacum	XVII	17
	468,5	Calcaria	VIIII	9
	468,6	Camboduno	XX	20
	468,7	Mamucio	XVIII	18
	469,1	Condate	XVIII	18
	469,2	Deva leg. XX Vici	XX	20
	469,3	Bovio	X	10
	469,4	Medialano	XX	20
	469,5	Rutunio	XII	12
	469,6	Urioconio	XI	11
	469,7	Uxacona	XI	11
	470,1	Pennocrucio	XII	12
	470,2	Etoceto	XII	12
	470,3	Manduesedo	XVI	16
	470,4	Venonis	XII	12
	470,5	Bannaventa	XVII	17
	470,6	Lactodoro	XII	12
	471,1	Magiovinto	XVII	17
	471,2	Durocobrivis	XII	12

267

Appendix 9: User's Guide to the Outlining of Rivers and Routes on Barrington Atlas Bases (C–F), with Associated Texts: Antonine Itinerary

268

Appendix 9: User's
Guide to the
Outlining of Rivers
and Routes on
Barrington Atlas
Bases (C–F), with
Associated Texts:
Antonine Itinerary

	471,3	Verolamio	XII	12
	471,4	Sulloniacis	VIIII	9
	471,5	Londinio	XII	12
	472,1	Noviomago	X	10
	472,2	Vagniacis	XVIIII	19
	472,3	Durobrovis	VIIII	9
	472,4	Durolevo	XIII	13
	472,5	Duroruerno	XII	12
	472,6	Ad portum Ritupis	XII.	12
239	473,1	Item a Londinio ad portum		
	473,2	Dubris	LXVI, sic:	66
	473,3	Dubobrius	XXVII	27
	473,4	Durarueno	XXV	25
	473,5	Ad portum Dubris	XIIII.	14
240	473,6	Item a Londinio ad portum		
	473,7	Lemanis	LXVIII	68
	473,8	Durobrivis	XXVII	27
	473,9	Duraruenno	XXV	25
	473,10	Ad portum Lemanis	XVI.	16
241	474,1	Item a Londinio Luguvalio ad		
	474,2	vallum	CCCCXLII:	442
	474,3	Caesaromago	XXVIII	28
	474,4	Colonia	XXIIII	24
	474,5	Villa Faustini	XXXV	35
	474,6	Icinos	XVIII	18
	474,7	Camborico	XXXV	35
	474,8	Duroliponte	XXV	25
	475,1	Durobrivas	XXXV	35
	475,2	Causennis	XXX	30
	475,3	Lindo	XXVI	26
	475,4	Segeloci	XIIII	14
	475,5	Dano	XXI	21
	475,6	Legeolio	XVI	16
	475,7	Eburaco	XXI	21
	476,1	Isubrigantum	XVII	17
	476,2	Cataractoni	XXIIII	24
	476,3	Levatris	XVIII	18
	476,4	Verteris	XIIII	14
	476,5	Brocavo	XX	20
	476,6	Luguvalio	XXI.	21
242	476,7	Item a Londinio Lindo	CLVI, sic:	156
	476,8	Verolami	XXI	21
	476,9	Durocobrius	XII	12
	476,10	Magiovinio	XII	12
	476,11	Lactodoro	XVI	16
	477,1	Isannavantia	XII	12
	477,2	Tripontio	XII	12
	477,3	Venonis	VIII	8
	477,4	Ratas	XII	12

	477,5	Verometo	XIII	13
	477,6	Margiduno	XII	12
	477,7	Ad Pontem	VII	7
	477,8	Crococalana	VII	7
	477,9	Lindo	XII.	12
243	477,10	Item a Regno Lundinio	XCVI, sic:	96
	478,1	Clausentum	XX	20
	478,2	Venta Belgarum	X	10
	478,3	Galleva Atrebatum	XXII	22
	478,4	Pontibus	XXII	22
	478,5	Londinio	XXII.	22
244	478,6	Item ab Eburaco Londinio	CCXXVII:	227
	478,7	Lagecio	XXI	21
	478,8	Dano	XVI	16
	478,9	Ageloco	XXI	21
	478,10	Lindo	XIIII	14
	478,11	Crococalano	XIIII	14
	479,1	Margiduno	XIIII	14
	479,2	Vernemeto	XII	12
	479,3	Ratis	XII	12
	479,4	Vennonis	XII	12
	479,5	Bannavanto	XVIIII	19
	479,6	Magiovinio	XXVIII	28
	479,7	Durocobrivis	XII	12
	479,8	Verolamo	XII	12
	479,9	Londinio	XXI.	21
245	479,10	Item a Venta Icinorum Lun-		
	479,11	dinio	CXXVIII, sic:	128
	480,1	Sitomago	XXXII	32
	480,2	Conbretovio	XXII	22
	480,3	Ad Ansam	XV	15
	480,4	Camoloduno	VI	6
	480,5	Canonio	VIIII	9
	480,6	Cesaromago	XII	12
	480,7	Durolito	XVI	16
	480,8	Lundinio	XV.	15
246	481,1	Item a Clanoventa Mediolano	CL, sic:	150
	481,2	Galava	XVIII	18
	481,3	Alone	XII	12
	481,4	Galacum	XVIIII	19
	481,5	Bremetonnaci	XXVII	27
	482,1	Coccio	XX	20
	482,2	Mamcunio	XVII	17
	482,3	Condate	XVIII	18
	482,4	Mediolano	XVIIII.	19
247	482,5	Item a Segontio Devam	LXXIIII, sic:	74
	482,6	Conovio	XXIIII	24
	482,7	Varis	XVIII	18
	482,8	Deva	XXXII.	32

269

*Appendix 9: User's
Guide to the
Outlining of Rivers
and Routes on*
Barrington Atlas
*Bases (C–F), with
Associated Texts:
Antonine Itinerary*

Appendix 9: User's Guide to the Outlining of Rivers and Routes on Barrington Atlas *Bases (C–F), with Associated Texts: Antonine Itinerary*

248	482,9	Item a Muridono Viroconi-		
	482,10	orum	CLXXXVI:	186
	483,1	Vindomi	XV	15
	483,2	Venta Belgarum	XXI	21
	483,3	Brige	XI	11
	483,4	Sorvioduni	VIII	8
	483,5	Vindogladia	XII	12
	483,6	Durnonovaria	VIII	8
	483,7	Muriduno	XXXVI	36
	483,8	Sca Dumnonniorum	XV	15
	484,1	Leucaro	XV	15
	484,2	Nido	XV	15
	484,3	Bomio	XV	15
	484,4	Iscae leg. II Augusta	XXVII	27
	484,5	Burrio	VIIII	9
	484,6	Gobannio	XII	12
	484,7	Magnis	XXII	22
	484,8	Bravonio	XXIIII	24
	484,9	Viriconio	XXVII.	27
249	484,10	Item ab Isca Calleva	CVIIII, sic:	109
	485,1	Burrio	VIIII	9
	485,2	Blestio	XI	11
	485,3	Ariconio	XI	11
	485,4	Clevo	XV	15
	485,5	Durocornovio	XIIII	14
	485,6	Spinis	XV	15
	485,7	Calleva	XV.	15
250	485,8	Item alio itinere ab Isca Calleva	CIII, sic:	103
	485,9	Venta Silurum	VIIII	9
	486,1	Abone	XIIII	14
	486,2	Traiectus	VIIII	9
	486,3	Aquis Sulis	VI	6
	486,4	Verlucione	XV	15
	486,5	Cunetione	XX	20
	486,6	Spinis	XV	15
	486,7	Calleva	XV.	15
251	486,8	Item a Calleva Isca Dumnonio-		
	486,9	rum	CXXXVI, sic:	136
	486,10	Vindomi	XV	15
	486,11	Venta Velgarum	XXI	21
	486,12	Brige	XI	11
	486,13	Sorbiodoni	VIII	8
	486,14	Vindocladia	XII	12
	486,15	Durnonovaria	VIII	8
	486,16	Moriduno	XXXVI	36
	486,17	Isca Dumnoniorum	XV.	15

(b) BORDEAUX ITINERARY (*ItBurd*) TEXT WITH JOURNEYS LETTERED (FAR LEFT COLUMN) AS ON MAP F

The edition followed is P. Geyer, *Itinerarium Burdigalense*, in *Itineraria et Alia Geographica*, Corpus Christianorum Series Latina 175 (Turnhout [Belgium], 1965), 1–26. However, **u** and **v** are distinguished, and the distance unit *milia* (for Roman miles) is omitted. Any distance figure with no distance unit attached can therefore be taken to be in Roman miles.

271

Appendix 9: User's Guide to the Outlining of Rivers and Routes on Barrington Atlas Bases (C–F), with Associated Texts: Bordeaux Itinerary

	549, 1	ITINERARIUM		
	549, 2	A BURDIGALA HIERUSALEM USQUE		
	549, 3	ET AB HERACLEA PER AULONAM		
	549, 4	ET PER URBEM ROMAM		
	549, 5	MEDIOLANUM USQUE		
	549, 6	SIC:		
A	549, 7	Civitas Burdigala, ubi est fluvius Garonna,		
	549, 8	per quem facit mare Oceanum accessa et		
	549, 9	recessa per leugas plus minus centum,		
	549, 10	mutatio Stomatas	leugae VII	7
	550, 1	mutatio Sirione	leugae VIIII	9
	550, 2	civitas Vasatas	leugae VIIII	9
	550, 3	mutatio Tres Arbores	leugae V	5
	550, 4	mutatio Oscineio	leugae VIII	8
	550, 5	mutatio Scittio	leugae VIII	8
	550, 6	civitates Elusa	leugae VIII	8
	550, 7	mutatio Vanesia	leugae XII	12
	550, 8	civitas Auscius	leugae VIII	8
	550, 9	mutatio Ad Sextum	leugae VI	6
	550, 10	mutatio Hungunverro	leugae VII	7
	550, 11	mutatio Bucconis	leugae VII	7
	551, 1	mutatio Ad Iovem	leugae VII	7
	551, 2	civitas Tholosa	leugae VII	7
	551, 3	mutatio Ad Nonum	VIIII	9
	551, 4	mutatio Ad Vicesimum	XI	11
	551, 5	mansio Elusione	VIIII	9
	551, 6	mutatio Sostomago	VIIII	9
	551, 7	vicus Hebromago	X	10
	551, 8	mutatio Cedros	VI	6
	551, 9	castellum Carcassone	VIII	8
	551, 10	mutatio Tricensimum	VIII	8
	552, 1	mutatio Hosverbas	XV	15
	552, 2	civitas Narbone	XV	15
	552, 3	civitas Beterris	XVI	16
	552, 4	mansio Cessarone	XII	12
	552, 5	mutatio Foro Domiti	XVIII	18
	552, 6	mutatio Sostantione	XV	15
	552, 7	mutatio Ambrosi	XV	15
	552, 8	civitas Nemauso	XV	15

272

Appendix 9: User's Guide to the Outlining of Rivers and Routes on Barrington Atlas Bases (C–F), with *Associated Texts: Bordeaux Itinerary*

A	552, 9	mutatio Ponte Aerarium	XII	12
	552, 10	civitas Arelate	VIII	8
	553, 1	Fit a Burdigala Arelate usque milia CCCLXXII,		372
	553, 2	mutationes XXX, mansiones XI.		30/11
	553, 3	mutatio Arnagine	VIII	8
	553, 4	mutatio Bellinto	X	10
	553, 5	civitas Avenione	V	5
	553, 6	mutatio Cypresseta	V	5
	553, 7	civitas Arausione	XV	15
	553, 8	mutatio Ad Letoce	XIII	13
	553, 9	mutatio Novem Craris	X	10
	553, 10	mansio Acuno	X	10
	554, 1	mutatio Bantianis	XII	12
	554, 2	mutatio Umbenno	XII	12
	554, 3	civitas Valentia	VIIII	9
	554, 4	mutatio Cerebelliaca	XII	12
	554, 5	mansio Augusta	X	10
	554, 6	mutatio Darentiaca	XII	12
	554, 7	civitas Dea Vocontiorum	XVI	16
	554, 8	mansio Luco	XII	12
	554, 9	mutatio Vologatis	VIIII	9
	555, 1	inde ascenditur Gaura mons		
	555, 2	mutatio Cambono	VIII	8
	555, 3	mansio Monte Seleuci	VIII	8
	555, 4	mutatio Daviano	VIII	8
	555, 5	mutatio Ad Finem	XII	12
	555, 6	mansio Vappinco	XI	11
	555, 7	mansio Catorigas	XII	12
	555, 8	mansio Ebreduno	XVI	16
	555, 9	inde incipiunt Alpes Cottiae		
	555, 10	mutatio Ramae	XVII	17
	555, 11	mansio Byrigante	XVII	17
	556, 1	inde ascendis Matronam		
	556, 2	mutatio Gesdaone	X	10
	556, 3	mansio Ad Marte	VIIII	9
	556, 4	civitas Segussione	XVI	16
	556, 5	inde incipit Italia		
	556, 6	mutatio Ad Duodecimum	XII	12
	556, 7	mansio Ad Fines	XII	12
	556, 8	mutatio Ad Octavum	VIII	8
	556, 9	civitas Taurinis	VIII	8
	556, 10	mutatio Ad Decimum	X	10
	557, 1	mansio Quadratis	XII	12
	557, 2	mutatio Ceste	XI	11
	557, 3	mansio Rigomago	VIII	8
	557, 4	mutatio Ad Medias	X	10
	557, 5	mutatio Ad Cottias	XIII	13
	557, 6	mansio Laumello	XII	12
	557, 7	mutatio Duriis	VIIII	9
	557, 8	civitas Ticino	XII	12
	557, 9	mutatio Ad Decimum	X	10

557, 10	civitas Mediolanum	X	10
557, 11	[mansio Fluvio Frigido	XII]	12
558, 1	Fit ab Arelate Mediolanum usque milia CCCCLXXV,		475
558, 2	mutationes LXIII, mansiones XXII.		63/22
558, 3	mutatio Argentea	X	10
558, 4	mutatio Ponte Aureoli	X	10
558, 5	civitas Bergamo	XIII	13
558, 6	mutatio Tellegate	XII	12
558, 7	mutatio Tetellus	X	10
558, 8	civitas Brixa	X	10
558, 9	mansio Ad Flexum	XI	11
558, 10	mutatio Beneventum	X	10
558, 11	civitas Verona	X	10
558, 12	mutatio Cadiano	X	10
558, 13	mutatio Aureos	X	10
559, 1	civitas Vincentia	XI	11
559, 2	mutatio Ad Finem	XI	11
559, 3	civitas Patavi	X	10
559, 4	mutatio Ad Duodecimum	XII	12
559, 5	mutatio Ad Nonum	XI	11
559, 6	civitas Altino	VIIII	9
559, 7	mutatio Sanos	X	10
559, 8	civitas Concordia	VIIII	9
559, 9	mutatio Apicilia	VIIII	9
559, 10	mutatio Ad Undecimum	XI	11
559, 11	civitas Aquileia	XI	11
559, 12	Fit a Mediolano Aquileia usque milia CCLI,		251
559, 13	mutationes XXIIII, mansiones VIIII.		24/9
559, 14	mutatio Ad Undecimum	XI	11
560, 1	mutatio Ad Fornolus	XII	12
560, 2	mutatio Castra	XII	12
560, 3	inde surgunt Alpes Iuliae		
560, 4	ad Pirum summas Alpes	VIIII	9
560, 5	mansio Longatico	X	10
560, 6	mutatio Ad Nonum	VIIII	9
560, 7	civitas Emona	XIIII	14
560, 8	mutatio Ad Quartodecimo	X	10
560, 9	mansio Hadrante	XIII	13
560, 10	fines Italiae et Norci		
560, 11	mutatio Ad Medias	XIII	13
560, 12	civitas Celeia	XIII	13
561, 1	mutatio Lotodos	XII	12
561, 2	mansio Ragindone	XII	12
561, 3	mutatio Pultovia	XII	12
561, 4	civitas Poetovione	XII	12
561, 5	transis pontem, intras Pannoniam		
561, 6	Inferiorem		
561, 7	mutatio Ramista	VIIII	9
561, 8	mansio Aqua Viva	VIIII	9
561, 9	mutatio Populis	X	10
561, 10	civitas Iovia	VIIII	9

273

Appendix 9: User's Guide to the Outlining of Rivers and Routes on Barrington Atlas *Bases (C–F), with Associated Texts: Bordeaux Itinerary*

274

Appendix 9: User's Guide to the Outlining of Rivers and Routes on Barrington Atlas Bases (C–F), with Associated Texts: Bordeaux Itinerary

A	561, 11	mutatio Sunista	VIIII	9
	562, 1	mutatio Peritur	XII	12
	562, 2	mansio Lentolis	XII	12
	562, 3	mutatio Cardono	X	10
	562, 4	mutatio Cocconis	XII	12
	562, 5	mansio Serota	X	10
	562, 6	mutatio Bolentia	X	10
	562, 7	mansio Maurianis	VIIII	9
	562, 8	intras Pannoniam Superiorem		
	562, 9	mutatio Serena	VIII	8
	562, 10	mansio Vereis	X	10
	562, 11	mutatio Iovalia	VIII	8
	562, 12	mutatio Mersella	VIII	8
	562, 13	civitas Mursa	X	10
	563, 1	mutatio Leutuoano	XII	12
	563, 2	civitas Cibalis	XII	12
	563, 3	mutatio Caelena	XI	11
	563, 4	mansio Ulmo	XI	11
	563, 5	mutatio Spaneta	X	10
	563, 6	mutatio Vedulia	VIII	8
	563, 7	civitas Sirmium	VIII	8
	563, 8	Fit ab Aquileia Sirmium usque milia CCCCXII,		412
	563, 9	mansiones XVII, mutationes XXXVIIII		17/39
	563, 10	mutatio Fossis	VIIII	9
	563, 11	civitas Bassianis	X	10
	563, 12	mutatio Noviciani	XII	12
	563, 13	mutatio Altina	XI	11
	563, 14	civitas Singiduno	VIII	8
	564, 1	fines Pannoniae et Misiae		
	564, 2	mutatio Ad Sextum	VI	6
	564, 3	mutatio Tricornia Castra	VI	6
	564, 4	mutatio Ad Sextum Miliarem	VII	7
	564, 5	civitas Aureo Monte	VI	6
	564, 6	mutatio Vingeio	VI	6
	564, 7	civitas Margo	VIIII	9
	564, 8	civitas Viminacio	X	10
	564, 9	ubi Diocletianus occidit Carinum		
	564, 10	mutatio Ad Nonum	VIIII	9
	565, 1	mansio Munecipio	VIIII	9
	565, 2	mutatio Iovis Pago	X	10
	565, 3	mutatio Bao	VII	7
	565, 4	mansio Idomo	VIIII	9
	565, 5	mutatio Ad Octavum	VIIII	9
	565, 6	mansio Oromago	VIII	8
	565, 7	finis Myssiae et Asiae		
	565, 8	mutatio Sarmatorum	XII	12
	565, 9	mutatio Caminitas	XI	11
	566, 1	mansio Ipompeis	VIIII	9
	566, 2	mutatio Rampiana	XII	12
	566, 3	civitas Naisso	XII	12
	566, 4	mutatio Redicibus	XII	12

566, 5	mutatio Ulmo	VII	7
566, 6	mansio Romansiana	VIIII	9
566, 7	mutatio Latina	VIIII	9
566, 8	mansio Turribus	VIIII	9
566, 9	mutatio Translitis	XII	12
566, 10	mutatio Ballanstra	X	10
566, 11	mansio Meldia	VIIII	9
566, 12	mutatio Scretisca	XII	12
567, 1	civitas Serdica	XI	11
567, 2	Fit a Sirmium Serdica usque milia CCCXIIII,		314
567, 3	mutationes XXIIII, mansiones XIII.		24/13
567, 4	mutatio Extuomne	VIII	8
567, 5	mansio Buragara	VIIII	9
567, 6	mutatio Sparata	VIII	8
567, 7	mansio Hilica	X	10
567, 8	mutatio Soneio	VIIII	9
567, 9	fines Daciae et Traciae		
567, 10	mutatio Ponte Ucasi	VI	6
567, 11	mansio Bona Mansio	VI	6
568, 1	mutatio Alusore	VIIII	9
568, 2	mansio Basapare	XII	12
568, 3	mutatio Tugugero	VIIII	9
568, 4	civitas Filopopuli	XII	12
568, 5	mutatio Sernota	X	10
568, 6	mutatio Paramvole	VIII	8
568, 7	mansio Cillio	XII	12
568, 8	mutatio Carassura	VIIII	9
568, 9	mansio Arzo	XI	11
568, 10	mutatio Palae	VII	7
568, 11	mansio Castozobra	XI	11
568, 12	mutatio Rhamis	VII	7
569, 1	mansio Burdista	XI	11
569, 2	mutatio Daphabae	XI	11
569, 3	mansio Nicae	VIIII	9
569, 4	mutatio Tarpodizo	X	10
569, 5	mutatio Urisio	VII	7
569, 6	mansio Virgoles	VII	7
569, 7	mutatio Narco	VIII	8
569, 8	mansio Drizupara	VIIII	9
569, 9	mutatio Tipso	VIII	8
569, 10	mansio Tunorullo	VIII	8
570, 1	mutatio Beodizo	VIII	8
570, 2	civitas Heraclea	VIIII	9
570, 3	mutatio Baunne	XII	12
570, 4	mansio Salambria	X	10
570, 5	mutatio Callum	X	10
570, 6	mansio Atyra	X	10
570, 7	mansio Regio	XII	12
570, 8	civitas Constantinopoli	XII	12
571, 1	Fit a Serdica Constantinopoli milia CCCCXIII,		413
571, 2	mutationes XII, mansiones XX.		12/20

*Appendix 9: User's
Guide to the
Outlining of Rivers
and Routes on*
Barrington Atlas
*Bases (C–F), with
Associated Texts:
Bordeaux Itinerary*

276
___

Appendix 9: User's Guide to the Outlining of Rivers and Routes on Barrington Atlas Bases (C–F), with Associated Texts: Bordeaux Itinerary

571, 3	Fit omnis summa a Burdigala Constantinopolim		
571, 4	vicies bis centena viginti unum milia,		
571, 5	mutationes CCXXX, mansiones CXII.		230/112
571, 6	Item ambulavimus Dalmatico et Zenophilo cons. III.		
571, 7	kal. Iun. a Calcedonia et reversi sumus		
571, 8	Constantinopolim VII kal. Ian. cons. suprascripto.		

B	571, 9	A Constantinopoli transis Pontum, venis Calcedo-		
	571, 10	niam, ambulas provinciam Bithyniam:		
	571, 11	mutatio Nassete	VII S<emis>	7.5
	572, 1	mansio Pandicia	VII S<emis>	7.5
	572, 2	mutatio Pontamus	XIII	13
	572, 3	mansio Libissa	VIIII	9
	572, 4	ibi positus est rex Annibalianus, qui fuit		
	572, 5	Afrorum		
	572, 6	mutatio Brunga	XII	12
	572, 7	civitas Nicomedia	VIIII	9
	572, 8	Fit a Constantinopoli Nicomedia usque mil. LVIII,		58
	572, 9	mutationes VII, mansiones III		7/3
	573, 1	mutatio Hyribolum	X	10
	573, 2	mansio Libum	XI	11
	573, 3	mutatio Liada	XII	12
	573, 4	civitas Nicia	VIIII	9
	573, 5	mutatio Schinae	VIII	8
	573, 6	mansio Mido	VII	7
	573, 7	mutatio Chogeae	VI	6
	573, 8	mutatio Thateso	X	10
	573, 9	mansio Tutaio	VIIII	9
	573, 10	mutatio Protunica	XI	11
	573, 11	mutatio Artemis	XII	12
	574, 1	mansio Dablae	VI	6
	574, 2	mansio Ceratae	VI	6
	574, 3	fines Bithiniae et Galatiae		
	574, 4	mutatio Fines	X	10
	574, 5	mansio Dadastano	VI	6
	574, 6	mutatio Trans Monte	VI	6
	574, 7	mutatio Milia	XI	11
	574, 8	civitas Iuliopolis	VIII	8
	574, 9	mutatio Hicronpotamum	XIII	13
	574, 10	mansio Agannia	XI	11
	574, 11	mutatio Petobrogen	VI	6
	575, 1	mansio Mnizos	X	10
	575, 2	mutatio Prasmon	XII	12
		mansio Malogordis	VIIII	9
	575, 3	mutatio Cenaxem Palidem	XIII	13
	575, 4	civitas Anchira Galatia	XIII	13
	575, 5	Fit a Nicomedia Anchira Galatia usque		
	575, 6	milia CCLVIII,		258
	575, 7	mutationes XXVI, mansiones XII.		26/12
	575, 8	mutatio Delemna	X	10
	575, 9	mansio Curveunta	XI	11
	575, 10	mutatio Rosolodiaco	XII	12

575, 11	mutatio Aliassum	XIII	13
575, 12	civitas Aspona	XVIII	18
576, 1	mutatio Galea	XIII	13
576, 2	mutatio Andrapa	VIIII	9
576, 3	fines Galatiae et Cappadociae		
576, 4	mansio Parnasso	XIII	13
576, 5	mansio Iogola	XVI	16
576, 6	mansio Nitalis	XVIII	18
576, 7	mutatio Argustana	XIII	13
576, 8	civitas Colonia	XV	15
577, 1	mutatio Momoasson	XII	12
577, 2	mansio Anathiango	XIII	13
577, 3	mutatio Chusa	XII	12
577, 4	mansio Sasima	XII	12
577, 5	mansio Andavilis	XVI	16
577, 6	ibi est villa Pammati, unde veniunt equi curules		
577, 7	civitas Thyana	XVIII	18
578, 1	inde fuit Apollonius magus		
578, 2	civitas Faustinopoli	XII	12
578, 3	mutatio Caena	XIII	13
578, 4	mansio Opodando	XII	12
578, 5	mutatio Pilas	XIIII	14
579, 1	fines Cappadociae et Ciliciae		
579, 2	mansio Mansucrinae	XII	12
579, 3	civitas Tarso	XII	12
579, 4	inde fuit apostolus Paulus		
579, 5	Fit ad Anchira Galatia Tarso usque milia CCCXLIII,		343
580, 1	mutationes XXV, mansiones XVIII.		25/18
580, 2	mutatio Pargais	XIII	13
580, 3	civitas Adana	XIIII	14
580, 4	civitas Mansista	XVIII	18
580, 5	mutatio Tardequeia	XV	15
580, 6	mansio Catavolo	XVI	16
580, 7	mansio Baiae	XVII	17
580, 8	mansio Alexandria Scabiosa	XVI	16
581, 1	mutatio Pictanus	VIIII	9
581, 2	fines Ciliciae et Syriae		
581, 3	mansio Pagrios	VIII	8
581, 4	civitas Antiochia	XVI	16
581, 5	Fit a Tarso Ciliciae Antiochia usque milia CXLI,		141
581, 6	mutationes X, mansiones VII.		10/7
581, 7	ad palatium Dafne	V	5
582, 1	mutatio Hysdata	XI	11
582, 2	mansio Platanus	VIII	8
582, 3	mutatio Baccaias	VIII	8
582, 4	mansio Catelas	XVI	16
582, 5	civitas Ladica	XVI	16
582, 6	civitas Gabala	XIIII	14
582, 7	civitas Balaneas	XIII	13
582, 8	fines Syriae Coelis et Foenicis		
582, 9	mutatio Maraccas	X	10

277

Appendix 9: User's Guide to the Outlining of Rivers and Routes on Barrington Atlas Bases (C–F), *with Associated Texts: Bordeaux Itinerary*

278

Appendix 9: User's Guide to the Outlining of Rivers and Routes on Barrington Atlas *Bases (C–F), with Associated Texts: Bordeaux Itinerary*

B	582, 10	mansio Antaradus	XVI	16
	582, 11	est civitas in mare a ripa milia II		2
	582, 12	mutatio Spiclin	XII	12
	583, 1	mutatio Basiliscum	XII	12
	583, 2	mansio Arcas	VIII	8
	583, 3	mutatio Bruttus	IIII	4
	583, 4	civitas Tripoli	XII	12
	583, 5	mutatio Triclis	XII	12
	583, 6	mutatio Bruttos alia	XII	12
	583, 7	mutatio Alcobile	XII	12
	583, 8	civitas Birito	XII	12
	583, 9	mutatio Heldua	XII	12
	583, 10	mutatio Parphirion	VIII	8
	583, 11	civitas Sidona	VIII	8
	583, 12	inde Sarepta	VIIII	9
	583, 13	ibi Helias ad viduam ascendit et petiit sibi cibum		
	583, 14	mutatio Ad Nonum	IIII	4
	584, 1	civitas Tyro	XII	12
	584, 2	Fit ab Antiochia Tyro usque milia CLXXIIII,		174
	584, 3	mutationes XX, mansiones XI.		20/11
	584, 4	mutatio Alexandroschene	XII	12
	584, 5	mutatio Ecdeppa	XII	12
	584, 6	civitas Ptolomaida	VIII	8
	584, 7	mutatio Calamon	XII	12
	584, 8	mansio Sicaminos	III	3
	585, 1	ibi est mons Carmelus, ibi Helias sacrificium faciebat		
	585, 2	mutatio Certha	VIII	8
	585, 3	fines Syriae Finices et Palestinae		
	585, 4	civitas Caesarea Palestina id est Iudaea milia VIII		8
	585, 5	Fit a Tyro Caesarea Palestina milia LXXIII,		73
	585, 6	mutationes II, mansiones III.		2/3
	585, 7	Ibi est balneus Cornelii centurionis, qui		
	585, 8	multas elymosynas faciebat.		
	585, 9	Inde est tertio miliario		
	586, 1	mons Syna, ubi fons est, in quem		
	586, 2	mulier est laverit, gravida fit.		
	586, 3	civitas Maximianopoli	XVIII	18
	586, 4	civitas Isdradela	X	10
	586, 5	ibi sedit Achab rex et Helias prophetavit;		
	586, 6	ibi est campus, ubi David Goliat occidit.		
	586, 7	Civitas Scithopoli	XII	12
	587, 1	Aser, ubi fuit villa Iob	XVI	16
	587, 2	civitas Neapoli	XV	15
	587, 3	Ibi est mons Agazaren: ibi dicunt Samaritani Abraham sacrificium obtulisse,		
	587, 4	et ascenduntur usque ad summum montem gradi numero MCCC. Inde ad pedem		1,300
	587, 5	montis ipsius locus est, cui nomen est Sechim. Ibi est monumentum, ubi positus		
	588, 1	est Ioseph in villa, quam dedit ei Iacob pater eius. Inde rapta est et		

588, 2	Dina filia Iacob a filiis Amorreorum. Inde passus mille locus est cui nomen		
588, 3	Sechar, unde descendit mulier Samaritana ad eundem locum, ubi Iacob puteum		
588, 4	fodit, ut de eo aquam impleret, et Dominus noster Iesus Christus cum ea locutus		
588, 5	est; ubi sunt et arbores platani, quas plantavit Iacob, et balneus, qui de eo		
588, 6	puteo lavatur.		
588, 7	Inde milia XXVIII euntibus Hierusalem in parte	28	
588, 8	sinistra est villa, quae dicitur Bethar.		
588, 9	Inde passus mille est locus, ubi Iacob, cum iret in Mesopotamiam, addormivit, et		
588, 10	ibi est arbor amigdala, et vidit visum et angelus cum eo luctatus est. Ibi		
588, 11	fuit rex Hieroboam, ad quem missus propheta, ut converteretur ad Deum		
589, 1	excelsum; et iussum fuerat prophetae, ne cum pseudoprophetam, quem secum		
589, 2	rex habebat, manducaret, et quia seductus est a pseudopropheta et cum eo		
589, 3	manducavit rediens, occurrit prophetae leo in via et occidit eum.		
589, 4	Inde Hierusalem	XII	12
589, 5	Fit a Caesarea Palestina Hierusalem usque milia CXVI,		116
589, 6	mansiones IIII, mutationes IIII.		4/4
589, 7	Sunt in Hierusalem piscinae magnae duae ad latus templi, id est una ad dexteram,		
589, 8	alia ad sinistram, quas Salomon fecit, interius vero civitati sunt piscinae gemellares		
589, 9	quinque porticus habentes, quae appellantur Bethsaida. Ibi aegri multorum		
589, 10	annorum sanabantur. Aquam autem habent hae piscinae in modum coccini		
589, 11	turbatam. Est ibi et cripta, ubi Salomon daemones torquebat. Ibi est angelus		
590, 1	turris excelsissimae, ubi Dominus ascendit et dixit ei is, qui temptabat eum,		
590, 2	et ait ei Dominus: *Non temptabis Dominum Deum tuum, sed illi soli servies.*		
590, 3	Ibi est et lapis angularis magnus, de quo dictum est: *Lapidem, quem reprobaverunt*		
590, 4	*aedificantes, hic factus est ad caput anguli.* Et sub pinna turris ipsius sunt cubicula		
590, 5	plurima, ubi Salomon palatium habebat. Ibi etiam constat cubiculus, in quo		
590, 6	sedit et sapientiam descripsit; ipse vero cubiculus uno lapide est tectus. Sunt ibi		
590, 7	et excepturia magna aquae subterraneae et piscinae magno opere aedificatae. Et		

279

Appendix 9: User's Guide to the Outlining of Rivers and Routes on Barrington Atlas Bases (C–F), with *Associated Texts:* Bordeaux Itinerary

*Appendix 9: User's
Guide to the
Outlining of Rivers
and Routes on
Barrington Atlas
Bases (C–F), with
Associated Texts:
Bordeaux Itinerary*

591, 1	in aede ipsa, ubi templum fuit, quem Salomon aedificavit, in marmore ante aram
591, 2	sanguinem Zachariae ibi dicas hodie fusum; etiam parent vestigia clavorum
591, 3	militum, qui eum occiderunt, per totum aream, ut putes in cera fixum esse.
591, 4	Sunt ibi et statuae duae Hadriani; est et non longe de statuas lapis pertusus,
591, 5	ad quem veniunt Iudaei singulis annis et unguent eum et lamentant se cum
591, 6	gemitu et vestimenta sua scindunt et sic recedunt. Est ibi et domus Ezechiae
591, 7	regis Iudae. Item exeuntibus Hierusalem, ut ascendas Sion, in parte sinistra
592, 1	et deorsum in valle iuxta murum est piscina, quae dicitur Siloa; habet quadriporticum;
592, 2	et alia piscina grandis foras. Haec fons sex diebus atque noctibus
592, 3	currit, septima vero die est sabbatum: in totum nec nocte nec die currit. In eadem
592, 4	ascenditur Sion et paret ubi fuit domus Caifae sacerdotis, et columna adhuc
592, 5	ibi est, in qua Christum flagellis ceciderunt. Intus autem intra murum Sion
592, 6	paret locus, ubi palatium habuit David. Et septem synagogae, quae illic fuerunt,
592, 7	una tantum remansit, reliquae autem arantur et seminantur, sicut Isaias propheta
593, 1	dixit. Inde ut eas foris murum de Sion, euntibus ad portam Neapolitanam
593, 2	ad partem dextram deorsum in valle sunt parietes, ubi domus fuit
593, 3	sive praetorium Pontii Pilati; ibi Dominus auditus est, antequam pateretur.
593, 4	A sinistra autem parte est monticulus Golgotha, ubi Dominus crucifixus est.
594, 1	Inde quasi ad lapidem missum est cripta, ubi corpus eius positum fuit et
594, 2	tertia die resurrexit; ibidem modo iussu Constantini imperatoris basilica
594, 3	facta est, id est dominicum, mirae pulchritudinis habens ad latus exceptoria,
594, 4	unde aqua levatur, et balneum a tergo, ubi infantes lavantur.
594, 5	Item ad Hierusalem euntibus ad portem, quae est contra orientem, ut ascendatur
594, 6	in monte Oliveti, vallis, quae dicitur Iosafath, ad partem sinistram, ubi sunt
594, 7	vineae, est et petra ubi Iudas Scarioth Christum tradidit: a parte vero
595, 1	dextra est arbor palmae, de qua infantes ramos tulerunt et veniente Christo

595, 2	substraverunt. Inde non longe quasi ad lapidis missum sunt monumenta duo
595, 3	monubiles mirae pulchritudinis facta: in unum positus est Isaias propheta,
595, 4	qui est vere monolitus, et in alio Ezechias rex Iudaeorum. Inde ascendis
595, 5	in montem Oliveti, ubi Dominus ante passionem apostolos docuit: ibi
595, 6	facta est basilica iussu Constantini. Inde non longe est monticulus, ubi
595, 7	Dominus ascendit orare et apparuit illic Moyses et Helias, quando Petrum
596, 1	et Iohannem secum duxit. Inde ad orientem passus mille quingentos est
596, 2	villa, quae appellatur Bethania; est ibi cripta, ubi Lazarus positus fuit,
596, 3	quem Dominus suscitavit.
596, 4	Item ad Hierusalem in Hiericho milia XVIII. Descendentibus
596, 5	montem in parte dextra retro monumentum est arbor sicomori,
596, 6	in qua Zachaeus ascendit, ut Christum videret. A civitate, passus mille
596, 7	quingentos est ibi fons Helisei prophetae. Antea si qua mulier ex ipsa aqua bibebat,
596, 8	non faciebat natos. Adlatum est vas fictile Heliseo, misit in eo sales et venit
596, 9	et stetit super fontem et dixit: *Haec dicit Dominus: sanavit aquas has.*
596, 10	Ex eo si qua mulier inde biberit, filios faciet. Supra eundem vero fontem
597, 1	est domus Rachab fornicariae, ad quam exploratores introierunt et occultavit eos,
597, 2	quando Hiericho eversa est, et sola evasit. Ibi fuit civitas Hiericho,
597, 3	cuius muros gyraverunt cum arca testamenti filii Israel et ceciderunt muri. Ex
597, 4	eo non paret nisi locus, ubi fuit arca testamenti et lapides XII, quos filii Israel
597, 5	de Iordane levaverunt. Ibidem Iesus filius Nave circumcidit filios Israel.
597, 6	et circumcisiones eorum sepelivit.
597, 7.8	Item ad Hiericho ad Mare Mortuum milia novem.
597, 9	Est aqua ipsius valde amarissima, ubi in totum nullius generis piscis est nec
597, 10	aliqua navis, et si qui hominum miserit se, ut natet, ipsa aqua eum versat.
598. 1.2	Inde ad Iordane, ubi Dominus a Iohanne baptizatus est, milia quinque.
598, 3	Ibi est locus super flumen, monticulus in illa ripa, ubi raptus est Helias in caelum.

Appendix 9: User's Guide to the Outlining of Rivers and Routes on Barrington Atlas Bases (C–F), *with Associated Texts: Bordeaux Itinerary*

18

282

Appendix 9: User's Guide to the Outlining of Rivers and Routes on Barrington Atlas Bases (C–F), with *Associated Texts: Bordeaux Itinerary*

598, 4	Item ab Hierusalem euntibus Bethleem milia quattuor super strata in		
598, 5	parte dextra est monumentum, ubi Rachel posita est, uxor Iacob. Inde milia		
598, 6	duo a parte sinistra est Bethleem, ubi natus est Dominus Iesus Christus;		
598, 7	ibi basilica facta est iussu Constantini. Inde non longe est monumentum Ezechiel.		
598, 8	Asaph, Iob et Iesse, David, Salomon, et habet in ipsa cripta ad		
598, 9	latus deorsum descendentibus hebraeis litteris scriptum nomina supra scripta.		
599. 1.2	Inde Bethasora milia XIIII, ubi est fons, in quo Philippus eunuchum baptizavit.		14
599, 3.4	Inde Terebinto milia VIIII, ubi Abraham habitavit et puteum fodit sub arbore terebintho		9
599, 5	et cum angelis locutus est et cibum sumpsit; ibi basilica facta est iussu		
599, 6	Constantini mirae puchritudinis.		
599, 7	Inde Terebinto Cebron milia II, ubi est		2
599, 8	memoria per quadrum ex lapidibus mirae pulchritudinis, in qua positi		
599, 9	sunt Abraham, Isaac, Iacob, Sarra, Rebecca et Lia.		

C 600, 1	Item ab Hierusolyma, sic:		
600, 2	civitas Nicopoli	XXII	22
600, 3	civitas Lidda	X	10
600, 4	mutatio Antipatrida	X	10
600, 5	mutatio Betthar	X	10
600, 6	civitas Caesarea	XVI	16
601, 1	Fit omnis summa a Constantinopoli usque Hierusalem		
601, 2	milia undecies centena LXIIII milia		64
601, 3	mutationes LXVIIII, mansiones LVIII.		69/58
601, 4	Item per Nicopoli Caesarea milia LXXIII S<emis>		73.5
601, 5	mutationes V, mansiones III.		5/3

D 601, 6	Item ab Heraclea per Machedonia:		
601, 7	mutatio Aerea	XVI	16
601, 8	mansio Registo	XII	12
601, 9	mutatio Bedizo	XII	12
601, 10	civitas Apris	XII	12
602, 1	mutatio Zesutera	XII	12
602, 2	finis Europae et Rhodopeae		
602, 3	mansio Sirogellis	X	10
602, 4	mutatio Drippa	XIIII	14
602, 5	mansio Gipsila	XII	12
602, 6	mutatio Demas	XII	12
602, 7	civitas Traianopoli	XIII	13
602, 8	mutatio Ad Unimpara	VIII	8
602, 9	mutatio Salei	VII S<emis>	7.5
602, 10	mutatio Melalico	VIII	8

602, 11	mansio Berozicha	XV	15
603, 1	mutatio Breierophara	X	10
603, 2	civitas Maximianopoli	X	10
603, 3	mutatio Ad Stabulodio	XII	12
603, 4	mutatio Rumbodona	X	10
603, 5	civitas Epyrum	X	10
603, 6	mutatio Purdis	VIII	8
603, 7	finis Rhodopeae et Macedoniae		
603, 8	mansio Hercontroma	VIIII	9
603, 9	mutatio Neapolim	VIIII	9
603, 10	civitas Philippis	X	10
604, 1	ubi Paulus et Sileas in carcere fuerunt		
604, 2	mutatio Ad Duodecimum	XII	12
604, 3	mutatio Domeros	VII	7
604, 4	civitas Amphipholim	XIII	13
604, 5	mutatio Pennana	X	10
604, 6	mutatio Peripidis	X	10
604, 7	ibi positus est Euripidis poeta		
605, 1	mansio Appollonia	XI	11
605, 2	mutatio Heracleustibus	XI	11
605, 3	mutatio Duo dea	XIIII	14
605, 4	civitas Thessalonica	XIII	13
605, 5	mutatio Ad Decimum	X	10
605, 6	mutatio Gephira	X	10
606, 1	civitas Polli, unde fuit Alexander, Magnus Ma-		
606, 2	cedo	X	10
606, 3	mutatio Scurio	XV	15
606, 4	civitas Edissa	XV	15
606, 5	mutatio Ad Duodecimum	XII	12
606, 6	mansio Cellis	XVI	16
606, 7	mutatio Grande	XIIII	14
606, 8	mutatio Melitonus	XIIII	14
606, 9	civitas Heraclea	XIII	13
607, 1	mutatio Parambole	XII	12
607, 2	mutatio Brucida	XVIIII	19
607, 3	finis Macedoniae et Ephyri		
607, 4	civitas Cledo	XIII	13
607, 5	mutatio Patras	XII	12
607, 6	mansio Claudanon	IIII	4
607, 7	mutatio In Tabernas	VIIII	9
607, 8	mansio Grandavia	VIIII	9
608, 1	mutatio Treiecto	VIIII	9
608, 2	mansio Hiscampis	VIIII	9
608, 3	mutatio Ad Quintum	VI	6
608, 4	mansio Coladiana	XV	15
608, 5	mansio Marusio	XIII	13
608, 6	mansio Absos	XIIII	14
608, 7	mutatio Stefanaphana	XII	12
608, 8	civitas Apollonia	XVIII	18
608, 9	mutatio Stefana	XII	12

*Appendix 9: User's
Guide to the
Outlining of Rivers
and Routes on
Barrington Atlas
Bases (C–F), with
Associated Texts:
Bordeaux Itinerary*

284

*Appendix 9: User's
Guide to the
Outlining of Rivers
and Routes on*
Barrington Atlas
*Bases (C–F), with
Associated Texts:
Bordeaux Itinerary*

608, 10	mansio Aulona treiectum	XII	12
609, 1	Fit omnis summa ab Heraclea per Machedoniam		
609, 2	Aulona usque milia DCLXXXVIII,		688
609, 3	mutationes LVIII, mansiones XXV.		58/25
609, 4	Trans mare stadia mille, quod facit milia centum,		
609, 5	et venis Odronto mansio mille passus:		
609, 6	mutatio Ad Duodecimum	XIII	13
609, 7	mansio Clipeas	XII	12
609, 8	mutatio Valentia	XIII	13
609, 9	civitas Brindisi	XI	11
609, 10	mansio Spilenaees	XIIII	14
609, 11	mutatio Ad Decimum	XI	11
609, 12	civitas Leonatiae	X	10
609, 13	mutatio Turres Aurilianas	XV	15
609, 14	mutatio Turres Iuliana	VIIII	9
609, 15	civitas Beroes	XI	11
609, 16	mutatio Butontones	XI	11
610, 1	civitas Rubos	XI	11
610, 2	mutatio Ad Quintumdecimum	XV	15
610, 3	civitas Canusio	XV	15
610, 4	mutatio Undecimum	XI	11
610, 5	civitas Serdonis	XV	15
610, 6	civitas Aecas	XVIII	18
610, 7	mutatio Aquilonis	X	10
610, 8	finis Apuliae et Campaniae		
610, 9	mansio Ad Equum Magnum	VIII	8
610, 10	mutatio vicus Forno Novo	XII	12
610, 11	civitas Benevento	X	10
610, 12	civitas et mansio Claudiis	XII	12
610, 13	mutatio Novas	VIIII	9
610, 14	civitas Capua	XII	12
611, 1	fit summa ab Aulona usque Capua		
611, 2	milia CCLXXXVIIII, mutationes		289
611, 3	XXV, mansiones XIII		25/13
611, 4	mutatio Ad Octavum	VIII	8
611, 5	mutatio Ponte Campano	VIIII	9
611, 6	civitas Sonuessa	VIIII	9
611, 7	civitas Menturnas	VIIII	9
611, 8	civitas Formis	VIIII	9
611, 9	civitas Fundis	XII	12
611, 10	civitas Tarracina	XIII	13
611, 11	mutatio Ad Medias	X	10
611, 12	mutatio Appi Foro	VIIII	9
612, 1	mutatio Sponsas	VII	7
612, 2	civitas Aricia et Albona	XIIII	14
612, 3	mutatio Ad Nono	VII	7
612, 4	in urbe Roma	VIIII	9
612, 5	Fit a Capua usque ad urbem Romam milia CXXXVI,		136
612, 6	mutationes XIIII, mansiones VIIII		14/9
612, 7	Fit ab Heraclea per Aulona in urbe Roma usque		

612, 8	milia undecies centena XIII, muta-		13
612, 9	tiones CXVII, mansiones XLVI.		117/46

285

*Appendix 9: User's
Guide to the
Outlining of Rivers
and Routes on
Barrington Atlas
Bases (C–F), with
Associated Texts:
Bordeaux Itinerary*

E 612, 10	Ab urbe Mediolanium:		
612, 11	mutatio Rubras	VIIII	9
613, 1	mutatio Ad Vicensimum	XI	11
613, 2	mutatio Aqua Viva	XII	12
613, 3	civitas Ucriculo	XII	12
613, 4	civitas Narniae	XII	12
613, 5	civitas Interamna	VIIII	9
613, 6	mutatio Tribus Tabernis	III	3
613, 7	mutatio Fani Fugitivi	X	10
613, 8	civitas Spolitio	VII	7
613, 9	mutatio Sacraria	VIII	8
613, 10	civitas Trevis	IIII	4
613, 11	civitas Fulginis	V	5
614, 1	civitas Foro Flamini	III	3
614, 2	civitas Noceria	XII	12
614, 3	civitas Ptanias	VIII	8
614, 4	mansio Herbelloni	VII	7
614, 5	mutatio Ad Hesis	X	10
614, 6	mutatio Ad Cale	XIIII	14
614, 7	mutatio Intercisa	VIIII	9
615, 1	civitas Foro Semproni	VIIII	9
615, 2	mutatio Ad Octavo	VIIII	9
615, 3	civitas Fano Furtunae	VIII	8
615, 4	civitas Pisauro	<milia VIII	8
615, 5	civitas Ariminum>	XXIIII	24
615, 6	<Fit a Roma> usque Ariminum <milia CCXXIIII,		224
615, 7	mutationes XXIIII, mansiones XIIII>		24/14
615, 8	mutatio Conpetu	XII	12
615, 9	civitas Cesena	VI	6
616, 1	civitas Foro Populi	VI	6
616, 2	civitas Foro Livi	VI	6
616, 3	civitas Faventia	V	5
616, 4	civitas Foro Corneli	X	10
616, 5	civitas Claterno	XIII	13
616, 6	civitas Bononia	X	10
616, 7	mutatio Ad Medias	XV	15
616, 8	mutatio Victoriolas	X	10
616, 9	civitas Mutena	III	3
616, 10	mutatio Ponte Secies	V	5
616, 11	civitas Regio	VIII	8
616, 12	mutatio Canneto	X	10
616, 13	civitas Parme	VIII	8
616, 14	mutatio Ad Tarum	VII	7
616, 15	mansio Fidentiae	VIII	8
616, 16	mutatio Ad Fonteclos	VIII	8
616, 17	civitas Placentia	XIII	13
617, 1	mutatio Ad Rota	XI	11
617, 2	mutatio Tribus Tabernis	V	5

286

*Appendix 9: User's
Guide to the
Outlining of Rivers
and Routes on
Barrington Atlas
Bases (C–F), with
Associated Texts:
Bordeaux Itinerary*

617, 3	civitas Laude	VIII	8
617, 4	mutatio Ad Nonum	VII	7
617, 5	civitas Mediolanum	VII	7
617, 6	Fit omnis summa ab urbe Roma Mediolanum		
617, 7	usque milia CCCCXVI,		416
617, 8	mutationes XLIIII, mansiones XXIIII.		44/24
617, 9	Explicit itinerarium.		

NOTES

Introduction

1. See A. Gall, "Atlantropa: A Technological Vision of a United Europe," in E. van der Vleuten and A. Kaijser (eds.), *Networking Europe: Transnational Infrastructures and the Shaping of Europe, 1850–2000* (Sagamore Beach, MA, 2006), 99–128; more fully, id., *Das Atlantropa-Projekt. Die Geschichte einer gescheiterten Vision. Herman Sörgel und die Absenkung des Mittelmeers* (Frankfurt, 1998).

2. It was wholly extraordinary for the entire map to be displayed – on just a single day (November 26, 2007) – in celebration of its inclusion in UNESCO's Memory of the World Register.

3. C. Hicks, *The Bayeux Tapestry: The Life Story of a Masterpiece* (London, 2006), 72.

4. See further the edition by J. B. Rives (Oxford, 1999), 69–74.

5. See in brief, most recently for example, D. Woodward (ed.), *The History of Cartography* [= *HistCart*], vol. 3: *Cartography in the European Renaissance* (Chicago, 2007), pt. 1, chap. 1; and J. M. Headley, *The Europeanization of the World: On the Origins of Human Rights and Democracy* (Princeton, NJ, 2008), chap. 1.

6. "De hoc variae sunt conjecturae, sed tollit omnem nobis ambiguitatem charta militaris, quam apud Chunradum Peutingerum nostrum Augustae vidimus." Arnold (1682), 769; see further below, Chap. 1, sec. 2 (c).

7. "Existimabant homines eruditi, hoc finium regundorum judice, qui omnem exceptionem superaret, multas tantum non immortales geographorum dissensiones componi, multos inextricabiles in historicorum libris nodos solvi posse." Welser (1591), 5; see further below, Chap. 1, sec. 2 (a).

8. G. Uggeri, *La viabilità della Sicilia in età romana, Journal of Ancient Topography/Rivista di Topografia Antica*, Supplement II (Rome, 2004); note especially chap. 3.2.2.

9. P. Barber, "England I: Pageantry, Defense, and Government: Maps at Court to 1550," in D. Buisseret (ed.), *Monarchs, Ministers, and Maps: The Emergence of Cartography as a Tool of Government in Early Modern Europe* (Chicago and London, 1992), 26–56 at 42, 26; id., *King Henry's Map of the British Isles: B. L. Cotton MS Augustus I.i.9* (London, 2009), 43. For the frequency, character, and purposes of Henry VIII's progresses through England, see

K. Sharpe, *Selling the Tudor Monarchy: Authority and Image in Sixteenth-Century England* (New Haven [CT] and London, 2009), 173–74.

Chapter One: The Surviving Copy: History, Publication, Scholarship

1. As a synthesis of the map's discovery, fortunes, and perceived importance through the early eighteenth century, J. G. Lotter's neglected work, *Dissertatio de Tabula Peutingeriana* (Leipzig, 1732, pp. 58) remains fundamental. For a summary of the wide variety of names devised to refer to the map, note K. Miller, *Itineraria Romana: Römische Reisewege an der Hand der Tabula Peutingeriana dargestellt* [= *ItMiller*] (Stuttgart, 1916), p. XXIX, n. 2; on this work, see further below, sec. 6.

2. See N. Henkel, "Bücher des Konrad Celtis," in W. Arnold (ed.), *Bibliotheken und Bücher im Zeitalter der Renaissance*, Wolfenbütteler Abhandlungen zur Renaissanceforschung 16 (Wiesbaden, 1997), 129–66, at 153.

3. On his career, see D. Wuttke, "Celtis, Conrad(us)," in W. Killy (ed.), *Literaturlexikon. Autoren und Werke deutscher Sprache*, vol. 2 (Gütersloh/Munich, 1989), 377–84 (plates) and 395–400 (text). Note also P. H. Meurer, in *HistCart*, 3.2 (2007), 1190–91; L. Silver, *Marketing Maximilian: The Visual Ideology of a Holy Roman Emperor* (Princeton [NJ] and Oxford, 2008), esp. 19–20, 107–108, 188–90.

4. See below, Chap. 2, sec. 1.

5. See below, Conclusion, sec. 2 (c).

6. As it happens, Konrad Peutinger (see further below) studied at the university in Padua during the 1480s. Conceivably, he saw the bishop's map, learned the story of its origin, and informed Celtis.

7. The library at Speyer immediately became a favored location: note the review by Lotter (1732), 23. For skeptical appraisal of this location and others, see P. Gautier Dalché, "La trasmissione medievale e rinascimentale della *Tabula Peutingeriana*," in F. Prontera (ed.), *Tabula Peutingeriana: Le antiche vie del mondo* (Florence, 2003), 43–52, at 47, 49–50; and further below, Chap. 2, sec. 2 (e).

8. C. Celtis (ed.), *Opera Hrotsvite* (Nuremberg, 1501; facsimile reprint Hildesheim: Olms, 2000), 1. This translation is adapted and expanded from L. W. Spitz, *Conrad Celtis: The German Arch-Humanist* (Cambridge, MA, 1957), 97. A notorious instance of a manuscript found, taken, and published by Italians was that of Tacitus' minor works, including *Germania*.

9. On his career and role as humanist, see H. Kugler, "Peutinger, Konrad," in Killy, vol. 9 (1991), 136–37; *Brill's New Pauly*, Classical Tradition, vol. 2, s.v. "Germany," esp. sec. C1, cols. 633–36; Silver (2008), 4–5, 14, 20–21, 30–31, 43, 77–79. Note also K. A. Vogel and T. Haye, "Die Bibliothek Konrad Peutingers. Überlegungen zu ihrer Rekonstruktion, Erschliessung und Analyse," in W. Arnold (1997), 113–28.

10. See H.-J. Künast and H. Zäh, *Die Bibliothek Konrad Peutingers, Edition der historischen Kataloge und Rekonstruktion der Bestände, Band 1: Die autographen Kataloge Peutingers; Der nicht-juristische Bibliotheksteil* (Tübingen, 2003), 580.

11. The text of the grant is reproduced in full by F. A. Veith, *Historia Vitae atque Meritorum Conradi Peutingeri post J. G. Lotterum* (Augsburg, 1783), 123–24.

12. "... licet interim huius promissionis me poenituerit, quod res sit maximi laboris et gravior pene, quam his humeris ferre possim" ("... although

in the meantime I have come to regret this promise, because the task is extremely laborious and almost heavier than I can sustain on these shoulders"). Letter 256 (Hummelberg to Beatus, April 6, 1526), in A. Horawitz and K. Hartfelder (eds.), *Briefwechsel des Beatus Rhenanus* (Leipzig, 1886).

13. See H. Meyer, "Rhenanus, Beatus," in Killy, vol. 9 (1991), 415–16 and 425; J. Hirstein, "Rhenanus (Beatus)," in C. Nativel (ed.), *Centuriae Latinae: Cent une figures humanistes de la Renaissance aux Lumières*, vol. 1 (Geneva, 1997), 679–85.

14. Horawitz and Hartfelder (1886), Letter 257 (Hummelberg to Beatus, May 20, 1526); cf. Letter 250 (January 13, 1526) for the same pride.

15. On June 29, 1531, Michael's brother Gabriel asks Beatus if he has any information: Horawitz and Hartfelder (1886), Letter 279. To date, it is impossible to evaluate Miller's ambitious claim (*ItMiller*, XXI–XXII) that he saw some of these sheets in the Museo San Martino, Naples, in 1912, because the "Codex R 35" containing them can no longer be found even with the expert help of Dr. Gianluca Del Mastro. The principal contents of the Codex were evidently some, or all, of the very rare set of twenty-one maps engraved by Francesco Cassiano de Silva and published by Antonio Bulifon as *Nuova ed esattissima descrizione del Regno di Napoli colle sue XII provincie* (Naples, 1692). On this work, see further G. Amirante and M. R. Pessolano, *Immagini di Napoli e del Regno: Le raccolte di Francesco Cassiano de Silva* (Naples, 2005), esp. 291–96.

16. Horawitz and Hartfelder (1886), Letter 250. The map offered much to attract Francis, with his taste for ceremonies, Roman antiquarianism, and the display of treasured objects; his court, moreover, was a traveling one. See R. J. Knecht, *The French Renaissance Court 1483–1589* (New Haven, CT, 2008), esp. chap. 7.

17. For further discussion see P. Gautier Dalché (2003), 51, with Horawitz and Hartfelder (1886), s.v. "Peutingersche Tafel" in the *Namenverzeichnis*.

18. Greater detail on many aspects may be found in three successive overviews of the history of the map's publication: (1) M. A. P. d'Avezac[-Macaya], *Mémoire sur Éthicus et sur les ouvrages cosmographiques intitulés de ce nom*, in *Mémoires présentés par divers savants à l'Académie des Inscriptions et Belles-Lettres, Ière Série: Sujets divers d'érudition*, vol. 2 (Paris, 1852), 230–551, at 415–25, Article III in 3ème sec.: "De divers ouvrages qui n'appartiennent pas à Éthicus" [rejecting any notion that the map and texts attributed to Aethicus were both the work of the same individual]; (2) E. Desjardins, *Géographie historique et administrative de la Gaule romaine*, vol. 4 (Paris, 1893), chap. 6, posthumously published; this chapter stops just short of the appearance of any contribution made by Konrad Miller; (3) F. Cabrol and H. Leclercq (eds.), *Dictionnaire d'archéologie chrétienne*, vol. 7 (Paris, 1927), s.v. "Itinéraires VIII" (by Leclercq), cols. 1865–83.

19. J. G. Lotter, *Historia Vitae atque Meritorum Conradi Peutingeri Augustani* (Leipzig, 1729), presents a stemma between pp. 20–21 showing the five generations of descendants.

20. Künast and Zäh (2003), 17–19.

21. Killy, vol. 12 (1992), 243–44; J. Papy, "Welser (Marcus)," in C. Nativel (ed.), *Centuriae Latinae: Cent une figures humanistes de la Renaissance aux Lumières*, vol. 2 (Geneva, 2006), 831–35.

22. For his career and publications, see, for example, R. W. Karrow, *Mapmakers of the Sixteenth Century and Their Maps: Bio-Bibliographies of the Cartographers*

of Abraham Ortelius, 1570 (Chicago, 1993), 1–31; M. P. R. van den Broecke, *Ortelius Atlas Maps: An Illustrated Guide* (Westrenen [Netherlands], 1996); P. van der Krogt in *HistCart*, 3.2 (2007), chap. 44, esp. p. 1303. For the broader context, see W. Goffart, *Historical Atlases: The First Three Hundred Years, 1570–1870* (Chicago, 2003), especially 30–35. Ortelius' much revised and enlarged atlas *Theatrum Orbis Terrarum* (1st ed., 1570) first began to include a section ("Parergon") of historical maps in 1579; this gained its own title page in the 1595 edition and was published separately in 1624. See further below, subsection (c).

23. J. H. Hessels (ed.), *Abrahami Ortelii et Virorum Eruditorum ad Eundem et ad Jacobum Colium Ortelianum Epistulae* (Cambridge, 1887), 126.3.

24. Hessels (1887), Letter 117. 2 and 5.

25. See B. Bischoff, *Latin Palaeography: Antiquity and the Middle Ages* (Cambridge, 1990), 34.

26. "Ex ea cum testimonia nonnulla produxisset, plerosque illius videndae desiderio vehementi incendit" (p. 5).

27. This sketch is a doublespread (as such, approx. 26 cm [10¼ in.] wide), with a foldout extending 12 cm (4¾ in.) to the right. Its height falls not far short of the 19 cm (7½ in.) page height.

28. Hessels (1887), Letter 306.1–3.

29. For a transcription of the text, see Appendix 1. Altogether I rely here upon the invaluable study by C. Piérard, "Un exemplaire de la *Tabula itineraria* ou *Tabula Peutingeriana* édition Moretus 1598, conservé à Mons," *Quaerendo* 1.3 (1971): 201–16, and I warmly thank the Bibliothèque de l'Université Mons-Hainaut, Belgium, for the opportunity to inspect and reproduce this copy. At some stage its nine sheets were mounted side by side on linen and evidently left on display; hence they have darkened somewhat from this exposure, but otherwise they remain in remarkably good condition.

30. So claims Balthasar Moretus (twice) in his *Theatrum Orbis Terrarum Parergon* (1624, see further next subsection [c] below). Even so, the possibility that his own father wrote the text should not be discounted.

31. The edition comprised nine loose sheets, therefore. The eight map sheets are made conveniently accessible today in the attractive double-pamphlet (*Kaart, Commentaar*) publication of the Museum Het Valkhof te Nijmegen, Netherlands (1991): A. M. Gerhartl-Witteveen and P. Stuart, *Museumstukken: De Tabula Peutingeriana*. Caution is in order, however, insofar as this publication reproduces in monochrome a heavily colored reprint of the original, and omits the SPECTATORI s. text. Much the same must be said of the copy held by the Royal Geographical Society, London, cataloged mistakenly as a 1598 original.

32. The point is made by P. H. Meurer in *HistCart*, 3.2 (2007), 1242.

33. See below, sec. 4 (g).

34. See, for example, *ItMiller*, XXVI, LXXVI, 603–604, with sec. 6 and Chap. 2, sec. 1 below.

35. For this observation, and that at the end of the preceding paragraph, my thanks to Gannon Hubbard.

36. G. D. J. Schotel, *Biographisch Wordenboek der Nederlanden*, vol. 8, fasc. 2 (Haarlem, n.d.), 207–208.

37. C. Arnold, *Marci Velseri Opera in Unum Collecta* (Nuremberg, 1682), 829–30.

38. Ibid., 830–31.

39. Pp. 4–5 of this section (pages not numbered).

40. *HistCart*, 3.2 (2007), 1339.

41. In this instance, however, there is not the opportunity to reassemble the map in strip form, because text is printed on the reverse sides of the relevant pages.

42. Here headed: "Eiusdem Velseri de eadem tabula postquam integram nactus esset, sub alieno nomine iudicium" ("An assessment by Welser again, under a different name, of the same map after he had secured the whole of it").

43. Amsterdam, page size 30 cm wide × 49 ($11\frac{3}{4} \times 19\frac{1}{4}$ in.). From 1653 onward (through 1741!), this atlas was reissued with a text by the Leiden professor Georg Horn (1620–70): for the complex details, see C. Koeman, *Atlantes Neerlandici: Bibliography of Terrestrial, Maritime and Celestial Atlases and Pilot Books, Published in the Netherlands up to 1880*, vol. 2 (Amsterdam, 1969), 147, 151, 185.

44. Koeman (1969), 180–81, 499–507; note also *HistCart*, 3.2 (2007), 1328–29, 1339.

45. *ItMiller*, XXIV.

46. It now reads: "Porro si haec quoque referat: Autographum membranaceum est, pelliculis accurate conglutinatis, latum pedem Augustanum unum circiter, longum ultra viginti duos: scalptori ad istam mensuram contrahere visum commodius."

47. "Instar additamenti integrum hoc *Cap. XXIII. ex Petri Bertii lib. 1. Rer. German.* consulto et de industria adscripsimus; quoniam *sex prope segmenta priora* quam apertissime planissimeque inibi explicantur." In Bertius' volume (unpaginated), the text occupies five pages, with one additional page offering four quotations from ancient sources.

48. See briefly Lotter (1732), 55–57; Veith (1783), 121; *ItMiller*, XXIV, n. 3. The manuscript of a commentary by the Dutch scholar Menso Alting "the Younger" (1637–1713) that was never published is held by the Austrian National Library (MS 9588); cf. W. Kubitschek, *Gött. gel. Anz.* 179 (1917): 19.

49. Each pullout with two folds, except the first with three, because its greater length includes the title as a header, the same "short" one used by Jansson and Arnold.

50. For over a century now, from Miller onward, all accounts of the map's fate during these years have simply followed his (*Die Weltkarte* 12–13 = *ItMiller*, XVI). It should be recognized, however, that for the most part he copies without acknowledgment from Lotter (1732), 17–19.

51. Lotter (1732), 18.

52. See E. Weber, "Das 'Verkaufsinserat' der Tabula Peutingeriana aus dem Jahr 1715 – Ein kleiner Beitrag zur Wissenschaftsgeschichte," in U. Fellmeth et al. (eds.), *Historische Geographie der Alten Welt: Grundlagen, Erträge, Perspektiven* [Festschrift Olshausen] (Hildesheim, 2007), 367–79. In addition to tracing the notice itself, Weber provides a most welcome explanation of its learned allusions.

53. My thanks to Professor Adelheid Eubanks for assistance with this translation.

54. Von Scheyb, in his 1753 edition of the map (*Dissertatio*, p. 38; see below, sec. 4 [a]), contributes these details, although without specifying a date for Kühtze's death. As von Scheyb explains (ibid., note [p]), he benefited from information conveyed by Nicolò de Forlosia, prefect of the imperial library in Vienna when it acquired the map, who in turn had enjoyed frequent contact with Prince Eugen's *Bibliopegus artificiosissimus*, Etienne Boyet.

55. For the map in the context of the prince's extensive collection of manuscripts, see O. Mazal, *Prinz Eugens Schönste Bücher: Handschriften aus der Bibliothek des Prinzen Eugen von Savoyen* (Graz, 1986), 6–7 and Abb. 1–2.

56. S.v. "Passionei," *Biographisch-Bibliographisches Kirchenlexikon* 6 (1993), cols. 1582–88 (by H. H. Schwedt).

57. From an extensive quotation preserved by J. Cristianopoulo, *Tabula Itineraria*, p. XII (Iesi, 1809; see below, sec. [d]), in which Passionei proceeds to elaborate upon the appropriateness of a great commander in contemporary far-flung campaigns possessing this map featuring the "military" routes of the ancient Roman Empire. The translation quoted (p. 105) is an anonymous one entitled *An Oration on the Death of Eugene Francis, Prince of Savoy*, and published by T. Edlin (London, 1738).

58. See J. Stummvoll (ed.), *Geschichte der Österreichischen Nationalbibliothek, I: Die Hofbibliothek (1368–1922)* (Vienna, 1968), 210–13.

59. For the wide range of publications relating to the map's history and significance accumulated by the library, see its Web site, www.onb.ac.at, under "Literatur zu Handschriften."

60. Stummvoll (1968), 296.

61. Ibid., 332.

62. Ibid., 344.

63. Ibid., 430.

64. E. Trenkler (ed.), *Geschichte der Österreichischen Nationalbibliothek, II: Die Hofbibliothek (1922–1967)* (Vienna, 1973), 119, 208.

65. On his career, which included six years based in Rome during the 1730s, see C. von Wurzbach (ed.), *Biographisches Lexikon des Kaiserthums Oesterreich*, vol. 29 (Vienna, 1875), 248–49; W. Kriegleder, "Scheyb, Franz Christoph von," in Killy, vol. 10 (1991), 204; and, most fully, I. Tuma (Holzer), "Franz Christoph von Scheyb (1704–1777). Leben und Werk. Ein Beitrag zur süddeutsch-österreichischen Aufklärung," diss., University of Vienna, 1975, especially 49–53.

66. Reprinted and discussed by F. Römer, "Geographie und Panegyrik: Beobachtungen zu Franz Ch. v. Scheybs Praefatio [*sic*] seiner Edition der Tabula Peutingeriana," in F. Beutler and W. Hameter (eds.), *Festschrift Ekkehard Weber*, Althistorisch-Epigraphische Studien 5 (Wien, 2005), 615–26.

67. The first attestation offered is a joint one by Nicolò de Forlosia and Adam Franz Kollar, who in 1753 were First Custos and Second Custos of the library respectively: see Stummvoll (1968), 246, 248.

68. (1) (pp. 1–15), on ancient geography, mapping, itineraries; (2) (pp. 15–29), on the commissioning of the map and its date [by Theodosius I in A.D. 393, according to von Scheyb]; (3) (pp. 29–38), the map's history to the mid-eighteenth century; (4) (pp. 39–48), the shortcomings of previous editions of the map, and the merits of the present one; (5) (pp. 48–65), the nature of the map, and its use in antiquity; (6) (pp. 66–69), comparison of the map and the Antonine Itinerary.

69. For indexing, each of the twelve numbered engravings is divided into six divisions lettered A–F; A–C span the top, D–F the bottom. The midpoint in each vertical margin is marked on either side of the engravings, as are also the points one-third and two-thirds along the upper and lower margins.

70. Each is a single sheet 66 cm wide × 51 (26 × 20 in.), thus permitting generous margins all round the engraving; only segment numbers are printed on the intervening pages, so that reassembly of the map into strip form is entirely feasible.

71. The engravings omit to indicate the points where one parchment ends and the next begins.

72. *Praefatio*, p. x. Peter Barber kindly drew to my attention a copy of the map reassembled in strip form and neatly colored in the King's Topographical Collection (formed by George III) at the British Library, London. For whatever reason, this coloring is only partial (routes in particular are left untouched), and certain color choices do not match von Scheyb's specifications; notably, blue is used for roofs.

73. As will emerge (see below, secs. 4 [b], 4 [g] and 6), three of the most vocal nineteenth-century critics, Mannert, Desjardins, and Miller, in due course issued revisions of von Scheyb's presentation rather than making a wholly fresh start. Miller's chiding of von Scheyb, and later Desjardins, for failure to replicate the forms of lettering on the map more faithfully seems overdemanding (*ItMiller*, XXIV, XXVI). As early as 1598, the SPECTATORI S. text accompanying the first publication of the map (admittedly at reduced size) had drawn attention to the impracticality of attempting such replication.

74. Tuma (1975), 178.

75. I thank my colleague, Professor Terence McIntosh, for this explanation of an otherwise puzzling initiative that Tuma does not account for.

76. For these events, see P. Fuchs, *Palatinatus Illustratus: Die historische Forschung an der Kurpfälzischen Akademie der Wissenschaften* (Mannheim, 1963), 157–58, 570 (no. 49); for Schöpflin, see ibid., 566 (no. 2).

77. *Nova Acta Eruditorum* 34 (1766): 76–80.

78. C. Häffelin, "Observations sur l'Itinéraire de Théodose, connu sous le nom de Table de Peutinger," *Acta Academiae Theodoro-Palatinae* 5 (1783): 105–26 at 111.

79. For this affair, see W. Kubitschek, *Gött. gel. Anz.* 179 (1917): 16–17; Fuchs (1963), 158–60 and n. 361 on Goens. For Lamey, see Fuchs, 566 (no. 4); for Häffelin, ibid., 569 (no. 43).

80. Häffelin (1783), 108, note (a).

81. Letters 7–17 in J. Hahn, *Bartholomäus Kopitar und seine Beziehungen zu München*, Geschichte, Kultur und Geisteswelt der Slowenen 17 (Munich, 1982).

82. Fuchs (1963), 385–89.

83. Mannert, *Tabula Itineraria*, 1–2 (Leipzig, 1824; see below); Thiersch compliments Kopitar on July 11, 1819: "Ihr gebührt der Verdienst, sie aus den Händen eines Juden gerissen und um den billigen Ersaz des Metallwerthes von dem Einschmelzen gerettet zu haben" ("The Academy deserves the credit, it wrenched [them] from the hands of a Jew who wanted to have them melted down for cheap profit"); Hahn (1982), Letter 10, p. 45. Thiersch does not date these developments.

84. *Allgemeine Deutsche Biographie*, vol. 38 (Leipzig, 1894), 7–17.

85. *Biographisches Lexikon des Kaiserthums Oesterreich*, vol. 12 (Vienna, 1864), 437–42; Stummvoll (1968), 363.

86. *Biographisches Lexikon des Kaiserthums Oesterreich*, vol. 8 (Vienna, 1862), 463–64; Stummvoll (1968), 259. Manuscripts were among Heyrenbach's special interests long before he eventually joined the staff of the Hofbibliothek in 1773.

87. It seems not to have been published until 1852 (in Vienna) by T. G. von Karajan, who wrote a two-page introduction and added the subtitle *Ein nachgelassenes Werk*.

88. *Allgemeine Deutsche Biographie*, vol. 32 (Leipzig, 1891), 125–27. Breslau is today Wrocław in Poland.

89. For this appointment, see further E.-M. Hüttl-Hubert, "Bartholomäus Kopitar und die Wiener Hofbibliothek," *Österreichische Osthefte* 36 (1994): 521–88, at 545.

90. Later, Thiersch's letter of April 12, 1820, appears to confirm the original idea as Kopitar's, when he writes: "Ihnen gehört auf jeden Fall das Lob und bleibt das Verdienst, dass Sie zuerst auf die Nothwendigkeit einer neuen Vergleichung hingewiesen haben." ("You in any event are due praise, and the credit remains yours, that you were the first to draw attention to the need for a new comparison"; Hahn [1982], Letter 14, p. 51).

91. Ibid., Letter 9, p. 44.

92. Ibid., Letter 10, esp. pp. 45–46.

93. *Allgemeine Deutsche Biographie*, vol. 20 (Leipzig, 1884), 199–200.

94. It was to be moved to Munich in 1826 in order to become the Bavarian capital's university.

95. Hahn (1982), Letter 11, p. 47.

96. Ibid., Letter 12, p. 48.

97. Ibid., Letter 13, p. 49.

98. Joseph Maximilian Ossolinski: see Stumvoll (1968), 343–69.

99. Hahn (1982), Letter 14, esp. pp. 50–51.

100. Ibid., Letter 15, p. 52. Kopitar's concern was presumably a potential dispute over the right to use the material. In the event, Schneider raised no objection (Mannert [1824; see below], II, 39).

101. Hahn (1982), Letter 16, p. 53. Vodnik had been a Franciscan by training (see next subsection) and did in fact recognize that von Scheyb presented the map's eleven parchment segments on twelve plates (see Appendix 3).

102. Hahn (1982), Letter 17, esp. p. 55, n. 137.

103. Stumvoll (1968), 262–63, 365.

104. Note Thiersch's Praefatio to Mannert's edition (1824; see n. 106 below), p. II.

105. To judge by the brief entry in J. French (vols. 1–2) and V. Scott (vols. 3–4) (eds.), *Tooley's Dictionary of Mapmakers*, 4 vols., rev. ed. (Riverside, CT, 1999–2004), s.v. "Johann Baptist Seitz (1786–1850)," he is likely to have worked in Munich or its vicinity.

106. *Tabula Itineraria Peutingeriana, primum aeri incisa et edita a Franc. Christoph. de Scheyb* MDCCLIII. *Denuo cum codice Vindoboni collata, emendata et nova Conradi Mannerti introductione instructa, studio et opera Academiae Literarum Regiae Monacensis*. The Index, however, was printed in Munich.

107. *Tabula Itineraria*, 39.

108. *Biographisches Lexikon des Kaiserthums Oesterreich*, vol. 51 (Vienna, 1885), 128–36. The fullest recent studies of this renowned figure, whose activities and influence were extensive, are mostly in Slovenian. This difficulty thus adds to the value of M. Šašel Kos, "Valentin Vodnik and Roman Antiquities in the Time of Napoleon," *Antichità Altoadriatiche* 64 (2007): 405–30. I am most grateful to Dr. Šašel Kos for bringing Vodnik's work to my attention and assisting my investigation of it. Surprisingly, when the tireless W. Kubitschek made enquiries, he was frustrated by how little he could discover: see *Gött. gel. Anz.* 179 (1917): 10.

109. M. Michaud (ed.), *Biographie universelle*, vol. 39 (Paris, n.d.), 273–74; A. Vigi Fior, "Etienne Marie Siauve," *Antichità Altoadriatiche* 40 (*Gli scavi di Aquileia: Uomini e Opere*) (1993): 83–101. Siauve was subsequently assigned

to Napoleon's Russian campaign and died during the retreat from Moscow in 1812. The responsibilities of a Napoleonic *commissaire-ordonnateur* were quite literally the commissariat – the billeting, supply and transport of troops.

110. For these and subsequent events, see J. Kastelic, "Vodnikova kopija Tabule Peutingeriane," *Glasnik Musejskega društva za Slovenijo* 23 (1942): 98–100; Appendix 2 offers an English translation by G. Stone.

111. My warmest thanks to the director, Dr. P. Kos, and to Dr. P. Bitenc, for the opportunity to inspect it and reproduce it. Its survival in sound condition seems miraculous; by contrast, the copy of von Scheyb's edition, which we know Zois was eventually able to purchase for his library sometime after 1809, has gone missing since 1942. On the copy made by Vodnik, see further Appendix 3.

112. In print (1852), the essay extends to twenty-one pages. Vodnik's twelve handwritten pages (with his own heading "Censura") therefore constitute a more drastic precis of the German, albeit a fair one, than Kastelic (1942) was able to appreciate, having never seen the essay in manuscript or print.

113. My thanks to the library and to Dr. J. Hrovat for the opportunity to study and reproduce this Latin summary. See further Appendix 4. The manuscript copy in German sent by Kopitar is lost.

114. Hahn (1982), Letter 16, p. 53: "Neshics ist ein scholasticus obscurus, den ich Vodnik'en als Gesellen aus dem Lesesaal herausgegriffen hatte" ("Neshics is an odd intellectual whom I drafted from the reading room as a helper for Vodnik").

115. *Tabula Itineraria* (1809; see text below), XIII.

116. Ibid.

117. S.v. "Garampi," *Biographisch-Bibliographisches Kirchenlexikon* 2 (1990), col. 177 (by F. W. Bautz). Garampi had been made a cardinal in February 1785.

118. *Tabula Itineraria* (1809), XV. On these events, see briefly, for example, D. Gregory, *Napoleon's Italy* (London, 2001), esp. chap. 1; C. Duggan, *The Force of Destiny: A History of Italy since 1796* (London, 2007), chaps. 1–2.

119. *Tabula Itineraria* (1809), XVI.

120. Ibid.; the novelty of the typeface led to errors, however, which could only be noted in a final *Monitum* (following Index, p. XXVI).

121. See above, n. 43.

122. Even so, his insights on letter forms had to be based exclusively on their rendering in engravings, because he had never seen the map itself.

123. *ItMiller*, XXV, n. 2, terms the volume rare. I am most grateful for permission to inspect the copies held by the Robinson Library (Special Collections), University of Newcastle, England, and by the Widener Library, Harvard University. Cristianopoulo's title page and the map's Segment IV as engraved by him are reproduced in R. B. Parlapiano (ed.), *Biblioteca Planettiana, Iesi* (Fiesole, 1997), 124–25.

124. *Tabula Itineraria* (1824), 40.

125. *Gött. gel. Anz.* 3 (1817): 1846–48.

126. (1852), 420, n. 3.

127. *Biographisches Lexikon des Kaiserthums Oesterreich*, vol. 11 (Vienna, 1864), 30–32.

128. This is not to forget that efforts to extend the commentary had been begun by others (most recently by von Scheyb), although for various reasons none had succeeded: see above, n. 48.

129. *Vetera Romanorum Itineraria, sive Antonini Augusti Itinerarium, Itinerarium Hierosolymitanum, et Hieroclis Grammatici Synecdemus* (Amsterdam, 1735). For *ItAnt* alone, Wesseling's text and commentary run to 529 large pages in small print. The commentary incorporates notes by three earlier scholars, J. Simlerus, A. Schottus, and H. Surita; Wesseling does not link his commentary to a contemporary atlas, nor does he provide any maps himself.

130. Katancsich elects not to number the routes that he creates, but otherwise his approach and that of Emmanuel Miller later (who creates 235; see below, sec. 4 [f]) are comparable. The routes of both these scholars tend to be shorter and less arbitrary in span than the 141 created by Konrad Miller later still (see below, sec. 6). Katancsich groups routes by continent, region, and subregion (thus Italia is subdivided into Transpadana, Venetia, Liguria, Cispadana, Tuscia, Etruria, etc.). He also incorporates routes within the scope of the map but not marked there (added from *ItAnt* especially), as well as isolated settlements on the map, and (separately, pp. xcvii–cviii) routes attested west of the map's surviving coverage.

131. "Lectori philologo s.," two pages dated July 31, 1824, Buda.

132. Of the two, only Karacs (1770–1838), a widely known letter- and map-engraver, achieves an entry (with portrait) in French and Scott (1999–2004).

133. In the copy known to me (in the Harvard Map Collection, where the twelve sheets are folded and bound with vol. 2), red is used extensively throughout – to fill the upper and lower borders of the map, for symbols (the dominant color of the largest symbols in particular), and traced thinly under route line work and around display capitals as required. Rivers and open water appear light-green in sheets 1 and 9–12, but gray in sheets 2–8; shorelines are highlighted in a darker shade of the same color. Both *Silvae* appear green, and some mountain ranges brown; but altogether the variety of colors in which these ranges appear on the map itself is not reproduced. The later attempts by Desjardins and Miller to convey the map's color (see below, secs. 4 [g] and 5) are more painstaking and more successful, not least because they create a background color for the parchment itself, which Katancsich does not.

134. The only visit to Vienna that he mentions – at the opening of his Prooemium – occurred in August 1779 "urbis visendae gratia," when he took the opportunity to go to the imperial library in hope of seeing the map, and was shown instead (or in addition; the point is left ambiguous) von Scheyb's edition.

135. It did not appear in time to be noted in the long and learned entry "Peutingeriana Tabula" contributed by K. Eckermann to J. S. Ersch and J. G. Gruber (eds.), *Allgemeine Encyclopädie der Wissenschaften und Künste in alphabetischer Folge*, vol. 3.20 (Leipzig, 1845), 14–34; immediately preceding (1–14) is "Peutinger" by the same author.

136. M. Michaud (ed.), *Biographie universelle*, vol. 14 (Paris, 1856), 429–32.

137. The full "text" is accessible through http://gallica.bnf.fr/ as well as in the Map-Appendix (CD-ROM) to R. Talbert, "A Forgotten Masterpiece of Cartography for Roman Historians: Pierre Lapie's *Orbis Romanus ad Illustranda Itineraria* (1845)," in H. M. Schellenberg et al. (eds.), *A Roman Miscellany: Essays in Honour of Anthony R. Birley on His Seventieth Birthday* (Gdansk, 2008), 149–56.

138. The top-right corner of sheet 3 is occupied by a large inset for Rome and its environs ("Urbs cum adjacentibus regionibus") at a scale of approximately

1:1,000,000; immediately below is a tiny Campanian inset, untitled, that covers Atella-Cumae-Aenaria ins.-Neapolis at approximately 1:800,000.

139. Identified only as "Flahaut sculpt." in tiny letters under the map title on sheet 1. The entries s.v. Flahaut in French and Scott (1999–2004) confirm that two individuals using no more than this single name engraved many of Lapie's maps between the 1820s and 1840s; at least one ("Mlle") was female.

140. M. Michaud (ed.), *Biographie universelle*, vol. 23 (Paris, n.d.), 228–29 (by A. Maury).

141. *GGM*, vol. I, Praefatio, p. v; for Müller's plans, see further D. Marcotte, *Géographes Grecs*, vol. 1 (Budé series, Paris, 2000), XIII–XIX. The selection of texts eventually published by A. Riese, *Geographi Latini Minores* (Heilbronn, 1878), included neither the itineraries nor the map.

142. These efforts are reflected in his entry "Itinéraires," cols. 616–37 in E. Carteron et al. (eds.), *Complément de l'Encyclopédie Moderne* 6.1 (Paris: Firmin Didot, 1857).

143. W. Smith and G. Grove (eds.), *Atlas of Ancient Geography Biblical and Classical* (London, 1872–74).

144. On Müller and his extensive contribution to Smith's Atlas, see R. J. A. Talbert, "Mapping the Classical World: Major Atlases and Map Series 1872–1990," *JRA* 5 (1992): 5–38, at 6–9 and 31–32; id., "Carl Müller (1813–1894), S. Jacobs, and the Making of Classical Maps in Paris for John Murray," *Imago Mundi* 46 (1994): 128–50. Whether Müller inspected the Peutinger map before Maury and Desjardins (see below) or after, and whether they were in contact with one another, I cannot say.

145. R. d'Amat and R. Limouzin-Lamothe (eds.), *Dictionnaire de biographie française*, vol. 10 (Paris, 1965), 1403–1404.

146. "Note sur un nouvel examen de la partie de la carte de Peutinger où est figurée la Gaule," *Revue Archéologique* 9 (1864): 60–63. Later, Desjardins would claim to have identified as many as 387 slips in Mannert's presentation of the entire map, "sans compter les erreurs ou omissions de points et les inexactitudes de dessin, qui sont innombrables" (*Rapport*, p. v). Even so, his total may be considered inflated, no doubt in order to impress the minister. The table of categories into which Desjardins divides the slips reveals that some fifty are simply stretches of red line work added along river courses on segments 1–4 – embellishment predictably ignored in the production of an engraving that was to be uncolored.

147. *Rapport*, p. IV.

148. Later (p. v), taking into account all the presentations of the map, Desjardins condemns von Scheyb's as "la plus inexacte de toutes." Nonetheless, it was this one that *Gaule: Bulletin de la Société d'Histoire, d'Archéologie et de Tradition Gauloises*, 2ème série 7 (July 1965) chose to reissue at reduced size (12 sheets with a single fold, each map plate 23 cm [9 in.] in height and between 35 [13¾ in.] and 41 cm [16 in.] in width, a reduction that renders names in open water difficult to read) along with a pamphlet entitled *La Table de Peutinger* (pages numbered 105–23) offering brief essays and bibliography by R. Chevallier, E. Thevenot, and O. Pagès.

149. He successfully applied for a pension in November 1867: see Stummvoll (1968), 440, 449.

150. *Rapport*, p. IV. Note that Desjardins misrepresents von Bartsch as an engraver; in fact the title *scriptor* simply designates a junior member of the imperial

library staff. It is intriguing to realize that von Bartsch (who joined the staff in January 1814) might even have recalled Vodnik's visit in October 1815.

151. See his thoughtful discussion in *Rapport*, p. IV; his conclusion may seem overly conservative, but it must have been genuinely open to question whether photography was yet capable of fulfilling his needs.

152. Seven *livraisons* in 1869, two in 1870 and (after the series had been "interrompue par les événements") in 1872, one in 1873, two in 1874.

153. In 1887, K. Miller (*Die Weltkarte*, 3) mentions 140 francs as the price for the map.

154. "Katanc-" [sich].

155. Pp. 191–93, in *Livraison* 12.

156. Note the extensive *Observations particulières sur la Gaule*, pp. 66–79, in *Livraison* 5 (with some of his most elaborate tables).

157. This map is not supplied until *Livraison* 13, even though the presentation of Gaul spans *Livraisons* 1–5. It is reprinted in E. Desjardins, *Géographie historique et administrative de la Gaule romaine* IV (Paris, 1893), facing p. 76. The other two maps accompany *Livraison* 14. All three carry scale bars, but no scale figure; those given are my own approximations. Ancient names appear in black, with the modern equivalent immediately below in red.

158. Faults he found in Desjardins's revisions are itemized in *ItMiller*, XXVI, n. 1 (lefthand column).

159. The Library of Congress, Washington, DC, holds a copy.

160. Both works have the same publisher, Strecker and Schröder, Stuttgart. *Die Peutingersche Tafel* now gains sixteen pages of introductory text, followed by twelve pages of route sketch maps either reproduced from, or derived from, *Itineraria Romana*. The modern equivalent names added along the bottom of the main map are updated.

161. See further below, Appendix 5.

162. Strecker and Schröder, Stuttgart.

163. Brockhaus, Stuttgart. Even after such a long interval, the modern equivalent names appearing along the bottom (last revised in 1916) were not updated.

164. Endpaper foldout in Prontera (2003).

165. Notably, *Tübinger Atlas des Vorderen Orients* B S 1 *Weltkarten der Antike/Ancient Maps of the World*, 1.2 *Tabula Peutingeriana*, with accompanying text by J. Wagner (Wiesbaden, 1984), reproduces Miller's segments VIII 5 to XII 5, but without his modern equivalent names along the bottom. Instead, certain ancient names on the map that may give the reader difficulty are spelled out here (in capital and lower-case lettering), while ancient names (in capitals) are supplied for certain unnamed symbols.

166. The route is missing from von Scheyb's engraving, too, but not from that of Moretus. M. Calzolari (in Prontera [2003], 67) draws attention to the absence of the course of Fl. Arsia (4A1) and other slips in marking rivers in Italy.

167. See further below, Chap. 3, sec. 4 (c).

168. See Stummvoll (1968), 466.

169. See A. Auer et al. (eds.), *Geschichte der Fotografie in Österreich* (Bad Ischl, 1983), vol. 2, p. 96.

170. By this date such photography itself, while still challenging, was no longer novel. The South Kensington Museum, London, had successfully commissoned full-size photographs of the entire Bayeux Tapestry in 1872: see A. J. Hamber, *"A Higher Branch of the Art": Photographing the Fine Arts in England, 1839–1880* (Amsterdam, 1996), 440–41.

171. Reproduced as Map B (i).
172. The British Library and Harvard University are among the few holders. However, according to Stummvoll (1968), 483, during the early 1890s the Hofbibliothek presented sets of the photographs to other major European libraries in the hope that they would reciprocate correspondingly. Chapel Hill's Ancient World Mapping Center secured the Eric W. Wolf Collection copy in 2001 (Waverly Auctions, Bethesda, MD, Sale 174).
173. Weber, *Tabula Peutingeriana, Codex Vindobonensis 324*, Akademische Druck-u. Verlaganstalt, Graz, with a separate *Kommentar* volume (see further below, sec. 7). The map volume alone, without the *Kommentar*, was subsequently reissued in Italy by U.C.T. Trento (n. d.).
174. Edizioni Edison, Bologna. On this book, see further sec. 7 below.
175. Note the two memoirs by his grand-niece, Gertrud Husslein: in H. Gaube (ed.), *Konrad Miller, Mappae Arabicae, TAVO*, Beihefte B65 (Wiesbaden, 1986), IX–XIII; and more fully in *Orbis Terrarum* 1 (1995): 213–33 with Tafeln 13–17. Husslein was responsible for one of the reprintings of Miller's *Itineraria Romana* (Bregenz, 1988).
176. Page size 24 cm wide × 34 ($9\frac{1}{2}$ × $13\frac{1}{4}$ in.).
177. Note the long, harsh reviews by W. Kubitschek in *Gött. gel. Anz.* 179 (1917): 1–117, and *Zeitschrift für die deutsch-österreichischen Gymnasien* 68 (1917/18): 740–54 and 865–93, in some instances repeating criticisms already made (by Kubitschek himself and others) at the end of the 1880s.
178. Miller's passionate advocacy of Castorius has found little support; see further below, Chap. 5, sec. 1.
179. This choice of numbering on his part was novel and has not been followed by scholars who have since contributed major publications on the map.
180. *ItMiller*, XL.
181. As an equally practical step – but still arbitrary and prone to mislead in certain respects – compare the division of the frieze on the Column of Trajan into 154 scenes, and on that of M. Aurelius into 116, by C. Cichorius, *Die Reliefs der Traianssäule* (Berlin, 1896–1900), and by E. Petersen et al., *Die Marcus-Säule auf Piazza Colonna in Rom* (Munich, 1896) respectively. For discussion, see V. Huet, " Stories One Might Tell of Roman Art: Reading Trajan's Column and the Tiberius Cup," in J. Elsner (ed.), *Art and Text in Roman Culture* (Cambridge, 1996), 9–31, at 9–24.
182. Cols. 107–108.
183. For a rare reference to the relevant photograph, note the entry for Gerainas, *ItMiller*, 136 and n. 1. Five small illustrations in the introduction (on pp. XXX, XLVI, XLVII) are cropped from the photographs; for the last of these five, two consecutive parchments are joined. It is understandable that Miller's aversion to reliance upon photographs of the Peutinger map may have been reinforced by his far from satisfactory experience with the photographic record made of the Ebstorf Map in the 1890s: see E. Michael, "Das wiederentdeckte Monument – Erforschung der Ebstorfer Weltkarte, Entstehungsgeschichte und Gestalt ihrer Nachbildungen," in H. Kugler (ed.), *Ein Weltbild vor Columbus: Die Ebstorfer Weltkarte – Interdisziplinäres Colloquium 1988* (Weinheim, 1991), 9–22, at 12–14.
184. This impatient, opinionated approach was perhaps characteristic. Compare the observation by S. D. Westrem, *The Hereford Map: A Transcription of the Legends with Commentary* (Turnhout [Belgium], 2001): "Miller, by his own admission, never saw the Hereford Map. His published facsimile [1896], which is 3/7 the size of the map itself, includes altered text that corresponds

to his readings (incorrect, and apparently derived from what he thought a reading ought to be); in some cases his readings and facsimile clearly disagree" (xxvi, n. 35). Miller did at least examine the Peutinger map himself.

185. A further unavoidably disorienting feature for today's readers is the fact that so many of the modern equivalent place-names have changed out of all recognition since the early twentieth century.

186. Second edition, in three volumes (Hamburg, 1877). Miller clearly sought to keep abreast of newly published volumes in the great ongoing epigraphic corpora, especially *CIL* (to whose material he does offer full citations). But it seems that he chose to ignore the *Real-Encyclopädie der classischen Altertumswissenschaft*, which began to appear in 1894 and had reached "Imperator" by 1914, along with a single volume ("Ra-Ryton," 1913) in its Zweite Reihe.

187. *ItMiller*, XXV, LIII.

188. Coverage in this section is inevitably selective. Needless to say, the map regularly merits an entry in reference works of many kinds.

189. *RE*, 10 (1919), 2126–44. His extensive related entry "Itinerarien" appeared earlier in *RE*, 9 (1916), 2308–63.

190. S.v. "Peutingeriana," *RE*, 19 (1938), 1405–12.

191. See below, Chap. 3, sec. 4 (c).

192. Bologna, 1978; see further above, sec. 5.

193. Rimini: Maggioli Editore.

194. Université de Paris IV, 1990. My thanks to Professor Arnaud for generously furnishing a microfiche copy.

195. Pp. 855–56 in part 3, chap. 3.

196. It is reflected previously in his article "L'origine, la date de rédaction et la diffusion de l'archétype de la Table de Peutinger," *Bulletin de la Société Nationale des Antiquaires de France* (1988): 302–21.

197. Paris (2007), esp. pp. 182–88 (with much recent scholarship ignored).

198. *HistCart*, 1 (1987), 238–42. For some additional detail, compare O. A. W. Dilke, *Greek and Roman Maps* (London, 1985), esp. 112–20 and Appendix V.

199. Hildesheim (1995), esp. 186–87; see further below, chap. 5, n. 50.

200. The circumstances are outlined by R. Talbert, "Greek and Roman Mapping: Twenty-First Century Perspectives," 9–27 in R. J. A. Talbert and R. W. Unger (eds.), *Cartography in Antiquity and the Middle Ages: Fresh Perspectives, New Methods* (Leiden, 2008), at 9–15.

201. For recent empire-wide perspectives in this connection, note in particular *NP*, ss.vv. "Strassen," "Viae Publicae" (both in vol. 12/2, 2002) with Suppl. 3 (*Historischer Atlas der antiken Welt*, 2007), 194–99, 261; J. Wilkes in *CAH*, vol. 12, 2nd ed. (2005), 233–41. For the countless discussions with a regional or local focus, search *L'Année philologique* ss.vv. "Tabula Peutingeriana" (or vice versa), "Itineraria et geographica," and the online *Database of Classical Bibliography*.

Chapter Two: The Surviving Copy: The Material Object and its Paleography

1. I.e., calfskin; cf. Woodward in *HistCart*, 1 (1987), 324, n. 190.

2. In the case of vellum the two sides hardly differ. Parchment tends to roll itself in toward the hair side. The map's sheets, by contrast, seem to curl

away from the viewer: their edges lie flat, while the middle presses against the top of the container.

3. Weber, *Tabula Peutingeriana, Kommentar*, 23–28.

4. In 4A1, for example.

5. In 4A2, for example.

6. Note Weber, *Kommentar*, 11 and 23, n. 32; and further below.

7. This important insight is contributed by M. Steinmann. The most visible such holes are top left on Segment 1; bottom center on 4; top and bottom in the margin (righthand) of 6, and correspondingly in the margin (lefthand) of 7 at the top only (the bottom is broken off); top and bottom right on 11. Other possible such holes, although not so well preserved, occur at the bottom of 7 in the righthand margin, and correspondingly on 8; also at the top of 10 in the lefthand margin, and below at the far bottom left of the map itself.

8. The discovery is discussed in my Chap. 1 sec. 1. For a *mappamundi* hung on the wall of an Oxford college's library in the 1470s, together with other details (from college accounts) about the making and repair of maps there, see R. Thomson, "Medieval Maps at Merton College, Oxford," *Imago Mundi* 61 (2009): 84–90.

9. See Chap. 1, sec. 4 (a).

10. *Dissertatio*, 38, in von Scheyb (1753). At the time when Forlosia's predecessor, Pius Nikolaus Garelli, died (July 1739), the map was actually at his house, and was retrieved by Forlosia as acting head of the library (Stummvoll [1968], 224).

11. Note Weber's discussion in *Kommentar*, 11.

12. See M. K. Lawson, *The Battle of Hastings 1066* (Stroud [England], 2002), 264, and further below. For a drawing of this cylinder for the Bayeux Tapestry, see T. F. Dibdin, *A Bibliographical, Antiquarian and Picturesque Tour in France and Germany*, vol. 1, 2nd ed. (London, 1829), 247. By the mid-nineteenth century, a second cylinder had been introduced, allowing the tapestry to be wound from one to the other. The tapestry is of course a much longer object than the Peutinger map, although not a great deal taller.

13. E. Edwards, *Memoirs of Libraries: Including a Handbook of Library Economy*, vol. 2 (London, 1859), 397. For his summary of the map's history (reflecting the mistaken belief that there are twelve parchment segments, not eleven), see pp. 388–90.

14. Maury (1864), 60: "La carte. . . . forme un long rouleau actuellement déposé, en partie déroulé, sous une vitrine, dans une salle à part du grand établissement. . . . "

15. Stummvoll (1968), 466; during October and November, according to Desjardins (1869–74), *Rapport*, p. III. No doubt the cloth backing was removed now, at the latest.

16. Trenkler (1973), 210; Weber, *Kommentar*, 10.

17. See M. Flieder and E. Irblich (eds.), *Texte, Noten, Bilder: Neuerwerbungen, Restaurierungen, Konservierungen 1977–1983* (Vienna, 1984), 145–47; and E. Irblich, "Die Konservierung von Handschriften unter Berücksichtigung der Restaurierung, Reprographie und Faksimilierung an Hand von Beispielen aus der Handschriftensammlung der Österreichischen Nationalbibliothek Wien," *Codices Manuscripti* 11 (1985): 15–32 at 18–22.

18. In certain spots (e.g., 3B2, 8B5), these tops have suffered scratching, which is visible on the scanned images. In addition, the airholes in the tops, and

the shadows cast by them, can confuse and obstruct the viewer; see, for example, *Ptolomaide* (9C2).

19. Miraculously, it survives (incomplete) as a succession of eight linen strips, 68.38 meters ($224\frac{1}{4}$ ft.) in length, varying between 45.7 (18 in.) and 53.6 cm (21 in.) in height, embroidered with wools of eight different colors. It was probably produced within fifteen years of the Battle of Hastings (1066), in England, possibly by designers at Canterbury or trained there. There is no known record until 1476, and even a partial drawing was not published until 1729. Neither of the two academicians in Paris who first alerted the scholarly world to the tapestry in the 1720s ever went to Bayeux to view it. See further Hicks (2006), esp. chap. 5.

20. It survives complete, pentagonal in shape, drawn on calfhide, approximately 160 cm in height × 130 (63 × 51 in.), produced around 1300. The earliest record dates to 1684, and drawings were only published for the first time during the 1840s. Even in the early nineteenth century it was thickly covered by dirt and had lanterns piled up against it. See P. D. A. Harvey (ed.), *The Hereford World Map: Medieval World Maps and Their Context* (London, 2006), esp. 45. An important discussion of where in the cathedral the map's makers would have placed it, why, and how they intended it to be viewed, is offered by D. Terkla, "The Original Placement of the Hereford *Mappa Mundi*," *Imago Mundi* 56 (2004): 131–51.

21. By the first method, the new parchment was overlaid by the pricked exemplar, fine powder ("pounce") was applied, and this filtered through the holes to show the placement of the pricks. The second method left holes in both the exemplar and the new parchment, but there are none to be seen in our copy of the map. An alternative means to achieve accurate reproduction of line work in particular was to trace it onto thin, transparent parchment and then to copy from that, much as Kleiner and Cristianopoulo each did – using paper – in the eighteenth century (above, Chap. 1, secs. 4 [a] and [d] respectively). See in general R. W. Scheller, Exemplum: *Model-Book Drawings and the Practice of Artistic Transmission in the Middle Ages (ca. 900– ca. 1470)* (Amsterdam, 1995), 70–71.

22. The pigments have never been chemically analysed. It remains to be explained why they have undergone little, if any, change over the margins; perhaps they have been preserved by the glue that was used.

23. Use of light washes rather than full colors was not more economical; rather, two different techniques were involved.

24. The two rings encircling ROMA could have been made with a compass, but it is impossible to establish whether the center – above ROMA's two girdles – has been pricked.

25. Weber, *Kommentar*, 15.

26. Examples: *Conpito Anagnino* (5B1) on top of a route that continues unbroken; *Teano scedicino* (5B3), a simplified symbol; *Iovnaria* (5A2), incomplete (only in red).

27. See below, Chap. 3 sec. 2 (c).

28. "Black" is the conventional description; it is really a shade of brown.

29. Compare below in black ink and distinctly smaller lettering (as used for place-names): *Hic legem accepervnt i(n) monte Syna.*

30. Marked above the identical name for the city written in regular black minuscules.

31. *Fl. Nilvs qui dividit asiam (et) libiam* (8C1) is similar but somewhat smaller.

32. For two instances, note PANNONIA SVPERIOR, PANNONIA INFERIOR (4A3–5A4).

33. Note that *Adpvblicanos* (4A2) is fitted either side of a red display capital **R**, and that the next place-name, *Adrante*, overwrites the next such capital **I**. Observe how by contrast the **P** of PALESTINA (9C2) in red capitals is placed to avoid *Tyberias* in black minuscules, a shift that the copyist could no doubt have noted in advance from the exemplar.

34. The same applies to round **d** and **o** in *Mindo fl.* (4B2). For **pp** to be run together – as in *Via appia* (4B5) – is an older practice.

35. But note "round" capital **S** in *Svessvla* (5B4), *Assaria* (6C3).

36. For examples, see above, Introduction, "Presentation of the Map."

37. But note *Fossa Facta P(er) Servos Scvtarvm* (8A1).

38. See further below, Chap. 3, sec. 2 (f).

39. The text that accompanies the illustrations for the fourth-century Quedlinburg Itala, for example, is written in uncial: see I. Levin, *The Quedlinburg Itala: The Oldest Illustrated Biblical Manuscript* (Leiden, 1985), with facsimile. However, it is quite possible that capitals were used alongside uncial as a display script.

40. See the invaluable overview by J. J. G. Alexander, *Medieval Illuminators and Their Methods of Work* (New Haven, CT, 1992), chap. 1; the only regret is that his scope fails to include maps.

41. For the few early modern corrections and amendments, see section (f) below.

42. Database entry IN ALPE MA[..]T[.]MA.

43. *HistCart*, 1 (1987), 324.

44. Note M. Gullick, "How Fast Did Scribes Write ? Evidence from Romanesque Manuscripts," 39–58 in L. L. Brownrigg (ed.), *Making Medieval Books: Techniques of Production* (Los Altos [CA] and London, 1995), esp. 43.

45. That is, from "Praegothica" to "Übergangsschriften" and "Frühgotische Schriften." For the former, see A. Derolez, *The Palaeography of Gothic Manuscript Books: From the Twelfth to the Early Sixteenth Century* (Cambridge, 2003), 56–71; for the two latter, K. Schneider, *Gotische Schriften in deutscher Sprache. Teil 1, Vom späten 12. Jahrhundert bis um 1300, Textband* and *Tafelband* (Wiesbaden, 1987).

46. Schneider (1987), *Textband*, 9–162, with Derolez (2003) for "Praegothica" throughout Europe.

47. Compare Weber, *Kommentar*, 11.

48. (1987), 71–75.

49. Compare Derolez (2003), 95.

50. See Schneider (1987), 15 and s.v. in "Sachregister" (305).

51. H. Lieb, "Zur Herkunft der Tabula Peutingeriana," in H. Maurer (ed.), *Die Abtei Reichenau: Neue Beiträge zur Geschichte und Kultur des Inselklosters* (Sigmaringen, 1974), 31–33. The claim is taken up again by E. Albu, "Rethinking the Peutinger Map," in Talbert and Unger (2008), 111–19.

52. For the long-standing but unjustified preoccupation with Speyer, see above, Chap. 1, n. 7.

53. Note that Henry VI went to Rome to be crowned by Pope Celestine III in 1191.

54. GES after NITIOBRO (1A4–1A5); **L** above the **R** in *Fl. Riger* (1A5); ETRVR(*i*)A (4B1); LA(*c*)ONICE (6B5); ARCA(*d*)IA (6C5).

55. *ida* on mountain range no. 97 (8B2); an illegible name below unnamed symbol no. 1 on island no. 3 (1B3–1C3).

56. *Regenspurg* added below *Regino*, and *Salzpurg* below *Ivavo* (both 3A4).
57. See the database entry for *Fl. Rhamma*.
58. Most clearly seen in the vicinity of *Avgvsta Pretoria* (2B4).

Chapter Three: The Design and Character of the Map

1. See, for example, Weber, *Kommentar*, 12; *TAVO*, B S 1 *Weltkarten der Antike/Ancient Maps of the World*, 1.2 *Tabula Peutingeriana* (text by J. Wagner, 1984); Brodersen (1995), 187.
2. The fact that copyists have chosen to reproduce it on a varying number of parchments, sheets, or plates is irrelevant to the conception of the design.
3. Chap. 2, sec. 1.
4. For Miller (*ItMiller*, XLII; cf. *Mappaemundi*, Heft VI [1898], 90, 94), Rome is only the center point of the Mediterranean, not of the entire map. Weber, *Kommentar*, 13, is ready to think otherwise.
5. Letter 256 (Hummelberg to Beatus, April 6, 1526), in Horawitz and Hartfelder (1886), 364.
6. See further below, Conclusion, sec. 1.
7. See above, Chap. 1, sec. 2 (b) and Plate 4.
8. 7.5.1–16 Stückelberger = J. L. Berggren and A. Jones, *Ptolemy's Geography: An Annotated Translation of the Theoretical Chapters* (Princeton [NJ] and Oxford, 2000), 108–11. Although this work by Ptolemy – written around the mid-second century A.D. at Alexandria – is commonly called the *Geography*, its actual title was *Guide to Drawing a World Map* (γεωγραφικὴ ὑφήγησις). If Ptolemy himself drew maps to accompany the text (as he might well have done), all are lost; the surviving "Ptolemy" maps often presented with the text are in fact medieval work or later.
9. See further below, sec. 4 (b).
10. See further below, Chap. 5, sec. 3.
11. These are themselves loose terms: see, for example, S. P. Mattern, *Rome and the Enemy: Imperial Strategy in the Principate* (Berkeley, CA, 1999), 41–66; W. V. Harris, "The Mediterranean and Ancient History," in id. (ed.), *Rethinking the Mediterranean* (Oxford, 2005), 1–42, at 15–16.
12. Our copy does not preserve any name(s) for it. For the persistent conviction that the *oikoumene* was surrounded by Ocean, see J. S. Romm, *The Edges of the Earth in Ancient Thought: Geography, Exploration, and Fiction* (Princeton, NJ, 1992), 12–17, 33–36, 41–44.
13. This section draws upon my earlier study, "Peutinger's Roman Map: The Physical Landscape Framework," 221–230 and Tafeln 15–16 in M. Rathmann (ed.), *Wahrnehmung und Erfassung geographischer Räume in der Antike* (Mainz, 2007).
14. Refer to the separate layers for each on Map A.
15. At 8A1, the Golden Horn (on which Sycas lies) is in turn exaggerated.
16. For discussion of sources, Chap. 5, sec. 2.
17. 2B5–3C1.
18. By contrast, the map prescribed by Ptolemy affords Sardinia and Sicily equal coverage (see Ptol. *Geog.* 8.9.1–4, Stückelberger with the latter's Ptolemaic map *Europa, 7*).
19. 5C5–6C1, island no. 42.
20. *BAtlas*, Map 48, and *Directory*, p. 736.

21. This is Ptolemy's recommendation (*Geog.* 2.1.4).

22. The marking of two settlements (Diotahi, Derta) linked by a route on unnamed island no. 107 is extraordinary.

23. See further below, Conclusion, sec. 1.

24. On this latter aspect, see further below, Chap. 5, sec. 3.

25. As already mentioned, the North African coastline is lowered in turn for a brief distance (5C5–6C1) to accommodate the island of Djerba (no. 42, unnamed).

26. All in 7B1–7B3. To place Cytera much closer to the Peloponnese would seem to pose no difficulty, however; so the choice not to do so remains a puzzle.

27. For Delphi as geographic center, protecting the earth's navel (*omphalos*), see S. G. Cole, "'I know the number of the sand and the measure of the sea': Geography and Difference in the Early Greek World," in K. A. Raaflaub and R. J. A. Talbert (eds.), *Geography and Ethnography: Perceptions of the World in Pre-Modern Societies* (Oxford, 2010), 197–214.

28. 7B5–8C2.

29. To the left of the Bosporus, by contrast, there are no such consequences to ringing the Black Sea with settlements that actually lie on its west coast (*BAtlas* 22 F4 – 52 D2).

30. From, say, Lamasco (8B2) to Chidvm (= Cnidos, 9B1).

31. From, say, Chidvm to Aregea (= Aegeae, 9B4).

32. 8C3–9B4.

33. Elsewhere, too, such stretches can be found in close proximity (along Segment 4 above the Adriatic's upper shoreline, for example, and above Antiochia at the righthand end of Segment 9), but not to the same extent as in North Africa.

34. Originating in 8C1.

35. See *BAtlas*, 87 E4-G2; the route could regarded as the counterpart, so to speak, to the western one from Tomis (7A4).

36. No wonder that Hummelberg, who labored to copy the entire map accurately for the first time, was unimpressed by its final part. In offering Beatus Rhenanus a glimpse on April 6, 1526, he writes: "Eius itineris extremam tabellam his adnexam tibi mitto, ut videas, qualis tota sit farrago" ("I am sending you the final segment of the itinerary attached to this letter so that you may see the kind of complete hotchpotch that it is"). Letter 256 in Horawitz and Hartfelder (1886), 364.

37. = Ecbatanis Partiorvm (11C1).

38. = Persepoliscon Mercivm persarvm (11C2).

39. Mare Hyrcanivm, leading into unnamed Ocean (10A5–11A2).

40. These are initially a single range (from 2B2), which soon splits; the Apennines continue for far longer (to 6B2) than the Alps (to 3A2, although with separate offshoots thereafter).

41. 9B1–11B5.

42. To 1B2.

43. Named "Fl." only, 3A5 (no. 27A).

44. Unnamed (no. 119) but for the crossing at 9C5.

45. Nos. 109 and 110 (9A2).

46. Italy's west coast close to the north coast of Africa, for example; Verona (3A3) to Ivavo (3A4); Actanicopoli (6B3) to Leptimagna col. (6C4); Pergamo (8B3) to Alexandria (8C3).

47. For example, Vesontine (2A1) to Avgvsta Rvracvm (2A4); Verona (3A3) to Hostilia (3B4) and in turn to Ravenna (4B1); Vtica colonia (4C3) to Chartagine colon (4C5).

48. See further Chap. 5, sec. 3.

49. In addition, the copy of a map in *P.Artemid.* should not be overlooked: see C. Gallazzi, B. Kramer, and S. Settis (eds.), *Il Papiro di Artemidoro* (Milan, 2008), 273–308. Doubts have been expressed about the authenticity of this document in whole or in part, however, and in any event the map in its unfinished nature proves frustratingly difficult to interpret. For discussion, see R. Talbert, "P.Artemid.: The Map," in K. Brodersen and J. Elsner (eds.), *Images and Texts on the "Artemidorus Papyrus,"* Historia Einzelschrift 214 (Stuttgart, 2009), 57–64.

50. O. A. W. Dilke, in *HistCart*, 1 (1987), 220–25.

51. See http://formaurbis.stanford.edu with J. Trimble, "Visibility and Viewing on the Severan Marble Plan," in S. Swain, S. Harrison, and J. Elsner (eds.), *Severan Culture* (Cambridge, 2007), 368–84.

52. Small fragments of other city plans on marble survive from Rome and else-where, but there is no knowing how any of these plans were displayed or how large they were when complete: see J. Trimble, "Process and Trans-formation on the Severan Marble Plan of Rome," in Talbert and Unger (2008), 67–97, at 69–76.

53. See my entry in P. Barber (ed.), *The Map Book* (London, 2005), 24–25, with Brodersen (1995), 145–48, and S. James, *Excavations at Dura-Europos 1928–1937, Final Report: The Arms and Armour and Other Military Equipment* (London, 2004), 25, 39 (Tower 2) for findspot and *comparanda*.

54. See further on this perspective G. W. Bowersock, "The East–West Orien-tation of Mediterranean Studies and the Meaning of North and South in Antiquity," in Harris (2005), 167–78.

55. 14.6.10, ". . . a primo ad ultimum solem se abunde iactitant possidere."

56. Ptol. *Geog.* 2.1.5.

57. Further discussion by B. Salway, "Putting the World in Order: Mapping in Roman Texts," in R. J. A. Talbert (ed.), *Ancient Perspectives: Maps and Their Place in Mesopotamia, Egypt, Greece, and Rome* (Chicago, forthcoming).

58. *HistCart*, 1 (1987), 222.

59. Trimble (2007), 368, with http://formaurbis.stanford.edu.

60. See B. Salway, "Sea and River Travel in the Roman Itinerary Literature," in Talbert and Brodersen (2004), 43–96, at 92–95.

61. See M. H. Crawford, "Tribus, tessères et régions," *CRAI* (2002): 1125–35.

62. Note the placement of the two regions of both Pannonia (4A3, 5A2) and Moesia (5A5, 6A2).

63. On its coloring, see also above, Chap. 2, sec. 2 (a).

64. The occasional instance where red, not black, is used to demarcate coastline (for example, island no. 27; the left end of Sicily on Segment 5; compare the small islands no. 15 and no. 16, colored entirely red) must surely be a copyist's error. Likewise it seems no more than a copyist's clumsiness to mark out each letter in LVCCANIA (5B5–6B1) by a red stroke or blob, and then to add the letters themselves in black.

65. The shade of red chosen as fill for mountain ranges on our copy may vary from dark to light: see, for example, no. 109A in 11B2–11B3.

66. See the layer for Map A "River courses: supplementary line work."

67. Note the discussion by Salway (2004), 87–88. In his *Rapport*, p. III, Desjardins (1869–74) is convinced that this lining signified frontiers; at first the uncomprehending copyist reproduced some of it, but then he simply ceased to bother.

68. See further below, sec. 4 (c).

69. For example, lakes nos. 1, 2 (2A5); 21 (11B3); 22 (11C5).

70. Our copyist has not troubled to serrate some parts of the Apennines (range no. 15) or of the long range (no. 11) along the bottom of the map as sharply as others; range no. 120, too, is less sharply serrated than others in its part of the map.

71. See further below, n. 137.

72. Especially along range no. 109A on Segments 10–11.

73. Chicanes that turn upward can be found. In some instances, though not all, their departure from the norm is manifestly deliberate (particularly to overcome the constraints of limited space), but has no special significance. Instances include: Riobe (1A4); Varcia (1A5); +allio (2A1); Gemenello (2B3); Cirta colonia (2C5) – Castellvm Fabatianvm (3C1); Tarnasici (4A1); Svrpicano (4B4); Adrvbras (4B5); Adlefas (5B4); Stenas (6B5); Mandis (7C5); Phara (8C4); Miletvm – Mindo Fl. (9B1); Lazo (11B1). The upward chicane after Nemetaco (1A2) may well be a copyist's slip.

74. See further below, Chap. 4, sec. 3.

75. Compare *BAtlas*, 17 D2, southward.

76. "Fines" is a common name or component of one; at the provincial level, note Tvcca fines affrice et mavritanie (1C5); Fines cilicie (8B4 and note in database entry; 9B3).

77. On its potential impact, see below, Chap. 5, sec. 3.

78. For example, Port(vs) Calovitanvs (5A3); AMAXOBIISARMATE (6A2); M++ASCOLPVS, LA(c)ONICE (both 6B5); perhaps also Levcopetra (6B2); Salolime (8A1), if this is a garbling of Greek Kalos Limen.

79. See further above, Chap. 2, secs. 2 (b) and (c).

80. There seems to be no significance to such exceptions as Fl. Tanno (6B2), Fl. Agalingvs (7A3); they may well reflect the oversight or carelessness that Steinmann suggests above, Chap. 2, sec. 2 (b) (i).

81. Uniquely in the case of PROVINCIA AFRICA (2C5–6C3, the most elongated name on the map), two different colors are used – black for the first word, red for the second. It seems no more than oversight or decoration that one-word names in red may be followed by a stop in black: HACI, VAPII (both 1A2); or that two-word names in black may be divided by a stop in red: note SAGAES CYTHAE (11A1), ABYOS CYTHAE (11A3).

82. In 9A1, for example, PONTICI and PAFLAGONIA run close enough for a viewer to confuse them; for the former to appear in red and the latter in black is welcome guidance. The same may be said of QVADI and IVTVGI (3A5); PALESTINA and SYRRIA PHOENIX (9C2); and ARGENE SVPERIORIS and MONS TAVRVS (11B2).

83. See further below in this connection, sec. 4 (b).

84. The placement of Fl. Nigella (3B2) is therefore atypical, especially as this name could have been written horizontally and closer to the source of the river (no. 10Q). Likewise puzzling is the island name Crocira Port(vs) on its side when there is no visible need to place it thus (no. 53, 6B2).

85. Note the Avlona–Actanicopoli route (6B3).

86. Notable instances where care is exercised to avoid such overrunning include Avgvstvm (1) (2B1); Ac[.]lovm Fl., Calidon Fl. (both 6B4); Ptolomaide (9C2); Coclisindor(vm) (11C5).

87. Names and figures that accordingly overrun open water or river courses include ragvrio (5A2); Caprasia (6B1); Melena (6B5); Macomadase l(orvm) (7C1); Epifania (9C4); Hispa (10B2); and the remarkable route from Tigvbis (10C3) to Hatris (10C5). By contrast, lettering for Ad Horrea (5C2), which extends into open water, need not have done so.

88. Note, for example, Iovnaria (5A2); Tessalonic(a)e (7B2); Ptolomaide (7B4); Phemenio (8B2); Appollonia (8B3).

89. Among exceptions, typically arising from constraints upon space, note the stretches for Diolindvm (1B2); Vindonissa (2A5); Lepidoregio (3B3); Foro Gallorvm (3B4); Vico mendicoleo (5B5); Tanno Fl. (6B2); Stenas (6B5); Ceroni (7B1); Macomadase l(orvm) (7C1); Sagari(vs) Fl. (8A3); Stratonicidi (8C4); Celenderis, Lapheto (both 9B3); Roschirea, Tigvbis, Hadia (all 10C3).

90. If [..]NTVS POLEMONI[. . .]s (9A2) names a region, as seems likely, then its placement wholly within open water is exceptional but understandable in context (see its database entry). Likewise exceptional, and without obvious justification, is such placement of two isolated settlement names in 7C4, TARICEA and ON[– ? –]RO.

91. Predictably, exceptions occur, typically where space is limited: for example, in 3B5 Fl. Brintesia (no. 10jj); in 4B5 Fl. [– ? –]a[– ? –] (no. 40); three in 5B1 (nos. 46, 47, 48). The name for Fl. Bag+[– ? –]da (no. 42, 4C3) is also needlessly written thus.

92. Note Fl. Patabvs no. 3 (1A1); Fl. Nigrinvm no. 131, Fl. Oxvs no. 132, Fl. Sygris no. 133 (all 11A2); no doubt also no. 7 (1B1), where the name would be within the lost part of the map. Fl. Renvs no. 2A (1A1), and probably also Fl. Tygris no. 127 (10C4), are named twice at their mouths.

93. Note Fl. Riger no. 5 (1B2–1A5). In 2A5–3A1 the viewer who inferred from the stopping point Ad Renvm that the river (unnamed here) beginning its course immediately above is the Rhine would be correct, as it happens; on the river's course here, see further the database entry for Ad Renvm.

94. Exceptions do occur, but seldom. Note, for example, the second I in ITALIA (4B3); C in PICENVM (4B4).

95. See further below, sec. 3 (f).

96. The otherwise curious figure IIX on the Navpactos stretch (6B5) is perhaps to be regarded as another 28 originally written thus, but now missing its initial xx. Compare IIXXX on a milestone (*CIL*, XVII.4.1 no. 188).

97. Comparable instances of IX: Tartvrsanis (4A1); Adaqvas (4B3); Astvra (5B1); Avidvvicvs (5C2); So[– ? –]tv (8B5); Monogami (8C3); Hatita (9C1). Instances of XXIX: Agatinno (6B1); Coridallo (9B2); Calcida (9B5). Instances of XXXIX: Sagari(vs) Fl. (8A3); Tyana (9B2).

98. Also IX for Ebvtiana (5B3), XIX for Viciano (6A3), XXIX for Mandvris (6B1).

99. Compare the choice of IX for the successive stretches Pretorio and Ad Pannonios (6A4), where space is more limited.

100. For other instances of numerals divided simply by a space, see Hadrianopoli (6B3); Cortin[.] (8B1); possibly also Pestv (5B5).

101. Further instances: unnamed no. 31 (4B1); Foro clodo (4B2); Conflventib(vs) (5A5); Invinias (5B3); fons (7B3); also AD SCM PETRVM added later (4B4).

102. See the summary of views by Bosio (1983), 127–28.

103. Note, for example, three peninsulas and associated bays on the Adriatic coast in 5A2–5A3; three likewise along Italy's Mediterranean coastline in 5C2–5C5; and two along the African coast (5C2, 5C5).

104. Consideration of the map's use of the term would have been welcome in *TLL* s.v. Comparable use in another cartographic context is perhaps to be found in the dedicatory verses written for a map commissioned by Theodosius II ("Hoc opus egregium, quo mundi summa tenetur,/ Aequora quo, montes, fluvii, portus, freta et urbes/ Signantur...*"; see below, Chap. 5, n. 19). Salway (2004), 92, believes that *port(vs)* can be considered a scribe's slip for *pro(mvn)t(vrivm)* (promontory) in at least one instance on the Peutinger map, but more generally this explanation lacks conviction; a slip for *positio* (anchorage) might seem rather more plausible.

105. Sinvs Pestanvs (5C5) appears comparable, with the terms *sinvs* and *portvs* seemingly interchangeable in this context.

106. Map C outlines those rivers that can be identified (many cannot) as far east as the Euphrates and Tigris on a *BAtlas* base. For the importance of rivers in Romans' view of the world, note I. Östenberg, *Staging the World: Spoils, Captives, and Representations in the Roman Triumphal Procession* (Oxford, 2009), 230–45.

107. *NH*, 4.79.

108. Note, for example, nos. 10V, 62, 97, 99.

109. Note nos. 49, 50, 55 (all in 5B2); no. 43b; Cynips (no. 81); no. 120.

110. Note in particular the Escvs (no. 15E) and the unnamed Margus (no. 15C).

111. *BAtlas*, 40 B1.

112. For example, rivers nos. 95, 97, 98, 99.

113. For example, Adenvm (3A3); Arnvm Fl. (3B2); Sinnvm Fl. (3B5); Vbvs Flvmen, Armoniacvm Fl. (both 3C3); Arrabo Fl. (4A3); Mindo Fl. (4B2); Misco Fl. (4B3); Flvsor Fl. (4B4); Armascla Fl. (4C1); Hapsvm Fl. (6A2).

114. See, for example, rivers nos. 18, 39, 70, 114, 115, 125.

115. See, for example, rivers nos. 22, 44, 49, 53, 63, 66, 89, 90, 91, 94, 109.

116. Normally, "Fl." preceding a name signifies a river, whereas "Fl." following a name signifies a route stretch that takes its name from a river.

117. See, for example, rivers nos. 2A (in 2A5–3A1), 15C, 26C, 57, 64, 71, 72, 73, 95, 98, 100.

118. For example, rivers nos. 69B, 97, 99, 112.

119. Note rivers nos. 94, 124; compare unnamed river no. 8, where our copyist corrected this error made either by himself or by a previous copyist.

120. Note, however, river no. 111.

121. No. 126A and no. 127 Fl. Tygris drain into marsh; cf. Philostratus, *Life of Apollonius* 1.20.2 (Jones).

122. Note rivers nos. 26b Fl. Pallia, 86A, 86B, 92, 116; compare the copying errors corrected in rivers nos. 10S Ambrvm and 10T, also in nos. 26A (4B5) and 59.

123. [– ? –]A[– ? –] (2A5).

124. It is conceivable, as Salway (2004), 92, argues, that he is working from sources of different types, and failing to combine their data satisfactorily. Islands hereabouts and their names are muddled too: see next section below.

125. See in general s.v. "Insel," *RAC*, 18 (1998), cols. 312–28 (F. Prontera). For a large mosaic "map" of sites connected with the goddess Aphrodite on

Mediterranean islands from Sicily eastward (late third/early fourth century A.D. ?), note F. Bejaoui, "Iles et villes de la Méditerranée sur une mosaïque d'Ammaedara," *CRAI* (1997): 827–60.

126. More could have been related thus, however, among them Corsica and Sardinia in particular; see further above, sec. 1 (b).

127. See 2C5, 6B2, 10C4, in each instance with all islands named; 3C3 without individual names.

128. 5A3; cf. *BAtlas*, 20 D6 and discussion below, Chap. 4, sec. 1.

129. As no. 51 (6A2) and no. 62 (6B3).

130. As no. 60 (6B3) and no. 64 (6C3).

131. In addition, Salway (2004), 92 is willing to credit that Corcyra/Corfu is duplicated as Crocira (no. 53, 6B2) and Cassiopa (= no. 65 Ins. C[– ? –], 6C3).

132. No. 6 Ins. Ari[.]aria; no. 8 ango portvs insvla.

133. No. 7 Ins. Galliata.

134. *ItMiller*, 396, makes the point. It is tempting, but surely too speculative, to imagine that the lower of the two Sason islands (no. 62, 6B3) was originally meant to be Malta.

135. An unfortunate consequence of the elimination of Euboea is that the well-known spa on the island at Aidepsos (*BAtlas*, 55 E3) cannot be marked.

136. Note, for example, Inmonte Bvlsinio (5A4); Inmontecarbonario, Inmontegrani (both 5B1); Monte avreo (6A1).

137. In this connection, note Bosio (1983), 48.

138. Note, however, several road stations that take their names from the range: for example, In alpegraia (2B3); Inalpe ivlia (3A5).

139. The people Cavcasi are marked (8A5), but inconspicuously.

140. Thus, if the name "Boecolen Montes" (7C3) does refer to mountain range no. 80, it seems inappropriately small. Yet there are names of peoples extending immediately above and below the range, and they are permitted to attract attention instead.

141. Nominative is the norm, but note also, for example, NORICO (4A1–4A3); IEPIRVM NOVVM (6B3); and several genitive plurals in North Africa, where a collective noun in the nominative has to be supplied, such as NATIOSELOR(VM) (6C5) retains. These plurals include MVSONIORVM (1C2); GEDALVSIVM (1C4); MVSVLAMIORVM, NVMIDARVM (both 1C5).

142. Among the cases of doubt are LOCIDEREGI (7A3); Sorsdesertvs (7A5); Sorices (8A1); Amyrni, Brvani, Seracoe (all 8A2); Sardetae (8A3); Sanyigae (8A5); Achei (9A1); Acheon, Malichi (both 9A2); AROTE (11A5); CATACE (11B2); CASPYRE (11B4).

143. Gallia COMATA (1B3) – inappropriately small, as well as clumsily placed – is perhaps a copyist's addition.

144. LIGVRIA, too, is spread wide (2B3–3B1), whereas ETRVR(i)A is not (4B1). Elsewhere, CILICIA is spread out extensively (9B3–9B5), CARIA and LYCIA (both 9B1) not at all.

145. In particular, several peoples in 1A1–1A2. Note also the proximity of MARCOMANNI and VANDVLI (3A3), and the interweaving of QVADI and IVTVGI (both 3A5–4A2).

146. But note INSVBRES (2B5, 3A1); PSACCANI (8A2) and Psacccani (8A4); MONS TAVRVS (10B5–11B2, 11B1–11B3); and further below, Chap. 4, n. 16.

147. Map D outlines the network on a *BAtlas* base as far as Maps 87 and 89; to continue farther east in this way is hardly practical. Note the thorough

(but sometimes incautious) attempt to establish the map's routes within and from northeast Asia Minor by R. H. Hewsen, *Armenia: A Historical Atlas* (Chicago and London, 2001), 64–65, 68–69, and Map 59 (p. 70).

148. See further below, Chap. 5, sec. 3.

149. For the two principal surviving collections of such listings, the Antonine Itinerary (*ItAnt*) and Bordeaux Itinerary (*ItBurd*), see Maps E and F respectively, with Appendix 9 and discussion in Chap. 5, sec. 2 below.

150. Ptolemy's standard practice in the *Geography*, by contrast, is to present names in the nominative.

151. See further below, Chap. 5, secs. 1 and 2.

152. With the map alone as guide, the natural plan would be to proceed on from Nicea (8B2) by one of the routes that goes down, rather than by the one that goes up to unnamed Ancyra (no. 53, 8B4). Compare D. French, *Roman Roads and Milestones of Asia Minor, fasc. 1: The Pilgrim's Road*, BAR International Series 105 (Oxford, 1981), 13.

153. In Egypt, for example, to show the route from the Nile to Berenice (8C2–8C5), but not to Myos Hormos (*BAtlas*, 80 E1), was adequate, as was the sketchy rendering of the Nile Delta (8C3–8C4).

154. See further below, sec. (b).

155. Compare *BAtlas*, Map 12. On the direct route that is not shown, there would be many fewer stopping points.

156. Compare *BAtlas*, Map 34.

157. For discussion, see Conclusion, sec. 1.

158. Between 4A1 and 4A5, for example, note Pola, Vindobona, Adprotoriv(m), Sabarie, Brigantio, Aqvinco, Sardona, Siscia.

159. See further below, sec. 4 (c).

160. Note the partial study by T. J. Allen, "Roman Healing Spas in Italy: The Peutinger Map Revisited," *Athenaeum* 91 (2003): 403–15; more generally, *NP*, s.v. "Aquae."

161. Observe that the entire route from Serdica to Heraclea Sintica, on which the well-known spa at Scaptopara lies, is omitted (*BAtlas*, 49 F1; *CIL*, III.12336 of A.D. 238).

162. Note, for example, Arelato (1B5) to Valentia (2B1); along the North African coast in 7C1.

163. Consider, for example, Casarodvno (1B3) to Cenabo (1A3); Nicopolistro (7A2) to Marcianopolis (7A3).

164. Travelers who lacked a complete grasp of stopping points could of course find themselves seriously disadvantaged. Insufficient caution in this regard may have contributed to the deaths suffered by Licinius' escort when it was caught in a snowstorm traversing the Julian Alps too precipitately in February 313: see T. D. Barnes, *The New Empire of Diocletian and Constantine* (Cambridge, MA, 1982), 71; A. McCabe, *A Byzantine Encyclopaedia of Horse Medicine: The Sources, Compilation, and Transmission of the* Hippiatrica (Oxford, 2007), 186–88 (Theomnestus).

165. Note also Catara (9B4) to Samosata (10B3), where ten successive stretches are all between two and five.

166. This sequence represents the map's figures for Troesmis (7A3) to Tomis (7A4). Travelers' typical capacity for a day's journey is reflected better in *ItAnt* and above all in *ItBurd*, which records stopping points every few miles, even differentiating between *mansiones* and more modest *mutationes*.

167. See further below, Chap. 4, sec. 3.

168. It would suffice to extend the upper route ending at Tivisco so that it descends to join the route below on which Tivisco appears.

169. Note the stretches Cambete–Arialbinvm–Avgvsta Rvracvm (2A3, 2A4); Lvria and Cvria (both 3A1); Avodiaco (3A1) and Abodiaco (3A2); Inter-amnio and Inter manana (both 4B4). Duplication of Adhercvlem (6A4) and Adhercvle (6B4) evidently reflects more serious confusion. Instances where duplication could have been introduced by either the mapmaker or a copyist: Noreia (both 4A1); Temsa (both 6B1).

170. In the former area, Abrostola is marked twice, either side of Amvrio.

171. Two other possible duplications (and if so, by the mapmaker?) are Aegonne (9A1) and Evgoni (9B1); Stabvlvm and Ad stabvlvm (both 9B2). However, the second occurrence of Lamasco (8B1, 8B2, both with symbol) seems better explained as a copyist's careless substitution for Apamea.

172. With and without symbol: Berya (9B5) and Bersera (10C1); Nisibi (10B4, 10B5); Singara (10B5) and Sirgora (10C4). In addition, Rana (11C3) and Rhana (11C4); +ntiochia (11A5) and Antiohia tharmata (11B5).

173. Note J. C. N. Coulston, "Three New Books on Trajan's Column," *JRA* 3 (1990): 290–309, at 303.

174. See Chap. 5, sec. 2.

175. See further below, Chap. 5, sec. 3.

176. Instances occur where a river crossing may be deliberately intended to substitute for a chicane in marking the start of a stretch: for example, Sestias (4B3); Heraclea (8A4); Appollonia (9B2); Salmalasso (10A1). It is impossible to say whether copyists are responsible for some, or even all, rather than the mapmaker.

177. The type of claim made by T. Bekker-Nielsen, *The Roads of Ancient Cyprus* (Copenhagen, 2004), rests on a false premise, therefore: "In the northwest of the island, the name of Marion/Arsinoë has been omitted, but the station is shown as a kink in the road" (p. 160). On the contrary, this settlement is simply omitted.

178. For further discussion of the means and criteria by which he chose places to be marked with a symbol, see the next section.

179. Note Ptol. *Geog.* 1.22.5 and 1.24.9 (*semeiosis*).

180. Note the extreme case on a small island (no. 107 in 10C3) where Diotahi and Derta (neither considered to merit a symbol) are linked by a vertical route.

181. As a result, the wide spacing of letters for an isolated settlement such as HERMONASSA (9A1) can offer viewers merely a general impression of its location. No more than two settlements isolated from the route network are considered to merit a symbol: Tvrribvs (3C1, in Sardinia) and Antiohia tharmata (11B5, in India).

182. Observe Perintvs–Apris (7B5), where four distance figures and three intermediate place-names must be accommodated.

183. Further instances where a stretch is recognized to be over-long (even if the distance figure is omitted): Dertona (2B5)–Iria (3B1)–comeli magvs; Verona (3A3)–Hostilia (3B4)–Ravenna; Hadre (4A4)–Bvrno; Veresvos (4C2)–Thasarte (4C4)–Si[lesv]a (5C2)–Adaqvas; Actanicopoli (6B3)–Larissa; Synnada (8B4)–Evforbio (8B5)–Apamea ciboton; Inco-macenis (10B1)–Heracome; Hierapoli (10C1)–Zevgma; Hierapoli (10C1)–Ceciliana; Tigvbis (10C3)–Fons scabore.

184. Very high figures include: LXXX: [– ? –]++ia (8C4); Antiochia pisidia (9B2); XC: Acori (8C3); CXX: Berdanna (11C1); CXXX: Nicopolistro (7A2); CLX:

Paricea (11C4). For the special case of the route from Tazora (11B3) through to an unnamed settlement symbol (no. 77, 11C5), see below.

185. In some instances where names and distance figures seem to have been inserted, there is inevitably no knowing whether the mapmaker is correcting his own oversight or introducing an afterthought, or whether a copyist is responsible. Consider, for example, Bricianis (3A3); Marinianio (3A4, with note in database entry for Blaboriciaco); Svrontio (3A5); Castris novis (6A4).

186. Compare Dertona–Avgvsta Tavrinor(vm) (2B5); Sostra (7A2).

187. Because it is regular practice for the name associated with a symbol to be placed above it, only the distance figure for any stretch beyond has to occupy route line work. Even so, occasionally, the map layout requires the name to occupy space to the left of the symbol; a chicane may then be drawn to mark the start of such a stretch (whereas typically the preceding stretch runs to the symbol direct). Note Sammarobriva (1A3); Baca conervio (1A4); Ipponte diarito (4C1).

188. Possibly Iovnaria (5A2) and Petris (8C5) have been fitted in by this means. Elsewhere, in a crowded area of the map, to mark Selinvnte (9B2) with a symbol is plainly advantageous; but it probably merited one anyway.

189. Avsere fl.–Pvtea–Lamini(a)e–Veri (6C1–6C2).

190. Approximate equivalents are 1,618 yards and 1,475 meters.

191. 1 Gallic league = 1.5 Roman miles. On this league, see further M. Rathmann, *Untersuchungen zu den Reichsstrassen in den westlichen Provinzen des Imperium Romanum* (Mainz, 2003), chap. 3.7.4.

192. Compare Ammianus Marcellinus (15.11.17), who notes of the confluence of the Rhone and Arar rivers (i.e., the site of Lugdunum), "Exindeque non millenis passibus sed leugis itinera metiuntur."

193. See R. J. A. Talbert and T. Elliott, "New Windows on the Peutinger Map of the Roman World," in A. K. Knowles (ed.), *Placing History: How Maps, Spatial Data, and GIS Are Changing Historical Scholarship* (Redlands, CA, 2008), 199–218.

194. *ItMiller*, XLIX.

195. Non-Roman sources and their units are discussed further below, Chap. 5, sec. 2.

196. See the database entry for Traiect(vs) Stadior(vm) CC (7B1). Conversion of this distance figure into Roman miles might have been expected, although it is true that the *Itinerarium Maritimum* (*ItMarit*) collection readily uses miles for some routes and stades for others; see Salway (2004), 77–85, 91. Eight stades were typically taken to be equivalent to one Roman mile: see D. R. Dicks, *The Geographical Fragments of Hipparchus* (London, 1960), 42–46.

197. It is just possible that such a distance was given in connection with island no. 8 (ango portvs insvla, 2C4). Miller's suspicion of another instance depends upon a reading that I reject: see the database entry for Is[– ? –] (3B1).

198. See further Salway (2004), 90–91 with fig. 11.

199. Other possible instances are Navpactos (6B5), or even Actanicopoli (6B3)–Pache (6B5); across the Nile delta to Pelvsio (8C4); and indeed all the routes along the Nile. It would be instructive to know how the route along the African coast westward from Tingi was presented on the lost part of the map; see below, Appendix 5, n. 8.

200. See above, n. 53.

201. Superbly presented in M. Piccirillo and E. Alliata (eds.), *The Madaba Map Centenary 1897–1997. Travelling through the Byzantine Umayyad Period*

(Jerusalem: Studium Biblicum Franciscanum, 1998). Its symbols are compared with those on the Peutinger map by G. W. Bowersock, *Mosaics as History: The Near East from Late Antiquity to Islam* (Cambridge, MA, 2006), 19–25.

202. Such symbols are also outlined on the Artemidorus map (above, n. 49).

203. See B. Campbell, *The Writings of the Roman Land Surveyors: Introduction, Text, Translation and Commentary* (London, 2000), especially pp. xxi–xxvi.

204. Above, n. 51.

205. Note Ovid's breezy advice to the young man seeking to impress a girlfriend as they watch a triumphal procession (*Ars Amatoria* 1. 219–28), discussed by M. Beard, *The Roman Triumph* (Cambridge [MA] and London, 2007), 183–85. For a Roman surveyor's acknowledgment that slabs set up to record the width of a river (*trapeadi*) are liable to be mistaken for mileposts (*miliarii*), see Campbell (2000), 248, lines 19–21.

206. For exceptions, note variants (b7) and (c7).

207. Variant (a32), which joins the tops of the towers, may be viewed as a copyist's slip.

208. The map offers no lack of names incorporating *castellum, castrum, praetorium, pons*, etc; note also, for example, Insvmmo pyreneo (1B2); Insvmmo Pennino (2B4) in connection with passes.

209. Ac1 (22 instances) is the exception; otherwise, Aa1 (131 instances), Aa2 (89 instances), Ab1 (43 instances), and Ab2 (21 instances) are very alike.

210. Aa3, C1.

211. The same would seem to be true of the symbols on the Dura shield (above, n. 53).

212. Thus, for example, the space between the two towers for Pvteolis (5B4) is colored red; some, but not all, the red coloring for Tarento (6B1) is missing; a red blob occupies the space between the towers for Aenos (7B5); the center line of the three linking the two towers of Singara (10B5) is red, not black.

213. For example, Sena Ivlia (3B3); Simitv Colonia (3C5); Volsinis (4B1); Senia (4B2); Castro novo (4B3); Sirmivm (5A4); Benebento (5B4); Tacape col. (5C5); Clampeia (6B1); Petris (8C5); Cesaria (9C1).

214. For example, Ad zizio (5A5).

215. For example, Nicea (6B5); Perintvs (7B5); Ascalone (9C1); Melentenis (10B2); Nagae (11B2).

216. For example, Theleote col. (3C5); Depanis (5C5); Scobre (6A2); Faliatis (6A3). Instances can be found, too, where the frame was drawn in black and then traced over in red: Amiternvs (4B5); Terracina (5B2).

217. Many symbols are colored thus in Segments 3 and 4, just conceivably an attempt at embellishment comparable to tracing some river courses additionally in red; see above, section 2 (c).

218. Note C 12, 13 (both), 16, 19, 21, 23, 24; this last might better be regarded as a variant of Ac2 rather than of C. In the similar case of C7, the symbol may signify a bath/spa because Vacanas (4B3) does happen to be situated on a lakeshore, even though the lake is not shown.

219. On copyists' handling of symbols, see further below, Chap. 4, sec. 1.

220. That is, a junction where two routes (only) merge and continue as one, or where one route forks into two.

221. For example, at Gesogiaco qvod nvnc Bononia (1A2); [–?–]araco (1A3); Riobe (1A4); Argantomago, Casarodvno (both 1B3); Degetia (1B4); Tamannvna Mvnicipivm et castellvm (1C2).

222. For example, Adnovas (3B4); *either* THVRRIS *or* Sicilibba (4C4; see database entry for Risca); Adlefas (5B4); Dissio Aqva Amara (6C5), if this be regarded as one stretch, not two; Dorileo (8B3), where it would in fact be far more awkward to fit a symbol than a regular route stretch; adtygrem (10B4); probably also Mompsistea (9B4); Cito (9C3).

223. Note, for example, the instances of Dertona (2B5); Z[.]gaza[.]na (7C1).

224. See further Chap. 5, sec. 2.

225. 2C1, 5A3, 5B3, 6B3 (twice), 8C5.

226. With a symbol at 6A4; without at 6B4, 10C4.

227. With a symbol at 3C5, 4C5; without at 3C3, 5C1, 10A3.

228. 3B1, 4B4.

229. In addition, Fanomartis (1B2) is only a regular stretch; so, too, is the single occurrence Ad veneris (5B5).

230. Also only regular stretches: Aqvis Neri (1B3); Adaqvas Albvlas (4B5); Ad aqvas (6A4); Aqvas Aravenas (9B1); Aqve Frigide (10B4).

231. Tivisco (6A4, twice); Adhercvlem (6A4), with Adhercvle (6B4); Prvsias, with Cio (both 8B2); Pompeiopolis (9B3, twice); Berya (9B5), with Bersera (10C1); Nisibi (10B4), with Nisibi (10B5); Singara (10B5), with Sirgora (10C4).

232. Note that by contrast both Mvslvbio Horreta (1C5) and Ad Horrea (2B2) are only regular stretches.

233. And by extension categories (E) and (F) likewise.

234. *ItBurd*, 613.

235. On the unique clustering in 5A2–5A4, see further below, Chap. 4, sec. 1.

236. For example, Caspiae (10A3); Sanora, Teleda (both 10A5); Thvrae (10B1); Lazo (11B1).

237. Camvlodvno (1A1); Albe[– ? –]+imillo (2B3); Albi[– ? –]avno (2B4); Lambese (2C2); Thamvgadi (2C4); Tergeste (3A5); Cremona (3B3); Bvlla Regia (3C5); Noviodvni (4A2); Gigti (5C5); Romvla (6A5); Marcianopolis (7A3); Heraclea (8A4), awkward though it would be to fit in a symbol hereabouts; Hormvcopto (8C2); Hecantopolis (11B2), assuming that Hecatompylos (*BAtlas*, 96 C4) is meant.

238. (1967), especially 169–76.

239. Most notably Egypt in the Palestrina Nile mosaic (c. 100 B.C.?): see B. Andreae, *Antike Bildmosaiken* (Mainz, 2003), 78–109.

240. For a late first century A.D. fresco from Rome that seems to depict an idealized city, see E. La Rocca, "L'affresco con veduta di città dal colle Oppio," in E. Fentress (ed.), *Romanization and the City: Creation, Transformations, and Failures* (Portsmouth, RI, 2000), 57–71. Rome itself is displayed in accurate detail (of no practical use) on the Marble Plan (c. A.D. 200): see above, n. 51.

Chapter Four: Recovery of the Original Map from the Surviving Copy

1. Ptol. *Geog.* 1.18.2.

2. The Severan Marble Plan of Rome illustrates the need for caution in these respects: the data that it incorporates for certain locations is demonstrably outdated, while elsewhere obvious minor slips in presentation remain uncorrected. See T. Najbjerg and J. Trimble, "The Severan Marble Plan since 1960," in R. Meneghini and R. S. Valenzani (eds.), *Formae Urbis Romae: Nuovi frammenti di piante marmoree dallo scavo dei Fori Imperiali* (Rome, 2006), 75–101, at 92–97.

3. Note in this connection, for example, Ricina (2B5); Adponte, Tarnasici (both 4A1); Salinis (5B3); Flacci Taberna (6C3); Secvrispa (7A1); Fossa Facta P(er) Servos Scvtarvm (8A1); Valcaton (8B3); Salaberina (9B1).

4. Compare the liberties taken by Peutinger's two artists and Johannes Moller in the sixteenth century, as well as by one of Vodnik's pupils in the early nineteenth, to refashion and decorate symbols according to their own taste: see Chap. 1, sec. 2 (a) and (b) with Plates 3 and 4, and Appendix 3 with Plate 8, respectively. The problem is widespread of course, and affects the copying of much other work besides maps: see, for example, J. J. G. Alexander, "The Illustrated Manuscripts of the Notitia Dignitatum," in R. Goodburn and P. Bartholomew (eds.), *Aspects of the* Notitia Dignitatum, BAR Supplementary Series 15 (Oxford, 1976), 11–25.

5. Following Steinmann above, Chap. 2, sec. 2 (e).

6. Aqvileia's symbol seems to extend into the lake immediately to its right. Ravenna's symbol almost encroaches upon the name Cvrita cesena; a previous smaller symbol here might have allowed a straighter onward route to Sabis and the addition of a chicane.

7. Consider the pair of Arephilenor(vm) altars (7C2), the three altars for Alexander (11A3, 11B4 twice), and even the unique unnamed tunnel (?) taken to represent the Crypta Neapolitana (no. 43, 5B4).

8. Separation of "in" and "habitabiles" (10B2) – implying that the copyist did not understand what he was writing here – is an exceptional lapse.

9. Quite possibly, Admatricem was not even marked by a symbol on the original map.

10. See further above, Chap. 3, sec. 4 (c).

11. See above, Chap. 3, n. 128.

12. Compare the practice of the Ravenna Cosmography (below, Conclusion, sec. 2 [a]).

13. Gesogiaco qvod nvnc Bononia (1A2); Anteadicta Hervsalem mo helyacapitolina (9C1). Users of the map after its rediscovery, however, could not resist the temptation to make further such additions: see above, Chap. 2, sec. 2 (f). In the case of a people, it may be that the second word of CHAMAVI QVIELPRANCI (1A1–1A3; = "qvi et Franci" ?) represents a copyist's addition that was subsequently garbled.

14. As Chapter 1 (esp. secs. 2 and 4) demonstrates, this problem also bedeviled engravers' efforts to copy the map as late as the nineteenth century.

15. See, for example, Actanicopoli (6B3)–Larissa (6B5); Hierapoli (10C1)–Zevgma (10C3) and Ceciliana (10C2); Tigvbis (10C3)–Fons scabore (10B4).

16. Note PSACCANI (8A2) and Psacccani (8A4); SAGAES CYTHAE (11A1) and SAGAE SCYTHAE (11A4); CIRRABE INDI and CIRRIBE INDI (both 11B4); perhaps also MEDIA MAIOR (10A4) and MEDIO MINOR (11B3).

17. Compare later engravers' failure to recognize the "tall" lower-case **z**.

18. See, for example, Convetoni (1A1); Gerainas (2B2); Spoletio (4B3); Adscrofvlas (6A3); Lvcis (6B2); Centvrippa (6C1); Evcarpia (8B4). It would seem that although a slip in Ad Preto+ivm (4C1) was recognized and erased, no correction was then made.

19. For the widespread absence of river names, see above, Chap. 3, sec. 3 (b). On Map A unnamed route stretches are overlaid in purple.

20. The successive stretches Adpvblicanos and Adrante (both 4A2) may furnish an unusual case where our copyist himself evidently realized that he had

failed to copy the two names and their distance figures from the exemplar, and then added them; Botivo (4A4) may be a similar case.

21. Among names omitted for symbols presumably for this reason, note no. 37 (5A3), no. 40 (5B2), no. 42 (5B4).

22. See, for example, Tincollo (1B4); Antvnnaco (2A1); Polentia (2B5); Vennv (3A3); Pallanvm (5B2); Anxia (6B1); Agris (6C2); Leptimagna col. (6C4); Cyrenis col. (7C5); Bylevm Fl., Heraclea (both 8A4); Haila (8C5); Neapoli (9C1); Gelvina (10A5).

23. See, for example, Cabios (5B1); Cytmon (7C1).

24. See, for example, Avaricvm (1B3); BRIGANTIO–Clvnia (2A5); In Alpe Maritima (2B3); Vadis Sabates (2B4); Neapoli (9C1).

25. See, for example, Optatiana (7A2); Cortin[.] (8B1); Dasevsa (10B2).

26. See the "Route stretches with no distance figure (orange)" overlay on Map A, which includes, for example, Pisis–Tvirtta (3B1); Aqva viva (4B4); Aholla, Vsilla Mvn (both 5C3); Semnvm, Solvnto (both 6B1); Tyemnvm (8B4); Panopoli, Tasdri (both 8C3); Cassio (8C5); Lavdicivm pilycvm (9B1); Tetra (9B2); Balbyblos (9C2); Thalama (10B3). A display capital A occupies the space where the figure for the Ezetiv stretch ought to be (5B5).

27. For such figures, see above, Chap. 3 sec. 2 (f). For two distance figures on the same stretch, note Risca (4C4); Scilatio (6B2); Ortosias–Demetri (9C3).

28. See in this connection Chap. 3, n. 184.

29. For example, isaria–Animvrio XV (9B2).

30. See, for example, Revessione (1B4); Batiana (2B1); Evrone (3B5); Cvsvm (5A3); Lvcis (6B2); Ponte vetere (7A1); Magnesia (8B5).

31. See above, Chap. 2, sec. 2 (d).

32. It is conceivable – but much less likely in my view – that instead the artist produced the map, and the scribe wrote an accompanying gazetteer or *commentarii*: see Cameron (2002), 125 and n. 36, with discussion below, Chap. 5, n. 19.

33. Possibly three at Ad plvmbaria (2C5), for example.

34. See the "Routes: one stretch drawn as two or more (black)" overlay on Map A.

35. Note, for example, Gabris (1B3); Presidio Silvani (5C4); P[–?–]scv (8C2); Adammontem (9C2).

36. For example, Evdracinvm (2B4); Bittio (5A4); Adponte campanv (5B3); Germizera (7A1); Castris rvbris (7B2); Plotinopoli (7B3).

37. For example, Arenatio (1A4); Vesontine–Loposagio (2A1); Igiligili Col. (2C1); Adsextvm (3B3); Ipponte diarito (4C1); Natiolvm (5B4); Carambas (8A5).

38. See, for example, Narona (5A4); Pestv (5B5); Regio-Levcopetra (6B2); Stenas (6B5). In the two latter instances, there is no practical alternative to running the line work above the names rather than below them.

39. See the "Route stretches with no start marked (yellow)" overlay on Map A.

40. Note the care taken on our copy that the Iria (3B1) and Melena (6B5) stretches, which begin on Segments 2 and 6 respectively, should continue without slippage on Segments 3 and 7.

41. See, for example, Divo Dvrimedio Matricorvm–Addvodecimvm (2A1); Ad Horrea (2B2); villagai (4A2).

42. See, for example, Vicvs (10B3).

43. For the omission of route line work for the preceding Pestv (5B5) stretch, see above, n. 38.

44. See, for example, Conpito Anagnino (5B1); Teano Scedicino (5B3); Sertica (6A5); Lacedemone (7C1); Mileopoli (8B3); Petris (8C5).

45. See, for example, Gesogiaco qvod nvnc Bononia – Castello Menapiorv (1A2, lower stretch); Aqvas Apollinaris – Pvnicvm (4B3).

46. See, for example, Cos[..]ianvm–Grvmento (6B1); Palmyra (9C5).

47. Elsewhere, it is possible that the first of two distance figures on the long Dyrratio–Clodiana stretch (6A2) really belongs on the route immediately below.

48. Were it to be proven that a copyist introduced the duplication, then the question would arise of how the original map linked Ravgonia and Isvmbo, if at all.

49. Nowhere else on the map is the course of missing route line work traced thus. It is impossible to determine whether this was done by our copyist or later; see above, Chap. 2, sec. 2 (f).

50. See the database entry for Naharra (10C4).

51. See, for example, Advicesimvm (4A2); Clefantaria (4C3); Risca (4C4); Ostia Eterni (5B1); Barivm (5B4); Capvae–Pvteolis and on to Neapoli (5B4); Cydonia down to Cisamos (7B5); Cyrenis col.–Appollonia (7C5); Amvrio–unnamed symbol no. 53 (8B4); Hatris (10C5)–Thelser (10B5); Nicea Nialia (11C1).

52. For example, Nasic–[– ? –]ndesina (1A5); Artane–Templ(vm) Hercvlis (8A3); Magnesia–Ephesvm (8B5); Melantvm (9A3); Phaselis–Atalia–Sidi (all 9B2); Tamiso (9B3)–Cito (9C3); compare Narona (5A4)–Ad zizio (5A5).

53. Further possible instances: Bobiano–Clvtvrno (5B3); Rvdas (5B4); Ad pirvm (5B5).

54. See, for example, Avg Svessor(vm)–Baca conervio (1A4); Bibe (1A4); Monte (1C3); Gerainas (2B2); Libarnvm (2B5); Svrpicano–Firmoviceno (4B4); Marrvbio–Svblacio (5B1); Ad Pyr–Avfidena (5B3); Foro novo (5B4); Oplont[.]s–Pompeis (5B5, lower route); Grvmento–Tarento (6B1, lower route); Amavante–Cofna–helyacapitolina (9C1).

55. Further instances: on the ground, the Tentira stretch should immediately follow the Lato and Diospoli Q[–?–]tibe stretches, which it precedes on the map (all 8C2); likewise, Dydymos should precede Affrodites, not follow it (8C3). It seems possible that our copyist was about to transpose Genesis Fl. and Hapsvm Fl. (both 6A2), but then corrected himself rather clumsily.

56. See above, Chap. 1, secs. 2 and 4, with Appendix 3.

Chapter Five: The Original Map

1. *ItMiller*, XXVI–XXXVI.

2. See L. Dillemann, *La cosmographie du Ravennate* (Brussels, 1997), 47–58, especially 52–53; for a trenchant summary, Gautier Dalché (2003), 43–44. It remains possible that the cosmographer's Castorius was a real person who lived and wrote at another date; but any such speculation is irrelevant here.

3. M. Giacchero (ed.), *Edictum Diocletiani et Collegarum de Pretiis Rerum Venalium*, vol. 1 (Genoa, 1974), 7, 9.

4. For all these practical arrangements, see R. Ling, *Roman Painting* (Cambridge, 1991), 212–20.

5. For some discussion, see R. J. A. Talbert, "Rome's Marble Plan and Peutinger's Map: Continuity in Cartographic Design," in Beutler and Hameter (2005), 627–34. On the Plan, see further above, Chap. 3, n. 51.

6. The title Dacicus Maximus, taken by Constantine in 336, suggests successful campaigning there: see *AE* (1934), 158, with T. D. Barnes, *Constantine and Eusebius* (Cambridge, MA, 1981), 250.

7. The relationship between the map and the Cosmography is discussed further below, in my Conclusion, sec. 2 (a).

8. E. Albu, "Imperial Geography and the Medieval Peutinger Map," *Imago Mundi* 57 (2005): 136–48; ead., "Rethinking the Peutinger Map," in Talbert and Unger (2008), 111–19.

9. Note the doubts expressed successively by B. Salway, "The Nature and Genesis of the Peutinger Map," *Imago Mundi* 57 (2005): 119–35, in particular concerning the relationship between the map and the Ravenna cosmographer's sources (125–27); and by P. Gautier Dalché, "L'héritage antique de la cartographie médiévale: les problèmes et les acquis," in Talbert and Unger (2008), 29–66, at 47–50.

10. For instructive analysis of how Carolingian scholars preserved the Roman geographical tradition and exploited it for contemporary purposes, see N. Lozovsky, "Roman Geography and Ethnography in the Carolingian Empire," *Speculum* 81 (2006): 325–64, especially 355.

11. For Constantinople as an addition to the map, see Chap. 4, sec. 1. For the map's evident failure to recognize the standard fourth-century route from Constantinople across Asia Minor to Syrian Antioch, see Chap. 3, n. 152.

12. For useful overviews of the regime, see especially R. Rees, *Diocletian and the Tetrarchy* (Edinburgh, 2004); *CAH*, 2nd ed., vol. 12 (2005), 67–89 (by A. K. Bowman), 170–81 (by E. Lo Cascio).

13. The scrappy testimony for the map is assembled in *GLM*, 1–8. For the Porticus Vipsania (its precise location still uncertain), see s.v. in *LTUR*, vol. 4 (1999), 151–53.

14. The claim is made by Brodersen (1995), 268–87, and gains support from S. Carey, *Pliny's Catalogue of Culture: Art and Empire in the* Natural History (Oxford, 2003), chap. 3.

15. For an overview, see K. Geus, "Space and Geography," in A. Erskine (ed.), *A Companion to the Hellenistic World* (Oxford, 2003), 232–45; more fully, K. Geus, *Eratosthenes von Kyrene. Studien zur hellenistischen Kultur- und Wissenschaftsgeschichte* (Munich, 2002). For the *diaphragma*, see O. A. W. Dilke in *HistCart*, vol. 1 (1987), 152.

16. There are no remains of this school; even its site within the city has yet to be identified. See A. Rebourg (ed.), *Carte archéologique de la Gaule* 71/1 and 2, *Autun* (Paris, 1993), especially 1, p. 32.

17. G. Woolf, *Becoming Roman: The Origins of Provincial Civilization in Gaul* (Cambridge, 1998), 1–3 and 12–13, re-creates the scene. For discussion of the speech, see R. Rees, *Layers of Loyalty in Latin Panegyric, AD 289–307* (Oxford, 2002), chap. 4.

18. *Panegyrici Latini* 9(4).20.2.–21.3 (Mynors). See further C. E. V. Nixon and B. S. Rodgers, *In Praise of Later Roman Emperors: The* Panegyrici Latini (Berkeley, CA, 1994), 171–77, on whose translation mine is based. As Riese notes in his Prolegomena to *GLM* (p. xvii), it is conceivable that the pair of curious Latin texts *Dimensuratio Provinciarum* and *Divisio Orbis*

Terrarum – each distinctly different, despite many identical elements – comprise the captions (thirty and twenty-five respectively) to accompany sets of regional maps for school use (*GLM*, 9–14, 15–19)

19. *GLM*, 19–20, with Meyer's "priorum" in line 10. These verses are preserved in several manuscripts of the ninth to twelfth centuries: see N. Lozovsky, "Maps and Panegyrics: Roman Geo-ethnographical Rhetoric in Late Antiquity and the Middle Ages," in Talbert and Unger (2008), 169–88, at 172–73.

20. For persuasive arguments that the author of these verses is the expert copyist Aemilius Probus, and that the concluding mention of Theodosius' instructive wisdom refers to his well-known interest in calligraphy, see A. Cameron, "Petronius Probus, Aemilius Probus and the Transmission of Nepos: A Note on Late Roman Calligraphers," in J.-M. Carrié and R. Lizzi Testa (eds.), *"Humana Sapit": Etudes d'antiquité tardive offertes à Lellia Cracco Ruggini* (Turnhout [Belgium], 2002), 121–30, at 125–26. It is fitting that the only Roman emperor's signature that happens to have survived is that of Theodosius: see D. Feissel and K. A. Worp, "La requête d'Appion, évêque de Syène, à Théodose II: P.Leid. Z révisé," *Oudheidkundige Mededelingen van het Rijksmuseum van Oudheden te Leiden* 68 (1988): 97–111.

21. See further below, Conclusion, sec. 1.

22. For this private compilation, which is loosely organized, repetitive, and far from comprehensive, see Map E and Appendix 9 (a), with discussion by R. J. A. Talbert, "Author, Audience and the Roman Empire in the *Antonine Itinerary*," in R. Haensch and J. Heinrichs (eds.), *Der Alltag der römischen Administration in der Hohen Kaiserzeit* (Cologne, Weimar, Berlin, 2007), 256–70.

23. For perceptive appreciation of one private record made in the early 320s, note J. Matthews, *The Journey of Theophanes: Travel, Business, and Daily Life in the Roman East* (New Haven, CT, 2006), especially 56–61, 130–32.

24. For instances, see Chap. 3, sec. 4 (b). Maritime itineraries are discussed by Salway (2004), 77–87.

25. See Map F and Appendix 9 (b).

26. From M. Calzolari, "Ricerche sugli itinerari romani. L'Itinerarium Burdigalense," in *Studi in onore di Nereo Alfieri* (*Atti dell'Accademia delle Scienze di Ferrara* 74 Supplemento, 1997), 127–89, at 147–51. Naturally, some differences in distance figures may have been introduced by copyists' slips.

27. On his practice, see further above, Chap. 3, sec. 4.

28. Compare, for example, the Late Antique catalog of names for peoples and various categories of physical feature, all extracted from poets and attributed to Vibius Sequester, *De Fluminibus, Fontibus, Lacubus, Nemoribus, Paludibus, Montibus, Gentibus per Litteras* (*GLM*, 145–59).

29. As Vibius uses, and as is also the map's typical practice for the names of physical features.

30. The former's description of, say, Italy (in Book 3) is too full and breathless. Readers of the latter might fairly conclude that any place listed in the *Geography* has some significance (the more so if *kolonia* is appended to the name), but the relatively few cities Ptolemy distinguishes as *episemoi* (notable) seem to be marked thus only for establishing a map framework. As it happens, several cities in Italy listed by him are not marked by a symbol on the Peutinger map, including Tergeste and Cremona, both termed *kolonia* by Ptolemy (3.1.27 and 31). See further in general Berggren and Jones

(2000), 19–20. Observe that in the reconstructed Ptolemy maps presented by C. Müller (*Claudii Ptolemaei Geographia: Tabulae XXXVI* [Paris, 1901]) to accompany his text of the *Geography*, many of the cities distinguished by larger type as more important are merely his own choices.

31. See C. Nicolet, *Financial Documents and Geographical Knowledge in the Roman World*, J. L. Myres Memorial Lecture (Oxford, 1996), 22–23. The late fifth-early sixth-century listing of cities province by province attributed to Hierocles no doubt has its origin in such *formulae*; see E. Honigmann (ed.), *Le Synekdèmos d'Hiéroklès et l'Opuscule Géographique de Georges de Chypre* (Brussels, 1939), with *BAtlas*, Map 102.

32. See A. J. Silverstein, *Postal Systems in the Pre-Modern Islamic World* (Cambridge, 2007), 7–28; and P. Briant, "From the Indus to the Mediterranean: Administration and Logistics on the Highroads of the Achaemenid Empire," in Talbert, Bodel, and Alcock, *Highways* (forthcoming).

33. *SEG* 45 (1995): 1879, 1880, with P. Callieri and P. Bernard, "Une borne routière grecque de la région de Persepolis," *CRAI* (1995): 65–95. Although Bernard's contribution in particular greatly enlarges upon the original topic, his discussion happens not to take into consideration data from the Peutinger map.

34. *FGH*, 781. See further F. Millar, "Caravan Cities: The Roman Near East and Long-distance Trade by Land," in id., *Rome, the Greek World, and the East*, vol. 3 (Chapel Hill, NC, 2006; originally published 1998), 275–99, and literature cited there, 277, n. 5.

35. *Annals* 11.8.3, where some slip or misunderstanding seems probable, because 3,000 stades can hardly have been covered in only two days.

36. Note especially Pliny, *NH* 6.63 with G. Parker, *The Making of Roman India* (Cambridge, 2007), 51–53.

37. 15.1.50, ὁδοποιοῦσι δὲ καὶ κατὰ δέκα στάδια στήλην τιθέασι, τὰς ἐκτροπὰς καὶ τὰ διαστήματα δηλοῦσαν.

38. R. Thapar, *Asoka and the Decline of the Mauryas*, rev. ed. (Oxford, 1997), 265. For discussion of how the distance interval specified here should be read, see Callieri and Bernard (1995), 90. The length of a *kos* is in turn uncertain, perhaps 2 km.

39. See above, Chap. 3, sec. 4 (b).

40. See R. H. Hewsen, *The Geography of Ananias of Sirak: The Long and the Short Recensions*, *TAVO* Beihefte B77 (Wiesbaden, 1992), 281 and Appendix VI.

41. Hewsen (1992), 15.

42. The *Geography* itself demonstrates comparable attention to different units: see Hewsen (1992), sec. 6 on 43, 43A with 80–81.

43. Greek Doubios (*BAtlas*, 88 C4). Compare Ecbatanis Partiorvm (11C1) as nodal point on the Peutinger map.

44. See further above, Chap. 3, sec. 4 (a).

45. See Chap. 2, secs. 1 and 2 (e) above, and Conclusion, sec. 2 (c) below, respectively.

46. For a comparable attempt, note R. Brilliant, "The Bayeux Tapestry: A Stripped Narrative for Their Eyes and Ears," *Word and Image* 7 (1991): 93–125, reprinted in R. Gameson (ed.), *The Study of the Bayeux Tapestry* (Woodbridge, England, 1997), chap. 10.

47. Note in this connection P. Gautier Dalché, "Les sens de *mappa (mundi)*: IVe-XIVe siècle," *Archivum Latinitatis Medii Aevi* 62 (2004): 187–202; id., "Agrimensure et inventaire du monde: La fortune de '*Mappa (Mundi)*' au

Moyen Âge," in D. Conso et al. (eds.), *Les vocabulaires techniques des arpenteurs romains* (Besançon, 2005), 163–71, at 163–65.

48. 3.6.4; the date is discussed by M. D. Reeve in his edition (Oxford, 2004), v and viii–x.

49. See above, Chap. 1, sec. 1.

50. See Brodersen (1995), 59–65, with K. Garland, *Mr Beck's Underground Map* (London, 1994), especially Fig. 13 by comparison with Fig. 7. More recently, K. Brodersen, "Die Tabula Peutingeriana: Gehalt und Gestalt einer 'alten Karte' und ihrer antiken Vorlagen," in D. Unverhau (ed.), *Geschichtsdeutung auf alten Karten: Archäologie und Geschichte*, Wolfenbütteler Forschungen 101 (Wiesbaden, 2003), 289–97.

51. Garland (1994), 17.

52. See above, Chap. 1, sec. 4 (a).

53. See W. A. Johnson, *Bookrolls and Scribes in Oxyrhynchus* (Toronto, 2004). The map matches the standard height of between 25 and 33 cm ($9\frac{3}{4}$ and 13 in.) for a roll of text during the Roman period in Johnson's sample (141–43); he finds no standard length for such a roll, although many were clearly much longer than the map (143–52).

54. The friezes on the Columns of Trajan and Marcus Aurelius can in turn be considered to recall scrolls, as discussed by F. Coarelli, *The Column of Trajan* (Rome, 2000), 11.

55. For this monument, see below, Conclusion, n. 5.

56. Fourth-century Roman senators' boasts about their travels, as mockingly represented by Ammianus Marcellinus (28.4.18), come to mind.

57. Note Suetonius, *Domitian* 10 with *PIR²* M 570 (Mettius Pompusianus), and P. Arnaud, "L'affaire Mettius Pompusianus ou le crime de cartographie," *MEFRA* 95 (1983): 677–99.

58. The literature on this theme is vast. See, for example, P. J. Holliday, *The Origins of Roman Historical Commemoration in the Visual Arts* (Cambridge, 2002), especially 104–21; Beard (2007), 143–86; Östenberg (2009), 189–261.

59. *De Mortibus Persecutorum* 5.3, ed. J. L. Creed (Oxford, 1984).

60. For a tapestry world map (of unknown size) presented by a high-ranking lady to a Roman emperor no later than Nero, see *Anthologia Palatina*, 9.778 (Philip of Thessalonica), with discussion by J. M. Scott, *Geography in Early Judaism and Christianity:* The Book of Jubilees (Cambridge, 2002), chap. 1. The size (each approximately 4 meters high by 6.5, 13 x 20 ft.) and colorful topographic detail of the four late-sixteenth-century "Sheldon" tapestry maps of English counties demonstrate what may be achieved in wool and silk: see H. L. Turner, "The Sheldon Tapestry Maps: Their Content and Context," *Cartographic Journal* 40 (2003): 39–49, and studies cited there.

61. For bibliography, see L. Lavan, "Political Life in Late Antiquity: A Bibliographic Essay," 3–40, in W. Bowden et al. (eds.), *Social and Political Life in Late Antiquity* (Leiden and Boston [MA], 2006), at 6–11 and 37–40; I. Uytterhoeven, "Housing in Late Antiquity: Thematic Perspectives," in L. Lavan et al. (eds.), *Housing in Late Antiquity: From Palaces to Shops* (Leiden and Boston [MA], 2007), 25–66, at 33–39. For discussion, see R. Smith, "The Imperial Court of the Late Roman Empire," in A. J. S. Spawforth (ed.), *The Court and Court Society in Ancient Monarchies* (Cambridge, 2007), 157–232, especially 187–96. Multiple means designed to impress visitors to the Byzantine

court are appreciated in F. A. Bauer (ed.), *Visualisierungen von Herrschaft. Frühmittelalterliche Residenzen. Gestalt und Zeremoniell* (Istanbul, 2006), valuably reviewed by R. Pfeilschifter, "The Great Palace at Constantinople Put into Context," *JRA* 21 (2008): 727–33.

62. For sketches see, for example, N. Duval, "Existe-t-il une 'structure palatiale' propre à l'Antiquité tardive?" in E. Lévy (ed.), *Le système palatial en Orient, en Grèce et à Rome* (Strasbourg, 1987), 463–90, at 474, 476; and J. Arce, "Emperadores, palacios y *villae* (A propósito de la villa romana de Cercadilla, Córdoba)," *Antiquité Tardive* 5 (1997): 293–302, at 295–96.

63. See J. J. Wilkes, *Diocletian's Palace, Split: Residence of a Retired Roman Emperor,* rev. ed. (Oxford, 1993), 60, 62, 72–73, with fig. 4 and n. 173 for comparative dimensions. The hall measures 32 meters by 14 (105 × 46 ft.); the curving course of the apse wall measures 12.1 meters ($39\frac{3}{4}$ ft.) between the spurs at either side. For further discussion of the hall, see S. McNally et al., *Diocletian's Palace: American-Yugoslav Joint Excavations,* vol. 5 (Minneapolis, 1989), 27–28.

64. The map could be conveniently extended as open water to any desired extent left and right. Appropriate decoration for such expanses can be seen on the "Dura shield" map (see above, Chap. 3, n. 53), not to mention the medieval Gough map (see my Conclusion, sec. 3).

65. Michael Hummelberg's description in 1526: see above, Chap. 3, n. 36.

66. *Geography* 1.1.1.

67. See R. R. R. Smith, "*Simulacra gentium*: The *ethne* from the Sebasteion at Aphrodisias," *JRS* 78 (1988): 50–77, at 51–53, with plate VII (3) and (4). Wholly imaginary, but still instructive, is the setting remarked upon by Philostratus (*Vita Apollonii* 1.25.3) when Apollonius of Tyana and his companions visit the men's quarters in the palace at Babylon, "... with a domed roof imitating a kind of sky, roofed with sapphire (this stone is very blue and heavenly to look at)," φασὶ δὲ καὶ ἀνδρῶνι ἐντυχεῖν, οὗ τὸν ὄροφον ἐς θόλου ἀνῆχθαι σχῆμα οὐρανῷ τινι εἰκασμένον, σαπφειρίνῃ δὲ αὐτὸν κατηρέφθαι λίθῳ (κυανωτάτη δὲ ἡ λίθος καὶ οὐρανία ἰδεῖν). Translation by C. P. Jones in the Loeb series (2005); notionally, in Jones's view (7), Philostratus imagines this visit to have taken place around the mid-first century A.D.

68. Rees (2004), 50; see further S. G. MacCormack, *Art and Ceremony in Late Antiquity* (Berkeley, CA, 1981), 176–77.

69. *NP* s.v. "Zone 2," with G. Irby-Massie, "Mapping the World: Greek Initiatives from Homer to Eratosthenes," in R. J. A. Talbert (ed.), *Ancient Perspectives: Maps and Their Place in Mesopotamia, Egypt, Greece, and Rome* (Chicago, forthcoming).

70. See Romm (1992), 60–67; and more fully, T. P. Bridgman, *Hyperboreans: Myth and History in Celtic-Hellenic Contacts* (New York and London, 2005), chaps. 1–4.

71. Appian, *Roman History*, Preface 7; Plutarch, *Life of Theseus* 1.1, 'Τὰ δ' ἐπέκεινα θῖνες ἄνυδροι καὶ θηριώδεις' ἢ 'πηλὸς ἀΐδνὴς' ἢ 'Σκυθικὸν κρύος' ἢ 'πέλαγος πεπηγός'·

72. Note, for example, Y. Shahar, *Josephus Geographicus: The Classical Context of Geography in Josephus* (Tübingen, 2004), 169–89; P. Hardie, *Virgil's Aeneid: Cosmos and Imperium* (Oxford, 1986), chap. 7; C. Nicolet, *Space, Geography and Politics in the Early Roman Empire* (Ann Arbor, MI, 1991) 29–56.

73. For the full context, see C. Schuler, "Augustus, Gott und Herr über Land und Meer. Eine neue Inschrift aus Tyberissos im Kontext der späthellenistischen Herrscherverehrung," *Chiron* 37 (2007): 383–403.

74. S. Şahin and M. Adak, *Stadiasmus Patarensis: Itinera Romana Provinciae Lyciae* (Istanbul, 2007), 36–37 (Left Face, lines 3–4).

75. For wide-ranging reflections on cartography and empire, note, for example, C. Jacob, *The Sovereign Map: Theoretical Approaches in Cartography Throughout History* (Chicago and London, 2006), 318–27; J. R. Akerman (ed.), *The Imperial Map: Cartography and the Mastery of Empire* (Chicago, 2009).

76. Note especially C. R. Whittaker, "'To Reach Out to India and Pursue the Dawn': The Roman View of India," in id., *Rome and Its Frontiers: The Dynamics of Empire* (London and New York, 2004), 144–62; and Parker (2007), 203–27 and 240–50.

77. While this ivory's representation of the emperor and Christ as virtual partners in cosmic rule is not in doubt, the specific identifications of Justinian and of Indians among his subjects cannot be verified. See H. Maguire, *Earth and Ocean: The Terrestrial World in Early Byzantine Art* (University Park [PA] and London, 1987), 75–76; Parker (2007), 128–31 = his "Images of Mediterranean India: Representing the Subcontinent in Ancient Greek and Roman Art," in G. Parker and C. M. Sinopoli (eds.), *Ancient India in Its Wider World* (Ann Arbor, MI, 2008), 106–26, at 113.

78. See J. R. Curran, *Pagan City and Christian Capital: Rome in the Fourth Century* (Oxford, 2000), 43–90; Lavan, in Bowden et al. (2006), 29–31; C. Machado, "Building the Past: Monuments and Memory in the *Forum Romanum*," in ibid., 157–92, at 161–68.

79. That is, twenty years of rule, and ten, respectively.

80. That is, in effect into provinces like the rest of the empire, although the choice of *regio* was intended as a tactful means to obscure the effect of the demotion; even so, use of the term *provincia* is also found. See further G. A. Cecconi, "Sulla denominazione dei distretti di tipo provinciale nell'Italia tardoantica," *Athenaeum* 82 (1994): 177–84.

81. For all these themes see, for example, Rees (2002).

82. The metaphor is used by Constantine, responding in the mid-330s to a request from Hispellum in Umbria to erect a temple to the imperial family (*ILS*, 705, line 11).

83. For this outlook see, for example, R. J. A. Talbert, "Rome's Provinces as Framework for World-view," in L. De Ligt et al. (eds.), *Roman Rule and Civic Life: Local and Regional Perspectives* (Amsterdam, 2004), 21–37; B. Campbell, "'Setting up True Boundaries': Land Disputes in the Roman Empire," *Mediterraneo Antico: Economie, Società, Culture* 8.1 (2005): 307–43. Hellenistic cartography, too, as reflected in Ptolemy's *Geography*, shares a preoccupation with boundaries.

84. See Rees (2002), 1–5. For the Tetrarchs' travels in detail, see Barnes (1982), 47–87.

85. Giacchero (1974), lines 148–50 (p. 137).

86. Ibid., lines 16–26 (p. 134). For discussion of the edict's preamble, see S. Corcoran, *The Empire of the Tetrarchs: Imperial Pronouncements and Government AD 284–324*, rev. ed. (Oxford, 2000), 207–13, who also draws attention to the recurrence of its themes on Tetrarchic coinage (*pacatores gentium*; *pax aeterna*; *securitas orbis*) and elsewhere.

87. See Barnes (1982), 201–25, and compare *BAtlas*, Map 100 with 101.

88. See Corcoran (2000), especially 259–60, 295–96.

89. In this connection, and others treated below, note R. MacMullen, "Some Pictures in Ammianus," in id., *Changes in the Roman Empire: Essays in the Ordinary* (Princeton, NJ, 1990; originally published 1964), 78–106, at p. 101.

90. See M. Roberts, *The Jeweled Style: Poetry and Poetics in Late Antiquity* (Ithaca [NY] and London, 1989), 111–18, with M. R. Salzman, *On Roman Time: The Codex-Calendar of 354 and the Rhythms of Urban Life in Late Antiquity* (Berkeley, CA, 1990), 34.

91. Roberts (1989), 73–76.

92. This is J. O. Thomson's reaction; see his *History of Ancient Geography* (Cambridge, 1948), 379–81, and my Preface above.

93. See R. Syme, *Emperors and Biography: Studies in the Historia Augusta* (Oxford, 1971), especially 63–64, 273–74.

94. Note the observations by T. Murphy, *Pliny the Elder's* Natural History: *The Empire in the Encyclopedia* (Oxford, 2004), 45–48.

95. Cf. Pliny, *NH* 3.101.

96. Note Roberts (1989), 59–62.

97. This is the visual impact achieved earlier by the Severan Marble Plan of Rome. Texts of comparable force are a fourth-century Latin catalog enumerating multiple features of each of Rome's fourteen regions (R. Valentini and G. Zucchetti [eds.], *Codice topografico della città di Roma*, vol. 1 [Rome, 1940], 89–192), and a fifth-century equivalent for Constantinople (O. Seeck [ed.], *Notitia Dignitatum* [Berlin, 1876], 227–43). A fragment of an earlier such catalog for Alexandria is also known: see P. M. Fraser, "A Syriac Notitia Urbis Alexandrinae," *Journal of Egyptian Archaeology* 37 (1951): 103–108; and, more generally, J. Arce, "El inventario de Roma: *Curiosum* y *Notitia*," in W. V. Harris (ed.), *The Transformation of Vrbs Roma in Late Antiquity* (Portsmouth, RI, 1999), 15–22.

98. See Roberts (1989), 57–58; S. McGill, *Virgil Recomposed: The Mythological and Secular Centos in Antiquity* (Oxford, 2005).

99. See J.-J. Aillagon (ed.), *Rome and the Barbarians: The Birth of a New World* (Milan, 2008), 86–91, 611–13 (by C. Panella).

100. Compare the *mappamundi* taken by King Henry VIII of England on his royal progresses (noted above, Introduction, n. 9).

Conclusion: The Map's Place in Classical and Medieval Cartography

1. For overviews see, for example, s.v. "Karte (Kartographie)," *RAC*, vol. 20 (2001), cols. 187–229 (F. Prontera); s.v. "Cartography," *Brill's New Pauly* 2 (2003), cols. 1138–43 (Talbert).

2. Ptolemy (*Geog.* 8.1.2) deplored maps known to him that showed Asia or Africa as smaller than Europe because the two former were "emptier" regions; but these are maps of a scientific type all the same. The Caspian Sea and Persian Gulf occupy the center of his own world map at a uniform scale, and this map was consciously austere and "unpolitical" in character, as A. Jones emphasizes in the conclusion to his "Ptolemy's Geography: Mapmaking and the Scientific Enterprise," in R. J. A. Talbert (ed.), *Ancient Perspectives: Maps and Their Place in Mesopotamia, Egypt, Greece and Rome* (Chicago, forthcoming).

3. See above, Chap. 5, sec. 2.

4. See, for example, A. Vasaly, *Representations: Images of the World in Ciceronian Oratory* (Berkeley, CA, 1993), esp. 133–39; E. Dench, *Romulus' Asylum: Roman Identities from the Age of Alexander to the Age of Hadrian* (Oxford, 2005), esp. 60.

5. See *LTUR*, vol. 3 (1996), 250–51, s.v. "Miliarium aureum." A corresponding μίλιον was erected at Constantinople: see W. Müller-Wiener, *Bildlexikon zur Topographie Istanbuls* (Tübingen, 1977), s.v. "Milion." The monument erected at Patara in Lycia during the 40s A.D. (see above, Chap. 5 n. 74) may have been intended to recall Rome's *miliarium aureum;* notably, much of its information about routes can have had no more than symbolic value, because it would have been set too high up for viewers to read.

6. See further B. Salway, "Putting the World in Order: Mapping in Roman Texts," in Talbert (ed.), *Ancient Perspectives*.

7. Ed. T. Mommsen (Berlin, 1895).

8. The sole unequivocal instance is no more than a product of the imagination. In Apollonius Rhodius' third-century B.C. epic (*Argonautica* 4.277–81, Race trans.), Argus tells Jason and the Argonauts of a possible alternative route for their return from Aia. Aia, Argus explains, is by origin an Egyptian foundation of long ago; it still exists. Moreover, its people "preserve writings of their ancestors, tablets on which are all the routes and limits of the sea and the land for those who traverse them in every direction." οἳ δή τοι γραπτῦς πατέρων ἔθεν εἰρύονται, / κύρβιας, οἷς ἔνι πᾶσαι ὁδοὶ καὶ πείρατ᾽ ἔασιν / ὑγρῆς τε τραφερῆς τε πέριξ ἐπινισσομένοισιν. Identification of line work on the unfinished Artemidorus map as routes remains open to doubt: see Gallazzi (2008), 289–91, 296–97, with Talbert (2009), 61–62.

9. On these issues, see further R. Talbert, "Roads Not Featured: A Roman Failure to Communicate?" in id., J. Bodel and S. Alcock (eds.), *Highways, Byways and Road Systems in the Pre-Modern World* (forthcoming).

10. Ptolemy begins his *Geography* (1.1) by explaining the distinction, as he sees it, between *geographia* (world cartography) and *chorographia* (regional cartography).

11. Another version reads: "in rotulo I." As it happens, this is the earliest attested use of the term *mappamundi:* see Gautier Dalché, *Archivum Latinitatis Medii Aevi* (2004); id. (2005).

12. For documentation and further discussion of both records, see Gautier Dalché (2003), 46–47.

13. The standard edition is by J. Schnetz in *Itineraria Romana*, vol. 2 (Leipzig: Teubner, 1940), reissued with an index by M. Zumschlinge (Stuttgart, 1990).

14. On the character and aims of his work, note N. Lozovsky, *"The Earth Is Our Book": Geographical Knowledge in the Latin West ca. 400–1000* (Ann Arbor, MI, 2000), esp. 30–33, 145–46.

15. The complex issues concerning his sources are discussed best by Dillemann (1997), part 1, esp. 38–40 with reference to the Peutinger map.

16. These shortcomings, and others, inevitably hamper efforts to reconstruct the lost lefthand end of the Peutinger map on the basis of data preserved by the cosmographer. In this regard, the boldness of A. L. F. Rivet and C. Smith, *The Place-Names of Roman Britain* (London, 1979), esp. chap. 5, is rightly appraised with caution by B. Jones and D. Mattingly, *An Atlas of Roman Britain* (Oxford, 1990), 29–33.

17. For illustration with reference to Pannonia and Numidia, see Dillemann (1997), 41–42.

18. See ibid., 167–80.

19. Discussion by Dillemann in ibid., 47, 113–14.

20. For a definitive study of this aspect, see J. Williams, *The Illustrated Beatus: A Corpus of the Illustrations of the Commentary on the Apocalypse*, 5 vols. (London, 1994–2003). A valuable overview of the commentary, with special reference to the map, is offered by E. Edson, *Mapping Time and Space: How Medieval Mapmakers Viewed Their World* (London, 1997), 149–59.

21. Williams (1994–2003), vol. 1, p. 51.

22. See J. Williams, "Isidore, Orosius and the Beatus map," *Imago Mundi* 49 (1997): 7–32.

23. Williams (1994–2003), vol. 2, no. 2, and plates 27–28.

24. Ibid., vol. 4, no. 4, and plate 5.

25. Ibid., vol. 3, no. 13, and plate 392 (with color reproduction in vol. 1, plate 8).

26. For a complete annotated listing, see K. Miller, *Mappaemundi*, vol. 1 (1895), 41–61.

27. The claim is made in detail by E. Schweder, "Über eine Weltkarte des achten Jahrhunderts," *Hermes* 24 (1889): 587–604, and supported by H. Gross, *Zur Entstehungs-Geschichte der Tabula Peutingeriana* (Bonn, 1913), 89–95.

28. See the edition and discussion by P. Gautier Dalché, *La "Descriptio Mappe Mundi" de Hugues de Saint-Victor* (Paris, 1988), 62–66, 173–78.

29. Westrem, in his indispensable edition (2001), takes the Antonine Itinerary to be the source of many names marked, especially in Africa (xxix–xxx, 429–31); but some, if not all, of these could equally well have been transmitted through maps such as the Peutinger map.

30. Gautier Dalché (2003), 47–48; more fully in id., "Du nouveau sur la transmission et la découverte de la *Tabula Peutingeriana*: La 'Cosmographia vetustissima' de Pellegrino Prisciani (+1518)," *Geographia Antiqua* 13 (2004): 71–84. When attention was first drawn to this sketch in an article published in 1981, its significance for the circulation and impact of the Peutinger map was entirely overlooked (Gautier Dalché [2004], 74, n. 21).

31. *BAtlas Directory*, p. 593 (Map 40, unlocated toponym).

32. M. L. King, *Venetian Humanism in an Age of Patrician Dominance* (Princeton, NJ, 1986), 284–85, 421–22.

33. Ibid., 447–49.

34. Prisciani's fullest Latin account (paraphrased above) reads: "Ha/buit nanque Italia picturam ipsam concilii Basiliensis tempore ut ab magistro quondam. P./ D. Tadeo Quirinio nobili Veneto quondam cathedralis ęcclesię ipsius Paduanę/ archipresbytero. accepimus: oratorum Venetorum: serenissimi dominii illius nomine et/ summi pontificis precibus et opera. Praecariam nanque nimis Germania designationem/ ipsam habebat. Quam postea Jacobus Zeno patritius Venetus et Paduę episco/ pus habuit et episcopio moriens reliquit." (Gautier Dalché [2004], 82). Zeno's successors were first Pietro Foscari (to 1485; King [1986], 373–74), and then Pietro Barozzi (1487–1507; King [1986], 333–35).

35. See, for example, J. W. Stieber, *Pope Eugenius IV, the Council of Basel and the Secular and Ecclesiastical Authorities in the Empire: The Conflict over Supreme Authority and Power in the Church* (Leiden, 1978), 10–57.

36. See, for example, in brief, D. Romano, *The Likeness of Venice: A Life of Doge Francesco Foscari, 1373–1457* (New Haven [CT] and London, 2007), 120, 124, 135–36; in detail, A. Niero, "L'azione veneziana al Concilio di Basilea (1431–1436)," in id. et al., *Venezia e i Concili* (Venice, 1962), 3–46.

37. King (1986), 370–72; more fully, *Dizionario biografico degli italiani*, vol. 40 (1991) cols. 789–94, s.v. "Donà, Pietro" (by A. Menniti Ippolito). Note further the wide-ranging study by I. Holgate, "Paduan Culture in Venetian Care: Bishop Pietro Donato (Padua 1428–47)," *Renaissance Studies* 16 (2002): 1–23.

38. At least the Carolingian manuscript listed (no. 94) in the inventory of Donato's library (see below) as *Eusebius de Temporibus in littera vetustissima*, now in Merton College, Oxford (MS 315), is thought to have been brought by him from Reichenau to Padua; see J. Martineau (ed.), *Andrea Mantegna* (New York and London, 1992), 123–25.

39. See R. Sabbadini, *Le scoperte dei codici latini e greci ne' secoli XIV e XV*, vol. 1 (Florence, 1905), 119–20.

40. Canon. Misc. 378 = no. 599 in O. Pächt and J. J. G. Alexander, *Illuminated Manuscripts in the Bodleian Library Oxford*, vol. 2 (Oxford, 1970), superseding the entry no. 666 in vol. 1 (1966). As a word of caution, it should be stressed that Donato's discovery of this volume at Speyer, let alone a Eusebius at Reichenau, does not make it any more likely that either library also held our copy of the Peutinger map; see further in this connection above, Chap. 1, n. 7 and Chap. 2 sec. 2 (e).

41. Most notably *ItAnt* and *Notitia Dignitatum*. The full contents of the volume are listed by Seeck (1876), p. x; Sabbadini (1905), 119–20.

42. No. 209. See P. Sambin, "La biblioteca di Pietro Donato (1380–1447)," *Bollettino del Museo Civico di Padova* 48 (1959): 53–98.

43. Nor any mention, Gautier Dalché notes (*Geographia Antiqua* [2004], p. 75), in a comparable inventory of Zeno's library made in 1482 by Foscari and witnessed by Quirini.

44. Two further points of note are that Donato's scribes continued to maintain extensive contacts in Germany (Holgate [2002], 13–14), and that he himself befriended the "father of classical archaeology," Cyriacus of Ancona, who visited him in Padua in 1437 and again in 1442–43: see Holgate (2002), 19–21, with E. W. Bodnar and C. Foss (eds. and trans.), *Cyriac of Ancona: Later Travels*, I Tatti series (Cambridge, MA, 2003), esp. plate II.

45. King (1986), 357–59.

46. The term does not appear in the detailed examination of palace records (*Registri Spese* in particular) offered by R. Zanocco in the first and second parts of his article "Il palazzo vescovile attuale nella storia e nell'arte (1309–1567)," *Bollettino Diocesano di Padova* 13 (1928): 175–92, 243–58, 334–42. There is ample confirmation here of the immense amount of building and decorating work commissioned by Zeno (182–83) and Barozzi ("il piccolo Papa di Lombardia," 258). For background, note M. C. Miller, *The Bishop's Palace: Architecture and Authority in Medieval Italy* (Ithaca [NY] and London, 2000).

47. See further above, Chap. 1, sec. 1.

48. See further below, Appendix 6 and Plate 26.

49. Miller, in his single reference to the discovery (*ItMiller*, xxvi, n. 1, righthand column), notes the misidentification, but does not document it. He makes

no mention of the matter previously, either in *Die Weltkarte* (1887; cf. p. 40) or in *Mappaemundi*, vol. 6 (1898).

50. See, in the first instance, N. Millea, *The Gough Map: The Earliest Road Map of Britain?* (Oxford, 2007), with http://143.117.30.60/website/GoughMap/viewer.htm. For further discussion of certain aspects, note C. D. Lloyd and K. D. Lilley, "Cartographic Veracity in Medieval Mapping: Analyzing Geographical Variation in the Gough Map of Great Britain," *Annals of the Association of American Geographers* 99.1 (2009): 27–48; K. D. Lilley and C. D. Lloyd, "Mapping Places: A New Look at the Gough Map of Great Britain (c. 1360)," *Imago Mundi* 61 (2009): 1–28; P. Barber (2009), 21–34.

51. On the roads, see especially B. P. Hindle, "The Towns and Roads of the Gough Map (c. 1360)," *Manchester Geographer* 1 (1980): 35–49, who recognizes similarities to the Peutinger map. Note, however, that his categories of main, secondary, and local roads and branches are not reflected on the Gough map itself; all roads appear alike there, as they do on the Peutinger map.

52. At the end of his discussion, D. Birkholz, *The King's Two Maps: Cartography and Culture in Thirteenth-Century England* (New York and London, 2004), 83–88, comes closest to formulating this claim but never develops it. Some comparison of the Peutinger and Gough maps is also made by C. Delano-Smith, "Milieus of Mobility: Itineraries, Route Maps, and Road Maps," in J. R. Akerman (ed.), *Cartographies of Travel and Navigation* (Chicago, 2006), 16–66, at 58–59.

53. The body of scholarship on the origin and development of *mappaemundi* is immense. Note in particular Harvey (2006); Gautier Dalché (2008), 36–53; Lozovsky (2008).

Appendix Two: English Translation of J. Kastelic, "Vodnikova Kopija Tabule Peutingeriane"

1. L. Prijatelj, Veda 1, 1911, 130 n. 1. On Siauve (died 1812 during the retreat from Russia), see also J. M. Quérard, La France littéraire ix, 1838, 125f.; F. Kidrič, Slovstvo, 371, 374, 417.

2. Zois's correspondence (ZK) 1809–1810, 97ff. and index of persons under Heyrenbach, Peutinger, Scheyb, and Siauve.

3. ZK, 138.

4. ČJKZ 4, 1924, 161 Prijatelj.

5. For this journey, see F. Levec, LZ, 9, 1889, 408ff.

6. For Vodnik's comparisons, see also Mannert, loc. cit., p. II and esp. p. 39; K. Miller, Die Weltkarte des Castorius, Einleitender Text, 1888, 35; K. Miller, Itineraria Romana, 1916, xxv. Neither of these two of course knows of the Ljubljana copy. For a correct assessment of Vodnik's comparisons, cf. (in addition to the editions quoted) Welser-Arnoldus, Opera Velseri, 1682, 705–784.

7. J. Mal, Doneski k Vodnikovemu življenjepisu [Contributions to Vodnik's biography], DS, 31, 1918, 183ff.

8. Evidence: Vodnik als Archäolog und Historiker, Vodnik-Album, publ. by E. H. Costa, 37–39.

9. Evidence: Die Peutingersche Tafel und die Geographie des Ptolemäus im Bezug auf Krain, MhVK, 19, 1864, esp. 81 n. 1. – Hitzinger was the first to draw attention to Ptolemy, and the first to publish Ptolemy's map was L. Jelić, Mitth. aus Bosnien u. der Hercegovina, 7, 1900, plate VII. Jelić is of

course superseded by the monumental edition, which J. Fischer produced in vol. 18 of the facsimile series of Vatican manuscripts, 1932.

10. For Slovene archaeology of that time, see R. Ložar, Razvoj in problemi slovenske archeološke vede [Development and Problems of Slovene Archaeological Scholarship], ZUZ, 17, 1941, 112–116.

11. First published as: I. Grafenauer, Iz Kastelčeve zapuščine [From the Legacy of Kastelic], 1911, 34–36 (= Čas 4, 1910, 217–219).

Appendix Three: Reflections on Vodnik's Copy of Von Scheyb's Engraving

1. The tear has taken more from the upper part of the copy (which does not continue beyond the distance figure XXII following Oscanidati) than from the lower (B is the last remaining letter in TAPROBANE).

2. See Plate 4.

3. See above, Chap. 1, n. 133 and Plate 11.

Appendix Five: Miller's Reconstruction of the Map's Western End

1. This appendix draws upon my earlier study "Konrad Miller, Roman Cartography, and the Lost Western End of the Peutinger Map," in Fellmeth (2007), 353–66.

2. *Mappaemundi*, vol. VI. 90. "Nicht schwer," he later says likewise of reconstructing the Iberian Peninsula in the 1916 reissue of *Die Peutingersche Tafel* (7).

3. See above, Chap. 3, sec. 1 (a).

4. See ibid., sec. 2 (e).

5. As noted in ibid., sec. 1 (b).

6. See further ibid., sec. 2 (d).

7. It has to be doubted, too, whether the mapmaker marked the wall itself; for certain, he marked none of the empire's northern *limites*, nor any overtly military features. The altars (of Alexander) in 11A3 and 11B5, matched by Miller in northern Spain and Africa, may best be regarded as medieval embellishment.

8. Note *BAtlas*, 25 A2–D2, and 28, 29 respectively; *ItAnt*, 9, 1–2, "A Tingi litoribus navigatur usque ad Portus Divinos."

9. See above Chap. 3, sec. 4 (b).

10. See ibid., secs. 4 (a) and (b).

11. Numerical references are to Miller's five vertical subdivisions of the reconstruction; he makes no horizontal subdivision.

12. Also adequate, for example, are Belone (1 middle); Asturica (3 high); Mediolano (5 high) – provided that in each instance the applicable distance figure were to be a short one.

13. Esco to Adpvtea (7A1), for example, lacks both distance figure and chicane.

14. For example, Limea to Iria (1–2 high); horizontal route from Aug Bracaria (1–2 high); route from P(er)ora (2 low), three routes from Lagubalio (4 high).

15. See above, Chap. 3, n. 73.

16. See ibid., n. 186.

17. See ibid., nn. 221–23.

18. Compare, for example, the setting of all the names for symbols along the North African coast in the reconstruction with their counterparts in Segments 1–4. See further above, Chap. 3, sec. 2 (e).

19. See above, Chap. 3, n. 89.
20. Three routes from Lagubalio; from Seguntio, Mancunio, Isca Aug (all 4 high). Compare the route from P(er)ora (2 low).
21. See *BAtlas Directory*, p. 18.
22. Note most recently A. Santana Santana, *El Conocimiento Geográfico de la Costa Noroccidental de Africa en Plinio: La Posición de las Canarias*, Spudasmata 88 (Hildesheim, 2002).
23. *NP* s.v. "Thule." If a depiction of an Arctic zone was originally associated with the map, Thule could equally have been sited there.
24. See above Chap. 3, sec. 3 (c).

Appendix Six: Wyttenbach's Claim: A Lost Piece of the Map Discovered

1. The most recent account of the claim, albeit incomplete, is by G. Gross, "Verschollen – entdeckt – verschollen: Befand sich ein verlorener Teil der Tabula Peutingeriana in Trier?" *Kurtrierisches Jahrbuch* 39 (1999): 89–96.
2. My thanks to Professor Adelheid Eubanks for assistance with this translation.
3. See P. Barber, "Old Encounters New: The Aslake World Map," in M. Pelletier (ed.), *Géographie du monde au Moyen Âge et à la Renaissance* (Paris, 1989), 69–88, at 70–71; and *HistCart*, 3.1 (2007), 44–46.
4. See *HistCart*, 1 (1987), plate 14, and G. Haslam, "The Duchy of Cornwall Map Fragment," in Pelletier (1989), 33–44 at 34–35.
5. See Gross (1999), 94–95.
6. See Michael (1991), 11–12.
7. For example, *Neue Jahrbücher für Philologie und Paedagogik* 13.4 (1835): 456–57; *Zeitschrift für Alterthumswissenschaft* 43 (1835): col. 352.
8. D'Avezac[-Macaya] (1852), 417, n. 4, reprints the Academy's letter.
9. J. Murray, *A Hand-book for Travellers in Southern Germany. . . . and the Danube from Ulm to the Black Sea*, 5th ed. (London, 1850), 203.
10. J. Freudenberg, "IV. Miscellen," *Jahrbücher des Vereins von Alterthumsfreunden des Rheinlands* 14 (1849): 167–69. I thank K. Brodersen for bringing this report to my attention.
11. My thanks to the library's archivist, Dr. R. Nolden, for matching this sheet with Freudenberg's report.
12. Compare Müller (1901), Europae Tabula II.
13. For discussion, see D. B. Durand, *The Vienna-Klosterneuburg Map Corpus of the Fifteenth Century: A Study in the Transition from Medieval to Modern Science* (Leiden, 1952), 145–50 with Plate VI; P. H. Meurer, in *HistCart*, 3.2 (2007), 1179, and more fully id., *Corpus der älteren Germania-Karten: Ein annotierter Katalog der gedruckten Gesamtkarten des deutschen Raumes von den Anfängen bis um 1650* (Alphen aan den Rijn, 2001), 33–38 (with focus primarily on the Koblenz fragment, which is mistakenly said to have been discovered before those from Trier).

BIBLIOGRAPHY

For the most part, standard reference works and entries within them are omitted.

(a) Works with a Specific Focus on the Peutinger Map

No author. *Peutingeriana Tabula Itineraria in Bibliotheca Palatina Vindobonensi asservata nunc primum arte photographica expressa.* Vienna, 1888.

Albu, E. "Imperial Geography and the Medieval Peutinger Map." *Imago Mundi* 57 (2005): 136–48.

————. "Rethinking the Peutinger Map." In R. J. A. Talbert and R. W. Unger (eds.), *Cartography in Antiquity and the Middle Ages: Fresh Perspectives, New Methods,* 111–19. Leiden, 2008.

Allen, T. J. "Roman Healing Spas in Italy: The Peutinger Map Revisited." *Athenaeum* 91 (2003): 403–15.

Arnaud, P. "L'origine, la date de rédaction et la diffusion de l'archétype de la Table de Peutinger." *Bulletin de la Société Nationale des Antiquaires de France* (1988): 302–21.

Bosio, L. *La Tabula Peutingeriana: Una descrizione pittorica del mondo antico.* Rimini, 1983.

Brodersen, K. "Die Tabula Peutingeriana: Gehalt und Gestalt einer 'alten Karte' und ihrer antiken Vorlagen." In D. Unverhau (ed.), *Geschichtsdeutung auf alten Karten: Archäologie und Geschichte,* 289–97. Wolfenbütteler Forschungen 101. Wiesbaden, 2003.

Chevallier, R., E. Thevenot, and O. Pagès. "La Table de Peutinger." *Gaule: Bulletin de la Société d'Histoire, d'Archéologie et de Tradition Gauloises,* 2ème sér. 7 (July 1965): 105–23, with reissue of the map as published by F. C. von Scheyb, *Peutingeriana Tabula Itineraria.*

Cristianopoulo, P. [J. D. P.] *Tabula Itineraria Militaris Romana Antiqua Theodosiana, et Peutingeriana Nuncupata quam ex Vindobonensi editione clar. Viri Christophori de Scheyb anni MDCCLIII accurate descripsit.* Iesi, 1809.

Desjardins, E. *La Table de Peutinger, d'après l'original conservé à Vienne.* Paris, 1869–74. Incomplete, only 14 *livraisons* published.

Eckermann, K. In J. S. Ersch and J. G. Gruber (eds.), *Allgemeine Encyclopädie der Wissenschaften und Künste in alphabetischer Folge,* vol. 3.20, ss. vv. "Peutinger" (cols. 1–14) and "Peutingeriana Tabula" (cols. 14–34). Leipzig, 1845.

Elliott, T. "Constructing a Digital Edition for the Peutinger Map." In R. J. A. Talbert and R. W. Unger (eds.), *Cartography in Antiquity and the Middle Ages: Fresh Perspectives, New Methods*, 99–110. Leiden, 2008.

Fortia d'Urban, A. *Recueil des Itinéraires Anciens comprenant l'Itinéraire d'Antonin, la Table de Peutinger et un choix des périples grecs, avec dix cartes dressées par M. le Colonel Lapie.* Paris, 1845.

Freudenberg, J. "IV. Miscellen," *Jahrbücher des Vereins von Alterthumsfreunden des Rheinlands* 14 (1849): 167–69.

Gautier Dalché, P. "La trasmissione medievale e rinascimentale della *Tabula Peutingeriana.*" In Prontera (2003), 43–52.

_____. "Du nouveau sur la transmission et la découverte de la *Tabula Peutingeriana*: La 'Cosmographia vetustissima' de Pellegrino Prisciani (+1518)." *Geographia Antiqua* 13 (2004): 71–84.

Gerhartl-Witteveen, A. M., and P. Stuart. *Museumstukken: De Tabula Peutingeriana [Kaart, Commentaar].* Museum Het Valkhof te Nijmegen, 1991.

Gross, G. "Verschollen – entdeckt – verschollen: Befand sich ein verlorener Teil der Tabula Peutingeriana in Trier?" *Kurtrierisches Jahrbuch* 39 (1999): 89–96.

Gross, H. *Zur Entstehungs-Geschichte der Tabula Peutingeriana.* Bonn, 1913.

Häffelin, C. "Observations sur l'Itinéraire de Théodose, connu sous le nom de Table de Peutinger." *Acta Academiae Theodoro-Palatinae* 5 (1783): 105–26.

Heyrenbach, J. B. *Anmerkungen über die Tabula Peutingeriana: Ein nachgelassenes Werk.* Vienna, 1852.

Kastelic, J. "Vodnikova kopija Tabule Peutingeriane." *Glasnik Musejskega društva za Slovenijo* 23 (1942): 98–100.

Katancsich, M. P. *Orbis Antiquus ex Tabula Itineraria quae Theodosii Imp et Peutingeri Audit ad systema geographiae redactus et commentario illustratus.* 2 vols. with 12 map sheets. Buda, 1824–25.

Kubitschek, W. Review of *ItMiller*, in *Gött. gel. Anz.* 179 (1917): 1–117.

_____. Review of *ItMiller*, in *Zeitschrift für die deutsch-österreichischen Gymnasien* 68 (1917/18): 740–54 and 865–93.

Levi, A., and M. Levi. *Itineraria Picta. Contributo allo studio della Tabula Peutingeriana.* Rome, 1967.

_____. *La "Tabula Peutingeriana."* Rome, 1978.

Lieb, H. "Zur Herkunft der Tabula Peutingeriana." In H. Maurer (ed.), *Die Abtei Reichenau: Neue Beiträge zur Geschichte und Kultur des Inselklosters*, 31–33. Sigmaringen, 1974.

Lotter, J. G. *Dissertatio de Tabula Peutingeriana.* Leipzig, 1732.

Mannert, C. *Tabula Itineraria Peutingeriana, primum aeri incisa et edita a Franc. Christoph. de Scheyb MDCCLIII. Denuo cum codice Vindoboni collata, emendata et nova Conradi Mannerti introductione instructa, studio et opera Academiae Literarum Regiae Monacensis.* Leipzig, 1824.

Maury, A., "Note sur un nouvel examen de la partie de la carte de Peutinger où est figurée la Gaule." *Revue Archéologique* 9 (1864): 60–63.

Miller, K. *Die Weltkarte des Castorius genannt die Peutingersche Tafel.* Ravensburg, 1887.

_____. *Die Peutingersche Tafel.* Ravensburg, 1888. Expanded edition 1916; reissued 1929 and 1962 (all from Stuttgart).

_____. *Map of the World by Castorius generally known as Peutinger's Tabula.* London and Edinburgh, 1892. English version of *Die Peutingersche Tafel.*

Piérard, C. "Un exemplaire de la *Tabula itineraria* ou *Tabula Peutingeriana* édition Moretus 1598, conservé à Mons." *Quaerendo* 1.3 (1971): 201–16.

Prontera, F. (ed.). *Tabula Peutingeriana: Le antiche vie del mondo*. Florence, 2003.

Salway, B. "The Nature and Genesis of the Peutinger Map." *Imago Mundi* 57 (2005): 119–35.

von Scheyb, F. C. *Peutingeriana Tabula Itineraria Quae in Augusta Bibliotheca Vindobonensi Nunc Servatur Adcurate Exscripta*. Vienna, 1753.

————. [untitled]. *Nova Acta Eruditorum* (Leipzig) 34 (1766): 76–80.

Talbert, R. J. A. "Cartography and Taste in Peutinger's Roman Map." in R. J. A. Talbert and K. Brodersen (eds.), *Space in the Roman World: Its Perception and Presentation*, 113–41. Münster, 2004.

————. "Rome's Marble Plan and Peutinger's Map: Continuity in Cartographic Design." In Beutler and Hameter (2005), 627–34.

————. "Konrad Miller, Roman Cartography, and the Lost Western End of the Peutinger Map." In Fellmeth (2007), 353–66.

————. "Peutinger's Roman Map: The Physical Landscape Framework." In M. Rathmann (ed.), *Wahrnehmung und Erfassung geographischer Räume in der Antike*, 221–230 and Tafeln 15–16. Mainz, 2007.

————. "A Forgotten Masterpiece of Cartography for Roman Historians: Pierre Lapie's *Orbis Romanus ad Illustranda Itineraria* (1845)." In H. M. Schellenberg et al. (eds.), *A Roman Miscellany: Essays in Honour of Anthony R. Birley on His Seventieth Birthday*, 149–56. Gdansk, 2008.

————, and T. Elliott. "New Windows on the Peutinger Map of the Roman World." In A. K. Knowles (ed.), *Placing History: How Maps, Spatial Data, and GIS Are Changing Historical Scholarship*, 199–218. Redlands, CA, 2008.

Tübinger Atlas des Vorderen Orients [*TAVO*] B S 1 *Weltkarten der Antike/Ancient Maps of the World*, 1.2 *Tabula Peutingeriana*, with accompanying text by J. Wagner. Wiesbaden, 1984.

Weber, E. *Tabula Peutingeriana, Codex Vindobonensis 324*, with separate *Kommentar* volume. Graz, 1976.

————. "Das 'Verkaufsinserat' der Tabula Peutingeriana aus dem Jahr 1715 – Ein kleiner Beitrag zur Wissenschaftsgeschichte." in Fellmeth (2007), 367–79.

Welser, M. *Fragmenta tabulae antiquae, in quis aliquot per Rom. provincias itinera. Ex Peutingerorum bibliotheca*. Venice, 1591.

————. *Tabula itineraria ex illustri Peutingerorum bibliotheca quae Augustae Vindel. est beneficio Marci Velseri septemviri Augustani in lucem edita*. Antwerp, 1598.

(b) Other Works Cited

Aillagon, J.-J. (ed.). *Rome and the Barbarians: The Birth of a New World*. Milan, 2008.

Akerman, J. R. (ed.). *The Imperial Map: Cartography and the Mastery of Empire*. Chicago, 2009.

Alexander, J. J. G. "The Illustrated Manuscripts of the Notitia Dignitatum." In R. Goodburn and P. Bartholomew (eds.), *Aspects of the* Notitia Dignitatum, 11–25. BAR Supplementary Series 15. Oxford, 1976.

————. *Medieval Illuminators and Their Methods of Work*. New Haven, CT, 1992.

Amirante, G., and M. R. Pessolano. *Immagini di Napoli e del Regno: Le raccolte di Francesco Cassiano de Silva*. Naples, 2005.

Andreae, B. *Antike Bildmosaiken*. Mainz, 2003.

Anonymous. *An Oration* [by D. Passionei, originally in Italian] *on the Death of Eugene Francis, Prince of Savoy*. London, 1738.

Arce, J. "Emperadores, palacios y *villae* (A propósito de la villa romana de Cercadilla, Córdoba)." *Antiquité Tardive* 5 (1997): 293–302.

———. "El inventario de Roma: *Curiosum* y *Notitia*." In W. V. Harris (ed.), *The Transformation of* Vrbs Roma *in Late Antiquity*, 15–22. Portsmouth, RI, 1999.

Arnaud, P. "L'affaire Mettius Pompusianus ou le crime de cartographie." *MEFRA* 95 (1983): 677–99.

———. "La cartographie à Rome." Thèse d'état, Université de Paris IV, 1990.

Arnold, C. *Marci Velseri Opera in Unum Collecta*. Nuremberg, 1682.

Arnold, W. (ed.). *Bibliotheken und Bücher im Zeitalter der Renaissance*. Wolfenbütteler Abhandlungen zur Renaissanceforschung 16. Wiesbaden, 1997.

Auer, A. et al. (eds.). *Geschichte der Fotografie in Österreich*. 2 vols. Bad Ischl, 1983.

d'Avezac[-Macaya], M. A. P. *Mémoire sur Éthicus et sur les ouvrages cosmographiques intitulés de ce nom*. In *Mémoires présentés par divers savants à l'Académie des Inscriptions et Belles-Lettres, Ière Série: Sujets divers d'érudition*, vol. 2, 230–551. Paris, 1852.

Barber, P. "Old Encounters New: The Aslake World Map." In Pelletier (1989), 69–88.

———. "England I: Pageantry, Defense, and Government: Maps at Court to 1550," In D. Buisseret (ed.), *Monarchs, Ministers, and Maps: The Emergence of Cartography as a Tool of Government in Early Modern Europe*, 26–56. Chicago and London, 1992.

——— (ed.). *The Map Book*. London, 2005.

———. *King Henry's Map of the British Isles: B. L. Cotton MS Augustus I.i.9*. London, 2009.

Barnes, T. D. *Constantine and Eusebius*. Cambridge, MA, 1981.

———. *The New Empire of Diocletian and Constantine*. Cambridge, MA, 1982.

Bauer, F. A. (ed.). *Visualisierungen von Herrschaft. Frühmittelalterliche Residenzen. Gestalt und Zeremoniell*. Istanbul, 2006.

Beard, M. *The Roman Triumph*. Cambridge [MA] and London, 2007.

Bejaoui, F. "Iles et villes de la Méditerranée sur une mosaïque d'Ammaedara." *CRAI* (1997): 827–60.

Bekker-Nielsen, T. *The Roads of Ancient Cyprus*. Copenhagen, 2004.

Berggren, J. L., and A. Jones. *Ptolemy's* Geography: *An Annotated Translation of the Theoretical Chapters*. Princeton [NJ] and Oxford, 2000.

Bergier, N. *Histoire des grands chemins de l'empire romain*. Paris, 1622. Reissue with the Peutinger map added, Brussels, 1728.

Bertius, P. *Theatrum Geographiae Veteris*. Amsterdam, 1619.

Beutler, F., and W. Hameter (eds.). *Festschrift Ekkehard Weber*. Althistorisch-Epigraphische Studien 5. Vienna, 2005.

Birkholz, D. *The King's Two Maps: Cartography and Culture in Thirteenth-Century England*. New York and London, 2004.

Bischoff, B. *Latin Palaeography: Antiquity and the Middle Ages*. Cambridge, 1990.

Bodnar, E. W., and C. Foss (eds. and trans.). *Cyriac of Ancona: Later Travels*. I Tatti series. Cambridge, MA, 2003.

Bowden, W. et al. (eds.). *Social and Political Life in Late Antiquity*. Leiden and Boston [MA], 2006.

Bowersock, G. W. "The East–West Orientation of Mediterranean Studies and the Meaning of North and South in Antiquity." In Harris (2005), 167–78.

———. *Mosaics as History: The Near East from Late Antiquity to Islam.* Cambridge, MA, 2006.

Briant, P. "From the Indus to the Mediterranean: Administration and Logistics on the Highroads of the Achaemenid Empire." in R. J. A. Talbert, J. Bodel, and S. Alcock (eds.), *Highways, Byways and Road Systems in the Pre-Modern World.* Forthcoming.

Bridgman, T. P. *Hyperboreans: Myth and History in Celtic-Hellenic Contacts.* New York and London, 2005.

Brilliant, R. "The Bayeux Tapestry: A Stripped Narrative for Their Eyes and Ears." *Word and Image* 7 (1991): 93–125. Reprinted in R. Gameson (ed.), *The Study of the Bayeux Tapestry*, chap. 10. Woodbridge [England], 1997.

Brodersen, K. *Terra Cognita: Studien zur römischen Raumerfassung.* Hildesheim, 1995.

Van Den Broecke, M. P. R. *Ortelius Atlas Maps: An Illustrated Guide.* Westrenen [Netherlands], 1996.

Callieri, P., and P. Bernard. "Une borne routière grecque de la région de Persépolis." *CRAI* (1995): 65–95.

Calzolari, M. "Ricerche sugli itinerari romani. L'Itinerarium Burdigalense." In *Studi in onore di Nereo Alfieri. Atti dell'Accademia delle Scienze di Ferrara* 74 Supplemento, 1997, 127–89.

Cameron, A. "Petronius Probus, Aemilius Probus and the Transmission of Nepos: A Note on Late Roman Calligraphers." In J.-M. Carrié and R. Lizzi Testa (eds.),"*Humana Sapit*": *Etudes d'antiquité tardive offertes à Lellia Cracco Ruggini*, 121–30. Turnhout [Belgium], 2002.

Campbell, B. *The Writings of the Roman Land Surveyors: Introduction, Text, Translation and Commentary.* London, 2000.

———. "'Setting up True Boundaries': Land Disputes in the Roman Empire." *Mediterraneo Antico: Economie, Società, Culture* 8.1 (2005): 307–43.

Carey, S. *Pliny's Catalogue of Culture: Art and Empire in the* Natural History. Oxford, 2003.

Cecconi, G. A. "Sulla denominazione dei distretti di tipo provinciale nell'Italia tardoantica." *Athenaeum* 82 (1994): 177–84.

Celtis, C. (ed.). *Opera Hrotsvite.* Nuremberg, 1501. Facsimile reprint, Hildesheim: Olms, 2000.

Cichorius, C. *Die Reliefs der Traianssäule.* 2 text vols., 2 of plates. Berlin, 1896–1900.

Coarelli, F. *The Column of Trajan.* Rome, 2000.

Cole, S. G. "'I know the number of the sand and the measure of the sea': Geography and Difference in the Early Greek World." In K. A. Raaflaub and R. J. A. Talbert (eds.), *Geography and Ethnography: Perceptions of the World in Pre-Modern Societies,* 197–214. Oxford, 2010.

Corcoran, S. *The Empire of the Tetrarchs: Imperial Pronouncements and Government AD 284–324.* Rev. ed. Oxford, 2000.

Coulston, J. C. N. "Three New Books on Trajan's Column." *JRA* 3 (1990): 290–309.

Crawford, M. H. "Tribus, tessères et régions." *CRAI* (2002): 1125–35.

Creed, J. L. (ed. and trans.). *Lactantius, De Mortibus Persecutorum.* Oxford, 1984.

Curran, J. R. *Pagan City and Christian Capital: Rome in the Fourth Century.* Oxford, 2000.

Delano-Smith, C. "Milieus of Mobility: Itineraries, Route Maps, and Road Maps." In J. R. Akerman (ed.), *Cartographies of Travel and Navigation,* 16–66. Chicago, 2006.

Dench, E. *Romulus' Asylum: Roman Identities from the Age of Alexander to the Age of Hadrian.* Oxford, 2005.

Derolez, A. *The Palaeography of Gothic Manuscript Books: From the Twelfth to the Early Sixteenth Century.* Cambridge, 2003.

Desjardins, E. *Géographie historique et administrative de la Gaule romaine.* Vol. 4. Paris, 1893.

Dibdin, T. F. *A Bibliographical, Antiquarian and Picturesque Tour in France and Germany.* Vol. 1. 2nd ed. London, 1829.

Dicks, D. R. *The Geographical Fragments of Hipparchus.* London, 1960.

Dilke, O. A. W. *Greek and Roman Maps.* London, 1985.

Dillemann, L. *La cosmographie du Ravennate.* Brussels, 1997.

Duggan, C. *The Force of Destiny: A History of Italy since 1796.* London, 2007.

Durand, D. B. *The Vienna-Klosterneuburg Map Corpus of the Fifteenth Century: A Study in the Transition from Medieval to Modern Science.* Leiden, 1952.

Duval, N. "Existe-t-il une 'structure palatiale' propre à l'Antiquité tardive?" In E. Lévy (ed.), *Le système palatial en Orient, en Grèce et à Rome,* 463–90. Strasbourg, 1987.

Edson, E. *Mapping Time and Space: How Medieval Mapmakers Viewed Their World.* London, 1997.

Edwards, E. *Memoirs of Libraries: Including a Handbook of Library Economy.* Vol. 2. London, 1859.

Feissel, D., and K. A. Worp. "La requête d'Appion, évêque de Syène, à Théodose II: P.Leid. Z révisé." *Oudheidkundige Mededelingen van het Rijksmuseum van Oudheden te Leiden* 68 (1988): 97–111.

Fellmeth, U. et al. (eds.). *Historische Geographie der Alten Welt: Grundlagen, Erträge, Perspektiven.* [Festschrift Olshausen]. Hildesheim, 2007.

Flieder, M., and E. Irblich (eds.). *Texte, Noten, Bilder: Neuerwerbungen, Restaurierungen, Konservierungen 1977–1983.* Vienna, 1984.

Forbiger, A. *Handbuch der alten Geographie.* 3 vols. 2nd ed. Hamburg, 1877.

Fraser, P. M. "A Syriac *Notitia Urbis Alexandrinae,*" *Journal of Egyptian Archaeology* 37 (1951): 103–108.

French, D. *Roman Roads and Milestones of Asia Minor, fasc. 1: The Pilgrim's Road.* BAR International Series 105. Oxford, 1981.

French, J. (vols. 1–2), and V. Scott (vols. 3–4) (eds.). *Tooley's Dictionary of Mapmakers.* 4 vols. Rev. ed. Riverside, CT, 1999–2004.

Fuchs, P. *Palatinatus Illustratus: Die historische Forschung an der Kurpfälzischen Akademie der Wissenschaften.* Mannheim, 1963.

Gall, A. *Das Atlantropa-Projekt. Die Geschichte einer gescheiterten Vision. Herman Sörgel und die Absenkung des Mittelmeers.* Frankfurt, 1998.

————. "Atlantropa: A Technological Vision of a United Europe." In E. van der Vleuten and A. Kaijser (eds.), *Networking Europe: Transnational Infrastructures and the Shaping of Europe, 1850–2000,* 99–128. Sagamore Beach, MA, 2006.

Gallazzi, C., B. Kramer, and S. Settis (eds.), *Il Papiro di Artemidoro.* Milan, 2008.

Garland, K. *Mr Beck's Underground Map.* London, 1994.

Gaube, H. (ed.). *Konrad Miller, Mappae Arabicae. TAVO* Beihefte B65. Wiesbaden, 1986.

Gautier Dalché, P. *La "Descriptio Mappe Mundi" de Hugues de Saint-Victor*. Paris, 1988.

———. "Les sens de *mappa (mundi)*: IVe–XIVe siècle." *Archivum Latinitatis Medii Aevi* 62 (2004): 187–202.

———. "Agrimensure et inventaire du monde: La fortune de '*Mappa (Mundi)*' au Moyen Âge." In D. Conso et al. (eds.), *Les vocabulaires techniques des arpenteurs romains*, 163–71. Besançon, 2005.

———. "L'héritage antique de la cartographie médiévale: les problèmes et les acquis." In R. J. A. Talbert and R. W. Unger (eds.), *Cartography in Antiquity and the Middle Ages: Fresh Perspectives, New Methods*, 29–66. Leiden, 2008.

Geus, K. *Eratosthenes von Kyrene. Studien zur hellenistischen Kultur- und Wissenschaftsgeschichte*. Munich, 2002.

———. "Space and Geography." In A. Erskine (ed.), *A Companion to the Hellenistic World*, 232–45. Oxford, 2003.

Giacchero, M. (ed.). *Edictum Diocletiani et Collegarum de Pretiis Rerum Venalium*. Vol. 1. Genoa, 1974.

Goffart, W. *Historical Atlases: The First Three Hundred Years, 1570–1870*. Chicago, 2003.

Gough map. http://143.117.30.60/website/GoughMap/viewer.htm.

Gregory, D. *Napoleon's Italy*. London, 2001.

Gullick, M. "How Fast Did Scribes Write? Evidence from Romanesque Manuscripts." in L. L. Brownrigg (ed.), *Making Medieval Books: Techniques of Production*, 39–58. Los Altos [CA] and London, 1995.

Hahn, J. *Bartholomäus Kopitar und seine Beziehungen zu München*. Geschichte, Kultur und Geisteswelt der Slowenen 17. Munich, 1982.

Hamber, A. J. *"A Higher Branch of the Art": Photographing the Fine Arts in England, 1839–1880*. Amsterdam, 1996.

Hardie, P. *Virgil's Aeneid: Cosmos and Imperium*. Oxford, 1986.

Harris, W. V. "The Mediterranean and Ancient History." In W. V. Harris (ed.), *Rethinking the Mediterranean*, 1–42. Oxford, 2005.

Harvey, P. D. A. (ed.). *The Hereford World Map: Medieval World Maps and Their Context*. London, 2006.

Haslam, G. "The Duchy of Cornwall Map Fragment." In Pelletier (1989), 33–44.

Headley, J. M. *The Europeanization of the World: On the Origins of Human Rights and Democracy*. Princeton, NJ, 2008.

Henkel, N. "Bücher des Konrad Celtis." In W. Arnold (1997), 129–66.

Herrmann, P. *Itinéraires des voies romaines de l'Antiquité au Moyen Âge*. Paris, 2007.

Hessels, J. H. (ed.). *Abrahami Ortelii et Virorum Eruditorum ad Eundem et ad Jacobum Colium Ortelianum Epistulae*. Cambridge, 1887.

Hewsen, R. H. *The Geography of Ananias of Sirak: The Long and the Short Recensions*. TAVO Beihefte B77. Wiesbaden, 1992.

———. *Armenia: A Historical Atlas*. Chicago and London, 2001.

Hicks, C. *The Bayeux Tapestry: The Life Story of a Masterpiece*. London, 2006.

Hindle, B. P. "The Towns and Roads of the Gough Map (c. 1360)." *Manchester Geographer* 1 (1980): 35–49.

Holgate, I. "Paduan Culture in Venetian Care: Bishop Pietro Donato (Padua 1428–47)." *Renaissance Studies* 16 (2002): 1–23.

Holliday, P. J. *The Origins of Roman Historical Commemoration in the Visual Arts*. Cambridge, 2002.

Honigmann, E. (ed.). *Le Synekdèmos d'Hiéroklès et l'Opuscule Géographique de Georges de Chypre*. Brussels, 1939.

Horawitz, A., and K. Hartfelder (eds.). *Briefwechsel des Beatus Rhenanus*. Leipzig, 1886.

Huet, V. "Stories One Might Tell of Roman Art: Reading Trajan's Column and the Tiberius Cup." In J. Elsner (ed.), *Art and Text in Roman Culture*, 9–31. Cambridge, 1996.

Husslein, G. "Konrad Miller." *Orbis Terrarum* 1 (1995): 213–33.

Hüttl-Hubert, E.-M. "Bartholomäus Kopitar und die Wiener Hofbibliothek." *Österreichische Osthefte* 36 (1994): 521–88.

Irblich, E. "Die Konservierung von Handschriften unter Berücksichtigung der Restaurierung, Reprographie und Faksimilierung an Hand von Beispielen aus der Handschriftensammlung der Österreichischen Nationalbibliothek Wien." *Codices Manuscripti* 11 (1985): 15–32.

Irby-Massie, G. "Mapping the World: Greek Initiatives from Homer to Eratosthenes." In R. J. A. Talbert (ed.), *Ancient Perspectives: Maps and Their Place in Mesopotamia, Egypt, Greece, and Rome*. Chicago, forthcoming.

Jacob, C. *The Sovereign Map: Theoretical Approaches in Cartography Throughout History*. Chicago and London, 2006.

James, S. *Excavations at Dura-Europos 1928–1937, Final Report: The Arms and Armour and Other Military Equipment*. London, 2004.

Janssonius, J. *Accuratissima Orbis Antiqui Delineatio sive Geographia Vetus, Sacra, et Profana*. Amsterdam, 1652.

———. *Novus Atlas sive Theatrum Orbis Terrarum*. Amsterdam, 1658.

———. *Atlas Major*. Amsterdam, 1662.

Johnson, W. A. *Bookrolls and Scribes in Oxyrhynchus*. Toronto, 2004.

Jones, A. "Ptolemy's Geography: Mapmaking and the Scientific Enterprise." In R. J. A. Talbert (ed.), *Ancient Perspectives: Maps and Their Place in Mesopotamia, Egypt, Greece, and Rome*. Chicago, forthcoming.

Jones, B., and D. Mattingly. *An Atlas of Roman Britain*. Oxford, 1990.

Jones, C. P. (ed. and trans.). *Philostratus, The Life of Apollonius of Tyana*. 2 vols. Loeb Classical Library. Cambridge, MA, 2005.

Kamal, Y. *Monumenta Cartographica Africae et Aegypti*. Vol. 2, fasc. 2. Cairo, 1932.

Karrow, R. W. *Mapmakers of the Sixteenth Century and Their Maps: Bio-Bibliographies of the Cartographers of Abraham Ortelius, 1570*. Chicago, 1993.

King, M. L. *Venetian Humanism in an Age of Patrician Dominance*. Princeton, NJ, 1986.

Knecht, R. J. *The French Renaissance Court 1483–1589*. New Haven, CT, 2008.

Koeman, C. *Atlantes Neerlandici: Bibliography of Terrestrial, Maritime and Celestial Atlases and Pilot Books, Published in the Netherlands up to 1880*. Vol. 2. Amsterdam, 1969.

Künast, H.-J., and H. Zäh. *Die Bibliothek Konrad Peutingers, Edition der historischen Kataloge und Rekonstruktion der Bestände, Band 1: Die autographen Kataloge Peutingers; Der nicht-juristische Bibliotheksteil*. Tübingen, 2003.

La Rocca, E. "L'affresco con veduta di città dal colle Oppio." In E. Fentress (ed.), *Romanization and the City: Creation, Transformations, and Failures*, 57–71. Portsmouth, RI, 2000.

Lavan, L. "Political Life in Late Antiquity: A Bibliographic Essay." In Bowden et al. (2006), 3–40.

Lawson, M. K. *The Battle of Hastings 1066*. Stroud [England], 2002.

Leclercq, H. s.v. "Itinéraires." In F. Cabrol and H. Leclercq (eds.), *Dictionnaire d'archéologie chrétienne*, vol. 7, cols. 1841–1922. Paris, 1927.

Levin, I. *The Quedlinburg Itala: The Oldest Illustrated Biblical Manuscript.* Leiden, 1985.

Lilley, K. D., and C. D. Lloyd. "Mapping Places: A New Look at the Gough Map of Great Britain. (*c.* 1360)." *Imago Mundi* 61 (2009): 1–28.

Ling, R. *Roman Painting.* Cambridge, 1991.

Lloyd, C. D., and K. D. Lilley. "Cartographic Veracity in Medieval Mapping: Analyzing Geographical Variation in the Gough Map of Great Britain." *Annals of the Association of American Geographers* 99.1 (2009): 27–48.

Lotter, J. G. *Historia Vitae atque Meritorum Conradi Peutingeri Augustani.* Leipzig, 1729.

Lozovsky, N. *"The Earth Is Our Book": Geographical Knowledge in the Latin West ca. 400–1000.* Ann Arbor, MI, 2000.

————. "Roman Geography and Ethnography in the Carolingian Empire." *Speculum* 81 (2006): 325–64.

————. "Maps and Panegyrics: Roman Geo-ethnographical Rhetoric in Late Antiquity and the Middle Ages." In R. J. A. Talbert and R. W. Unger (eds.), *Cartography in Antiquity and The Middle Ages: Fresh Perspectives, New Methods,* 169–88. Leiden, 2008.

MacCormack, S. G. *Art and Ceremony in Late Antiquity.* Berkeley, CA, 1981.

Machado, C. "Building the Past: Monuments and Memory in the *Forum Romanum.*" In Bowden et al. (2006), 157–92.

MacMullen, R. "Some Pictures in Ammianus." In R. MacMullen, *Changes in the Roman Empire: Essays in the Ordinary,* 78–106. Princeton, NJ, 1990. Originally published 1964.

Maguire, H. *Earth and Ocean: The Terrestrial World in Early Byzantine Art.* University Park [PA] and London, 1987.

Mannert, K. *Geographie der Griechen und Römer.* 10 vols. Leipzig, 1820–31.

Marcotte, D. *Géographes grecs* I. Budé series. Paris, 2000.

Martineau, J. (ed.). *Andrea Mantegna.* New York and London, 1992.

Mattern, S. P. *Rome and the Enemy: Imperial Strategy in the Principate.* Berkeley, CA, 1999.

Matthews, J. *The Journey of Theophanes: Travel, Business, and Daily Life in the Roman East.* New Haven, CT, 2006.

Mazal, O. *Prinz Eugens Schönste Bücher: Handschriften aus der Bibliothek des Prinzen Eugen von Savoyen.* Graz, 1986.

McCabe, A. *A Byzantine Encyclopaedia of Horse Medicine: The Sources, Compilation, and Transmission of the* Hippiatrica. Oxford, 2007.

McGill, S. *Virgil Recomposed: The Mythological and Secular Centos in Antiquity.* Oxford, 2005.

McNally, S. et al. *Diocletian's Palace: American-Yugoslav Joint Excavations.* Vol. 5. Minneapolis, 1989.

Merula, P. *Cosmographiae Generalis Libri Tres.* Leiden, 1605.

Meurer, P. H. *Corpus der älteren Germania-Karten: Ein annotierter Katalog der gedruckten Gesamtkarten des deutschen Raumes von den Anfängen bis um 1650.* Alphen aan den Rijn, 2001.

Michael, E. "Das wiederentdeckte Monument – Erforschung der Ebstorfer Weltkarte, Entstehungsgeschichte und Gestalt ihrer Nachbildungen." In H. Kugler (ed.), *Ein Weltbild vor Columbus: Die Ebstorfer Weltkarte – Interdisziplinäres Colloquium 1988,* 9–22. Weinheim, 1991.

Millar, F. "Caravan Cities: The Roman Near East and Long-distance Trade by Land." In F. Millar, *Rome, the Greek World, and the East*. Vol. 3, 275–99. Chapel Hill, NC, 2006. Originally published 1998.

Millea, N. *The Gough Map: The Earliest Road Map of Britain?* Oxford, 2007.

Miller, K. *Mappaemundi: Die ältesten Weltkarten*. 6 Vols. Stuttgart, 1895–98.

Miller, M. C. *The Bishop's Palace: Architecture and Authority in Medieval Italy*. Ithaca [NY] and London, 2000.

Mommsen, T. (ed.). *C. Julius Solinus, Collectanea Rerum Memorabilium*. Berlin, 1895.

Müller, C. s.v. "Itinéraires." In E. Carteron et al. (eds.), *Complément de l'Encyclopédie Moderne* 6.1, cols. 616–37. Paris: Firmin Didot, 1857.

———. *Claudii Ptolemaei Geographia: Tabulae xxxvi*. Paris, 1901.

Müller-Wiener, W. *Bildlexikon zur Topographie Istanbuls*. Tübingen, 1977.

Murphy, T. *Pliny the Elder's* Natural History: *The Empire in the Encyclopedia*. Oxford, 2004.

Murray, J. *A Hand-book for Travellers in Southern Germany . . . and the Danube from Ulm to the Black Sea*. 5th ed. London, 1850.

Mynors, R. A. B. (ed.). *xii Panegyrici Latini*. Oxford, 1964.

Najbjerg, T., and J. Trimble. "The Severan Marble Plan since 1960." In R. Meneghini and R. S. Valenzani (eds.), *Formae Urbis Romae: Nuovi frammenti di piante marmoree dallo scavo dei Fori Imperiali*, 75–101. Rome, 2006.

Nativel, C. (ed.). *Centuriae Latinae: Cent une figures humanistes de la Renaissance aux Lumières*. 2 vols. Geneva, 1997, 2006.

Nicolet, C. *Space, Geography and Politics in the Early Roman Empire*. Ann Arbor, MI, 1991.

———. *Financial Documents and Geographical Knowledge in the Roman World*. J. L. Myres Memorial Lecture. Oxford, 1996.

Niero, A. "L'azione veneziana al Concilio di Basilea (1431–1436)." In A. Niero et al., *Venezia e i Concili*, 3–46. Venice, 1962.

Nixon, C. E. V., and B. S. Rodgers. *In Praise of Later Roman Emperors: The Panegyrici Latini*. Berkeley, CA, 1994.

Ortelius, A. *Theatrum Orbis Terrarum Parergon, sive veteris geographiae tabulae commentariis geographicis et historicis illustratae*. Antwerp, 1624.

Östenberg, I. *Staging the World: Spoils, Captives, and Representations in the Roman Triumphal Procession*. Oxford, 2009.

Pächt, O., and J. J. G. Alexander. *Illuminated Manuscripts in the Bodleian Library Oxford*. Vols. 1 and 2. Oxford, 1966, 1970.

Parker, G. *The Making of Roman India*. Cambridge, 2007.

———. "Images of Mediterranean India: Representing the Subcontinent in Ancient Greek and Roman Art." In G. Parker and C. M. Sinopoli (eds.), *Ancient India in Its Wider World*, 106–26. Ann Arbor, MI, 2008.

Parlapiano, R. B. (ed.). *Biblioteca Planettiana, Iesi*. Fiesole, 1997.

Pelletier, M. (ed.). *Géographie du monde au Moyen Âge et à la Renaissance*. Paris, 1989.

Petersen, E. et al. *Die Marcus-Säule auf Piazza Colonna in Rom*. 1 text vol., 2 of plates. Munich, 1896.

Pfeilschifter, R. "The Great Palace at Constantinople Put into Context." *JRA* 21 (2008): 727–33.

Piccirillo, M., and E. Alliata (eds.). *The Madaba Map Centenary 1897–1997. Travelling through the Byzantine Umayyad Period*. Jerusalem: Studium Biblicum Franciscanum, 1998.

Race, W. H. (ed. and trans.). *Apollonius Rhodius, Argonautica*. Loeb Classical Library. Cambridge, MA, 2009.

Rathmann, M. *Untersuchungen zu den Reichsstrassen in den westlichen Provinzen des Imperium Romanum*. Mainz, 2003.

Rebourg, A. (ed.). *Carte archéologique de la Gaule* 71/1 and 2, *Autun*. Paris, 1993.

Rees, R. *Layers of Loyalty in Latin Panegyric, AD 289–307*. Oxford, 2002.

———. *Diocletian and the Tetrarchy*. Edinburgh, 2004.

Reeve, M. D. (ed.). *Vegetius, Epitoma rei militaris*. Oxford, 2004.

Rives, J. B. (ed. and trans.). *Tacitus, Germania*. Oxford, 1999.

Rivet, A. L. F., and C. Smith. *The Place-Names of Roman Britain*. London, 1979.

Roberts, M. *The Jeweled Style: Poetry and Poetics in Late Antiquity*. Ithaca [NY] and London, 1989.

Roldán Hervás, J. M. *Itineraria Hispana: Fuentes antiguas para el studio de las vías romanas en la Península Ibérica*. Valladolid, 1975.

Romano, D. *The Likeness of Venice: A Life of Doge Francesco Foscari, 1373–1457*. New Haven [CT] and London, 2007.

Römer, F. "Geographie und Panegyrik: Beobachtungen zu Franz Ch. v. Scheybs Praefatio [*sic*] seiner Edition der Tabula Peutingeriana." In Beutler and Hameter (2005), 615–26.

Romm, J. S. *The Edges of the Earth in Ancient Thought: Geography, Exploration, and Fiction*. Princeton, NJ, 1992.

Sabbadini, R. *Le scoperte dei codici latini e greci ne' secoli XIV e XV*. Vol. 1. Florence, 1905.

Şahin, S., and M. Adak. *Stadiasmus Patarensis: Itinera Romana Provinciae Lyciae*. Istanbul, 2007.

Salway, B. "Sea and River Travel in the Roman Itinerary Literature." In R. J. A. Talbert and K. Brodersen (eds.), *Space in the Roman World: Its Perception and Presentation*, 43–96. Münster, 2004.

———. "Putting the World in Order: Mapping in Roman Texts." In R. J. A. Talbert (ed.), *Ancient Perspectives: Maps and Their Place in Mesopotamia, Egypt, Greece, and Rome*. Chicago, forthcoming.

Salzman, M. R. *On Roman Time: The Codex-Calendar of 354 and the Rhythms of Urban Life in Late Antiquity*. Berkeley, CA, 1990.

Sambin, P. "La biblioteca di Pietro Donato (1380–1447)." *Bollettino del Museo Civico di Padova* 48 (1959): 53–98.

Santana Santana, A. *El Conocimiento Geográfico de la Costa Noroccidental de Africa en Plinio: La Posición de las Canarias*. Spudasmata 88. Hildesheim, 2002.

Šašel Kos, M. "Valentin Vodnik and Roman Antiquities in the Time of Napoleon." *Antichità Altoadriatiche* 64 (2007): 405–30.

Scheller, R. W. Exemplum: *Model-Book Drawings and the Practice of Artistic Transmission in the Middle Ages (ca. 900–ca. 1470)*. Amsterdam, 1995.

Schneider, K. *Gotische Schriften in deutscher Sprache. Teil 1, Vom späten 12. Jahrhundert bis um 1300, Textband* and *Tafelband*. Wiesbaden, 1987.

Schnetz, J. (ed.). *Ravennatis Anonymi Cosmographia et Guidonis Geographica*. In *Itineraria Romana*. Vol. 2. Leipzig: Teubner, 1940. Reissued with index by M. Zumschlinge. Stuttgart, 1990.

Schuler, C. "Augustus, Gott und Herr über Land und Meer. Eine neue Inschrift aus Tyberissos im Kontext der späthellenistischen Herrscherverehrung." *Chiron* 37 (2007): 383–403.

Schweder, E. "Über eine Weltkarte des achten Jahrhunderts." *Hermes* 24 (1889): 587–604.

Scott, J. M. *Geography in Early Judaism and Christianity:* The Book of Jubilees. Cambridge, 2002.

Seeck, O. (ed.). *Notitia Dignitatum*. Berlin, 1876.

Shahar, Y. *Josephus Geographicus: The Classical Context of Geography in Josephus*. Tübingen, 2004.

Sharpe, K. *Selling the Tudor Monarchy: Authority and Image in Sixteenth-Century England*. New Haven [CT] and London, 2009.

Silver, L. *Marketing Maximilian: The Visual Ideology of a Holy Roman Emperor*. Princeton [NJ] and Oxford, 2008.

Silverstein, A. J. *Postal Systems in the Pre-Modern Islamic World*. Cambridge, 2007.

Smith, R. "The Imperial Court of the Late Roman Empire." In A. J. S. Spawforth (ed.), *The Court and Court Society in Ancient Monarchies*, 157–232. Cambridge, 2007.

Smith, R. R. R. "*Simulacra gentium*: The *ethne* from the Sebasteion at Aphrodisias." *JRS* 78 (1988): 50–77.

Smith, W., and G. Grove (eds.). *Atlas of Ancient Geography Biblical and Classical*. London, 1872–74.

Spitz, L. W. *Conrad Celtis: The German Arch-Humanist*. Cambridge, MA, 1957.

Stanford Digital Forma Urbis Romae Project (http://formaurbis.stanford.edu).

Stieber, J. W. *Pope Eugenius IV, the Council of Basel and the Secular and Ecclesiastical Authorities in the Empire: The Conflict over Supreme Authority and Power in the Church*. Leiden, 1978.

Stummvoll, J. (ed.). *Geschichte der Österreichischen Nationalbibliothek, I: Die Hofbibliothek (1368–1922)*. Vienna, 1968.

Syme, R. *Emperors and Biography: Studies in the Historia Augusta*. Oxford, 1971.

Talbert, R. J. A. "Mapping the Classical World: Major Atlases and Map Series 1872–1990." *JRA* 5 (1992): 5–38.

———. "Carl Müller (1813–1894), S. Jacobs, and the Making of Classical Maps in Paris for John Murray." *Imago Mundi* 46 (1994): 128–50.

———. "Rome's Provinces as Framework for World-view." In L. De Ligt et al. (eds.), *Roman Rule and Civic Life: Local and Regional Perspectives*, 21–37. Amsterdam, 2004.

———. "Author, Audience and the Roman Empire in the *Antonine Itinerary*." In R. Haensch and J. Heinrichs (eds.), *Der Alltag der römischen Administration in der Hohen Kaiserzeit*, 256–70. Cologne, Weimar, Berlin, 2007.

———. "Greek and Roman Mapping: Twenty-First Century Perspectives." In R. J. A. Talbert and R. W. Unger (eds.), *Cartography in Antiquity and the Middle Ages: Fresh Perspectives, New Methods*, 9–27. Leiden, 2008.

———. "P.Artemid.: The Map." In K. Brodersen and J. Elsner (eds.), *Images and Texts on the "Artemidorus Papyrus,"* 57–64. Historia Einzelschrift 214. Stuttgart, 2009.

———. (ed.). *Ancient Perspectives: Maps and Their Place in Mesopotamia, Egypt, Greece, and Rome*. Chicago, forthcoming.

———. "Roads Not Featured: A Roman Failure to Communicate?" In R. J. A. Talbert, J. Bodel, and S. Alcock (eds.), *Highways, Byways and Road Systems in the Pre-Modern World*. Forthcoming.

Terkla, D. "The Original Placement of the Hereford *Mappa Mundi*." *Imago Mundi* 56 (2004): 131–51.

Thapar, R. *Asoka and the Decline of the Mauryas*. Rev. ed. Oxford, 1997.

Thomson, J. O. *History of Ancient Geography*. Cambridge, 1948.

Thomson, R. "Medieval Maps at Merton College, Oxford." *Imago Mundi* 61 (2009): 84–90.

Trenkler, E. (ed.). *Geschichte der Österreichischen Nationalbibliothek, II: Die Hofbibliothek (1922–1967)*. Vienna, 1973.

Trimble, J. "Visibility and Viewing on the Severan Marble Plan." In S. Swain, S. Harrison, and J. Elsner (eds.), *Severan Culture*, 368–84. Cambridge, 2007.

————. "Process and Transformation on the Severan Marble Plan of Rome." In Talbert and Unger (2008), 67–97.

Tuma (Holzer), I. "Franz Christoph von Scheyb (1704–1777). Leben und Werk. Ein Beitrag zur süddeutsch-österreichischen Aufklärung." Diss., University of Vienna, 1975.

Turner, H. L. "The Sheldon Tapestry Maps: Their Content and Context." *Cartographic Journal* 40 (2003): 39–49.

Uggeri, G. *La viabilità della Sicilia in età romana. Journal of Ancient Topography / Rivista di Topografia Antica*, Supplement II. Rome, 2004.

Uytterhoeven, I. "Housing in Late Antiquity: Thematic Perspectives." In L. Lavan et al. (eds.), *Housing in Late Antiquity: From Palaces to Shops*, 25–66. Leiden and Boston [MA], 2007.

Valentini, R., and G. Zucchetti (eds.). *Codice topografico della città di Roma*. Vol. 1. Rome, 1940.

Vasaly, A. *Representations: Images of the World in Ciceronian Oratory*. Berkeley, CA, 1993.

Veith, F. A. *Historia Vitae atque Meritorum Conradi Peutingeri post J. G. Lotterum*. Augsburg, 1783.

Vigi Fior, A. "Etienne Marie Siauve." *Antichità Altoadriatiche* 40 (*Gli Scavi di Aquileia: Uomini e Opere*) (1993): 83–101.

Vogel, K. A., and T. Haye. "Die Bibliothek Konrad Peutingers. Überlegungen zu ihrer Rekonstruktion, Erschliessung und Analyse." In W. Arnold (1997), 113–28.

Wesseling, P. *Vetera Romanorum Itineraria, sive Antonini Augusti Itinerarium, Itinerarium Hierosolymitanum, et Hieroclis Grammatici Synecdemus*. Amsterdam, 1735.

Westrem, S. D. *The Hereford Map: A Transcription of the Legends with Commentary*. Turnhout [Belgium], 2001.

Whittaker, C. R. "'To Reach Out to India and Pursue the Dawn': The Roman View of India." In C. R. Whittaker, *Rome and Its Frontiers: The Dynamics of Empire*, 144–62. London and New York, 2004.

Wilkes, J. J. *Diocletian's Palace, Split: Residence of a Retired Roman Emperor*. Rev. ed. Oxford, 1993.

Williams, J. *The Illustrated Beatus: A Corpus of the Illustrations of the Commentary on the Apocalypse*. 5 vols. London, 1994–2003.

————. "Isidore, Orosius and the Beatus Map." *Imago Mundi* 49 (1997): 7–32.

Woolf, G. *Becoming Roman: The Origins of Provincial Civilization in Gaul*. Cambridge, 1998.

Zanocco, R. "Il palazzo vescovile attuale nella storia e nell'arte (1309–1567)." *Bollettino Diocesano di Padova* 13 (1928): 175–92, 243–58, 334–42.

INDEX AND GAZETTEER

Index

Names and features on the Peutinger map (= PM), or within its scope and mentioned with reference to it, are indexed separately in the Gazetteer which follows.

Gazetteer

N.B. This listing does not extend to names and features on PM cited in the notes.

Ins. Dyme (island, no. 55) 6B2, 105

Ecbatanis Partiorvm (symbol, named =
    Ecbatana) 11C1, 94, 140
EGYPTVS (region) 8C3–8C5, 93, 99,
    108, 117
Fl. elevter (name, no symbol) 9C3, 129
Elvsa (name, no symbol) 9C1, 114
Epetio (symbol, named) 5A3, 121
Epirus, 99
Epitavro (symbol, named) 7B1, 117
Eribvlo (symbol, named) 8B2, 130
Ethiopia, 164
Euboea (omitted), 106
Euphrates river (unnamed, no. 126A),
    94–5, 104, 117
Evropos (name, no symbol) 11B2, 121
Evvenos Fl. (name, no symbol) 6B4, 131

Fano Fvgitivi (symbol, named) 4B3, 121
Fano Fvrtvn(a)e (symbol, named) 4B2,
    101
Ferrara, 166
Fines cilicie (name, no symbol) 8B4 and
    9B3, 113, 129
Fl. [– ? –] (river, no. 27A). *See* Savus
    river
fons (symbol, named) 7B3, 121
Foro Flamini (name, no symbol) 4B3,
    129
Foro Fvlvi (name, no symbol) 2B5, 113
Forum Alieni (omitted), 166
Fucinus lake (omitted), 105

GAETVLI (people) 2C5–4C1, 108
Fl. Ganges (river, no. 130A)
    11B2–11B5, 95
Gargara (symbol, named) 8B3, 121
Fl. Garvnna (river, no. 6) 1B1–1B5, 95
Gaul, 91, 99, 103, 107, 115, 117
Gesogiaco (name, no symbol) 1A2, 116
Gozo (omitted), 106
Gravinvm (name, no symbol) 1A2, 116
Gravisca (name, no symbol) 4B2, 121
Greece, 99, 106

Hadre (name, no symbol) 4A4, 126
Hadrianopol(is) (symbol, named) 7C4,
    121
HADRIATICVM PELAGVS (water)
    6B2–7B5, 105

Haila (name, no symbol) 8C5, 121, 131
Hasta (name, no symbol) 3B3, 103
Haste (name, no symbol) 10C4, 113
Hellespont, 89, 92
helyacapitolina (symbol, named) 9C1,
    130
Heraclea (symbol, named) 7B5, 129
Herichonte (symbol, named) 9C1, 130
Himalayas mountains, 137
Hostilia (name, no symbol) 3B4, 116
Hyppone Regio (symbol, named =
    Hippo Regius) 3C2, 155

IGEVM MARE (water = Aegean Sea)
    6C1, 89, 105, 106
Ilio (name, no symbol) 8B2, 128
Inalperio (symbol, named) 5A3, 121
Inaronia (symbol, named) 5A4, 121
Indenea (symbol, named) 5A2, 121
Indi, 108
INDIA (region) 11B2–11C5, 94, 99,
    102, 115, 117, 137, 140–1;
    significance on PM, 145, 149
Indian Ocean (unnamed), 89, 94, 105
Fl. Indvs (river, no. 136) 11C3–11C4, 94
iovisvri(vs) (symbol, named) 8A2, 129
Iovnaria (symbol, named) 5A2, 121
Ipponte diarito (symbol, named) 4C1,
    112
isaria (name, no symbol) 9B2, 111
Isvmbo (symbol, named) 10B5, 129
ITALIA (region) 2B5–4B5, 89, 91, 97,
    104–5, 107, 111, 129; Tetrarchs'
    commitment to, 150
Ivliobona (name, no symbol) 1A2, 116

Julian Alps, 311

Lacenivm (symbol, named) 6B2, 101
Lacvs et mons ciminvs (name, no
    symbol) 4B2, 129
Lambese (name, no symbol) 2C2, 109
Larinv (name, no symbol) 5B2, 131
Latium (omitted), 107
Leptimagna col. (symbol, named) 6C4,
    121
Levceris (name, no symbol) 3A2, 129
Libarnvm (name, no symbol) 2B5, 113
LVCCANIA (region) 5B5–6B1, 108
LVGDVNENSES (people) 1A1–1B5,
    107